LEARNING, PRACTICING, AND
LIVING THE NEW CAREERING

LEARNING, PRACTICING, AND LIVING THE NEW CAREERING

by

**Anna Miller-Tiedeman, Ph.D.
and Associates**

USA	Publishing Office:	ACCELERATED DEVELOPMENT *A member of the Taylor & Francis Group* 325 Chestnut Street Philadelphia, PA 19106 Tel: (215) 625-8900 Fax: (215) 625-2940
	Distribution Center:	ACCELERATED DEVELOPMENT *A member of the Taylor & Francis Group* 47 Runway Road, Suite G Levittown, PA 19057-4700 Tel: (215) 269-0400 Fax: (215) 269-0363
UK		ACCELERATED DEVELOPMENT *A member of the Taylor & Francis Group* 1 Gunpowder Square London EC4A 3DE Tel: +44 171 583 0490 Fax: +44 171 583 0581

LEARNING, PRACTICING, AND LIVING THE NEW CAREERING

1 2 3 4 5 6 7 8 9 0

Printed by Edwards Brothers, Ann Arbor, MI, 1999.

A CIP catalog record for this book is available from the British Library.

∞ The paper in this publication meets the requirements of the ANSI Standard Z39.48-1984 (Permanence of Paper).

Library of Congress Cataloging-in-Publication Data

Miller-Tiedeman, Anna, 1943-
   Learning, practicing, and living the new careering / Anna Miller-Tiedeman.
     p.   cm.
   Includes bibliographical references and index.
   ISBN 1-56032-740-5 (alk. paper)
   1. Vocational guidance.   2. Career development.   I. Title.
HF5381.M495   1999
331.7'02—dc21   98–54392
                                                    CIP

ISBN: 1-56032-740-5

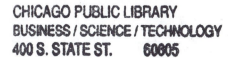

CONTENTS

3   The New (Quantum) Careering Model

4   Development, Decision Making, and the New (Quantum) Careering

PART II
PRACTICING THE NEW CAREERING:
THE *HOW* QUESTION   179

8 The New Careering (Lifecareer®) Practice

9 Money and the New Careering

TABLES AND FIGURES

ASSOCIATES

Barrie Day, Principal Partner
Life-Role Development Group Limited
Edmonton, Alberta

Hal A. Lingerman
San Marcos, California

Laurie McMenamin
Hellerwork–Ease
Tigard, Oregon

Eileen McCarthy
Bangor, Maine

Jim Puplava, President
Puplava Securities, Inc.
Poway, California

David Redekopp, Principal Partner
Life-Role Development Group Limited
Edmonton, Alberta

Calvin Rich
Canton, New York

Lee Joyce Richmond, Professor
Department of Education, Loyola College
Baltimore, Maryland

David V. Tiedeman, Vice President
The Lifecareer Group
Vista, California

PREFACE

From September 1973 to January 1981, I worked with hundreds of students at DeKalb (Illinois) High School. These students returned me to what I knew before I attended graduate school. Simply stated, Life, not job, is the big career. We do a lot of things as we go through life, some of which include working many jobs. All this gets together in ways we could not have planned or even imagined. As I worked my counseling job at DeKalb High School, I had no idea that I would write anything, much less the New Careering (Life-Is-Career®). I wanted to enjoy my life and relationship with David (V. Tiedeman), work in my garden, talk with my friends, and have some contemplative space. That was my hope, but life had other plans and I had a choice—grow and follow what I really came to do or get sick. I chose the former and received life's gift to me—the New Careering.

The main thesis in this book is that human beings are intelligent and capable of spinning their own personal career theories, telling their own stories, and directing their own destinies, using professionals when in need of support and/or when they need to hear an out-loud version of their story. Assuming intelligence and theory-making capability makes the client's thought (not the theorists' thoughts or techniques) primary and the professional's thought secondary, because the professional doesn't have access to the client's internal information or how that data co-mingles with other factors to move the client forward. Frequently, the client doesn't know that either, but time unfolds the answer.

When we get in a hurry for the answer, we seek out professional help which can spark a new insight, but it seldom brings the instant answer we sought. However, a professional who understands process can help midwife the unfolding of a client's life mission.

Living life as process means getting in touch with our inner e-mail, reading it, sitting with it, absorbing its meaning, while trying to keep our economics in balance.

Further, this book isn't just about the New Careering—it goes below the surface showing what I consider the engine of living—Paradigms, Development, and Decision Making—all three suspended in a sea of spirit. I devote a chapter to each of these topics and they find their way into most all the remaining chapters. That's how process continues to show us the connectedness of all things.

Joel Barker, in the video, *Creating the Future: The Business of Paradigms* said, "If you don't believe it, you won't see it." That idea plays out in this book. If you hold fast to the traditional career paradigm, you won't see the New Careering. In developmental terms, you will conform to what has been. From a paradigmatic standpoint, you will screen out the new because it won't fit how you see the world. Your decision making will then follow your developmental and paradigmatic position.

The book is divided into three sections: the What, How, and Why questions. The What question starts with painting, in broad brush, the 90-year history of the vocational psychology/career development theories. Next, the New Careering and its anchors—paradigms, development, and decision making—are discussed. The What section concludes with an allegorical introduction to Quantum Careering designed to deepen understanding of the practical application of physics to everyday life.

The How question starts with the practice and teaching of the New Careering. A chapter on money and the New Careering, was included since money or lack thereof anchors life (and its direction); and, in our downsized environment, money, for many, is less abundant. Therefore, professionals may want to consider working with individuals to help them start thinking about building a financial safety net.

Here's where paradigms enter again. If you hold the Allan Greenspan mindset, you'll think "Everything's fine. Why bother?" However, if you recognize the financial tight rope on which many people walk throughout life, then you will see the need for at least starting to mention money management as a safety net approach. If you think only those trained in investment can help clients think about building a financial safety net, you won't introduce the idea into your practice. While the teaching chapter chronicles its author's experience from 1983 in teaching Life-As-Career®, it's also a celebration of the life process in every one of us.

The alternative therapies chapter is included because my experience suggests that talk counseling or therapy can only access what we not only know but are willing to admit. Meditation, structural body work, and many other therapies including craniosacral therapy can help break up old behavior and thought patterns that we either have no or a marginal awareness of. We usually know that what we're doing or being blocked from doing frequently relates to old behavior patterns, but, in many instances, we can't quite access that information. Alternative therapies, like mainline therapies, tend to be time extended, but when they bring forth an understanding and awareness, the shift is often made rather instantly.

However, it usually takes time to work out the full import of the revelation.

A more open paradigm was needed for assessment. So Pythagorean assessment was introduced as it deals with heart's desire, along with destiny, offering decade markers for life's journey.

Health represents the major chapter in addressing the Why Question because of the direct relationship between stress and life direction. Stress, regardless of its origin, depresses the immune system and disassembles it for a period of time. While reassembling, the body remains unprotected and vulnerable to all kinds of large and small health problems. Furthermore, the body's stress mechanism was not designed to handle 20th Century stresses, such as downsizing, mortgages, and the like.

Finally, a brief review of vocational psychology/career theories is included in the Appendices.

The 21st Century will see a melt-down of the authority figure vis-à-vis having the last word on a particular concern. In its place will come a primary reliance on inner wisdom, personal research, and a co-relationship with professionals. Instead of being under the doctor's or therapist's care, the professionals will be under the client's or patient's care. Living the Life-As-Career® principles contribute to that emerging model.

— Anna Miller-Tiedeman, Ph.D.
The Lifecareer® Group
Vista, California
www.life-is-career.com

ACKNOWLEDGMENTS

This book is dedicated to my father, Elmer, and mother, Pearl Miller who always supported and never directed. To my wonderful husband and colleague, *David V. Tiedeman, who for eighteen years has supported—financially, emotionally and lovingly—the development of my gift to career development.* To Dr. Dean Hummel who admitted me to graduate study at Ohio University and then got out of my way. To Louise Boggess, my U.C. Berkeley writing teacher who gave me a deep appreciation of the value of active voice. Also to Anita Mitchell who was instrumental in bringing David and me to the University of Southern California, where I had time to think seriously about what I had learned in graduate school concerning career development. To Lee Joyce Richmond, my roommate in the 1983 *Assembly to Advance Career* at the University of Southern California, where I introduced the Life-Is-Career® idea. She has carried the torch for my work, and, when she could, gave me wonderful opportunities. To my family and particularly my sister Donna, who would not let me give up on my idea. A special appreciation to Dr. Betty Bosdell, a friend, neighbor, and colleague who has been a great support through many trying times.

Many along the way helped clarify my idea, including Dorothy Dallinger, Linda Kemp, George Pfister, Cynthia Miller, Pat Lambert, Muriel Niemi, Betty Bosdell, Andy Lawrence, Deborah Riepl, Deborah Bochinsky, Madeleine Schwab, Patti Elenz-Martin, Ann Medine, Jo Deverman, Gwendolyn Cooper, Susan Harris, Virginia Byrd, Donna Swanson, Ann Medine, Ruth Rounds, Sharon Smith, and other family members, Christopher Smith, Barbara Summer, Nancy Knapp, Evelyn Staus and many others too numerous to mention.

I also want to thank those people who stood in my way, who threw up barriers, and tried in many ways to thwart my work. They taught me that no human can stop what Life (God) wants to happen. Both the positive and the dispositive gave me great courage and insight.

Finally, I want to thank spirit, which for me is God, for its unfailing guidance and direction, for sticking with me when I veered from my path, for always sending me inner e-mail even though I failed to read it, for transmitting only what I could handle in the minute, for making possible great incidents of encouragement when I wanted to quit, for helping me catch those winds of grace in desperate emotional and psychological times, and for helping me finally understand one line in the 23rd Psalm in the Bible: "Yea, though I walk through the valley of the shadow of death" (of my insecurities, anxieties, self doubts, and disgust from time to time) "I will fear no evil..." I had repeated this line from childhood but failed to catch its life-enhancing meaning. The key word for me was *through*. As the wonderful minister Brian Anderson said in one of his sermons, "It doesn't say, 'Stop and buy a condo." At that point I realized I could get *through* the sticky wicket of coming from a different paradigm. Eighteen years into my endeavor, I now realize that spirit has been the wind under my wings, teaching me that life direction, when I paid attention, was as easy as breathing and as natural as the wind.

CHAPTER

Anna Miller-Tiedeman

Introduction to the New (Quantum) Careering: Foundations and Possibilities

Spotlight on a Major Universal Principle

The night was dark and stormy. A seaman ran into the captain's cabin and told the captain of a potential problem. "There's a ship in our sea lane about 20 miles away," he reported. The captain said, "Tell them to move." "They won't," replied the seaman. "I've tried." "Well, let's see what they do when *I* tell them," said the Captain. His signal sent out: "Move starboard 20 degrees." Signal came back: "Move starboard 20 degrees yourself." The Captain said, "I cannot believe this! Who does he think he is? Well, let them know who I am. I am the Captain." "This is the Captain Joe of the 26th. Move starboard 20 degrees. This is an order." Seaman comes back, "This is Seaman Bob Jones, III, I order you to move starboard 20 degrees at once." "What's going on here?" asked the Captain. We're a battleship! Let them know who we are." Signal sent out: "This is the mighty Flagship Missouri, 7th Fleet." Signal returned: "This is a lighthouse."

This story symbolizes what Stephen Covey (1997) suggested stands as the ultimate strength and advantage: "Principles that do not change are like lighthouses. We do not break them, we only break ourselves against them. Principles are timeless and self-evident."

You know a principle is self-evident when you try to argue for its opposite. See if you can talk about career without talking about life and see if that makes sense. Have you ever seen a career go to work and a life stay home?

When we fail to acknowledge the individual as a theory maker, we leave the life out of career. The result: We continue to break ourselves against life, ignoring *flow*, life's major demand.

Flow characterizes the overall principle in the New Careering model. People experiencing flow are more likely to feel "strong," "active," "creative," "concentrated," and "motivated" (Csikszentmihalyi, 1990). And, in order not to *break ourselves against life*, we need to: (a) cooperate with the approaching forces while assessing the situation; (b) value those decisions that offer pleasing results (right) as well as those that don't (left); (c) understand life as it unfolds using the best information at hand (first internal and then external); and (d) consider *life* as the big career, which resembles a rough draft requiring a lifetime of rewrites.

The New Careering model, built on the principle of *flow*, uses the following as foundational: (a) quantum physics; (b) self-organizing systems theory; (c) physicist David Bohm's notions about wholeness; (d) Buckminster Fuller's comments on the instructive nature of left turns (things that don't work out); (e) a focus on the now, as noted in the Sermon on the Mount; (f) timing and rhythm; and (g) various thoughts from the *Tao Te Ching* and Hawaiian Kahuna thought (see Figure 1.1).

The societal living of Life-As-Career resembles a musical fugue. A fugue, usually based on one theme (in Lifecareer®, it is process), gets played in different voices, different keys, different speeds, and at times upside down and backwards (Hofstadter, 1979). Does this sound like life? In life, senses of new living wholes come to us as intuition in seamless experiencing. The fugue usually begins with a single voice singing its theme (Bach's *Musical Offering* is a good example.). When done, a second voice enters, either five notes up the scale or four down. Meanwhile, the first voice goes on singing a secondary theme in order to provide harmonic and melodic contrasts. Each of the voices enters in turn, singing the theme often to the accompaniment of the secondary theme in some other voice, while remaining voices do whatever fanciful things enter the composer's mind. When all the voices have arrived, there are no rules (Hofstadter, 1979). The fugue is then the seamless whole as in truth.

In living Life-As-Career (life as process), we play our individual themes with different voices, different behaviors, and as in music, different speeds. Sometimes it works and sometimes it does not, but it all gets together and

---

*Lifecareer, Life-Is-Career, Career Compass and their derivatives are registered trademarks of Dr. Anna Miller-Tiedeman.

The New (Quantum) Careering provides the umbrella term for the following:

Process careering – The experience

Lifecareer™ Theory – The theory and its philosophy

Additional concepts David Bohm – B. M. Fuller – The Holy Bible The Tao – The Hawaiian Kahuna

The foundation: Quantum physics Self-Organizing Systems Theory

FIGURE 1.1. The New Careering Model

forms our unique life signature. Life then becomes an artistic endeavor that takes on the feeling of a healthy pleasure.

Beck and Beck (1987), in their book, *The Pleasure Connection: How Endorphins Affect Our Health and Happiness,* suggested that pleasure feelings emanate from the limbic brain located between the reptilian stem brain and the cortex. In the limbic brain, we bond to love and avoid or reject unpleasantness, thus prioritizing our physiological responses. Each brain—instinctual, limbic, and cortical—has its own priorities, its own corresponding biochemistry. Each directly affects our physiology with automatic responses. The cortex thinks, plans, analyzes, and provides a rational view of the world. But the deeper layers of the brain (limbic) give us a sense of ourselves in relationship to the world. Beck (1995) suggested that self-worth, emotions, a sense of well-being, the five senses (touch, smell, sight, hearing, and taste), health and healing, and passion/desire all rest in the limbic brain. In the limbic brain we decide who we are and how much that means to us. The limbic brain supports our breakthroughs. It gets passionate while the cortex makes mental constructs. Additionally, the limbic brain stays with the present and the cortical brain worries about the past, present, and future (Beck, 1995). Finally, when the limbic brain anchors the intellectual, it brings forth a powerful synergism.

Traditionally, career development has been expressed through the cortex, by discussion, analysis, and a parceling of this or that trait, this or that behavior, this or that choice, or this or that role. Whether or not someone exhibits career maturity also falls in this category. In this sense, the strobe light falls on the *cortical* consideration of the career phenomenon with little or only subtle consideration of the *feeling* aspect of career (as a path or course through life) and scant consideration of the cortical and limbic brains working as a system that together make them more than the sum of their parts.

When you live Life-As-Career, you place the limbic brain activity in a primary position, followed by that of the cortex. In this way, you place your mind behind what you feel coming from your inner knowledge (or inner e-mail). You do not send the mind forward without the deep knowledge of the limbic brain. As a result, you power up your "master system" or the core that organizes and reorganizes your life.

In summary, flowing with the rhythm of life, managing the *now*, while working to balance the limbic and cortical sections of the brain, and valuing both right- and left-brain choices (the latter, often assessed as wrong both by self and others) offers the best potential for surfing the twenty-first century. The Sermon on the Mount (The Holy Bible) puts it this way: "Take no thought for the morrow," (Matt. 6:34) and "To every thing there is a season, and a time to every purpose under heaven" (Eccles. 3:1). In the *Tao Te Ching* (Lao Tsu, 1972), you find "In action, watch timing" (p. 8). Finally, in *Ano Ano The Seed* (Zambucka, 1978), the Hawaiian Kahuna teachings suggest that, "We find our right place at the right time with the right person" (p. 39).

This introduction: (a) briefly reviews the old worldviews that shaped all disciplines, including career development into the early 1900s; (b) introduces the new worldview that now supports transformation (more about worldviews in Chapters 3 and 7); (c) reviews Buckminster Fuller's notions about honoring all your decisions; and, (d) presents some concepts that help us handle life in a way friendly to our immune system and which points to the interconnectedness of all things.

The Old Paradigm

The Newtonian Worldview

The theories of Rene Descartes and Sir Isaac Newton, two eminent scientists of the seventeenth century, dictated the worldview for more than 300 years. Descartes held that scientific knowledge should be certain (often referred to as the Cartesian worldview). He felt we should believe only those things that can be fully known and substantiated beyond all doubt. He also regarded nature as a perfect machine and the mind as a separate entity from the body. This represents a *logical positivistic viewpoint*, one that discounts metaphysics completely, and invalidates the mind and body connection (this viewpoint presently anchors counseling practice). In a similar vein, Newton saw the universe as a great clock: Take it apart and study its inner workings and you'll understand the universe. This notion worked well when applied to the movement of planets, manned space flights, and modern technology. However, when scientists applied Newton's theory to the atomic and sub-atomic worlds, it fell short as "... scientists became painfully aware that the basic concepts, their language, and their whole analytic way of thinking was inadequate to deal with the new atomic phenomena" (Capra, 1983, p. 5).

As Dick Bradley (1982), a sports writer, noted, life resembles a rickety card table. When we are born, God sets up an old-fashioned card table with rickety folding legs, places a huge jigsaw puzzle on it and says: "Okay, sort it out and when it is finished, you'll understand why you're here" (p. 14). Most people finish the puzzle in middle age and spend the remainder of their lives trying to protect it. Scientists do similarly, and many physicists have tried to protect the Newtonian worldview. But Einstein and other physicists emerged kicking the Newtonian puzzle table, relegating it to the level of a special case theory—useful in some cases, but not in all.

You can see the imprint of Newtonian thinking in the idea, "If you don't know where you're going, you'll probably end up somewhere else." This belief drives traditional career development, along with the value of planning and goal setting, which also has a flavor of Newtonianism.

In brief, then, the Newtonian worldview: (a) suggested that the parts equal the whole; (b) ignored erratic motion, thinking the universe operated like a machine; and (c) did not acknowledge the observer as part of the observed. This perspective takes an either/or not a both/and view. Separation names the former and inclusion the latter view.

Career Development Grew Up in the Newtonian Worldview

Following the worldview of the day, Career Development theorists and practitioners carved out their theories beginning with Parsons' 1909 trinity, considered necessary to making a wise vocational choice: (a) understanding self by looking at the parts, such as interests, abilities, aptitudes, ambitions, resources, and limitations; (b) knowing favored occupations and their conditions for success; and (c) applying true reasoning.

With this orientation, career took on the meaning of job or a series of jobs. Individuals talked about finding or losing a career, looking for second, third, and fourth careers. Education for these careers by technical institutes, proprietary schools, and colleges and universities followed. A subtle notion of the training led one to believe that with the right choice, positive outcomes would follow. Research emerged with the same orientation, surveying groups of people, suggesting remedies and/or more research. Professionals developed career materials to carry out the practice end of the research or theory. Over eighty years later, that imprint still exists, as can be seen on the cover of *Forbes* magazine (1997), "The Key to Successful Retirement: 2nd Career," with the inside article entitled, "Your Shadow Career" (Geer, 1997, p. 156).

Valiant efforts to turn traditional career theories into practice show up in *Career Choice and Development* (Brown, Brooks, & Associates, (1984, 1990, 1996) and in *Applying Career Development Theory to Counseling* (Sharf, 1992). But it's difficult at best to harmonize theories: (a) of career choice that moderately explain why people chose specific occupations, (b) of career development incorporating evolution of career choice, and (c) of career decision making that centers on the process of occupational selection.

Counselors, particularly beginning counselors, try to fit traditional practice to conventional theories, and often, with confusion. In fact, Morrissey (1996) suggested, "Beginning counselors have difficulty conceptualizing client problems from a consistent theoretical framework and then choosing appropriate technique" (p. 14). In trying to integrate various theories, helping professionals often exemplify the three blind men describing the elephant (Shah, 1972). One felt the elephant's trunk and described the elephant as being thin, like a snake. Another felt its leg and called it round, like a post. The third felt its side and said it felt flat like a house. All perceptions were partially correct. By considering only its parts, helping professionals tend to miss the whole theory and, more specifically, the most important theory, one not taught in graduate school theory courses—the client's *own* ever evolving career theory. This illustrates how the quantum physics principle of complimentarity—when you focus on one thing, you miss something else—parallels career development, even in practice.

On the other hand, Lifecareer counseling, tracking the individual's life stream, makes the crossover from theory to practice seamless because it does not clutter practice with a grab-bag of theories as the professional works with the client's career theory, supporting, empowering, educating about the changed work paradigm, challenging outdated paradigms whether related to work, relationships or self, listening and questioning negative self-talk—all of which offers the client a more open opportunity to move his or her life forward. Practice then follows as day to night. (See Chapter 8 for more details on practice.)

Career Development from the Business Perspective

Career development in organizations emerged from the fields of psychology, sociology, and political science. Specifically, Kurt Lewin's (1951) interest centered on an individual's life space and the person–environment interaction. Lewin believed individuals created their own reality (or view of the world) and acted accordingly. Everett C. Hughes, according to Hall (as cited in Brown et al., (1990) first used career in relation to formal institutions. He distinguished between the objective career (the way a career looks to others) and subjective career (the individual's view of his or her career experiences). On the other hand, the political scientists focused on the administrative practices that controlled the individual careers.

Influenced by work in social psychology, sociology, and political science, the field of organizational behavior began to emerge in the 1950s. As a protégé of Super, Hall did much to form a union of self-concept theory and the literature of organizational behavior. He oriented his work on issues of identity and psychological success and their relationship in time. Schein (1993) introduced *career anchors* or occupational self-concepts, which include self-perceived talents and abilities, self-perceived motives and needs, and self-perceived attitudes and values. Schein believed that career anchors act as guides and constraints and help stabilize and integrate the career (as in profession).

In general, then, vocational psychologists tended to focus on occupational choices of students in public and private education while organizational career researchers studied adult career development during a work life. And, even though psychologists started to study self perception, they tended to come from their own postulations rather than those elicited from the subject. However, Carl Rogers proved the exception. Mitchell (personal communication, May 1996) reports that a woman in one of Rogers' presentations asked him a question about a blind girl (the question illustrated a Newtonian separate-parts notion). Rogers asked the woman to repeat the question three times, saying, "I don't understand your question." He finally told the woman that she was masking the individual with a label which had little self information in it.

The Newtonian/Cartesian notion, that the parts equal the whole, presently plays out in the overall thinking of traditional career both in public and higher education, as well as in organizational career development. Since today's career paradigm sprang from the Newtonian framework, personal reality or personal knowledge takes second place to conventional wisdom and the objective view.

Training then follows the objectivity paradigm with professionals ignoring client career theories even when clients bring them in. For instance, Brooks (in Brown et al., 1984) declares "... the counselor who is able to conceptualize career problems from diverse theoretical systems may be better able to develop different treatments" (p. 338). Acting on that assumption, counselors consider the client's problems from theoretical systems, not from the client's theory or personal knowledge, nor from a process standpoint in which personal knowledge can participate. That points to the major difference between a self-concept theory and one that attributes self-conceiving to each individual as does the Lifecareer theory and its philosophy.

Life Renews Itself in Eastern Europe and the USSR

In the 1980s, while the career development field worked with a 70-year-old paradigm, freedom broke out in Eastern Europe, the Berlin Wall fell, followed by the break-up of the Soviet Union.

While freedom worked out its challenges in the world, technology advanced by the minute. Answering machines replaced receptionists. Then voice-mail, with its laundry list of choices, greeted callers. Numerous secretarial and management duties disappeared into the computer as did many jobs connected to book publishing—paste-up, graphics, cover design and the like.

In the world of business, many engage in world-telecommunication networks. For instance Met Life Insurance switches claims adjustment to Ireland via telephone (Barnet, 1993). More and more people process their income taxes on personal computers. Legal forms and ready-made legal templates available on software make hiring a lawyer frequently unnecessary. And lawyers rush to computers to markedly downsize their secretarial help, aided by pagers and voice mail. Accounting and editorial software offer both business and home access to services once purchased. Computer technology now softens many occupations once thought solid and stable even in the medical arena.

In the midst of the computer revolution, the Internet arrives. Large and small businesses scramble to put up their home pages offering products and services to millions, not hundreds, of people at reasonable costs. For instance, as you ride through the tunnel of cyberspace, you see the movement of retail stores back into the home. You also find universities offering wire degrees via e-mail (Gubernick & Ebeling, 1997). *Forbes* magazine rated the top twenty wire degrees in their June 16, 1997 issue. Executives of various businesses find themselves working in an international climate rather than a national or community climate. *Omni* and *Longevity* magazines have ceased publishing for the newsstand and for mailed subscriptions. They will only be available electronically, and will use 31 fewer workers to produce. E-mail rapidly replaces regular postal services. Priority two-day and overnight mail take precedence over first class. Today, changes happen in nanoseconds, not hours, days, or weeks, except for research, development, and personal development. But human beings don't change that rapidly, therefore, we face much larger challenges both economically and socially.

Almost every day, someone gets downsized in America. For example, in 1996, AT&T announced the downsizing of 40,000 workers (Ramstad, 1996). Newspapers across the country print similar headlines almost every day. American companies not only downsize their employees, they downsize commitment and loyalty from remaining workers, who experience anxiety that they may be the next to go. Another quantum physics principle emerges—Everything connects to everything else.

One man commented, "I was once a corporate president, and now, due to *downsizing,* I am working for minimum wage. Welcome to the real world." Endless street stories exist—from college graduates with two degrees, to Ph.D.s who cannot find work, to those with less than a high school education.

While everyone has his or her own version of job security, Robert Reich, former U.S. Secretary of Labor, commented (Meyers, 1996) that job-security disappeared because of competition, more pressure from Wall Street, and corporate loss of executive statesmen. Formerly corporations balanced their needs with community and shareholder needs, but those days are gone. Reich thought more job training and more humane concern by corporations might turn things around.

Reich's suggestions reflect an old industrial format in which the employer took care of his employees in exchange for loyalty. At that time, the employer had the majority of his manufacturing and business located in the U.S. However, with global movement of jobs and smarter technology, job training does not solve the post-industrial problems of work and job security. Further, it does not dovetail with the shift of career ownership from the employee–employer alliance to the working arrangement that now brings about more customization of life (The HayGroup, 1988). These notions—working arrangement, entrepreneurial ventures, and customization—gain strength each year and, as the HayGroup predicted, now emerge as a life force.

The New Paradigm

Noted physicist, David Bohm, in his book *Wholeness and the Implicate Order* (1980), advanced the idea that the whole logically organizes the parts, not the reverse, an idea that contributed to an emerging new perspective.

On studying tiny sub-atomic particles, scientists discovered that the observer's perspective determined the qualities of the particle studied. If the scientist looked for mass, the particle had mass. If he or she looked for energy, the same particle had energy. From this, scientists began to recognize that we truly do *create our own reality* (Capra, 1982).

The mass–energy duality introduced two other important principles of the new physics: *complementarity* and *uncertainty*. The principle of complementarity, akin to our notion of *opposites*, explains why body mass and energy *cannot* be observed at the same time in the same particle. A thing cannot be both black and white at the same time. But the new physics approaches this duality in another way. A particle actually may have *both* mass and energy. However, when you try to measure either, you can only look for one at a time. Therefore, you can only see *either* mass or energy (Capra, 1982). (See Chapters 3 and 7 for more detail.)

This brings up the principle of uncertainty. By focusing on measuring the mass of the particle, energy in that same particle cannot be observed with 100% accuracy. And since Descartes insisted that we regard reality as only those things observable, *we* say that it does not exist (Capra, 1982).

One of the problems with the principles of complementarity and uncertainty is that you never can dissect one from the other, as Newton would have proposed. This brings up an ever present third principle in the new physics: *connectedness*. Simply stated, this means the universe cannot be divided and still be a universe. "Uni" means one (Costello, 1991, p. 1456), and "universe," all of a whole (p. 1458). The universe is made up of relationships. For example, the centuries-old process of *bleeding* a patient to rid him or her of *bad blood* often resulted in death, because blood and life strongly connect.

Each of us has in some way found that the universe, a true unity, cannot be separated into independent parts. Vice Admiral James Bond Stockdale (1978), USN, learned this during his confinement as a prisoner of war in Vietnam. He remarked, "We found that over the course of time our minds had a tremendous capacity for invention and introspection, but had the weakness of being part of our bodies" (p. 102). He remembered how Descartes had separated mind and body. Stockdale's response, "Gosh, how I wish Descartes could have been right, but he's wrong" (p.102).

The ultimate insufficiency of the Newtonian theory shows that it is not the golden path, only a special-case theory. Though many applied this theory to people, their lives—and our interest here, their Life-As-Career— it became clear to increasing numbers that Newton's clockwork approach was not working. The great break came in the 1920s with the emergence of the so-called new physics. Sixty years later, we find ourselves just beginning to understand what it means to us personally and to our culture. (More detail on Quantum physics in Chapters 2 and 6.)

What does the new physics do that earlier scientific theories did not do? It confirms what we've all always known down deep—that the universe is complementary (e.g., day and night, two by two they marched into the ark, in and out, up and down), uncertain, and connected. In addition, scientists learned that you cannot separate the observer from what he or she observes. Each of these principles, in turn, supports the Life-As-Career idea.

A recurring theme in this book suggests that compelling parallels exist between the reality of the microscopic physical world and the social level of our everyday human experience. Zohar (1990) supports that parallel in her discussion of "A Physics of Everyday Life" (p. 17).

The Theory of Self-Organizing Systems

Living Life-As-Career means recognizing the self-organizing magic of life. (More about this in chapters 3 and 7.) Two major aspects of self-organizing systems (SOS) are (a) self-renewal; and (b) self-transcendence. In self-renewal, systems continually renew and recycle their components while maintaining the integrity of the overall system. In self-transcendence, living systems can grow beyond physical and mental boundaries (Capra, 1982), but growth remains a choice.

Life, that wonderful, mysterious balance between the vitality of being and the inertness of experience, continuously self-organizes and proves more dependable than most imagine. Without our help, life organizes on its own, given its inherent intelligence, even at the quantum particle level (Capra, 1982; Prigogine & Stengers, 1984; Zohar, 1990). Our cells, our organs, our bodies, the groups in which we interact, our communities, states, nations, universe, and even our lifecareers—all exemplify self-organizing systems. This does not necessarily mean we always like the results. It merely acknowledges that self-organization is built into life and continually unfolds and enfolds into itself (Bohm, 1980). Life does not ask our opinion about this. So, when we fail to organize, life often does it for us. And even when we do organize, life frequently reorganizes that too.

Buckminster Fuller

The late Buckminster Fuller (Wagschal & Kahn, 1979), inventor of the Dymaxion House, creator of the geodesic dome, philosopher and designer, held that valuing both the right and left decisions and events in life are necessary. He noted that we do not speak of walking on our right foot and wrong foot, but that both the right and left serve us well. Granted everyone would like things to go right, but life does not work that way. If everything went right, we people helpers would not have jobs. Miscues in human nature teach us. Miscues, mistakes, and left turns will carry the same meaning in this book: something that does not work. Even so, it will contain encrypted information for the next decision.

Fuller loved both the right and left in life. Once when working with university students on a project, immediately on completion, the project collapsed. Fuller merely said, "Well, let's see what we learned and start again" (personal communication, January 22, 1981). Like with driving, life continually calls for correction, action, and more correction.

Biblical Contributions, the Tao Te Ching, and the Kahuna

The Sermon on the Mount in the Bible suggests we take no thought for tomorrow. It does not say anything about today, a place where we make our tomorrow. If you make every day count, then you find interesting things happening in your life. Further, you will not live today under tomorrow's stress. You'll realize, as pointed out in Ecclesiastes 3:1, that "to every thing there is a season, and a time to every purpose under heaven." This means you *flow* with the rhythm of life, listening for the signals. You do not try to mold life to your limited vision. Sally Field, an Academy award-winning actress, made this very clear in her statement, "You have to give up the life you plan in order to get the life that is waiting for you" (Field, 1996). When at the crossover point of surrender, the 23rd Psalm may be useful, particularly the line, "Yea, though I walk through the valley of the shadow of death..." The key word *through* alerts us that we will come out on the other end eventually.

The Tao Te Ching (1972), sensitive to life's polarities, motion, and movement, suggested:

> Sometimes things are ahead and sometimes they are behind;
> Sometimes breathing is hard, sometimes it comes easily;
> Sometimes there is strength and sometimes weakness;
> Sometimes one is up and sometimes down (p. 29).

Capra (1975) provides a more powerful illustration of the movement of life. He tells of sitting by the ocean one late afternoon watching the waves and feeling the rhythm of his breathing. Being a physicist, he knew that the sand, rocks, water, and air were vibrating molecules and atoms, and that these interacted, creating and destroying particles; he also remembered that the Earth's atmosphere received continual showers of cosmic rays, but he had only experienced these ideas through concept and textbook. Then, suddenly, his former experiences came to life and "I 'saw' cascades of energy coming down from outer space in which particles were created and destroyed in rhythmic pulses; I 'saw' the atoms of the elements and those of my body participating in this cosmic dance of energy; I felt its rhythm and I heard its sound and at this moment I knew that this was the Dance of Shiva, the Lord of Dancers worshipped by the Hindus" (p. 11).

The Kahuna teachings acknowledge the whole, as does the Tao. It also has aspects of self-organizing systems, "Sometimes we are violently pitchforked away from someone or something that we have wanted. And we rage against the stroke of fate that breaks up the alliance. But it may have been disastrous had we stayed" (Zambucka, 1978, p. 39). Ordinarily, looking back we see that what happened was for the best, "... all evens out and harmony is restored in the end" (p. 39). However, the Kahuna teachings do acknowledge the influence of past lives on this existence. "We bring strange yearnings with us on our journey from the past, for somewhere along the line, we have been all things ... man and woman ... beggar and merchant ... pauper and potentate. Though mankind is only one, it wears a million masks" (p. 40). And finally, the recognition that we see ourselves reflected in those around us. They believed, as Confucius did, that outer problems often mirror the internal—correct yourself and your world will change)—and, Prigogine's notion (Lukas, 1980), that you can recognize yourself by your descriptions of anything and everything.

The New Careering Model: Reasons Why

The idea of living Life-As-Career developed when Miller-Tiedeman worked with high school students at DeKalb High School (Miller-Tiedeman, 1996) and found the students *breaking themselves against life* time and time again as traditional career focused more on individual items like tests, techniques, and control of life, not on *flow*. Even the National Board for Certified Counselors (NBCC) took a non-process approach for updating skills and knowledge. Their categories for continuing education—which resemble graduate school courses—reveal the assumption that counselors need more of the same, not something that naturally falls in their path. Further, traditional counseling practice often assumes a parent-child attitude between counselor and client.

On the other hand, the Lifecareer assumptions hold that life generally unfolds intelligently and each individual can identify what he or she needs to mature his or her individual career theory/philosophy. Remember that humanity (including Parsons himself) found its way long before Parsons (1909) began matching people to jobs early in the twentieth century. It seems reasonable to expect that individuals not only will continue to do that but also will be forced into doing that as jobs that support reasonable lifestyles become fewer. However, the New Careering Professional will enjoy a rewarding practice as he or she will hold a very different attitude, will subscribe to different assumptions, and will have had the experience that he or she seeks to support (not parent) in the client.

A second reason for process careering has to do with freeing individuals from the common reality or conventional wisdom and encouraging them to trust their own thinking. When they do, they place personal knowledge first and external information second, which helps them avoid *breaking themselves against life*. Those who follow their own notions will experience pain, but so will those who do not. However things turn out, those cooperating with the flow will encounter less stress, and, in additon, will enjoy the satisfaction of knowing they followed their own life signals and cues.

The attainment of balance in life provides a third reason to introduce the Life-Is-Career idea. When individuals consider Life-As-Career, they cooperate with the approaching forces while intelligencing the situation. They do not anchor their identity in a job. They know that all life experience contributes to the unfolding and developing of their life direction. As an editor once said to me, "I didn't start out with a plan to find an editor's job." It's this intelligent handling of life that reduces stress and enhances the immune system.

A fourth reason to go for the principle of process in career hinges on placing intentions and organizing the above goals and plans. Many individuals set goals then discover they cannot meet them. This frequently induces worry, stress, and physical problems, not to mention depression and lowered self-esteem. At this point, the value of setting intentions becomes crystal clear, as intentions work with life, not against it.

Goals tend to run in very narrow channels, suggested Deepak Chopra in *Creating Health: How to Wake Up the Body's Intelligence* (1991). He further says that the river of life does not work that narrowly, that the highest state of attention goes beyond goals and anchors internally with a balance between rest and activity. Both goal setting and traditional career attitudes encourage activity, with little focus on rest. Without the rests in music, little melody would emerge. The same holds true for maturing a life work.

Finally, and perhaps more importantly, health (another one of those self-evident principles) stands as one of the best reasons for moving to process careering. Without health, professional endeavor pales. However, *cooperating with the approaching forces* while assessing the situation engenders good feelings. This leads to a lowered risk of getting a disease that can make you sick (Sapolsky, 1994).

The New Careering, like the bread crumbs dropped by Hansel and Gretel, leads those ready for the personal journey back to their own knowing. At this point, the interest shifts from just making a living to making a life while making a living.

In summary, process careering

1. empowers the career theory of each individual; thereby helping the individual work with life,not break him or herself against it.

2. remains open, varied, and free, rather than limited by parts, levels, and stages;

3. encourages flexibility rather than dependence on pattern and prediction; and,

4. works well for all people in any situation.

Reason and Rowan (1981), in their book *Human Inquiry: A Sourcebook of New Paradigm Research*, advanced the idea that "we need to put people in positions where they may learn truth about themselves." The Lifecareer theory, convertible to a philosophy, does just that.

Major Differences

Major differences exist between the New Careering model and that of traditional career. Chapter 3 will show and explain those major differences. Generally, when you live Life-As-Career, you place personal knowledge above conventional wisdom. You gain a sense of balance and harmony. You do not rehearse what did not work. You accept the learning and move on. You stop looking for a career or worry about finding a second or third one. All of this becomes irrelevant when you live life as the big career. You learn that life works, not always the way you want it to, but it works. You know that cooperating with the approaching forces while intelligencing the situation makes for less stress, which enhances the immune system and that, in turn, effects your Lifecareer developing.

Intentions in This Manuscript

This book breaks into three sections, following this introductory first chapter. Part One, "Learning the New Careering: The *What* Question", has six chapters (Chapters 2 through 7). Chapter 2 briefly reviews vocational psychology paradigms; Chapter 3 presents the New Careering model; Chapter 4 discusses decision-making and its relationship to development and the New Careering. Chapter 5 shows how paradigms, development, and decision-making influence many aspects of the New Careering. Chapter 6 suggests how decision-making and worldview relate, as do paradigms and development, and Chapter 7 uses dialogue of a young professor.

In Part Two, "Practicing the New Careering: The *How* Question" (Chapters 8-13), application forms the major focus. Chapter 8 deals with Lifecareer practice; Chapter 9 discusses how money anchors career in the new forming economy; Chapter 10 presents alternative modalities useful to life direction discernment. Chapter 11 explains the usefulness of the Pythagorean numerical system as a more open paradigm for personal assessment. Chapter 12 showcases Canadian innovations in career development with a focus on *Engage Your Life*, published by the Centre for Career Development Innovation (1993) in Edmonton, Alberta, Canada. Chapter 13 tracks a university professor's experience in teaching Lifecareer.

Part Three, "Living the New Careering: The *Why* Question," includes brief information on the health benefits—both physiological and psychological. Since major volumes discuss Vocational Psychology theory and practice, this book only briefly summarizes those theories in Appendix A. Finally, Appendix B outlines a personal development lesson used with learning-disabled students; Appendix C, resumes; and Appendix D, Work-Career Paradigm Survey Key.

Acknowledging Another Kind of Intellectual Debt—
A Personal Note

Any writing ought to bear the mark of gratitude for those who labor in intellectual pursuits. They brought their best thinking to career concerns given their time and place in history.

However, not finding a hint of process in the career development field, I (Miller-Tiedeman) started reading in the area of science. I, therefore, thank all scientists and their assistants who provided a rich literature that now has utility in many different disciplines.

I also thank those career development theorists, both past and present, who failed to acknowledge the individual as theory maker. Their omissions provided content for my life's work. If these men (and they were mostly men) had experienced more development and vision, my contribution would have taken a very different direction. In that sense, we all serve each other.

My vision also has its limits, and those following will work out their understanding of process, free of my limits. They perhaps will wonder why I did not see many things. Those behind them will similarly wonder until inspiration brings a still more comprehensive form. But that's life's way of protecting each of our life missions while making a grander organization.

1

LEARNING THE NEW CAREERING: THE *WHAT* QUESTION

The Bohr-Heisenberg view of indeterminacy suggests that the foundation of reality itself is an unfixed, indeterminate maze of probabilities. This view serves as a good metaphor for perceiving reality. In everyday living we see the Uncertainty Principle and the Principle of Complementarity—the wave/particle duality—as offering a choice between different ways of looking at the same system. For example, when we sit on the beach and view the ocean, we see either massive undulations on the sea's surface or think of them as disturbed water particles (molecules). In the same way, we can think of nation states. We can break them down into individual cities, buildings, and people. We can take that further and think of the bricks in a building or cells in the people, or taken another step further the molecular or atomic makeup of each. It all depends on the perspective we choose (Zohar, 1990).

The New Careering (Lifecareer®, quantum careering, or living life as process) functions in that same quantum universe which suggests that any one topic has multiple possible perspectives and connects in a web of relationships. Therefore, you'll find quantum physics, development, paradigms, and the new careering, in various chapters with different slants, or with additional information.

If you're coming from a Newtonian perspective, you might call the multiple discussions redundant because they don't follow linear thinking. Ideas, like particles, show up in different places depending on the probability. Then you discover the old notion that seeing is believing reverses itself and becomes believing is seeing.

Anna Miller-Tiedeman
David V. Tiedeman

Vocational Theory in Broad Brush

Spotlight on Transition

Everything moves and changes, even career theory. In the time it took you to read the foregoing two sentences, several trillion reactions occurred in your body. Some of these changes were subtle, some more visible; and they go on without formal permission. As a result, we have the opportunity to grow.

Gary Zukav, author of *The Dancing Wu Li Masters* (1979), in search of a definition of a master, discovered it in a foreword written by Alan Watts in *Embrace Tiger: Return to Mountain* (Huang, 1973). Watts suggested that a master begins from the center, not from the edge. He teaches understanding of basic principles before going to the details, letting the student inquire as understanding progresses. In doing this, what works becomes the motif. Dancing with the process of each individual then becomes the guiding principle. This approach recognizes renewal as basic to life.

If you can learn to dance with change, satisfaction, like a butterfly, will light on your shoulder. You'll also drop a lot of "how it used to be" baggage which will lighten your load for the journey ahead. More importantly you will not *break yourself against life* as frequently.

☐ Looking Ahead

Watch for the following important topics:

1. The roots of vocational guidance: The Vocation Bureau of Boston

2. Parsons' short work history

3. Parsons' first and second propositions

4. First paper-and-pencil test

5. The birth of the *Strong Vocational Interest Blank* (*SVIB*)

6. The Hawthorne effect and prediction of occupational success

7. The first study of vocational choice and adjustment

8. The creation of the *Dictionary of Occupational Titles* (*DOT*)

9. Trait and factor theory goes to World War II for America

10. Vocational choice as a developmental process

11. The career pattern study

12. The Center for Research in Career

14. Career development hits mainstream America

15. Important terms and concepts:

    a. Vocational choice

    b. Trait and factor

    c. Hawthorne effect

    d. Career pattern study

    e. Vocational development

    f. Logical Positivism

Major Transitions

In the early part of the twentieth century, many people on the northeast coast of the United States moved to urban centers in order to find work. Greater Boston felt this effect as well as the unsettling effects arising from too many applicants for too few appealing jobs. To meet this need, greater Boston and its indigenous university, Harvard, together informally rose to the challenge of alleviating distress among the unemployed, thus ushering in the vocational guidance era.

As vocational guidance grew during the twentieth century in Boston and all over the United States, a three-era transition in career theory took place. Professional attention to the human career moved through vocational guidance (Parsons, 1909) to career development (Ginzberg, Ginsburg, Axelrad, & Herma, 1951) to defining life as the big career where the individual occupies primary position, not the professional. This position considers career as something one lives not something one chooses (Miller-Tiedeman, 1982, 1985, 1987, 1988, 1989, 1992; Miller-Tiedeman & Tiedeman, 1983). Vocational psychology discusses individual behavior in conjunction with occupational choice and decision-making. In contrast, Miller-Tiedeman used concepts from physics, the Bible, Buckminster Fuller's thought, and the Hawaiian Kahuna.

The Lifecareer® perspective suggests that the purpose of being alive is to develop our understandings and grow our vision to the fullest extent possible. To do this requires acknowledging ourselves as theory makers and followers of the great inner light leading to individual life mission. The human mission is not only to work, eat, sleep, and consume, but to awaken to a higher purpose.

Vocational Guidance Beginnings

The seeds of vocational guidance germinated in the Vocation Bureau of Boston in 1908. Professor Paul H. Hanus, Department of Education, Harvard University, and Chairman of the Massachusetts State Commission on Industrial Education, convinced the Commonwealth of Massachusetts of its stake in regional industrialization. He also served as a member of the executive committee for the Vocation Bureau of Boston during the early 1900s, the years of the Bureau's conception, birth, and early childhood (Brewer, 1942). Hanus thus had a range of responsibilities that empowered his vigorous participation in organizing the Vocation Bureau of Boston. Among other things, Hanus quickly saw to it that Frank Parsons, a founder of the Bureau, had time to write and speak for the Bureau's cause. Furthermore, Hanus' professorship at Harvard existed when Harvard's interests in education enlarged from a Department of Education into the

---

*LifeCareer, Life-Is-Career, Career Compass and their derivatives are trademarks owned by Dr. Anna Miller-Tiedeman.

Harvard Graduate School of Education. Vocational guidance got a boost of energy from the University's increased interest in general—not just collegiate—educational practice.

Brewer (1942) wrote of the remarkable effort on the part of the Bureau's executive committee and that "... the Vocation Bureau of Boston was formally opened on January 13, 1908" (p. 303) in the proud *Cradle of Liberty* in the United States of America. "[Frank] Parsons was given the title of Director and Vocational Counselor" (p. 59). Brewer credited Parsons with fathering vocational guidance.

Parsons lived only about eight months into the beginning of his dream to provide vocational guidance for youths in need of employment and life direction. His voluminous accomplishments in the eight months' direction of the Vocation Bureau astonish those familiar with administration and management. Besides creating and financing a new organization, and constructing teaching materials for both teaching counseling and working with clients, Parsons penned two sentences still in use today that simplistically define vocational guidance and career counseling. Imagine, just two sentences of this now-recognized father of vocational guidance set vocational guidance on an 80-plus year course into today's profession of career counseling. That exemplifies a parsimonious definition of a career development theory akin to the compactness sought in mathematics. It states a first model (theory) of career development. The two sentences are as follows:

Parsons' First Sentence. "In the choice of a vocation there are three broad factors: [1] a clear understanding of yourself; [2] a knowledge of the requirements and conditions for success ... in different lines of work; [3] true reasoning on the relation of these two groups of facts" (Brewer, 1942, p. 61).

Parsons' Second Sentence. "The Vocation Bureau is intended to aid young people in choosing an occupation, preparing themselves for it, finding an opening in it, and building up a career of efficiency and success" (Brewer, 1942, p. 61).

The first sentence concerns a single choice of vocation; the second one connects two or more choices from which a decision must be made either simultaneously or sequentially (see Tiedeman & Miller-Tiedeman, 1979). Both ideas include decision-making. But the second accommodates decision-making development as well, an important distinction, understanding it makes a difference in whether you deal with the job-career or a single occupation. Neither of these field-defining propositions, however, accommodated the idea that one's work should be pre-emptively self-satisfying.

Parsons' two powerful sentences gave form to the substance of a valuable process in American society—the individual balancing of dream and opportunity necessary for reasonable social order in a democracy (Kelley, 1940).

Brewer's (1942) account of Parsons' life suggested a brilliant man whose life attests to living his in-the-moment experience even though he advocated differently for other people. His paternal grandfather came to America from Cornwall, England, and his father, one of 11 children, spent his early life in the West. After Parsons' birth, his father went west again, taking a job with the Atchison, Topeka, and Santa Fe Railway. When his mother died, Parsons was sent east to live with his Aunt Kate and Aunt Bess. He lived with them until his death in 1908.

Parsons attended the Aaron Academy in Boston, one of a group of 15 academies that flourished during that time. Later he attended Cornell University, majoring in math and science, and graduated as a civil engineer. However, the panic of 1873 downsized many civil engineers so he started teaching in Southbridge, Massachusetts. He worked up from the district school to the high school, and then had charge of the drawing and painting instruction for all schools in town. He experienced success in this work and in mathematics. In addition, he helped organize a fine literary society in town and was so good at debate that a friend and leading lawyer urged him to study law and offered him considerable advantage. A few weeks later, Parsons was offered a professorship at Swarthmore College, but turned it down to study law with the Honorable F. P. Goulding of Worcester, considered one of the finest lawyers in New England. He then took a job as chief clerk at one of the largest Boston firms, but in 1892, he left to engage in legal writing, gaining a reputation for thoroughness, accuracy, and analytic power.

In addition to his law interests, he lectured in Boston on English literature, first at the Y.M.C.U., and after that in the Y.M.C.A. The clarity and brevity with which he treated the subject excited much interest, and his lectures were put into book form and published by Little, Brown, and Co., of Boston, as *The World's Best Books*. This led to an invitation from a New York publishing house to write introductory notes for a variety of books. Boston University also invited Mr. Parsons to lecture on Insurance Law in the university's law school.

Soon Parsons became well known at the state house and throughout Boston. His criticism of Herbert Spencer's philosophy, published by the New National Company, received the highest commendation from eminent thinkers of the country, as did his book on English literature. He also wrote a book entitled *Our Country's Need*. Parsons also contributed editorials to the *Boston American* (Brewer, 1942).

Frank Parsons was an accomplished, brilliant, and multi-talented man. His life-career developing did not follow a straight line. He lived life as process and since he fathered vocational guidance, we can assume he did not have access to what we call counselors. You might want to ask yourself, "What would a career counselor have said to Parsons? What kind of help did he really need? Parsons, very much like Thoreau in his multiple talents, let life inform him. Yet, this man came up with the matching of people to jobs. After reading Parsons' life, it is difficult to imagine anyone telling him anything. Yet, he found his way quite well. While the *wise decision* mantra came from Parsons, *Light, Information, Inspiration*, and *Co-operation* served as the Bureau's mottoes. It appears that the career development field jumped on the *information* aspect of the vocational bureau's concepts, not its orientation toward *light, inspiration*, and *cooperation*. Parsons, this author believes, would have understood process careering and he would have also been open to acknowledging the value of all decisions, not just the wise ones.

You could describe Parsons as a man who seized the moment, growing and changing when appropriate. If Parsons woke up today, he might say, "What? You are not still doing this match thing, even though valuable at times. Remember the winds of life continually blow and we have to bend with that change. Look how my life changed from 1854 to the time I made my transition. I did not follow the straight line, nor were all my decisions wise, but they all worked. Thank you for acknowledging my vision in 1908, now get on with process careering."

Vocational guidance, as set in motion by Parsons, grew substantially during World War I. The need for humanpower management during that war and the subsequent 1930s depression fueled that growth. In addition, with improvement of analytic methods and increased attention of the Harvard Graduate School of Education, more and more institutions of higher education supported the early construction of vocational guidance for everyone, not just those in public education.

The Bureau sustained its own life for a reasonable period because it embraced (a) strong and friendly interests of town and gown, (b) healthy debate of philosophic and practical purpose in vocational guidance, and (c) cooperation with approaching forces of income maintenance in a markedly fluctuating economy.

John Brewer (Harvard's first guidance professor) had a major hand in starting the National Vocational Guidance Association and getting its journal going. He also facilitated nationwide discussion of policy and projects required for (a) improvement of vocational guidance intentions, and, (b) construction and maintenance of a new infrastructure for empowerment of personal development as fostered in a union of liberal education, industrial education, vocational education, and, at present, professional and continuing education. Brewer brought this discussion to a head in a long-term debate of Guidance as Education and/or of Education being Guidance, a debate in which the President of Harvard participated from time to time.

Parsons spearheaded the vocational guidance movement because of his deep concern about the exploitation of workers by industrial monopolists. "This concern led him to propose reforms in business, to prevent exploitation of workers, and in education and other social institutions to help workers choose jobs that matched their abilities and interests" (Brown et al., 1990, p. 13). By sparking establishment of the Vocation Bureau of Boston, Parsons and his professional descendants helped individuals identify their strengths and hopes, and determine how they might use them in various jobs.

Vocational guidance began during the nineteenth and twentieth centuries—the third era of science. With the growing success of the natural sciences in highly structured observation, reasoning, and investigation, psychologists adopted Descartes' logic and Newton's mathematics and the direct querying of nature "untouched by uncontrolled human being." The philosophy of logical positivism and the science of behaviorism took hold in psychology. Logical positivism rejects all transcendental metaphysics, and accepts only those things with verifiable consequences in experience *and* in statements of logic, mathematics or philosophy. In other words, spontaneous healings of any kind would not get a logical positivistic nod.

Differential psychology and its handmaiden, psychometrics, followed almost naturally, just in time to attract Parsons' quest for " ... personal analysis, job analysis, and matching through scientific advising as the basis of occupational choice" (Brown et al., 1990, p. 14).

As noted, World War I initiated the need for large-scale selection and assignment of abilities of men selected for military service. With Robert M. Yerkes' leadership, the first group tests of intelligence—the Army Alpha (a verbal test) and the Army Beta (a nonverbal test)—were given to military personnel in an attempt to match duties with abilities. For the first time, occupational differences in measured intelligence entered research and practice. In all, 18,423 men took the tests, and the data were reported in *Memoirs of the National Academy of Sciences* (Yerkes, 1921, as cited in Crites, 1969).

In 1927, several major contributions to vocational psychology emerged. First, Edward K. Strong, Jr., at Stanford University, published the first edition of the *Strong Vocational Interest Blank (SVIB)*. Strong based the SVIB on research into interests done by James Burt Miner, Bruce V. Moore, and Walter V. Bingham at the Carnegie Institute of Technology (Crites, 1969). This inventory launched Strong's long career dedicated to interests, choice, and other vocational topics. At the same time, Elton Mayo and his colleagues at the Harvard School of Business Administration joined engineers at the Hawthorne Works of the Western Electric Company to conduct what turned out to be a most influential program of research on worker productivity—the Hawthorne study—which suggested that the positive change in worker productivity noted was due to the workers' perception of being singled out for the study, not just for unique patterning in their capabilities (Crites, 1969).

The Minnesota Employment Stabilization Research Institute (MESRI) in 1931 initiated the first programmatic study of vocational choice and adjustment designed to research a large number of workers over a span of several years. It had a three-fold intent: (a) to gain more information about the vocational aptitudes of unemployed workers; (b) to provide data on the re-education problems of the unemployed; and (c) to demonstrate methods of re-education and rehabilitation (Crites, 1969).

To accomplish these goals, D. G. Paterson and others of the University of Minnesota developed tests and psychometric instruments that provided helping professionals with tools to conduct the personal analysis necessary to make seemingly self-advantaged occupational choices. Numerous tests were used to empower Parsons-like intentions. Tests adopted dug into human behavior for traits considered to be (a) fundamental to personality, interests, abilities, and achievements; (b) fairly stable (reliable); and (c) valid enough to justify use in vocational guidance (Crites, 1969).

The Vocational Guidance Era

In the 1930s, vocational counselors generally did directive counseling (i.e., largely structured by the counselor) using the Parsons formula. However, in the early 1940s, Carl Rogers introduced non-directive or client-centered counseling (Rogers, 1951) which gave helping professionals a choice of both technique and philosophy. In what became a prolonged debate between the two camps, E. G. Williamson (1939) at the University of Minnesota strongly led the so-called directive debate. Carl Rogers (1942), at the University of Chicago, led the so called non-directive one.

In surprising parallelism between Parsons' second magic sentence in 1908 relative to vocational development, Williamson (1939) advocated a multi-step process of analysis, synthesis, diagnosis, prognosis, counseling, and follow-up in every step of Parsons' formula for facilitation of vocational development. Williamson recommended a number of counseling techniques designed to help clients explore their personal attributes, discover jobs, learn more about decision-making, relate jobs to themselves, and take action.

Congress, in 1933, passed the Wagner-Peyser Act authorizing the organization of the United States Employment Service (USES). This service acted then much as it does today—as a clearinghouse for job openings and the administration of unemployment insurance. Furthermore, during this period, 25,000 employers and more than 100,000 employees were surveyed (a) to gather job information from job analyses; (b) to develop measures of proficiency and potentiality (c) to establish job equivalence schedules for the transfer of skills; and (d) to write job descriptions for a *Dictionary of Occupational Titles* (*DOT*). The *DOT* became the bible of vocationalists (Crites 1969).

Career Development by the Dawn's Early Light. In 1941, the bombing of Pearl Harbor catapulted the United States into war. Vocational guidance went to war along with the millions of Americans in the Armed Services in one category or another: (a) regulars were ordered into active service immediately; (b) volunteers had some choice of service; and (c) draftees were ordered to serve at the point of greatest need. Service persons met with vocational guidance at induction, testing, and classification. In turn, vocational guidance met service persons while doing its established work of testing and interviewing in order to furnish Armed Forces with abilities matched to military need and, when possible, to personal choice in a small field of opportunity.

Soon, the first era vocational counselors found their clientele changing rapidly. The number of sick and wounded needing rehabilitation increased. The country realized that discharged military needed to be helped back into the civilian economy. Some went directly into similar work of the past. Others had to change fields, get different education, and start to build a new life.

The need to select and classify military personnel on such a grand scale grew vocational psychology overnight. Measurement and evaluation developed in coordinate fashion. Spurred by the need to specify human factors necessary for service in various duties, using new military hardware, psychology pioneers in factor analysis, such as L. L. Thurstone (1947) and John C. Flanagan, founder of the American Institutes for Research in Pittsburgh, Pennsylvania, and later in Palo Alto, California, created new tools, inventories, training specifications, and criterion measures. In a 1947 report on the Aviation Psychology Command's accomplishments in identifying human factors in military services, Brigadier General Flanagan wrote, "rather than the 10, or even 20, traits which many psychologists regarded as the maximum number of important independent traits only a few years ago, the number is almost certainly 50 or even 100, or even larger" (Flanagan, 1947, as cited in Crites, 1969, p. 8). The human mind was more intricate than psychometricians had assumed. This shifted emphasis from job requirements to individual characteristics and co-investigation by individuals and helping professionals. Matching individuals to jobs in the 1930s gave way to what in the 1940s became known as trait and factor theory.

"At the dawn's early light" of World War II's peace, vocational guidance was healthy even though the career development era bubbled beneath its surface like the geyser, Old Faithful.

The Career Development Era

A broad brush fails to trap all it sweeps, but it does pick up guiding principles for traditional career as we know it today. The twentieth century turned into a winner for Newtonian theory and related technologies. Science consolidated its place in the life of being human. Technological advance proceeded close behind. Although a century or two behind the emergence of Newtonian theory, as noted above, vocational guidance largely adopted science paradigms from its birth. (See Parson's sentences above.)

You have to invoke imagination to experience the feel of introducing the unusual in a conforming Western culture. Parsons and a few brave souls did just that in pioneering vocational guidance. We can well imagine the many specters of uncertainty hanging around the minds of those pioneers as they fired up vocational guidance. The step from nothing to something seldom happens easily. "Yes, but..." most likely came from many who watched this development. But somehow what life wants always wins. It then paves the way for more complexity and understanding.

In 1951, Eli Ginzberg brought together an interdisciplinary team— an economist, a psychoanalyst, a sociologist, and a psychologist— to study occupational choice. Ginzberg invited Paul Lazarsfeld, a sociologist, to review the European literature, and Donald Super, the American literature.

Lazarsfeld importantly recommended that Ginzberg's investigators ask *how* occupational choice is made, not *why*. Ginzberg accepted that recommendation. That one change of question marks the beginning of the study of occupational choice as a developmental process.

Time and the self-organizing nature of science obfuscates exact determination of scholarly credit for paradigm shifts such as Ginzberg's shift of his project from its original study of *why* individuals make occupational choices to *how* they make them. However, award of credit seems relatively clear. Both Lazarsfeld (1931) and Buehler (1933) had the idea. But Lazarsfeld introduced it into Ginzberg's project (1951) by suggesting that "instead of posing the question of 'Why,' a more constructive and meaningful approach would be to raise the issue of 'How" (p. 16) in regard to occupational choice. Ginzberg et al. (1951) accepted this notion and clearly credits Lazarsfeld with that shift. But historians report the event differently, as noted below:

Crites (1969) reported the incident as, "Ginzberg et al. (1951) introduced the idea that choice is a process which transpires over a prolonged period of time. Influenced by the work of Lazarsfeld (1931) and Buehler (1929) both of whom argued that *how* individuals make vocational choices may be more significant than *why* they make them (p. 126).

Brown (Brown et al., 1990) said, "Ginzberg, Ginsburg, Axelrad, and Herma set forth a radical new psychologically based theory of career development that broke with the static trait and factor theory of occupational choice" (p. 3). This quote fails to acknowledge Lazarsfeld's place in making the shift to process from which Ginzberg ultimately researched and constructed his theory of occupational choice.

In the early 1950s, Donald E. Super, at Teachers College, Columbia University, influenced by Ginzberg's work, reorganized his own work on *The Dynamics of Vocational Adjustment* (1942) and published his reconceptualization as *A Theory of Vocational Development* (1953). Vocational development was taken to be self-concept maturing through work experience. This paper was instrumental in moving vocational guidance forward to the career development theme. Furthermore, stressing *career patterning* as an organizing principle of logical positivistic research in career development, Super started "The Career Pattern Study" (Super, 1957), a 20-year longitudinal study of the vocational development of adolescents and young adults. Super deliberately excluded females because he lacked enough financial support and because he considered males more vocationally needy than females at that time.

In 1952, influenced by both Ginzberg and Super, David Tiedeman (1968) launched a research series in career development as part of the training program in guidance at the Harvard Graduate School of Education. This first series dealt with most aspects of *how* and *why* adolescents choose the occupations they do. These first studies were driven by method, the generalization of Fisher's two-group discriminant analysis to the *k*-group case and the application of multivariate statistical methods to problems of choice and classification of personnel (Rulon, Tiedeman, Tatsuoka, & Langmuir, 1967).

Tiedeman shifted the second phase of the Harvard Studies in career development from analytic method to theory construction emphasizing concepts drawn from Erikson's (1959) psychosocial theory of ego identity and current existential formulations stemming from the process of decision-making.

The third phase concentrated on the creation and establishment of a computer-involved information system for vocational decisions (ISVD) intended to allow the student to interact with personally chosen facts/data for unfolding of two types of awareness: (a) consciousness of the formed inside concept satisfying the reason for inquiry; and (b) awareness of developmentally becoming more conscious of self-formed understanding. *Tiedeman's care to not overwhelm the inquirer by programmers' intent represents an early effort, and perhaps the first in computer-involved vocational guidance, to place the individual's notions in primary position.*

As happens quite often in research, two or more persons in different locations may unknowingly be working on the same problem. This happened with Anne Roe and John Holland in their common search for a fairly inclusive structure of occupations.

Roe specifically sought such a structure in regard to the personality types and responsibility levels associated with a large number of occupations. Roe sought her structure so she could study the development of personality in the first 20 years of her subjects' parent-child interactions. Roe also studied the kind and responsibility level of their occupational predilection. Her schema, detailed in *The Psychology of Occupations* (1956), included the following categories: Service, Business Contact, Organization, Technology, Outdoor, Science, General Culture, and Arts and Entertainment (see Appendix A, Table A-1). The National Institutes of Mental Health facilitated the latter part of her work with a research grant enabling her acceptance of a professorship at Harvard with co-direction (with Tiedeman) of the Center for Research in Career.

A decade later, John Holland concentrated on prediction of such variables as vocational choice, occupational membership, and the work history, using an individual's resemblance to one or more personality types. Holland evolved an occupational grouping system quite substantially reflecting Parsons' trait and factor theory. To do so, Holland had to devise (a) an interest inventory solidly reflecting human vocational interests; (b) an environmental characterization of a large number of vocations constructed in parallel with his interest inventory, so the match of person and job had strong correspondence; and (c) a self-administered delivery system (see Appendix A, Table A-1, p. 328).

This work resulted in his *Self-Directed Search* (SDS)(1977), which has six occupational categories:

1. realistic;
2. investigative;
3. artistic;
4. social;
5. enterprising; and
6. conventional.

The depth, care, integrity, and usefulness of his delivery system has kept the SDS as generally number one on the helping professional's hit list of career development support materials. Crites (1969) put Holland's popularity in these logical positivistic terms (a definition of logical positivism appears earlier in this chapter): "It is characteristic of Holland's research that it involves analyses of data on large numbers of variables obtained from large numbers of subjects" (p. 11).

In the very comprehensive Project Talent study (McLaughlin & Tiedeman, 1974), both the Roe (1956) and the Holland (1966) categories resembled one another logically and empirically. The study was based on numerous occupational data, a scientifically specified, five percent random sample of the seniors of all American high schools. In accordance with principles of longitudinal career studies, students in the sampled schools were followed up 1, 5, and 11 years later. That same cohort of students reported their educational and occupational preferences each time.

Initial and follow-up career designations were coded according to three criterion systems: Holland's 6-group; Roe's 8-group; and Flanagan's 12-group systems. Hit rates of 11-year occupations by high school choice proved to be relatively similar after correction for difference in the number of groups in the three classification systems.

In small measure, Flanagan's system rated highest, Holland's second highest, and Roe's third. But Flanagan's system included both educational and occupational categories; Holland's and Roe's only occupational categories. Four of Holland's six categories had definite one-to-one correspondence with four of Roe's. Holland's remaining two categories spread themselves over the four remaining Roe categories quite logically, as expected from the order of groups in Holland's hexagon and Roe's circle. (See Appendix A for more detail on the Roe and Holland theories.)

Career Development Goes Public

Even though traditional careerists continue searching for predictive factors of occupational membership using logical positivism, their concepts did not seep deeply into mainstream America. Vocational guidance mostly served professionals, college students, and other middle-class people. However, that changed markedly in November, 1972, when Richard Bolles published *What Color Is Your Parachute? A Practical Manual for Job-Hunters and Career Changers*. By 1974, *What Color Is Your Parachute?* leaped to the top of the best-seller lists, first in the Northwest and then throughout the country in succeeding years. It has stayed current by annual updates. Its success lay in presentation of old ideas in new ways. Key ideas in *What Color is Your Parachute?* include "The Party Exercise," "The Quick Job-Hunting Map," "The Practice Field Survey," and the "Information Interview."

Each of these ideas has been used extensively by many helping professionals (Bolles, 1994).

Pieces Seeking Puzzles. By 1960, the literature of career development theory, study, and practice attained a national and potentially international corpus sufficient to support construction and dissemination of collections of the several emerging theories of career development (see Table 2.1).

As career development theories increased further between 1960 and today, authors of books presenting two or more theories (e.g., Osipow, 1973) began a search for integrating theories. They collected two or more separate parts hinting at a vague but as yet inexpressible unity, and hoped that these parts together would coalesce into a more inclusive general theory even though the parts were not designed to be together.

In the early '80s, Brown, Brooks, and Associates (1984) created an excellent compendium of traditional career theories. They solicited 10 select career theories written by their originators, with the exception of Frank Parsons' theory. Brown et al. (1984) included Holland's Theory of Careers, Roe's Personality Theory, Bordin's Psychodynamic Model of Career Choice, Krumboltz's Social Learning Theory, Super's Life-Span Life-Space Theory, Hotchkiss and Borow's Sociological Perspectives on Work and Career Development, Tiedeman's Career Decision Theory, and Douglas Hall's Theory of Career Development in Organizations. Each theorist used a simple research structure for presentation of his or her theory, and applied his or her theory to The Case of K.

Brown, who wrote the trait and factor chapter and developed K's case, asked questions like "What do you (K) know about the work of an entry level accountant?" Weinrach and Srebalus viewed K's case from the Holland perspective, identifying where K's vocational activities fit on Holland's hexagonal model. Lunneborg used the Roe approach—personality and occupation—and asked questions about needs, interests, work values, and personality traits closest to identity. Bordin started with a series of probes like job satisfaction, current job frustrations, and so forth. Super asked how many times K had changed goals, and whether or not she would stay with the current preference, the relative importance of her work and homemaking roles, among other things. Krumboltz and Mitchell looked at K's dilemma through the lens of the social learning theory of career decision making (SLTCDM). Since Miller-Tiedeman and Tiedeman took an individualistic approach and the case summary contained mostly trait and factor data, they chose to contrast the individualistic approach with the trait and factor notions in general.

TABLE 2.1. Chronology of Vocational Guidance & Career Development

1909	F. Parsons	Father of vocational guidance
1939	E. G. Williamson	Directive counseling
1942	C. R. Rogers	Non-directive counseling
1951	P. Lazarsfeld	Switched the question from *why* people make certain occupational choices to *how* they make them, opening the way for studying occupational choice as a developmental process.
1951	E. Ginzberg	Conducted a study validating occupational choice as a developmental process, posing a theory of occupational choice
1952	D. V. Tiedeman	Research series in career development
1953	D. E. Super	Self-concept maturing through work experience; Career patterning as an organizing principle
1956	A. Roe	Personality and responsibility associated with occupation
1961	D. V. Tiedeman	Decision-Making Theory Information System for Vocational Decisions (ISVD)
1966	J. L. Holland	Occupational choice related to personality type
1972	R. Bolles	Packaging of career development concepts for mainstream America in *What Color Is Your Parachute?*
1979	J. D. Krumboltz	Social learning theory/behaviorism; Managed development
1983	A. Miller-Tiedeman	Process careering suggesting each individual is his or her own theory maker

All theorists followed the editors' instruction in traditional terms except for Miller-Tiedeman and Tiedeman, who looked at The Case of K and said, "Out of about 630 words in the case history, practically all of them are trait and factor words—that is, the words of our occupational scientism of seventy years or so. A mere 3 percent of the words resemble in any way K's personal words about herself" (Brown et al., 1990, p. 500). In traditional career, you can summarize for someone else, let the experts comment, and allegedly derive some learning. But when you work from the individual's perspective you need verbatim information from both the individual and the responding counselor in order not to fall into a trait and factor response. Further, summarized cases do not carry inflective voice information, which frequently proves to be more telling, and upon which a completely new line of thought often emerges from both the client and the counselor.

In addition, summaries frequently fail the accuracy test when applied to another research cohort. We see this in courts of law. A witness reports something and on cross-examination it often does not hold up. Further, what a witness hears from someone else is hearsay and not admitted into evidence. Also, we all know that ten people watching an accident will most likely offer ten different versions. That is one reason why in mediation, during the exchange, you ask the complaining parties to mirror what they heard the other one say so they can work on the problem with full information. And even with complete data, uncertainty is still there.

All the chapters in Brown et al. (1984, 1990, 1996) reflect selected part(s) of the career or vocational topic with a client and counselor orientation with the counselor's notions in primary position. Even Super with his rainbow and stage theories failed the individualistic test, as he does not entertain the notion that each individual is his or her own career-theory maker (Miller-Tiedeman, 1988). Rather, he looked to group data for generalizations derived from statistical models. In this instance, Super used different but quite similar concepts to those of Tiedeman and O'Hara (1963).

This suggests that two schools of thought now emerge (a) those who think their training makes them the better judge of an individual's life possibilities, and (b) those who acknowledge no one has all the information the individual has, therefore, the individual perspective occupies primary position. Using the latter, we give career development away to the individual, offer our support to them as they struggle to grow a more mature internal career theory, one that does not get dated or dependent on anyone else's interpretation.

Let the career theorists continue their probes into lifeless data and discussion, but let those who want an alive, lived experience move forward toward greater possibilities on the wings of process. Room exists for both approaches. We only need a shift up in development to initiate more conversation about the individualistic point of view. Kottler (1997) captures the necessity for this line of thinking in the following story:

> Most of us were taught very early in our career that experts exist who really do know what good counseling is and how to do it. However, few of these prominent counselors seem to agree with one another about which therapeutic ingredients are most important. At various times, I have been told that I should work on the relationship, correct cognitive distortions, interpret unconscious desires, reflect underlying feelings, excavate unresolved issues, construct alternative narratives, reframe problems strategically, deal with existential issues, structure specific goals, and a dozen other strategies I no longer remember. In most cases, the mentor or advocate felt strongly that his or her conception of good counseling was optimal and everyone else simply misinformed, ignorant or even incompetent. Needless to say, I found this a bit confusing.
>
> During a trip to Alberta to give a presentation on the essence of good counseling, I took a break to do some hiking in the mountains. As I made my preparation, I spoke with a number of people in the area, each of whom warned me, I might run into a bear in which case I had better know what to do.
>
> "Okay," I prompted, "What should I do if I see a bear?"
>
> "Back away slowly," the native Albertan warned me. "And whatever you do, don't make eye contact. Look at your feet."
>
> Sounded reasonable to me. Hadn't I once read somewhere about following similar advice when confronting a mountain gorilla? Something about showing, deference. Thus armed, I continued my inquiries about the best trails to visit.
>
> The next person I consulted, a shop keeper, also warned me about the bears. "You know what to do if you see one, don't you?"
>
> I broke into a big smile. "Why of course!" I said. When I began to explain about the downcast eyes, she began laughing.
>
> "You've got to be kidding," she laughed. "You don't actually believe that do you?" Before I could formulate an answer, she continued: "Actually, what works best is to immediately fall to the ground, curl yourself into a fetal position. Cover your head. And whatever you do, don't move. At worst, the bear will play with you a bit."

Right, I thought. I could just imagine myself doing that. Even if it did I'd prefer to die on my feet rather than just lying there waiting to see if the bear read the same books I did.

Some time later, while outfitting myself for the adventure, another long time resident of the town asked me once again if I knew what to do if I should encounter a bear.

"Yea, yea, I know. Curl into a ball and wait patiently for death, or life, depending on the bear's mood."

"Well, there is some truth to that. Actually though, you don't have to sit still."

I perked up considerably at this. "Yea?," I asked wearily. "What then?" "Bears, you see, can't run downhill very well. It throws off their gait. All you have to do is find a downward slope and run, roll, or fall as fast as you can."

I was skeptical at this point, and it showed on my face. "Come on," he urged. "Have you ever seen a bear running downhill?"

Come to think of it, I hadn't. Besides, this was advice I liked a lot. I'm a good runner. I like to run. There is no better way I'd rather get snatched by a bear than running for my life.

Later that day, someone again asked about my knowledge of bear lore. This time I was grateful for the opportunity to show off my obscure piece of intelligence that bears can't run downhill.

The woman thought this was hysterical. In fact, she found it difficult to catch her breath. She called others over to show them an especially dumb tourist. Once she regained control, she explained that bears like to run downhill. And besides, look at the laws of physics—a small body mass rolling downhill, and a very large, angry body mass moving down the same slope. Which do I think would make better time?

Yea, I challenged her a bit too stridently. "What should I do then?" "Why climb a tree, of course," she answered. "Grizzlies don't climb trees. I have a friend who, when chased, climbed a tree and angered the bear so much it camped beneath the branches, pacing back and forth, for hours until it finally gave up and left.

Now I could easily do that under the circumstances, even though I felt leery about the advice. The only bear I really knew much about was Winnie the Pooh and as I recall he climbed trees quite often to get at the honey. Now there may be a difference between what you should do with a Pooh bear, a black bear, and a grizzly, but I didn't trust my diagnostic judgment to tell the difference under the circumstances. For one, I was supposed to throw a rock to chase it away, the other I was supposed to crawl into a hole. And what if I couldn't tell which kind it was? Should I throw a rock at myself?

The peculiar variety of bear advice continued all day long. The more people I spoke with, the more advice I got. All of it different. Some people advised me to wear a bear bell, others to carry a gun, still others told me not to go into the mountains at all. Most amazing of all: each person felt confident that he or she was right and everyone else wrong. When I presented each of them with contradictory data, they met my challenge with an unconcerned shrug. Each had not the slightest doubts about what I should do.

Does this sound at all familiar? It sure did to me. And I felt immediate relief realizing that it isn't just some members of my profession who feel so certain they are right, and everyone else misguided. There seems to be so many people trying to find their way in the world by convincing themselves, and others, that no other truth except what they have discovered personally exists.

Fortunately, I never ran into a bear that day. It was a good thing, too, because I'm certain I would have just froze, overwhelmed with all the choices available. The bear would have had some story to tell her cubs that night. A story about some guy she met who, alternately, hit the ground, ran downhill and climbed a tree. I'm sure I would have tried them all.

To this day, I'm not sure what to do with a bear. That's all right though, because I'm not always sure about what to do with most of my clients. And when I talk to people about the essence of counseling, I may think I know what is most important, but I now remind myself that the world is filled with experts who believe they have found truth. By the way, many of them got snatched by bears" (p. 38).

The Statistics of Vocational Guidance and Career Development

Love and marriage may well "go together like a horse and carriage" and "you can't have one without the other." But, as Heisenberg has shown, human incapacity to know tomorrow perfectly, or even at all, has not surfaced in consciousness as yet. We only need look to weather prediction to understand uncertainty. Uncertainty does not readily surface when individuals each day continually face existential choices in a downsized environment.

Statisticians have labored mightily to help those in the helping professions put a science beneath their counseling purpose. This labor started early in the twentieth century, almost from the time of Frank Parsons. But statisticians have been unable to escape the one koan all existential constructionists face: STATISTICS AND GUIDANCE ARE LOGICALLY INCOMPATIBLE. You have to have one *without* the other because you cannot capture an individual life in a statistic, only moments in time, which have little bearing on the accumulated whole.

Additionally, statistics of vocational guidance ordinarily produce probabilities, usually for today's events, not tomorrow's necessities. The statistics of vocational guidance take those that believe them into the future looking backwards, ignoring the fact that the *Reader's Digest* openly informs hopeful entrants that the holder of only one, in the expected 900,000,000 participant chances, will drive home that single $35,000 automobile tendered as prize in its sweepstakes.

On the other hand, seekers of guidance, me, you, your parents, helping professionals, continue to want certainties to assuage that bugaboo of doubt present in a shifting economic environment. But this calls for a different scientific base than that provided statistically. This book intends to help you develop confidence that life dances in you and only awaits recognition. At this point, you can surf the probabilities and know that at the right moment, you'll know what to do. Take love—you do not usually ask someone, "Am I in love now?"

How did the vulnerable guidance paradox of statistics and guidance get embedded in vocational guidance in the United States? First, its foundations jumped the Atlantic pond in the nineteenth century along with other European psychology, turning to a logical positivistic view which gradually worked its way into psychology and counseling in U.S. universities, its professors, and the practitioners they trained. Statistics sounded scientific, like good hard science, and the need to look intelligent and keep up with other disciplines perhaps played no small part in the furrow statistics plowed in a field devoted to helping human beings, most of whom know or care little about statistics. They usually want to know, "How will it benefit me?" "Will it make a difference in my life?" Individuals choose counseling because they want to help people, not guide them by statistics.

Vocational Guidance and Career Development— Looking Back

Trait and factor logic and instrumentation presently underlies most career theories grounded in advising clients concerning choices of education, job, occupation, vocation, and career. Many of the theories in the first two editions of *Career Choice and Development* (Brown et al., 1984, 1990) reflect trait and factor application. The thinking that "each individual has a unique set of traits that can be measured reliably and validly" (1984, p. 12) reflects the narrow conception that an individual consists only of his or her measured traits. This misses the holistic quality of the individual as well as the fact that the whole is more than the sum of its parts. Brown (1996) goes on to say that most career development theorists cast their vote toward the matching of worker to occupation because they think it both possible and desirable.

The simplicity of the trait and factor model has kept its principal techniques pretty clear. Many tests have been developed over the past 90 years for analysis of the individual either at the individual's behest or some authority's request. Mountains of media and advertising materials also exist concerning analysis of school, college, job, occupation, vocation, and so on—quite a few of them free. "Youths just need them," many adults stress, especially as their youths need to be readied for a major American identity test—being able to support themselves. Matching individuals and jobs on the basis of all this out-formation (the opposite of in-formation) gets done by a bag full of guidance matching instrumentalities: self, parents, friends, teachers, helping professionals, consultants, interviewers, computers.

While clear and distinctive in their day, Parsons' two defining propositions strangle efforts to change the paradigm, values, concepts, and techniques upon which today's career development whale presently flounders, as did an actual whale in San Francisco Bay several years ago. It swam in the wrong direction, like current theorists who try to carry out the limited intent of vocational guidance developed toward the end of the industrial era at the beginning of the twentieth century.

Emerging Theories

The 1996 edition of *Career Choice and Development* continues to reflect the trait and factor imprint (Brown et al., 1996). It smacks of directive counseling notions where the client receives what the helping professional allegedly knows. What passes for emerging theories still lingers in the shadow of trait, factor, and logical positivism. The helping professional takes the lead for assessing the situation, not the client, in Brown's (1996) values-based model. A social cognitive perspective tracks career connections of all sorts (Lent, Brown, & Hackett, 1996); a cognitive information processing approach asks the question, "What can we do as helping professionals to enable individuals to acquire self-knowledge, occupational knowledge, career decision skills, and metacognitions to become effective and responsible career problem solvers and decision makers?" (Peterson, Sampson,

Reardon, & Lens, 1996, p. 427); and a contextual explanation uses action theory "cognitively and socially steered and controlled" (Young, Ladislav, & Valach, 1996, p. 483).

The language of all the emerging theories tends to place professional theory first, overlooking life as living art; suggesting that clients often lack self or occupational knowledge as well as career decision skills, and finally the client may not be an effective problem solver. A contextual explanation has more possibility in its notion of joint action. But, it does not respond to a major life principle—flow. Furthermore, none of these emerging theories tend to (a) place personal knowledge as primary; (b) values the individual as a theory maker; or (c) empowers the personal journey of the client in a framework larger than job. Finally, the litmus test for any theory is its usefulness. Can it be used for non-job-oriented situations? Nevertheless, it would be interesting to watch these theories develop.

Fortunately, the number of individuals imprinted by these over-cognitive theories stay small in contrast to those uncertified individuals like doctors, hair dressers, psychics, friends, ministers, and the like who today provide useful career counseling. Individuals seek what they need when they need it and use their practitioner of choice. If it works for the person choosing it, then it works. Many uncertified and untrained people presently help numerous individuals.

Here's where development and paradigms enter the discussion. Those who believe that one needs academic training to do career counseling would, of course, decide that uncertified practitioners do not qualify. But if you look at how one gets certified, you discover it's built primarily on memory, memory which conforms mostly to what has been. It may be that the most effective helping professional, when working with a client, forgets all he or she has been taught and remembers what he or she knows.

The On-Line Career Professional

While career development professionals work on aspects of theory, practice, certification, licensing, and registration, the on-line career centers flourish, offering a smorgasbord of career help. At present few universities offering career counseling degrees can compete with the information on the Internet that in some cases runs into the millions of pages. On-line you can search all kinds of job possibilities, go into chat rooms, file your resume, and look for job openings world-wide. (See Chapter 8 for more details and web addresses.) Could the helping professional-in-training five or ten years ago have imagined such a complete system, well removed from the halls of academia and certification? We ought to ask ourselves, what high-touch kinds of things can helping professionals do that could interlink with the high-tech on-line career centers?

The Career-as-Process Era: A Major Paradigm Shift—
Looking Forward

In the early 1980s, Miller-Tiedeman (Miller-Tiedeman & Tiedeman, 1983), introduced Life-Is-Career® at an Assembly to Advance Career, convened at the University of Southern California. She next wrote and published *How NOT To Make It ... And Succeed: Life on Your Own Terms* (1987, 1989); *LIFECAREER™: The Quantum Leap into a Process Theory of Career* (1988); and *LIFECAREER: How It Can Benefit You* (1982, 1985, 1992). She moved career from something to talk about, to a "lived and owned in the moment" process, from a definition of job as career to life as career, and from theorists spinning theory to the individual as theory maker. After 87 years, the individual's career theory and life process took center stage with career theorists and professionals standing in the wings. The individual now can see that career is not something out there, in your future, to be chosen, planned, pursued, reached or discussed by someone else. Career is here— *now*. It is you, who you are, your *Life* (Miller-Tiedeman, 1982, 1985, 1987, 1988, 1989, 1992). Life outlives all of us; and it passes the timeless and self-evident test.

☐ Looking Back

Significant Paradigm Shifts

Most traditional career theories relate in some way to Parsons' self knowledge, requirements for work, and true reasoning. Parsons' two sentences represent a paradigm establishment as he designed the vocational guidance model. In the late forties and early fifties, Ginzberg (Ginzberg et al., 1951) identified Lazarsfeld as the one who switched the occupational choice question from *why* people make certain choices to *how* they make them and did several studies. This proved a radical departure from the traditional paradigm and recognized vocational choice as a developmental process. Eli Ginzberg and his colleagures (1951) then assembled an interdisciplinary team to investigate occupational choice. His findings validated Lazarsfeld's wisdom of a switch in the question. This spawned many professional contributions that notched the field forward. (See Table 2.2.)

In the 1960s, Harvard University entered into contract with the U.S. Office of Education to develop prototypes for an *Information System for Vocational Decisions* (*ISVD*). Professor David V. Tiedeman served as principal

---

*Lifecareer, Life-Is-Career, Career Compass and their derivations are trademarks owned by Dr. Anna Miller-Tiedeman.

investigator of this project. While most remember the ISVD for just its information orientation, Tiedeman's vision, looking years ahead, designed prototypes of a system allowing the client to work interactively with the data and not get caught in the loop of the designer's paradigm (Tiedeman & Field, 1965). The required system technology reached commercial feasibility only in the 1990s and feasibility still has not reached the reality Tiedeman envisioned.

Richard Bolles' *What Color Is Your Parachute?*, written and published in the 1970s, probably contributed more to the actual career development of ordinary Americans than theorists and/or practitioners contributed before.

New contributions usually deviate from the norm and come from those not heavily invested in the old paradigm or who are in a position not to have their jobs threatened. Joel Barker (1990) in his video, *Discovering the Future: The Business of Paradigms*, suggests that new pioneers have nothing to lose by creating the new. They're already in the new, writing the new rules at the edge with great courage and trust in their own judgment. But it may also be that those who create the new, fulfill a life mission—and they may be more adept at listening to its *calling*.

If history has anything to teach us, it is that those who listen to new tunes and life callings help notch humanity forward even though they themselves face colleagues who disbelieve. As Hans Alfen, a Nobel scientist, once noted, the phrase, *"all knowledgeable people know"* has stopped many a contribution.

TABLE 2.2. Major Paradigm Shifts Occurring Pre-Process Careering

---

1931	Paul Lazarsfeld shifted the question from the *why* of occupational choice to the *how*, introducing occupational choice as a developmental process.
1951	Eli Ginzberg formulated a developmental theory of occupational choice.
1968	David V. Tiedeman designed an interactive computer system to facilitate the inquirer's escape from the program designer's teaching model.
1974	Richard Bolles packaged career development ideas for the public.

The End of a Century

Today, we have more opportunity to romance life, living our own process, than ever before, while trying to stay economically afloat in a transforming economy. Today's information superhighway proceeds across the wires rapidly and internationally. That's today's fast lane into which vocational psychology should move because the on-line career centers (see Chapter 3 for more detail) now far exceed anything being done in academic institutions vis-à-vis traditional career development, with the exception of theory development. But one might argue that theory is being constructed via the practice now in effect electronically. Those in vocational psychology might want to ponder the question, "What can we do that is not done better on-line?"

Furthermore, career today gets fashioned worldwide and calls for a new set of assumptions which frees individuals from old paradigms and myths. Recently, an entire issue of *The Counseling Psychologist* (Heppner, 1997) was devoted to the School-to-Work idea which indicates the parochial nature of some in vocational psychology. To bring that issue into the 1990s, we'd retitle it "School-to-World."

After all the theorizing, it comes down to how we can romance our Life-As-Career, loving both the ups and the downs. This means accepting life as it is and ourselves as we are, while keeping an eye out for improvement.

Robert James Waller, in his book *Old Songs in a New Cafe* (1994), wrote about the romance of life, that indescribable magic continually bumping up against us if we but pause to notice. Waller said you would know that had happened if, on your dying bed, after all the living and doing, you ran the following poem of R. M. Rilke through your mind:

I live my life in growing orbits
which move out over the things of this world.
Perhaps I never can achieve the last,
but that will be my attempt.

I am circling around God.
Around the ancient tower,
and I have been circling for a thousand years.
And I still do not know,
if I am a Falcon,
or a storm,
or a great song.

"When you have done that ... you can smile and nod quietly to yourself, you will have succeeded and romance will ride your shoulder as you turn for home. Go well. Remember the flowers. Remember the wind" (Waller, 1994, p. 51–52).

☐ Discussion Questions

1. What is transition? Name at least five important historical transitions that dramatically affected individual life direction.

2. Appendix A summarizes nine theories. Compare and contrast any one of those theories with the Lifecareer Theory.

3. Read one of the traditional career theories and be prepared to discuss the following questions:

   a. What assumptions are apparent in the theory you read?

   b. What about the individual as theory maker?

   c. Could the theory you chose be used in everyday situations outside of job search?

☐ Classroom/Group Exercises

1. Pair up with someone you don't know and listen to each other's definitions of transition.

   a. Look at your definition of transition and identify one of your major beliefs.

   b. Why is perception important?

   c. Why is it important to have a theory that encourages individuals to trust their own thought?

   d. What economical gains result when you trust your inner wisdom?

2. Name several historical happenings and discuss the role perception played.

3. Choose a classmate and discuss the following sharing back with the class:

   a.   Do you believe you live your life theory?

   b.   What is it?

   c.   How does it feel to have your career theory validated?

   d.   What do you think of the idea that Life-Is-Career?

   e.   Tell how you manage your life direction. What helps you the most?

☐ Homework Assignment

1. Using the questions in the Classroom/Group Exercise #3, interview someone in the community and report to the class.

Anna Miller-Tiedeman

The New (Quantum) Careering Model

Spotlight on Process

Early in James Michener's writing career, he received a letter from his agent saying that he had reached a regrettable conclusion that Michener had no future as a writer. Further, the agent said he was terminating the contract and returning the manuscript, as he doubted it would ever be publishable. He went on to say that Michener did not welcome constructive criticism, that his revisions had not improved the manuscript, and that he showed no promise whatever of developing into a writer whose works would find favor with the public.

This letter shattered Michener, but he said he did not get angry at the agent as he had always treated him fairly. He thought, "I guess he knows what he's doing" (1992, p. 284). Michener also acknowledged that the agent had been accurate and fair in his criticism because he (Michener) did not accept advice from others graciously, particularly when it touched on his writing (a Self-Aware response; see Chapter 4 for more detail on development). Michener had determined to do things his way and accept the consequences.

Walking to work, James Michener felt a kind of depression. But by the time he reached his office, he felt better. He decided to forget that letter and go on. So, he continued to work. While in a heated discussion with several editors over the use of words, someone knocked on the door. A colleague opened the door and said, "Jim, you've won the Pulitzer Prize!" (p. 286). Of course the rest is history.

One person's, *"you cannot write,"* for another person becomes a *Pulitzer Prize*—an illustration of the quantum physics principal which suggests you cannot separate the observer from what he or she observes. Or, reality depends on who is looking.

☐ Looking Ahead

Watch for the following Important topics:

1. Life-Is-Career®.

2. The value of personal experience.

3. Changed decisions for a changed paradigm.

4. Living Life-As-Career changes perspectives.

5. Selected Lifecareer (Quantum Career or process living) assumptions.

6. Selected Lifecareer Principles:

    a. No one of us has all it takes to make our dreams come true.

    b. Each individual has a personal theory that works for him or her.

    c. Life-Is-Career and self organizes on its own.

    d. Guiding from inner wisdom.

    e. Life goes both right and left (often called wrong).

    f. Life is self-organizing.

    g. Cooperating with the approaching forces while assessing the situation.

    h. Setting intentions and organizing versus setting goals and planning.

7. Important terms and concepts:

    a. Self-conceiving.

Lifecareer, Life-Is-Career, Career Compass and their derivatives are registered trademarks of Dr. Anna Miller-Tiedeman.

b. Whole organizes the parts.

c. Life direction happens each moment.

d. Making a life, a primary value; making a living, a secondary one.

e. Career is lived and becomes the path you leave behind.

f. Focus on inner wisdom.

g. Web of connections.

The New Careering Model

Life-Is-Career organizes the major thesis of the New Careering model, not for the purpose of academic discussion or assimilating someone else's opinion, but for the lived in the moment experience individually defined, differing each minute, and changeable *ad infinitum*. Therefore, most of the concepts in this chapter and book are conveyed by story. The theory for the New Careering comes from the Lifecareer theory used by individuals as a philosophy, and by professionals as a theory. Lifecareer stretches your beliefs about all aspects of life, whether about a job or an emergency room experience. When Life-Is-Career everything in life contributes to life-direction clarity. Even the confusion aspect, over time, contributes to the clarity. When you recognize and understand the flow of experience, then trust assumes a primary position. You see that growing does not have to be painful but may turn out that way, that the "there" you think is there may not be there when you get there. This brings a more relaxed attitude about life as you continue to advance a next step. At this point, you gain a greater awareness of how much of life falls outside of your control.

Professionals who work with Lifecareer act as New Careering Developers (NCDs) because they support, and encourage what is coming from the individual (assuming a healthy psychology), and only on rare occasions voice their career theory or use former career theories with clients. NCDs differ from counselors in that they make different assumptions (see Table 3.1) and their responses usually come from a higher level of development reflecting inclusiveness and potentiality for all ideas. Instead of working from trends or what has been, they help midwife the client's unfolding vision.

Further, New Careering Developers support the emerging story—they do not edit or co-author the story content, although any interaction does somewhat contaminate and change the story by virtue of another's involvement. They guard against interpreting the client's story, but they do help clients identify career development ideas and personal paradigms that have both served and not served them well. New Careering Developers rely on a time-tested principle—trial and error. In this sense they act more like mediators, working with the client's perception. But NCDs do encourage clients to consider all decision making valuable and instructive. The focus is on the action taken, not on outcome or getting it right.

Lifecareer encourages individuals to *cooperate with the approaching forces* in their lives while applying maximum intelligence to the situation. We all do this, but sometimes fail to recognize it because we look for something harder, thinking that no pain translates into no gain. In Lifecareer the opposite is true. Maturing your personal career theory advances more rapidly within a cooperation framework.

What Is an Approaching Force?

An approaching force is simply all of life that bumps into us, both positive and negative. The positive forces, we tend to handle fairly well. The dispositive ones present a challenge. Joan*, a writer, started working on her manuscript again at 6:00 p.m. after she had worked on it all day. She felt too tired to start an intellectual activity, as she knew that the approaching force of exhaustion usually took over, but she started anyway. The result: She wrote two impotent paragraphs. At that point, she quit. The next morning, she got up still feeling empty and without words. She started typing and the words fell out like water over the cliff. She could not stop them. She later remarked that had she cooperated with the approaching force of sleep (exhaustion), she could have saved her psychic and physical energy. But she, like many people, felt the need to push on.

Another example, illness. Often we try to work our bodies to where they finally say, "no." They break down. We get rest because our body forces us to cooperate. A little thought and awareness might have prevented the breakdown. Sometimes, we focus so intently on what we have to do that we ignore the body signaling, "Enough for now." When we do not pay attention, we often end up in the biggest life-direction center around—the hospital. Approaching forces come in all shapes and sizes in every aspect of our lives, and they do not ask our permission to interrupt. They appear without permission, as do the lessons we need to learn.

We All Live Life as Process

What does that mean? Simply that you handle what comes into your life, the overwhelming, the underwhelming, and the normal. "What do you

---

*All names in case vignettes have been changed to protect the confidentiality of the client.

mean by living life as process?" That question gets asked over and over again as if it is something strange and new. Miller-Tiedeman has shared panel discussions where people tell a part of their life story, which clearly reveals process. But when they take audience questions they revert back to the learned professional response. For instance, a very well-known person in career development told how he came to his current position (as a media spokesperson). His story revealed that his background did not include formal training in career development. Yet, he made a substantial place for himself as an expert in that area. When the audience asked questions, he reverted back to a traditional career response: *"You should do this."* This advice seemed light years away from the principles he had used in his life.

This separation of experience from conscious awareness illustrates another quantum physics principle—complementarity: When you focus on one thing, you miss others. If you do not look for the *life as process* theme in someone's story, you'll miss it as it then takes on the character of separate happenings. However, when you look for the principle of process, you realize how one experience followed another one, forming a pattern for the individual's life. Each experience carries an encryption useful in the next experience.

The major theme in the New Careering model revolves around the individual as theory maker, as a teller of his or her own evolving story. If we do not tell our own story both to ourselves and others, we live from dogma. But living one's own story takes courage. The core meaning of courage suggests having heart. It is the delicate imbalance of love and fear with love having the slight edge. Courage sustains us through life (Courion, 1997).

Theory is not separate from experience. Theory merely mirrors a story of someone's experience. You can look at any theory and piece together the theorist's story.

A few words here about story. The Western take on story suggests it useful mostly for and with children. This slices out an important technique for maturing our career theory because only when we know our story do we have the opportunity to revise it in cooperation with our life mission. Otherwise, we will break ourselves against life time and time again. But a perfect draft is not the intention, only a rough one that receives continual revision. You might think of it as unfinished nonfiction. Additionally,

Storywork (in its broadest definition) leads us into the life we yearn. In truth, we are the stories we tell ourselves and others. Stories connect us to the wisdom of our ancient past, clarify our chaotic present, and inspire us to reach toward the vision of what we sense is the possible in our future. Stories shape our beliefs, expectations, and actions.... To truly transform ourselves and our circumstances we need to: (a) fully recognize the attachment we have to our current story; (b) acknowledge how our current story may possess and limit us; and (c) be willing to reinterpret or change our relationship to our stories (Courion, 1997, p. 1, parentheses added).

Emmett and Harkins (1997) catch the spirit of *story* in suggesting the narrative technique for training counselors. They note that "A paradigm of career as story requires a shift in the role of the career counselor. Career counselors operating from a matching framework help clients fit into appropriate occupations, whereas career counselors operating from a narrative framework help clients find ways to belong and to matter" (p. 61).

Earlier, Savickas (1993) suggested that the role of the career counselor is one of a co-author or editor which, on the surface, appears to suggest altering client life information and viewpoint. But Savickas goes on to say that counselors can identify themes and tensions in the client's story-line which often prove useful and informative for the next step.

Many approaches can help individual clients clarify at different points in life even those that some might deem inappropriate. As in mediation, the question isn't, "what does it look like or sound like to someone else?", but rather, "does the client find it useful?"

How Does an Individual Make Theory?

Individuals make theory the same way professionals make theory—there's nothing magical about it. You do not need an academic degree, you only need what you already have—a life. But you might want to consider that you do not really have a life—life has you (Courion, 1997). Academic theorists create theory from their experience and observations which include everything that has had meaning and non-meaning in their lives. They do research to support their theoretical ideas. They, like the quantum scientists, tend to find what they look for. We all do that.

Most professional theorists do not veer too far from field-dominated literature. Therein lies one major weakness, particularly in vocational psychology, a field that focuses on individuals and aspects of their career development. But when you go to the adjectival form and talk about a career developing, you see that meaning for an individual life does not spring from concept and theory disconnected from story about human experiences, but from the story we tell ourselves as well as the story we tell our clients. Tests aside, but test interpretation included, career counseling, for the most part, reflects story telling, done either by the professional or the client; but it is seldom described that way.

Multidisciplinary reading fertilizes a career theory and life vision. For instance, poetry, literature, science, sociology, popular books that have a nugget of what your growth needs at the moment, children's books, plays, newspapers, magazines, all kinds of human stories (both in and outside of your culture), information from television and the Internet. All these sources will eventually form a pattern and one day you will recognize the red string (theme) of your life mission because it flows through everything you read. You recognize it by love. You find yourself continually drawn to different kinds of activities, ideas, books, events, and human interactions. These experiences fill in aspects of your career theory, your story.

A major Lifecareer principle suggests that career is *lived and owned* according to each individual's career theory, not *given and made* by a professional. Also, it is not something some get and other's don't. It represents life's gift to each of us, we need only recognize it.

Is Vocational Theory Useful in a Process Environment?

It all depends. However, Miller-Tiedeman did not find the vocational theory literature useful primarily because she did not perceive it as including principles of motion, complementarity, self-organizing systems ideas, uncertainty, and trial and error. Nor did it provide a philosophy that supports or values the individual as a theory maker. Further, vocational psychology reflects the dominant worldview of its time—Newtonian. Its first and major focus emphasized adolescent vocational choice, and occupational information for the school-to-work transition. Krumboltz and Ranieri (1996) called it the "learn, earn, and yearn" (p. 31) paradigm. Then professionals concluded that teaching better, best, and wise decision making would improve these transitions. This kind of thinking suggested getting your square peg self into that right occupational round hole, not surfing the process. Research on such things as real world accuracy (Walls, Fullmer, & Dowler, 1996), vocational maturity, and the like reflects the still-used, Newtonian worldview. So, quantum mechanics proved the only discipline large enough to handle the *Lifecareer* idea.

So, just as classical physics serves as a special case theory in the quantum physics framework, traditional career forms a special case of *Lifecareer* process theory. You can talk about traditional career within the *Lifecareer* paradigm but you cannot do the reverse because traditional career makes very different assumptions. For instance, it mostly:

- defines career as job;
- gives credence to first, second, and third careers;
- supports changing careers; and

- places the client in a subservient position.

This suggests that personal reality does not have the power of conventional wisdom, and that personal story matters most in the economic arena. Further, this perspective fails to recognize that the individual's career theory supersedes those developed by career theorists. These assumptions are untenable in Lifecareer because they do not support renewal and flow in life—two of life's major mandates. However, the assessment aspect, built on Newtonian assumptions, at various times, with selected people, remains appropriate with the caveat that all occupational areas need exploration, not just the area into which the test funneled the individual.

In the Lifecareer framework each individual is a whole system interacting within larger systems and their environments. Process anchors these transitional systems *ad infinitum*. The Newtonian reductionistic career paradigms, like Super's life roles and (in Super, D., Savickas, and Super, C., 1996) and Gysbers (circa 1975) general notion of life-career development (where Gysbers introduced a lifespan approach), do not serve as maps of *personal theories* which individuals can use to go from A to B to C in their everyday career developing.

For instance, after graduate school, Miller-Tiedeman sent out 60 resumes, and received 30 rejections. At that point, she notes that her thoughts did not return to career theory: "So I play many roles in life! So what? That's probably the last thing on my mind. Does self-concept theory or life-span discourse matter in my day-to-day life? Absolutely not, as I care most about my self-conceiving (not self-concept) within the context of my own career theory. Why? Because I wanted to earn money and have a theory that works for me daily, not a theory or theories professionals use for academic discussion. Finally, and most important, I need to use my own theory to grow my vision toward what I came on earth to do." For Miller-Tiedeman, the focus on life mission supersedes a career theory and practice which pushes schooling and then work.

In *The Turning Point*, Capra (1982) suggested that the problems biologists cannot solve today, apparently due to their narrow, fragmented approach, seems to result from treating holistic systems and their interactions with their environment reductionistically. That same problem confronts career development theorists and professionals today, as first jobs, occupational choice, decision making, and school-to-work transition are considered separately, not holistically and as primary in a life. In contrast, the Lifecareer theory considers the individual a living, interactive system which provides self-correcting information. This offers the individual an opportunity to grow and unfold his or her own career theory, not look outside himself or herself for more erudite models from theorists.

Literature That Inspired the New Careering

As noted in the introduction, the philosophical aspects of quantum physics form the foundation of the New Careering. Miller-Tiedeman introduced key concepts such as complementarity, uncertainty, and self-organizing systems Bohm, 1980; Capra, 1982; Prigogine, 1980; Wolf, 1981; and Zukav, 1979) beginning in the early '80s (Miller-Tiedeman, 1983, 1985, 1987, 1989, 1992). She used these ideas because they paralleled human life. "We're merely larger, more complex composites of the atomically small. From particles to humans (from humans to planets), we're all part of the life process functioning similarly although in different guises" (Miller-Tiedeman, 1989, p. 62, parentheses added). In complement, we are also smaller, less complex composites of the cosmologically large.

Further, since physics studies the behavior of the universe (mass and energy), it qualifies as the most appropriate literature Miller-Tiedeman uncovered for helping individuals form, understand, and live their life-direction dilemmas, as it's all particles and waves dancing to different tunes at different moments in life, taking various forms then disappearing and reappearing. Physics also offers timeless and self-evident principles (an idea that runs throughout this book) applicable to life in general and work in particular, and it supports motion and newness.

A vital link exists between thought processes and quantum processes and between ourselves and electrons.

Zohar (1990)

Another timeless and self-evident principle appears here: Synthesis and variety form the bases from which we grow. So while quantum physics anchors the foundation, it needs support from several perspectives: (a) Buckminster Fuller; (b) the Tao; (c) the Holy Bible; and (d) the Hawaiian Kahuna, which also suggests ageless principles. (Chapter 8 will detail how the science and its supporting foundation converts to practice in the New Careering model.)

General Scientific Assumptions

The New Careering model takes its lead from three principles upon which most scientists agree (Swimme, 1989): (a) Differentiation: Each moment differs from every other moment; (b) Subjectivity: Everything in the universe has an interior reality; (c) Communion: Everything relates to everything else. These timeless and self-evident principles support each of us in harvesting our own internal information.

Each Moment Differs from Every Other Moment. This means life continually changes and becomes new again, and again, and again with every minute differing from every other minute. Just imagine a world without change. Think how dull conversation would be. Life direction would not be a problem because everything would remain the same. Career development would not be an issue because there would not be a need for it. Getting together would not be interesting, as everything would be known. There would be no dissidents in any field, no protesters. Dislike or like would not exist, only sameness. There would be no old age, no new age, no age of any kind because nothing would have changed. Limited variety in jobs would exist because there would not be enough change to create new possibilities. People would bore themselves as well as everyone else. Even though change has its definite problems, you can see it has a great advantage—interest.

Everything Has an Interior Reality. With change we see that one person's treasure often translates into another person's junk. Said another way, one person's crisis is another person's opportunity. A Zen comic strip showed a snail going up the side of a frozen cherry tree and a bug coming down the other side looking quizzingly at the snail. The bug said, "Hey man, you're wasting your time. There are not any cherries up there. The snail replied, "There will be when I get there."

Since everything has a reality, we ought to develop more trust. For example, when you eat breakfast, your cells know what to do. They do not say, "Hey, what do we do with all this food that Joe dumps in on us?" The particles, atoms, cells, organs, and your entire body knows what to do and keeps busy at it. Even when a parasite gets in the body it knows what to do. Parasites have been called very good immunologists because some of them have figured out some very elegant ways of not getting detected.

For instance, after penetrating the body, the Bilharzia parasite can live in the veins for up to ten years without being rejected. How does it hide out in the body and conceal itself from the body's immune response? It coats its surface with protein from the host and within a few days, it has covered the surface antigens and for all practical purposes, it has disappeared. The body cannot see it, so it cannot reject it. The African trypanosome uses a more clever strategy, it continuously changes its antigens so it cannot be recognized by the body's immune system (NOVA, 1985).

At a level, a reality and a knowing intelligence (or whatever you wish to call it) exists in all living things. However, sometimes we fail to recognize it, like a frequently told story of the drowning minister. A man in a row boat said, "get in, we'll save you." The minister said, "God will save me." He kept floundering and someone in a helicopter came by and yelled, "Grab the ladder, we'll save you." The minister replied, "God will save me." Well, the minister drowned and when he got to the pearly gates he said to God, "What was wrong with you? You did not save me. I spent my life working for you and you did not help me." God replied, "Are you kidding? I sent you a row boat and a helicopter." Sometimes our beliefs (paradigms) are so narrow we find ourselves with one point of view, not points to view (Fynn, 1974).

We usually say, "Seeing is believing;" however, in paradigms if you don't believe it, you can't see it.

Joel Barker (1990)

Communion.   None of us can escape community, not even the recluse, as everything connects to everything else. We are communing creatures. Timothy Ferris (1985), in the program, *The Creation of the Universe,* said, "Every single atom in your body was once inside a star." In that sense, we're all related" (p. 2). Even those who deal with water-management problems have turned to the notion that damming up water and periodically flooding downstream will not solve some of their problems. Through research they discovered how that method has impacted plants, animals, and insects in the area. So, they now consider entire ecosystems when a water-management problem arises.

Similar consideration needs to take place when we decide to go to the hospital for anything. Depending on the statistic you read, anywhere from 150,000 to 300,000 people die each year in hospitals from hospital-contracted diseases, not from the initial condition.

Internal and external forces co-create, change, and produce changes which must, by definition, affect all. Many find this difficult to accept, as they often view certain changes within themselves as being forced on them because others refuse to change. For instance, "I'd like to change my life, but I'm locked in by society's rules. If I had my choice, I'd ... " This implies that an individual is being forced to do something against his or her will. "Inasmuch as an individual refuses to accept the choice to change, he or she limits society's ability to change" (Milani & Smith, 1985, p. 148). Since everything is connected, waiting for others to set you free or to make a way for you may end up counterproductive. "Rotationally, the only way to change any part of society is to change the self first (p. 148). However, any one change shuffles the entire universe in some way, as it's a web of relationships, even on the level of weeds.

It seems that the ecological balance in California and the Florida Everglades and in other places is being upset by maverick weeds that seem to be taking over the state's wild lands and threatening agricultural lands Schoch, 1998). So, the connectedness principles continues to be in force even though the public attaches very little credence to the problems it often generates.

The Ethics of Lifecareer

During the eighteen years of working with the Lifecareer idea, many questions have come up about its ethics. In short, the Lifecareer ethic is unbroken wholeness, unfoldment, evolutionary not revolutionary change. Lifecareer suggests no rupture in reality, rather steadily changing continuity. In a religious system there are injunctions—things that should be done and things that should not be done relating to good, evil, and those things undesirable in order to improve and prevent whatever the religious system encourages and forbids. In Lifecareer, anything that encourages the steady and continuous connection between the affective and cognitive, physical and spiritual is fostered. Lifecareering supports harmonious development in these four areas (Sarlos[1], personal communication, Summer, 1984). The above stories reflect that harmonious flow.

When anything in life threatens to disrupt this continuous *flow* taking action exemplifies the ethical imperative, not stoicism—total submission to natural law. Rather it suggests active participation in your development. To do this, you reflect with sensitivity, getting new organizations of personal experience, and coming up with concept-advancing holistic impressions.

In addition, Lifecareer has no violent aspects, only human development at peace with self. Lifecareer does not have to be earned; it is a gift to everything on Earth. Life is. In Lifecareer unfolding, you exercise responsible stewardship. You do not own life. You can never own it. You can only use it. In Lifecareer you can control knowledge about and sensitivity to life but life does not belong to anyone in particular. Responsible stew-

---

[1]In 1984, while teaching a summer class in Lifecareer at Loyola College, Professor Lee Richmond, my sponsor, arranged for me to lunch with Dr. Beatrice Sarlos, Professor of Philosophy at Loyola. She had read *How NOT to Make It ... And Succeed*, and I invited her comments. They proved a rare gift and burned themselves into my memory. So, I gratefully credit Professor Sarlos for her teachings. However, the section details my memory of that conversation, for which I take full responsibility.

ardship by each individual involves letting life unfold in everyone. Living the Lifecareer ethic requires *strenuous reflection* on where life appears to be headed and on all incoming information. You ask "What are the antecedents and direction of life?" Based on personal answers to this question, you cooperate and flow with life rather than trying to control it. This can be done without disadvantaging others' career development. Lifecareer is not career development in the selfish sense, it is career development in the higher sense of self—a self spirit in unity with universe in its entirety, a self continually seeking to know wholeness.

Prigogine (1980) and, lately, Zohar (1990) called this *the arrow of time* which continuously works in the chaos of self-organizing systems differentiating in harmony with continued reintegration in rhythm. When I (Miller-Tiedeman) walk on the beach, I see that rhythm in action. As I walk, I see a group of seagulls in my path. As I approach, they back off. I pass them, and they return to the edge of the water. Perfect orchestration.

In short, Lifecareer follows life non-intrusively. You do not rupture the stream of life. You are the stream. You are the current. You strive to stream well, divining direction, continually active and alert to the stream's movement.

However, during redefinition and while streaming, interruption frequently occurs. In fact regrouping is a messy process. In *Women Who Run With the Wolves*, Estes (1992) advances that wolves who have lost the scent scrabble to find it again and they appear rather funny in the process. They hop in the air, run in circles, plow up the ground with their noses, scratch the ground, run ahead, then back and then stand still. While it appears they have lost their wits, they are merely trying to pick up all the clues they can find by biting them down from the air, filling their lungs with scents at ground and shoulder level, and tasting to see who has passed through recently. Their ears rotate like satellite dishes as if picking up transmissions from afar. Once they have all the clues in place, they know what to do. Sometimes the redirection process for humans looks as strange as it does for wolves. But we, too, need to receive all necessary clues in order to know what to do. Sometimes these clues come quickly, but often they are time extended, causing us to believe nothing is working or will work. But in time situations resolve themselves.

Selected Principles That Support Living Life-As-Career

Principle 1: Life Self-Organizes

Self-organizing systems theory, an integral part of today's quantum physics, acknowledges that order comes from chaos. Specifically, the more coherent a system becomes, the more susceptible it is to falling apart. The break out of freedom in Eastern Europe and the dissipation of the U.S.S.R. serve as prime examples, as does our current downsizing problem.

When a belief exists in self organizing systems, then cooperating with the approaching forces, not fighting against them, becomes the motif. Ilya Prigogine, a Nobel winning chemist, pioneered the dissipative structures concept. He described them as open systems that maintain their structure by continually exchanging energy with their environment (Lukas, 1980). According to Prigogine (1980), fluctuation is the main process element of all self organization in all living systems. Periodically fluctuations are driven to their limits. This imbalance is frequently called stress. During such imbalance, two possibilities exist—maintenance or renewal (a restoring) or growth (a transition). Since all living things experience fluctuations, they constantly strive for balance by maintaining and growing. For instance, walking fast or running causes the heart to beat more rapidly and breathing to be faster and deeper. When the activity ceases, heart and breath return to normal. The body resumes its normal rhythm returning to a maintenance state. However, Prigogine (1983) suggested that living organisms always exist far from equilibrium.

Conversely, during crisis periods—downsizing, divorce, business failure, sickness and such—when nothing seems to work, it takes work to maintain balance and regain the former equilibrium. But the fluctuations may be too great, and instability results. Then mental and/or physical uncertainty can show up in the body, the behavior, and/or social and professional relationships. Physical symptoms like depression, headaches, or other physical problems can arise as a result of a depressed immune system. But, after a period, the system reorganizes and either maintains at a new level or reaches a breakthrough. One woman reported that she knows she's close to a breakthrough when she feels most confused and blocked. If she can live through *the valley and shadow of that confusion*, she experientially knows something new will emerge.

In this new state, she has grown and learned, and, at least for awhile, experiences more stability. This also happens after a serious illness where people report they have changed, grown, and evolved. They feel healthier than they did before the illness. Sometimes the system cannot adapt to such challenges. If it does not adapt to handle the change in energy or adapt quickly enough, then it will continue on as before or wither.

The New Careering Model in Action

A story in Ann Landers' column illustrates how life continues to self-organize. Two sisters wrote Ann about their 83 year old mother. After the mother's second husband died, she decided to move into a retirement home. From day one, she liked it, as it provided card games, square dancing, Scrabble, poker games, movies, concerts, and bus rides to the zoo. The sisters usually visited their mom on Sundays, but they decided to visit her on her birthday, which fell on Wednesday. They baked her a birthday cake and drove over to the retirement home. They decided to go straight to her room. When they opened the door, they found their 83 year old mom in her negligee on the sofa necking up a storm with an 84 year old resident whose wife had died the previous year. Mom, surprised, quickly blurted out that she and Eddy planned to get married (Landers, 1996).

Mom did not have to plan getting involved, she merely cooperated with the approaching forces and assessed the situation. She could have refused the advances, but that evidently did not feel right. Further, mom in her wisdom probably understood Ecclesiastes 3:1 that it is all timing.

Life detests disorganization, children's rooms in chaos not withstanding. Life continually self-organizes dependably, even at the particle level. Bodily cells, organs, groups, communities, states, nations, world, universe, and even individual Lifecareers—*all* self-organize. They cannot help it. It is built into the system, as life's career is renewal. Now this does not necessarily mean that we always like the results. Further, if we fail to organize, life does it for us. And even when we do organize, life often puts its spin on that organization. How many times have you thought you would do something, and a phone call, a knock on the door, or a toilet spillover changed your plans? Life happens without our permission.

Recognizing that life works, not always in pleasing ways, but it works, helps you relax and let your career develop naturally because you know that life will continue to inform you about necessary changes. This differs markedly from traditional career that suggests control of life, along with the needed prescription to make it, and, accompanying plans and goals. This comes with a preponderance for living in the future. In contrast, *Lifecareerists* cooperate with life. They recognize the necessity for a fit between what they want and how that matches life's current program.

Those who live Life-As-Career use plans sparingly and tend to follow inner wisdom—experience, intelligence, and intuition. This means working closely with inner wisdom. Everyone has inner wisdom, however, but only a few seem to plumb those depths and cooperate with their findings.

Cooperating with the approaching forces means seeking information when necessary. The major orientation is *flexibility* and *flow* while continually living in the now, taking action when necessary, knowing this will imprint data for the next moment. You might call this the basic process of being intelligent.

Motion constitutes the basic self-organizing systems activity, and is the central dynamic in *Lifecareer*. For every (re)action occurring in nature, some change in either mass or energy occurs" (Milani & Smith, 1985, p. 148). Even when the overall system remains stable and seems to produce no perceivable change, change happens.

Principle 2: Each Individual Has a Career Theory (Individual Story) That Matters Most

This should not surprise anyone, as each of us protects our own way of seeing the world and how we access our economic needs. When you think about your life, you recognize you do have direction. You get up in the morning, get dressed, have things to do, have ideas and dreams. In that sense, no individual lacks direction. But working with the data, waiting for the idea to mature in order to take action which will move toward a chosen intention, often presents a challenge.

Adverse circumstances tend to grow us toward a higher level of development. The outgrowth of that challenge rearranges and revises our story, which then shifts our career theory and philosophy. Around thirty years ago Marshall McLuhan (Ferguson, 1980) suggested that on Spaceship Earth everyone is crew, there are no passengers. Translate that for today and you find the environment encouraging more and more people to take command of their own destiny. They do this by coming to terms with their own theory (story), joyfully creating and recreating aspects of it, and keeping it in motion. Printed theories that do not include the individual as a theory maker stagnate as individual theory runs free of print, stays open for momentary changes and, most importantly, remains in the control of its owner. The collective consciousness now moves to liberate itself from old institutions, old ways of thinking, and the heavy hand of control. As a result, each of us, at a level, now feels the pull into our own story.

Believing that an individual can generate his or her own theory is not an egocentric or conceited view. The negative connotation of self-centeredness has long kept us alienated from ourselves and heavily dependent on authority. Such phrases as "Who do you think you are anyway?" "What makes you think you are so great?" and "What do you know?" have impeded progress to freeing up the self. Recently, a well respected professional in career development asked Miller-Tiedeman something like, "Do you really believe that most individuals know enough to make good decisions?" Miller-Tiedeman replied, "Everyone makes decisions. 'Good' is a value judgment that can only be determined by the individual. Furthermore, like the weather, what is good one minute can turn sour another." What you believe about individuals' capability to make decisions will show up in both your professional and personal life and represents a paradigm (see Chapter 5 for more on paradigms).

Once you acknowledge that your theory and philosophy works for you, even though not perfectly, you start taking a cooperative stance toward life. Then you began to see that *life has a career* which shows up in ourselves, other individuals, the environment, our health and body functioning, to name a few areas. Optimum physical, emotional, and mental health comes from a cooperative stance with all of life, as life has its own agenda which more frequently than not doesn't include *"make it happen" strategies*. However, sometimes life's intentions and ours do coincide. The following example is for those individuals who unsuccessfully (in their definition), have tried to make life match their agenda, but somehow it did not work.

Helen Schucman, a psychologist at the Columbia Presbyterian Hospital in New York City, and author of *A Course in Miracles* (Foundation for Inner Peace, 1975), more than once abandoned that writing, *but* William N. Thetford, a colleague, helped her see its value. However, on completion, she refused to place her name on it, as she felt it had come *through not from* her. Interestingly, she died feeling ambivalent about the work (Skutch, 1984). So, sometimes life chooses us even though we do not understand or even like what we receive.

Principle 3: Complementarity

If you change one thing in a system, other things change throughout the system. A system is of a whole. Additionally, when you focus on one thing, you miss others. For instance, hundreds of students enter counseling and psychology programs each semester hoping to work in private practice or for a health-related organization. They tend to believe their training will provide a livelihood. However, if you look on the other side—managed care, HMOs, and insurance companies—you find that talk therapy now gives way to drug therapy. For instance, some insurance companies allow four therapy sessions, then it's on to drug therapy. Greg Critser (1996), in his essay, "Oh How Happy We'll Be," said that in the late 1980s, of the nearly 16 million patients who visited doctors for depression, 70% ended up in drug therapy" (p. 44). Drug therapy is not coming, it's here big time. If an individual wanted to be on the up-side of the wave, she or he might consider training as a pharmacologist. When you focus on any discipline without looking at the totality in which that discipline is only a part, you miss other possibilities—one of which may be lowered income.

Principle 4: The Whole Is More Than the Sum of Its Parts

The whole is in each of its parts but the whole cannot be reconstructed from its parts. This synergistic quantum principle of growth stands in contrast to Boltzmann's second law of thermodynamics, which suggests that energy tends toward decay or entropy without overall growth.

Technologically, humans first experienced synergy in the 1860s when world navies began using metal alloys in ship construction because the tensile strengths of alloys are greater than the sum of tensile strengths of their pure metal parts.

In career psychology we presently overlook the wholeness phenomenon in the errors of our models of individual differences with which we presently guide the careers of our students, using antecedent and consequent models, such as a regression equation might be. Nonetheless, we can never transcend until we and our clients take our senses of living wholes into consideration in our systems of individual thought and action. It is the human's response to life's press for greater and greater complexity. Growth is built into life and constantly moves both forward and back.

Principle 5: The Observer Cannot Separate Himself or Herself from What He or She Observes

We find what we look for. This principle appears in each of our observations. If we look for elements in matter, we find them; if we look for quanta in matter, we find them.

We needlessly attempt to rid our instruments of ourselves. But we actually do our best in measuring when we not only read ourselves into our measurements, but also share responsibility for the measurement process and results with research participants, who have the ultimate responsibility for what they now know, think, and find.

You see this principle frequently when you look for something, and, if it's not in the shape or package you remembered, you fail to see it. If it's something that doesn't interest you, you don't see it. Here we collide with paradigms, suggesting that if you don't believe it you won't see it. (See Chapter 5 for more on Paradigms.) This is the reverse of "seeing is believing." Also notice how paradigms bleed into principles and you'll see in Chapter 5 the connectedness of paradigms to principles. This is reminscent of relativity theory that suggests that nothing exists in a place except in time, and nothing in time exists except in a place. That's the wonder of process.

In regard to seeing, remember that the Swiss invented the Quartz watch, but missed the market because they didn't believe it would replace the watch with bearings (Barker, 1990). The same thing happened when several large companies missed the Xerox invention. Could it be that paradigm blinders serve as life's protection against one person or corporation having it all?

Principle 6: Interrelationship, Interconnection, and Interpenetration Are the Rules Not the Exception

Contrary to Western cultural notions, independence does not exist in universe, rugged individualism notwithstanding. Wholeness perpetually works in universe. Conceptual consciousness works in the balance of particulars and wholes which we humans experience as paradox. Remember the Hang Seng index that tumbled 15% in October 1997. The Nikkie Stock average then lost 725.67 points and the next day the Dow dropped 7.18% (Myerson, 1997). This reminded everyone that we live in a web of relationships, universe wide. The meeting of 150 countries in Kyoto, Japan (Stevens, 1997) to work on an agreement requiring reductions in the emission of heat-trapping greenhouse gases by industrial countries reminds us again of our universal bond with each other.

Principle 7: Guiding by Inner Wisdom Using Intentions

In using your inner wisdom, ask yourself if the information you get reflects the cultural programming, what the majority agree upon, or is it placed there by you, as that information guides your decision making. As you think about it, consider that from birth parents tell you how it is; then teachers not only tell you how they think it is, but suggest you memorize how others think it is; and then to church where the rabbi, minister, or priest dictates his or her reality version. Not knowing two realities exist, personal and common, and not getting much practice in discerning the two, you are denied the option to consciously choose either, as you have to be aware a choice exists in order to deliberately make it. So, you might want to question the information that comes to you in quiet time or in meditation as well as what other people tell you.

Estes (1992) suggested that there are things that beckon to us and things that come from our soul. Imagine a smorgasbord. We look at it and see wonderful things, like croissants, different cheeses, great breads, and all these things that appeal to us. Frequently we choose things that beckon to us. We choose them because they happen to be in front of our face at that time.

But if we want to connect to the instinctual self, we ask, "For what am I hungry?" without looking at anything. We have to go inside and ask, "What do I want today?" Maybe I really want peanut butter in celery and it just may not be on the smorgasbord table. That's a metaphor for how to reconnect with the instinctual self.

You might use that same approach to go inside and ask, "Is this what I think and/or believe?" or "Have I accepted someone else's truth about it?" A young man separating from the military had a resume he had used to get three or four jobs. As a part of his separation package, he chose vocational counseling, testing, and some job-search help. However, the coordinating counselor working with his group looked at his resume and told him it would not work. The young man redid it, but did not feel good about it. When he had his individual session with a Lifecareer counselor, he brought up the resume incident. The counselor asked him what he thought about the old resume. He replied, "I've never had trouble with it. In fact, I've gotten three jobs using it." She then advised him to use the resume he had the most confidence in. This response (a) relaxed the client, (b) enhanced his immune system, (c) built his self esteem, and (d) increased his confidence. With one sentence, the counselor made a difference in the body, mind, and spirit of the client.

Guiding from inner wisdom means not allowing anyone to compress one's thoughts, ideals, values, or morals, or to step on dreams bubbling up. In that sense, no right, wrong, good, or bad decisions exist, only decisions that inform us. However, things that do not work out teach patience. Remember, a garden has to be turned in the fall to prepare it for the spring. It cannot bloom all the time. So, cycles have to be allowed because they occur as part of the growing up of our personal career theory.

If we do not allow that maturing, or if we conform to what people think we should do, or for that matter what *we* think we should do, those proclivities for expression get suppressed where they fester and mull around, until one day with the right amount of pressure, they burst out the side wall which causes us to act in some inappropriate way. Like, quitting a job, or walking out of a business or a relationship. Even more important, all that frustration goes straight into the body, setting up enormous stress (see Chapter 14 for more particulars on stress).

You have to allow yourself a little newness. Animals do this all the time. They may want to dig their cave or habitat the same way each year, but they have to adapt to the conditions around them. Say you decide you want your medical degree, but it's impossible because you have to work full time. Then you have to make the adaptation to become innovative instead of martyred by it. This holds true for any decision you make.

Estes (1992) suggests that when you connect with your instinctual self, you always have at least three choices. You have the two opposites and the middle ground. If you are not connected, you usually think you have only one choice, and not a good one at that, and further, you may feel that you should suffer about it.

In considering what you believe about inner wisdom—experience, intelligence, and intuition—remember that these three combine and form a more powerful information source than what is collectively agreed upon by others. You might call that your "cosmic Internet." If you do not log on (or in this case *in*), you miss the information.

In order to log on, you need quiet time. Meditation offers a good way to browse your internal Internet. Additionally, it relaxes the body. Benson (1975), at Harvard University, discovered this when he studied transcendental meditators. He found that meditation, or the relaxation response, can lower blood pressure and reduce drug use. Benson also suggested that many different meditation approaches can elicit the relaxation response producing health benefits. Tests at the Thorndike Memorial Laboratory at Harvard showed that similar technique used with any sound or phrase or prayer or mantra brings forth the same physiologic changes noted during Transcendental Meditation: decreased oxygen consumption; decreased carbon dioxide elimination; decreased rate of breathing. In other words, any one of the age-old or newly devised techniques produces the same physiologic results. Benson said, "We claim no innovation but simply scientific validation of age-old wisdom" (p. 114). So, even if you are not interested in listening to your inner wisdom, you might want to try meditation or the relaxation response for health reasons.

Goals or Intentions?   When you surf life's process, consider using goals for such things as joy and peace, college courses, degrees, financial planning—all those things mostly in your control. But even then, you'll discover that life flows in with or without your permission, so you modulate your goal setting, keeping an eye on life's agenda. Then you make an interpretation about the next step, but you do not lose time wondering about the missed goal. You thank life for the learning, and move on.

As Chopra (1991) suggested earlier, the channel of life does not run in a narrow band and refuses very often to be captured in goals. While contemplating a sought after goal, life slips through our fingers. The same holds true for a life developing, something in which we all participate.

So what alternatives exist? Consider setting intentions without time designations. Sometimes it takes only a few days for an intention to work, other times it takes months and even years. In the meantime, play with your intentions. Forget them. Remember them. Place them in various priority order. But keep unmet intentions on your list until you are sure they hold no meaning for you. Some people carry hundreds of intentions on their computer calendar. What seems a hot intention over time turns cold and vice versa. But by listing the intention, you do not lose it. Further, you'll discover that when your intentions coincide with life's rhythm, the answers manifest quickly. When they do not, the answers take longer and in some instances do not come at all.

Often when you set an intention, you do not know how to go about it. But if you keep it in attention, ideas will start popping into your mind. Write them on paper and place them in a folder, or log them on your computer.

It also works in reverse. Sometimes ideas come to you from time to time. If you keep them filed, you may discover a completely new idea forms. Or the ideas may suggest a potential book. If life followed a straight line, goals would work. But the universe consists of waves and particles, not straight lines. Goal setting becomes a problem when they do not work out because the individual spends time going over what might have happened. Most people appreciate a quick, easy, and convenient method. Setting intentions certainly fills that bill because when you set an intention, whatever works becomes the plan, the plan not working becomes a non-issue. Also, you continue to move forward. You do not look back and lose time wondering why something did not work. You chalk it up to experience and move on. Everything in life moves—seeds, pollens, pollution, people—all moving toward greater complexity.

Principle 8: Lifecareer Values Both Right and Left Decisions

Traditional career development mostly focuses on wise, better, or best decisions, frequently ignoring the wealth of information wrong decisions provide. When we look at quantum physics, we find duality essential. Consider the wave and particle notion that Zohar (1990) proposes is the most revolutionary statement quantum physics makes. At the subatomic level, everything can be described either as particles (little billiard balls) or waves (like on the ocean's surface). Further, neither particles nor waves contain the complete description, and both *must be* considered in order to understand the nature of things. You can see the Janus-like nature of quantum in the Complementarity principle which states that waves and particles complement each other and the whole picture is a packaged deal. All decisions, those that work out as well as those that don't, function as a unit and provide us with new information which enriches our career developing.

Even the body reveals the attention life pays (or God designed) to opposites. Buckminster Fuller (Wagschal & Kahn, 1979) realized the importance of this duality when he noted that people do not talk about walking on their right and wrong foot, but on their right and left one. It's the polarity that works both well and efficiently. Ask yourself, "How far could I go if I only had a right leg, a right hand, or a right ear?" Observing the efficiency of the body, using both its left and right sides, you know that life found balance primary.

Sometimes it's difficult to watch your children make decisions that your experience suggests will not work for them. But unless the decision constitutes bodily harm to him or her or to someone else, letting the child make those alleged dysfunctional decisions turns up valuable information which advances growth. On the other hand, children watch parents make decisions they perhaps think are not practical. Professionals also judge the decisions of their peers. You see this in the labels attached, like dull, boring, too advanced in thought, or weird because he or she crosses disciplines to learn more.

Karl Pribram, the famous neurosurgeon, frequently gets tarred and feathered by more conventional neuroscientists for his bold speculations and for seizing upon new findings outside his field in an effort to understand memory. Pribram recalls the pioneer memory researcher Ewald Hering's remark which suggests every scientist at some point in his work has to risk "looking foolish."

The scientist begins to be interested in his work and what his findings mean. Then Pribram said:

> ... he has to choose. If he starts to ask questions and tries to find answers to understand what it all means, he will look foolish to his colleagues. On the other hand, he can give up the attempt to understand what it all means, he won't look foolish and he'll learn more and more about less and less" (as cited in Wilber, 1982, p. 19).

Pribram concluded that you need the *courage to look foolish.* In living Life-As-Career, reading and following your inner wisdom could, somewhere along the way, require the courage to look foolish as well as the courage to continue, regardless of how others view your actions. May (1976) suggests that "Kierkegaard and Nietzche and Camus and Sartre have proclaimed that courage is not the absence of despair, it is, rather, the capacity to move ahead *in spite of despair"* (p. 3). And as Courion (1997) noted earlier in this chapter, courage means to have heart, to experience that fragile imbalance between love and fear with the scales tilting toward love.

When we do not consider right and wrong decisions a packaged deal, we judge results and this throws us: (a) back into the Newtonian *parts equal the whole mentality* where things exist separately (see Chapter 7 for more detail on classical physics); and, (b) locked into the conforming stage of development (see Chapter 4 for more information on development). Trying to deal with a fractured reality, failing to acknowledge and appreciate those things that do not work, saps energy and slows progress.

Often things fail because we rely too heavily on external information, attempting to jump on the right conveyor belt—known as *trends, high growth areas, or high income potentials*—from expert-driven information. Then we say, "Something went wrong." Language is key here. Nothing goes wrong, it just does what it does, sometimes it takes a direction we don't want or didn't intend. Think about that. Can you change how you feel by turning negative outcomes into positive statements? Chopra (1987) says that both happy and unhappy feelings change body chemistry and either enhance or depress the immune system.

One big problem in valuing both left and right decisions comes from worry about what others will say. Fear arises around not having the right education or the right job, the right clothes, doing the right interview, writing the right resume (Should I do a power resume, a strategic one, or one with a focus on key information?), presenting ourselves in the right way, saying the right thing, and on and on. All this requires energy better used for moving forward on your own thought and steam, as no one knows what is right for anyone else in any given moment in time.

No right or wrong way exists, as we can invoke many approaches on any one idea. A commencement speaker once told a group of cinema graduates at the University of Southern California, "I know you have paid good money to learn how to do it right ($60,000 for a four-year degree), but if you stick to what you have learned, you will never make a classic" (personal communication, Spring 1985). Those people who made classics stepped out of what everyone agreed on as the right way to do something. For instance, the entire body had never been filmed in a dance scene until Fred Astaire insisted they do it. In so doing he made cinema history.

Identifying experience as instructive removes the judgment and replaces it with discernment. Then you get on with living, correcting when necessary, adding to or stopping whatever needs doing. Then you learn the importance of trial and error which qualifies for one of the most important career skills. When you think, "I can't do that," remember how life works. Renalto Dulbecco, Nobel Winner in Medicine, in his book, *The Design of Life* (1987), wrote:

It may seem that Life aims at specific goals. But when analyzed in detail we find that there is no grand plan; the result is obtained by trial and error. The only beauty of this approach is that it works. This is a fundamental aspect of life; associations are established however possible through the use of a great hodgepodge of clues, signals, molecules. Associations that work are retained and the others are thrown away (p. 451).

Life takes a pragmatic approach, using those things that work to determine its successes. Sometimes life makes a seemingly wrong decision that turns right. For example, John had airline reservations. Because they oversold the seats, he could not get on. He fussed and fumed about it. However, the news that evening revealed that same flight crash-landed at the destination. What seemed left turned right for him. Sometimes life saves us from ourselves.

Henry David Thoreau made his living from pencil making and land surveying; and, his first writing project was *On Walden Pond*. Evidently Emerson felt that Thoreau had made many wrong decisions (left turns), as he wrote in Thoreau's obituary, "I so much regret the loss of his rare powers of action that I cannot help counting it a fault in him that he had no ambition" (Petroski, 1989, p. 16). What Emerson thought wrong turned right for Thoreau, in his lifetime as well as over time, as his writings now stand among the best classics. It also points out that one man's *no ambition* is another man's *classic legacy*, an illustration of different values and paradigms. It's also obvious Thoreau did not *conform to* Emerson's definition of ambition.

Principle 9: No One of Us Has All It Takes to Make Our Dreams Come True. It Takes Many Hands and Many Hearts

But our rugged individualism paradigm keeps us from noticing that it takes hundreds if not thousands of contacts with others to move us forward. Anyone who travels recognizes the many hands it takes to arrive at any destination. Start with the clothes you wear, the luggage carried, all made by someone else's labor. The shuttle for pickup, the baggage man who tags the luggage, the ticket agent who checks you in. The airport itself built by hundreds of individuals as well as the airplane that will carry the passengers. The pilot, co-pilot, and navigator, and the flight attendant all are part of getting passengers to their destinations. Another group of people prepares the food and its transportation to the plane. On arrival at the destination someone opens the baggage compartment of the plane and moves the bags into the baggage claim area. Then another shuttle awaits to taxi passengers to their destinations. It takes a collection of many people to keep life moving. This holds true in life direction.

Fredrick Tomblin graduated high school and then went on to work. However, a friend he met in high school talked him into going to college. Fred considered that and signed up. He graduated with a degree in Political Science and History and went on to get a Master's degree. However, while doing that work, a professor suggested he go to Chicago and finish his master's work. He applied and was accepted at the University of Chicago. While working on that degree, he had a night job at a residential hotel close to campus. One evening while studying for a test, someone walked up behind him. He thought at first it was a manager, but it turned out to be a widow of a circuit court judge who lived in the hotel. She asked him what he was doing and he told her studying for a test. She then asked him what he was going to do after he finished. He said, he was going to law school. She wanted to know what law school. He said, "Well, one of the night law schools because I have to work." She said, "Why don't you go to the University of Chicago?" He replied, "I'm out of that range. My grades are good enough but I don't think the University of Chicago is interested in a student with a B.A. from Marshall University. They probably haven't even heard of Marshall." The widow asked if his grades were good and he said, "Yes." She then said he could work at the hotel at night. The widow went on to say that the Dean of the law school owed her a favor. "He asked my late husband and I to recommend him for a Masters Degree at Yale University. We did that. So, he owes me a favor. I think I can get you accepted." She wrote the letter, and he was admitted.

While Frederick Tomblin earned the degrees, all of that might not have happened had it not been for the high school friend who casually told him he ought to go to college, and the widow who wrote the recommendation letter that got him admitted to the University of Chicago Law School. Frederick was one of 105 students in his beginning law class. At the end of the second year only 68 remained, and he not only stayed, he graduated and went on to become one of its most successful graduates, ending up as President of Commonwealth Title, one of the largest such companies in the United States. No one of us has all it takes to make our dreams come true, it takes many hands and many hearts.

Principle 10: Reality Continually Creates Itself in Our Mind; Therefore, Each Person Lives His or Her Own Mythology

The idea that reality continually creates itself each moment in our heads precludes allowing others to define that reality. Others include parents, teachers, counselors, friends, career theorists, and the like. This belief also precludes trying to create reality for someone else. Someone else includes those just mentioned, and especially clients.

The shift in how we consider reality comes from quantum physics. As stated before, the universe is made up of waves and particles. A major switch in physics occurred when physicists realized that scientists looking for a particle found a particle; when others looked for a wave, they found a wave. In other words, objectivity fell from grace in the scientific field. Zukav (1979) quoted John Wheeler, well-known physicist at Princeton, to note that "participator" strikes down the term "observer" of classical theory, the man who stands safely behind the thick class wall and watches without taking part. "It can't be done, Quantum mechanics says" (p. 54).

However, professors still ask students to be objective. Neither the students nor the professors can do this. You end up with different viewpoints. This means that no one has information beyond the moment and no one knows what anyone else ought to do, nor does anyone know how the transformation we now experience will affect our lives. On the other hand, as Zohar (1990) notes, we can objectively agree that a cat will not collapse into a kangaroo. But five of us can watch an accident and tell different stories about what happened. So, we need to approach objectivity with caution.

From another perspective, ask yourself, "What is real, English or Swimming?" In a Sufi tale (Courtland, 1976), a teacher hires a boatman to ferry him across a very wide river. As soon as they were afloat, the teacher inquired about the weather. The boatman said, "Don't ask me nothing about it," whereupon the teacher asked the man if he had ever studied grammar. "No," he replied. The teacher commented, "then half your life has been wasted." The boatman said nothing. Soon a terrible storm blew up. The boat began filling with water and the boatman leaned over to the teacher and asked, "Have you ever learned to swim?" The teacher said, "no." "In that case, schoolmaster, all your life is lost, for we are sinking" (p. 88). A different reality.

Another reality illustration comes from the 900 information industry. While knowledgeable people can comment on what they think will and will not sell, the truth reveals that no one knows. If they did, marketing would not exist as a course of study. One man developed a *Dial-an-Insult* line which now sells thousands of minutes per month at $1 a minute. He did not start out with jammed lines. He worked on the line, tested his ads, and eventually worked into 30,000 calls per month. A group of experts, using common wisdom, may have dampened what has become a very lucrative side business. The notion in the 900 industry is, let the people decide. A different reality.

When you trust your own thought and honor your reality, you lean heavily on the quantum idea that the whole organizes the parts. When you trust the whole to organize your life direction, you may not know where you are going, but you know that each step feels right. That is the litmus test of success.

The road to success is always a rough draft we work on as we move toward our hopes and dreams. The familiar saying, *If you don't know where you're going, you'll probably end up somewhere else* does not acknowledge that a large of number of people who thought they knew where they were headed also ended up somewhere else. That's life's way of helping us learn necessary lessons. The first lesson, we do not control life; nice as it sounds and as much as we might wish to, life's career dominates.

The twenty-first century will find all of us working through and out of someone else's definition of reality.

Principle 11: Support and Relatedness Exist in All of Life

As suggested in Principle 9, none of us have all it takes to make our dreams come true or to make it through life. Each of us needs help all along the way. Rugged individualism is only an illusion and an idea the mind evidently would like to boast of. As Brian Swimme (1994) said earlier, most all scientists agree that life goes around in communion not separateness. On the physiological level, our body cells commune with each other to do their work which keeps our bodies functioning. Humans commune with nature for psychological nourishment. We commune with each other because we are communing beings. And as mentioned earlier, all the atoms in our bodies were once inside a star (Ferris, 1985). In that sense, we are all related. No doubt we yearn to return to the closeness we once felt as we nestled together in that star. We need to commune with another for a reference, for an endorsement. We write to commune with larger audiences. When we start doing bigger things, we commune with more people.

We need each other to help us carry out our intentions. *Engage Your Life* (Centre for Career Development Innovations, 1993), a Canadian program, helps secondary school students embrace life in a broader sense. In one section they learn how many people it takes to help an individual realize his or her dream. For instance, the model who strikes the perfect pose. We usually forget those standing outside the photoshoot: her hairdresser, her make-up artist, her personal trainer, the image stylist, the photographer, the designer, the caterer, the magazine editor, the photo editor who computerizes the shot to rid the model of her blemishes, dark circles, body hair and other imperfections. Not to mention the people who sell her the clothes she wears, the landlord she rents her apartment from, the doctor she visits from time to time, her local supermarket. Well, you get the idea—it takes a village, many people working together to support any life on earth. Chapter 12 will tell you about the Canadian innovation, *Engage Your Life*, and the assumptions used to design it.

Faith Popcorn, author of *The Popcorn Report* (1991), came up with her future predictions using her allies, networks, magazines, and newspapers, and what she calls her "kitchen cabinet," a group of individuals with varying levels of education and backgrounds (see Chapter 8, Part II, for more details). She came up with the following ten trends: (a) Cacooning in a New Decade; (b) Fantasy Adventure; (c) Small Indulgences; (d) Egonomics; (e) Cashing Out; (f) Down-Aging; (g) Staying Alive; (h) The Vigilante Consumer; (i) 99 Lives; and (j) Save Our Society (p. xii).

Living life as process (quantum careering) means staying in the now. If you do, you'll never meet a moment you cannot handle. Check it out. Casting ahead frequently causes problems. This works in all aspects of life. For instance, in May 1990, when Miller-Tiedeman, decided to take David (V. Tiedeman) to the emergency room, her inner wisdom, not the doctor, informed her and the *now* worked. When she sat through two major operations within four days, each moment worked. Living through the intensive care situation with 90 days of "stable and holding," the *now* worked. At the end of this episode, she looked back and wondered how she survived. Then she remembered that she stayed in the *now* and it worked. That's true for any aspect of life, even death. It's only the thought of death, stepping out of the *now*, that frightens us. We'll all probably do just fine when our moment arrives. And, if we stay in the *now*, we'll all know what to do in each moment of our life even if that's waiting until the right moment arrives.

Important Connections to Our Past

Existentialism, Identity, and Phenomenology

The idea of the dominance of the individual has bubbled in Miller-Tiedeman's thought since graduate school, where she found the thinking of those in the human potential movement literature more attractive than that in vocational psychology. In retrospect, one might ask why the human potential movement did not show up in the career development literature with the exception of Tiedeman and Super's introduction of the self as central in occupational choice and vocational development.

Miller-Tiedeman asked Tiedeman, (personal communication, August 1, 1997), who at that time held a Professorship in the Harvard Graduate School of Education, why he thought that Harvard, a leader in career development, did not at least entertain, like the physicists do when they do not understand a theory, that there might be something to the human potential movement? David replied that a new professor stays busy trying to get the lay of the land. In addition, one of his measurement professors did not like the emphasis on the self that one of the guidance professors made, so Tiedeman felt he had to bridge that gulf. Then the amount of free time available after class preparation became a factor, along with needed family time. Add to that, your professional group not buying into the human potential movement along with your already established professional interest, and the human potential movement became a non idea.

However Tiedeman further stated that many of his colleagues remained unimpressed by the human potential movement, as they could not imagine how to measure the self, nevermind attribute to it the capacity to know for itself. Also remember that during the 1960s and early 1970s a not-so-quiet revolution was going on. People tried all kinds of new things—different kinds of relationships, dress, and behavior, as well as new ideas. Timothy Leary, then at Harvard, allegedly used some of his students in his experiments without official permission. Marijuana, LSD, and all kinds of experimental drugs were coming on the scene replacing alcohol as the drug of choice. The Beatles toured the United States for the first time. Wearing designer clothes with the name of the maker on the outside became chic. The youth rebellion reached its height in the summer of 1967, with tie-dyed shirts and bell-bottom jeans becoming the uniform (After the War, 1995). The Vietnam War raged as a controversy, ending with federal troops on the campuses of many universities and the well-remembered Kent State shootings. All this dovetailed with the human potential movement, T-Groups, and hot tubs (nude bathing) at Esalen Institute in Big Sur. During this time, a big push into a more Self-Aware level of development happened, sharpening the debate in American society about individual freedom versus public order, most always defined as rebellious (meaning a movement out of conformity).

In academia, the human potential movement defined itself more in terms of identity and existential experience, with Abraham Maslow (1968) writing a popular book, *Toward a Psychology of Being*, suggesting that existentialists, in general, discuss the experience of identity. American psychologists, in particular—such as Rogers' (1961) *On Becoming a Person*; Fromm's (1964) *The Heart of Man*; Erikson's (1959) *Identity and the Life Cycle*; Murray's (1962) *Prospect for Psychology*; Horney's (1942) *Self Analysis*; and May's (1975) *The Courage to Create*—and others, known and unknown, showed an interest in the emerging self and the quest for identity. The existential approach stressed starting from experiential knowledge rather than from abstract concepts or categories or, *a priori*, Existentialism. Likewise, the New Careering model uses personal, subjective experience as the foundation from which description emerges, not the reverse.

Neither early existentialists, the American psychologists interested in identity and phenomenology, nor the great thinkers of the human potential movement could penetrate the glass ceiling laid down by Isaac Newton's thought about a deterministic universe. But life, in its own time and way, now weaves spirit, self, and a growing universe alive with decisions and possibilities and ever expanding complexities, into a new vision for all of us.

Worldview Shift

The New Careering model seeks to make the individual dominant. This now converges with a worldview that includes holism, intentionality, and personal autonomy in which individuals search for authenticity through self knowledge; "legitimizing the *shift in authority* from belief systems, institutions, and professionals *to the individual*, a shift in authority from external to internal, recognizing that authentic individualism comes into being in the context of relationship" (Dacher, 1997, p. 14, italics added) not in our theories or research. This means the individual plays an active, responsible role in his or her life-direction development without the imprint from professional authority.

Kurt Lewin's life space theory that each person behaves in accordance with his or her world view (1951) provides support for starting and staying with the individual's notion of how his or her life should be designed. While Lewin's life space theory provided a holistic view, it remained mostly in the discussion arena, as not much use was made of it in vocational psychology vis-à-vis the client knowing more about his or her life and holding within the only theory that would ever work for him or her. But remember this idea came out in the 1950s during a time of major conformity, so to veer onto the edge and suggest clients needed mostly support not direction may have been heresy.

Rogers (1951) and his client-centered therapy had process intuitions. In a dialogue with Paul Tillich (Tillich & Rogers, 1966), Rogers said, "I find in my work as a therapist that if I can create a climate of the utmost freedom for the individual, I can trust the directions that he or she will move" (p. 5), perhaps against the odds of the logical positivistic approach and the stress of the mechanistic and highly deterministic point of view that sees man and woman as objects trying to match themselves to the world.

Maslow (1968), in his book *Toward a Psychology of Being*, notes that "no theory of psychology will ever be complete which does not centrally incorporate the concept that man (and woman) *have their future within them, dynamically active at this present moment*" (p. 15, italics added). This suggests another life principle—the future is unknown and unknowable.

It then follows that all "habits, defenses, and coping mechanisms are doubtful and ambiguous since they are based on past experience" (p. 16).

Further, Maslow (1968) described psychology as "... merely the study of tricks used to avoid the anxiety of absolute novelty by making believe the future will be like the past" (p. 16). In 1998, neither psychology nor career development are much closer to facing the truth that the future is not, cannot, and will never be like the past. Acknowledging that timeless and self-evident principle just may allow for the open and creative ingenuity of the individual to discern what he or she needs in any one minute. Otherwise, we perpetuate what we call *normal* in psychology, which Maslow (1968) called the "... psychopathology of the average, so undramatic and so widely spread that we don't even notice it ordinarily" (p. 16).

Why Lifecareer?

Living Life-As-Career can free you from major stress, thereby increasing motivation and creativity, resulting in a better-functioning immune system. It supports the maturing of each individual's career theory. For instance, when you live Life-As-Career:

- You do not have to search for a career, you have one. You do not look for second, third, or fourth careers or worry about losing a career or needing to find another one. Outcome: Reduced stress.

- You can trust your inner wisdom that comes from your experience, intelligence, and intuition. You feel joy in your own choices, and even though some do not work out, they provide pathways to newness. Outcome: Reduced stress.

- You do not have to know what you are doing all the time. Remember the bees that go in for nectar and in the process brush the pollen which, when carried to the next flower, causes cross-fertilization. This offers surprise in life. Outcome: Reduced stress.

- You know that life has a career and you work with it, not against it. Outcome: Reduced stress.

- You do not have to fit other people's notions of what you should do. You then free up considerable energy for exploration that opens up many new avenues. Outcome: Less fear, resulting in reduced stress.

- You know you can find ways to support your needs.

- You understand the importance of money management, distinguishing between need and want, knowing how quickly a sure bet can disappear. Outcome: Reduced stress.

- You know that you do not bring spirituality into your life and practice, but that it develops as a result of living the wholeness in life. Spirituality resembles development in that you can only offer to others what you've been able to gain yourself. So, the stress is off trying to bring it in.

Lifecareer and Wholeness

Lifecareer advocates a wholeness where individuals know they are part of it. Therefore, it is not restricted to Career Planning which many others take to be the new end of career theory. *Instead, Lifecareer is the dynamic, lived-in-the moment process defined by each person in individual moments.* It moves forward collecting all kinds of information both internal and external. It forms a pattern like crystals tumbling over each other in a kaleidoscope. It acts like all living things. The more you trust your inner wisdom—experience, intelligence, and intuition—the more you learn to value your own career theory. You then attune to your own cues for the next steps in life.

While in the flow, you seek information, or talk to one or several people. Then you internalize the information, work with new ways to use the information, and let time (the process) inform your next step. If you flow with the rhythm of life, you'll avoid major stress, feel good while you wait, and enjoy more satisfaction after you decide. In this way you support your immune system and experience improved health, probably one of the best reasons for living Life-As-Career.

When you live *your* Lifecareer theory, *you* determine what works and what doesn't. The real test of any career theory is, "does it work in your life?" Nevermind someone else's description or discussion of it. The physicists know this. Capra (1983) says that physicists hold a very common and practical attitude about an approach of any kind. "When you have a certain theory and you think it's not quite sound, mathematically or otherwise, but it works. Then you say, 'well, there must be something to it.' You then use the model and elaborate on it later" (p. 23). That attitude helped Capra return to the scientific community after his time out to write *The Tao of Physics* (1975) and *The Turning Point* (1982).

Lifecareer in Story

Each of Us Comes In With Different Data and Life Missions

Frequently what we think we ought or want to do just doesn't work out. For instance in the early 1960s, Jerrie Cobb tested in the top 2% of all male and female potential astronauts recruited for America's earliest space brigade. However, male experts, including John Glenn, spoke against women in space at congressional hearings in 1962. Glenn suggested that men fight war and fly airplanes and that women "... are not in this field is a fact of our social order" (Levine, 1998, p. E-2.). Having missed a much desired opportunity, Cobb brokenheartedly went forward looking for something else to do. She said, "Flying is what I do. It is my gift and my talent. It defines my life" (Levine, 1998, p. E-2). Given her dedication to flying, she looked for a place where she could use her flying talents and do the most good. She became a missionary pilot flying seeds and medical supplies to some of the world's most isolated, primitive, and starving people. She lives a rather nomadic life with no fixed address and she sleeps in a hammock in communal huts, and shares with these people she has grown to love, a life without benefit of modern conveniences like plumbing, electricity, medical care or even mail. In 1981 she was nominated for the Nobel Peace Prize. With the advent of John Glenn's space flight, friends set up a Web site for her (www.jerrie-cobb.org) and started a campaign to help her realize her dream—one space flight—which she calls "... the ultimate fly."

Life-as-Career Works Differently for Each of Us

Sometimes a simple incident like attending a concert can change your entire life. Gilbert Kaplan (1994), a former Wall Street journalist and businessman, graduated from Duke University in economics and made his first million by the age of 30 as founder and publisher of *Institutional Investor* magazine. He attended a concert and heard Mahler's Second Symphony. *He felt so overcome that, immediately afterwards, he began studying the score of the symphony with a Julliard instructor and for seven months, he spent five hours a day conducting a recording by George Solti, memorizing each nuance since he could not read music.* In 1994, Britain's Sunday Times voted Kaplan's upbeat recording of Mahler's Fifth Symphony, "Record of the Year." Kaplan still conducts Mahler's works and reports more love for it each day. That one evening at the concert hall changed Kaplan's life even though it appeared a leisure activity. What odds of success would a career counselor have given Kaplan, a man who could not even sight-read music?

Sometimes What Feels Right Can End in Tragedy

Jessica Dubroff, seven years of age, loved flying, and she wanted to break the existing world record. She followed her bliss, but when her plane took off, it climbed 400 feet, then nose-dived into the ground. She lost her life. Her mother said afterwards that she would not have made any different decision concerning Jessica's interest in flying. She remarked that Jessica died doing what she loved, and added, is not life itself a chance? (Sarche, 1996).

Frequently Students Major in a Field in Which They Never Find Work

At other times, they find work in a field for which they have no training or expertise and end up liking it better than what they trained for. Life has all kinds of twists and turns. As Lewis Thomas said, "I had no idea I'd end up an essayist and if a medical-journal editor had not suggested nine years ago that I try a regular column, I might never have started serious writing. Further, I grew up knowing I wanted to be a doctor but I did not know I'd go into research until I nearly finished medical school" (Leishman, 1980, p. 104). The war came, and Thomas accepted an assignment to the Rockefeller Institute medical research team.

A Childhood Experience Can Lead to a Life Work

The experience of living your own note can be as simple as one childhood experience that sent Ray Bradbury on what turned into a life of successful writing. It started with Poe. As Bradbury tells it, he fell in love with Poe's verbal jewelry. He began to imitate him from the age of 12 and continued until age 18. He attributes his success to Poe, the comics, the carnival and circus people in Northern Illinois, and old radio programs. However, he says Mr. Electrico permanently marked his life. He later wrote about it in *Something Wicked This Way Comes* (1962). Mr. Electrico, a carnival performer, came through Bradbury's hometown of Waukegan, Illinois, every autumn and sat in his electric chair each night. Someone would pull a switch and Mr. Electrico reached out with his sword and dubbed everyone in the front row with the electricity that sizzled from his sword. Fire prickled in his mouth and eyes and his hair stood on end. When he came to Bradbury, he touched him on the brow and chin and said, "Live forever." This sounded great to Bradbury. Enchanted with Mr. Electrico, Bradbury returned to the circus night after night. He and Mr. Electrico shared philosophies. Mr. Electrico said that he and Bradbury had previously met on the battlefield of the Argonne and Bradbury had died in his arms in the First World War in France. Bradbury said he did not know why Mr. Electrico told him that but it made a deep memory. Bradbury thought Mr. Electrico may have had a dead son, maybe no son at all, maybe was just lonely, and maybe a jokester. But within three months of his last meeting with Mr. Electrico in 1932, Bradbury begin writing full-time and never stopped. That was 48 years ago (Plummer, 1980).

On another level, a high school student scored 36 out of 36 on the ACT but did not want to attend college (personal experience in counseling, 1979). His parents tried to force him, but he resisted. Finally, they relented and he went to work. But two years later, he applied for college admission, and was accepted; four years later, he graduated. "To everything there is a season and a time to every purpose under Heaven" (Eccles. 3:1).

Each of these stories illustrates Life-As-Career at work in various circumstances unique to the individual. Each Life-As-Career looks different. None of these lives can be duplicated. That invalidates any one else's notion about how to do something. This dovetails with Kurt Lewin's life-space idea in which he suggested that each individual behaves in response to his or her world view (Lewin, 1951).

Living Life-As-Career means you form a cooperative bond with life (all forms). And we need to support each other's life journey, not judge it. Support increases confidence, self-esteem, and, potentially, motivation. It also enhances the immune system, making us less susceptible to various ailments and diseases.

Cindy Crawford attended DeKalb High School and graduated four years after Miller-Tiedeman left her counseling job there to move to California. Cindy, valedictorian of her class, went on to Northwestern University in Chicago. After one semester, she left to pursue a modeling career in New York. The rest is history, as she's now the most famous supermodel in America. Cindy jettisoned an opportunity for a college degree and followed her inner wisdom with support from her mother, Jennifer Moluf, who advised Cindy that if it (modeling) didn't work out, she would know that she tried. On the job, Cindy had support from her hairdresser, make-up artist, personal trainer, image stylist, photographer, designer, caterer, magazine editor, photo editor and more. Everyone needs support while pursuing his or her dream, even when it may not produce such astounding results.

About Work and Lifecareer

Earning a living is an essential part of life, but not to the exclusion of everything else, particularly health. Individuals whose main identity is wrapped up in their career face difficult psychological times with job loss. When they reconnect for work and experience another or multiple job losses, as in today's downsized environment, the trauma increases, affecting all in the immediate environment. When you think of Life-As-Career, everything you do figures into your life direction. When job loss occurs, it's momentarily painful, but not crippling. In addition, you free yourself from the traditional career assumptions like those noted in Table 3.1.

Choosing a Career

When Life-Is-Career, choosing and changing careers become obsolete concepts. Everyone has a career (a very present tense idea), which levels the playing field. However, we all engage in job choice all through our lives. Sometimes we make that choice to move into something new, but sometimes the employer makes that choice for us. The latter is called downsizing or rightsizing, depending on your perspective. At the moment, anyone who works for someone else holds an insecure job.

Choosing a career is probably a middle-class notion, as the rich do not need to think in those terms. They have connections already in place, schools lined up to attend, and money if they do not want to work a regular job. For instance, John F. Kennedy, Jr., worked in the legal profession for a while, and then, with money to live on (reported at 100 million), founded *George Magazine*. The poor are too busy surviving to consider the idea of career. It's the middle class that use it most. On the other hand, Life-As-Career serves everyone, rich and poor, able and disabled, educated and uneducated. In that sense, one-size-fits-all, but that's where the similarity ends, as each life looks different, acts different, and makes very different choices in order to fulfill an individual life mission.

Changing Careers

If you cling to the idea that job is career, you find yourself losing a career each time you receive a downsized notice. You'll also talk about first, second, and third careers, none of which matter when you live Life-As-Career. Dropping the notion of career as something out there that you may or may not ever have improves the immune system, as stress kills off immune cells, and feeling less than someone because you do not

TABLE 3.1. Assumptive Differences Between the New Careering (Used Situationally as LifeCareer, Life-Is-Career, and Quantum Careering) and Traditional Career*

Traditional Career	Lifecareer
Job defined as career	Life-Is-Career
Career theorists make all theory	Individual as theory maker
Control of life	Cooperate with approaching forces
Parts equal the whole	Whole organizes the parts
Sets goals	Sets intentions
Know where you are going	Learn as you go
Finding self	Self continually unfolds
External information primary	Internal information primary
Follows reality defined by experts	Individual creates own reality
Focus on doing	Focus on becoming
Plays career like a crap shoot	Plays career from personal knowledge
Relies heavily on other's opinions	Takes readings from experience, intelligence, and intuition, factoring in other's opinions when appropriate
Making a living a major focus	Making a life while making a living
Heavy emphasis on first job	Not age specific school-to-work transition
Mostly focused on getting a time job	Expands possibilities to include both full- getting a job and creating your own work
Focus on outcome	Focus on action
Stress not major focus	Helps individuals consider stress as a career factor
Focus on choosing a career	Acknowledges everyone has a career that he or she lives each day
Self-concept theory discussion	Self-conceiving experienced
Focus on right or wise decision making	Values both right and left decisions with focus on learning that comes with those things that do not work out
Low trust in life	High trust in life even when it does not work
Making it defined with future tense	Acknowledges everyone makes it daily— present tense

*These assumptive differences also reflect paradigms (see Ch. 5).

have a career, cannot find one, or simply do not think that way sets up enormous stress.

A Right Way Exists

Embracing Life-As-Career, you recognize that no right way exists, even one a counselor might suggest. Each moment shifts and rearranges everything, so you make the best decision possible and move on. Sometimes this means you invest in something that could bring you additional income. If you find it does not work, you can think of it as a lost investment or an investment with new information for your developing vision. Most classes, college or otherwise, seldom result in immediate income. The bottom line: exploration costs—another reason to take money management seriously.

You Need Continual Clarity About Life Direction

Clarity in life direction only stays around a short time because experiences bring in new ideas and information. However, some people experience stable notions about life direction at an early age. They train for their interest and end up working in that field, sometimes for a lifetime. But for most people, clarity comes and goes, popping in and out of existence like particles. You think you are clear until something else happens, and then you are uncertain again. That's the motion and continual shifting in life. So, consider clarity a gift when it comes but continue to cooperate with the approaching forces while you intelligence the situation, learning all you can, making decisions to bring in another moment of clarity.

You Can Control Your Life Direction

This idea epitomizes one of the biggest misconceptions around. If you believe that, you are a prime candidate for ocean front property in Montana. You can choose to attend school, but even that depends on admission, health, money, and time to study. Many people make plans for one endeavor only to end up doing something else because they could not find work in their major interest.

When you think about control, remember that none of life stands still. The atoms in the book you hold in your hand move at phenomenal rates of speed, you just cannot see them. Additionally, at a level, it's mostly empty space. So you might say that you hold space in your hand when you read a book. The same thing happens when you sit on a chair. At the subatomic level, it's mostly empty space. But our minds have been conditioned to believe it's solid.

If you think about an atom like a minute solar system, you would see a large nucleus in the center, like a sun, and various electrons circling about it in their individual orbits, each orbit representing a given energy state that an electron can occupy. Now, it turns out that electrons follow no set path as to when they might leap from one orbit to another or how big the leap might be. So, two things have emerged as predictable: (a) that the path would be bumpy, and (b) that the distance traveled, in retrospect, could be measured in whole quanta (Zohar, 1990). Humans are always orbiting around their possibilities, veering here and there, in order to sense their encoded life direction. Frequently, the turbulence feels scary and out of control.

When an electron makes a transition from one energy state to another within the atom, it does so in a completely random and spontaneous way, or without cause. It also can make a transition from a higher state to a lower one and vice-versa, and this happens simultaneously in every direction at once. But when humans try to emulate that pattern, judgments arise as to the effectiveness of the action (Zohar, 1990).

To make this even more strange, when an electron, in the guise of a probability wave, intends to move from one orbit to another, it smears itself out over a large region of space, displaying an omnipresence in many orbits. It temporarily feels out its own future stability by trying out, all at once, all the possible new orbits into which it might eventually settle (Zohar, 1990). Similarly, we smear ourselves around when we imagine various possibilities, or try on different notions to check out feelings; but, unlike the electron, we cannot do it all at once.

Dr. Jonas Salk (1973), in his book *The Survival of the Wisest*, suggests that "the genetic system contains the program for the possibilities of the organism" (p. 33). Trying to control all those electrons moving you toward your future possibilities requires enormous energy, often producing stress. On the other hand, when you work with the information encoded in your body for your life mission, and *cooperate with the approaching forces*, you do so effortlessly, which frees up energy for other things. Then you find yourself surfing life.

Most of us believe that life moves forward unperturbed. But quantum theory shows us that all motion—even that perceived as smooth and continuous—is structured like film frames, in that subatomic particles can leap several frames ahead, leaving out intermediate steps even though we perceive motion as moving forward smoothly (Zohar, 1990).

Describing motion as a series of disrupted leaps proved the most fundamental conceptual change to come out of quantum theory, in Zohar's opinion. It's like replacing the smooth flow of real life with jerky, broken stills like in individual film frames. Quantum theory showed us that ALL motion, even that perceived as smooth and continuous, is structured like the frames of a film. And just as a film might occasionally skip a bit, leaving out intermediate steps, so subatomic particles can leave out intermediate steps that might seem more natural (Zohar, 1990).

Can Professionals or Friends Create a Reality That Works for You?

Knowing how the electrons in your body continually nudge you toward new and possible futures, how could counselors, friends, or family create anything that could in any way compare with that level of information? This does not negate outside help. It merely means it's not the last word or even the first word necessarily. The feeling that comes from guiding your life from your internal program parallels the feeling you get when your body's pH level falls in the correct range, aches and pains disappear, and you feel almost euphoric.

How Do Decisions Differ When You Live Life-As-Career?

You recognize and value your decisions, but you do not get attached to any of them. You focus on action, not outcome. If you do not get a desired outcome, you make another decision and continue connecting until something of value happens or you give up.

Sometimes we decide to do things not in our life plan knowing they will never work, but we continue to press on. Some individuals recognize the futility and quit. Others work against the approaching forces, often trying in vain to make something happen. This frequently brings about major dissatisfaction with life direction occurs and you fall into the *Humpty Dumpty condition*, where all the queen's horses and all the queen's personnel could not spin that decision into something workable.

Consequently stress results. The more something does not work, the more frustrated, anxious, and stressed you may feel. You talk incessantly with others about it. You sometimes invest more money hoping to make it work. Then even more stress results. That stress then depresses the immune system and little health problems begin to show up (as mentioned before). And sometimes, if enough stress accumulates, larger health problems occur, all because you have tried to control life and make something happen that either will never happen or is outside the timing sequence.

For instance, a young woman wanted to start working on her Ph.D. in the Spring. She did not want to wait until Fall to get started even though she had been promised a good funding package from her first choice university. She wanted to push the river and take second best, but the second best school did not come through with the funding. She then decided to wait for her first choice. Sometimes, we have to go through our own issues before we learn that everything has a rhythm and right time.

What Changes for Those Who Live Life-As-Career?

Those who live Life-As-Career value the natural unfoldment of events. They do not try to rush life or focus on its outcome. Why not watch outcome? Because you can only do those things in your control. Trying to control outcome or worrying about it, only gives you something to do—it does not move you forward. If anything, it holds you back because you use good time worrying, stressing, and judging. Those who *cooperate with the approaching forces* keep their eye on their work and their action, not the outcome. All experience imprints the body and impacts the body either positively or dispositively. Everything we do has a health connection—physical and psychological.

Individuals who live Life-As-Career do not worry about searching for a career, losing one, or moving on to second or third careers. They treat life as a whole fabric. This perspective results in increased energy and potential.

In addition, Lifecareerists know they can trust their inner wisdom—experience, intelligence, and intuition—to guide them through the maze of life. Sometimes their inner guidance runs counter to their desires and sometimes they reject that information, particularly if it does not fit their paradigm. But it may return. Something that keeps returning usually has some nugget of gold in it.

People who live life as process do not have to know what they are doing all the time. Nor do they need an end result to start out and experiment. For instance, Sally, 14 years old, and her sister stayed home while the parents vacationed. They read that a New York production company put out bids for the part of Lolita. Sally went to the library and checked out the book, read it, and asked her sister to video tape her doing the part. She then sent the video to the production company. They called her, flew her to New York. She tried out, got the part, and they chauffeured her back to the airport in a stretch limousine. She did not know exactly how to do all this but she went ahead anyway and won the part (personal communication, September 10, 1996).

Those who live Life-As-Career do not fit other's notions of what they should be doing because they live from inner guidance. Why is that better? Because it has all the relevant information. It knows better than any-one the capabilities, drives, desires, and ambitions. For instance, a counse-lor might have advised Sally to forget it. Or the counselor might have said, "What you are thinking about is not realistic." Without the doubt and uncertainty, the young woman plunged into what could turn into a life-time commitment to the arts. Many a dream has been squashed by unin-formed (from the individual client's perspective) advice. On the other hand, a few dreams have been realized because a counselor wisely encouraged trial and error.

When you live life as process, you are better at saying, "no." You even learn how to say, either verbally or nonverbally, "I care, but I'm not interested in your comments." Or you do like Cindy Crawford, supermodel, did. When thinking about dropping out of college, she decided to talk her decision over with one of her former high-school teachers. He advised her to stay in school. Of course, she followed her own inner wisdom and suc-ceeded in becoming a world-class model. Her teacher later said that was probably the worst advice he has ever given anyone.

Those who have made it know how to embrace all of their experi-ence. They know how to follow their own vision despite others' "won't work" notions. For instance, if Chester Carlson had listened to IBM, Gen-eral Electric, or Kodak, that dry photographic process we now know as Xerox copying might have been longer coming into existence. Mozart dis-regarded his publisher's advice to write something more popular; and the rest is history. Ask yourself, "What does anyone know about anyone else's potential or possibilities?"

Lifecareer and Personal Development

Life direction and personal development intricately link both in language and behavior and reflect the worldview of their day. You can see this in Table 3.2 which indicates the differences in both traditional career and Lifecareer and where the paradigm shift may have occurred.

Also notice in Table 3.2, traditional career tends to function at the Conforming stage of development, where individuals follow already-laid-out pathways; it defines job as career, and teaches control of life based on making right and wise decisions using a socially agreed-upon agenda, like "a good education leads to a good job." Then, setting of goals and making plans follows. This dovetails with ignoring decisions that do not work and touting those that do. At this level, common knowledge (usually designed by those in authority) occupies top position and individuals receive unlim-ited information about what works and what doesn't. This can be clearly seen in regard to a resume, where a majority have argued the utility of the

TABLE 3.2.   LifeCareer, Its Four Core Propositions and Its Relationship to Personal Development

Quantum Worldview

Life-Is-Career (quantum careering, or living life as process)

Self-Aware Level of Development

Individual as theory maker (teller of your own story)

Cooperating with life

Individual reality primary (Self-conceiving)

Intentions/Scheduling

Co-creating with higher self

Self-aware: Life-Is-Career cooperates with the approaching forces

Values both right and wrong

Values setting intentions and cooperating with the approaching forces

Paradigm Shifting Point

Newtonian Worldview

Conforming Stage of Development

Professionals as theory makers

Job is career

Acts to control

Values right & wise

Works from Goal Setting/Planning, Common reality

Job is Career

Making life happen

Self-concept as an idea

Plans/Goals

Career Planning

one-page resume. Could it be they forgot to remember that the one-page resume came about when people changed jobs infrequently? Or is it possible for professionals to get stuck in their own conformity web?

Take a small step up from the Conforming stage to the Self-Aware level, where individuals consider life as the big career. They *cooperate with the approaching forces*, realizing that life goes both right and left, and personal reality occupies primary position. Individuals then work with intentions, and scheduling considering the socially acceptable agenda, but moves out of it from time to time. At the Self-Aware level, options and exceptions come into play more, confidence and trust occupy a higher position in the psyche, and one can live more flexibly and joyfully, learning what it's like to be more fully human. (See Chapter 4 for more detail on development.) Self aware individuals ask questions and question answers.

Development, paradigms, and decision making determine our lives. Those three work like the engines in our cars moving our lives along. Therefore, you will find a chapter on each one, as well as mention of them in most of the chapters, as they connect intricately to our everyday lives and resulting quality.

☐ Looking Back

1. Lifecareer, Life-Is-Career, Life-As-Career, living life as process, and quantum careering all refer to the New Careering, as suggested by context.

2. Most scientists agree that on the following three notions: (a) each moment of universe is different from every other moment; (b) everything has an interior reality; and (c) everything relates to everything else.

3. The New Careering builds its theory on: (a) the philosophy of Quantum Mechanics, specifically, Complementarity, the uncertainty principle, and connectedness; and (b) self-organizing systems theory.

4. Helping professionals: (a) use personal theory to guide their lives; and (b) support the client in identifying and using his or her own personal theory. This avoids the confusion of theory integration experienced by so many beginning counselors.

5. Personal reality occupies primary position, conventional wisdom secondary, but both get considered.

6. No one of us has all it takes to make our dreams come true. It takes many hands and many hearts.

7. The New Careering offers a more stress-free life direction approach.

8. Decision making occurs naturally and all life does it, even particles.

9. Living life as process means staying in touch with the whole of experience.

10. Life works, not always the way we want it to, but it works.

11. The Lifecareer ethic reflects unbroken wholeness, unfoldment, and streaming well. It's evolutionary, not revolutionary.

12. When Life-Is-Career, you do not choose it, you inherit it. Further, you don't speak in terms of second, third, and fourth careers, or of finding or losing a career.

13. No right way exists for individual journeys.

14. Focus on action, not outcome.

☐ Discussion Questions

1. What do you see in the idea that life is self-organizing?

2. Identify examples of life being self-organizing in your life. You may call it coincidence, luck, or God working in your life. However you see it, write it.

3. What impresses you about the idea that life is self-organizing?

4. What bothers you about that idea?

5. What is your reaction to the idea that you create your own reality?

6. What do you like about this idea?

7. What do you dislike about this idea?

8. How would your life be different if you became aware that you were creating at least some of the things that happen to you?

9. What connection does Lifecareer theory have to your life?

10. Given your current understanding of career theories and practice, what do you see as the major assumptive differences between traditional career and process careering (situationally identified as Lifecareer, Life-Is-Career, Life-As-Career, quantum careering, and/or living life as process).

11. Discuss the need for process careering (Lifecareer, quantum careering, etc.) in today's work arena.

☐ Classroom/Group Exercises

1. First, choose a partner, and the principle you most identify with. Second, discuss, telling why you chose your particular principle (sub-principle) and how it fits your experience.

2 Choose a different partner and discuss any one of the following four main ideas giving examples from your personal experience: (a) quantum physics (connectedness, the whole is more than the sum of its parts, complementarity, uncertainty); (b) Self-organizing systems theory; (c) Life is a right and left proposition; or (d) We each create reality. How do these ideas relate to your personal experience and vice versa?

3. With the same partner, discuss your view of *error*, mistakes, or so-called wrong decisions.

4. Compare Lifecareer with traditional career.

☐ Homework Assignments

1. Write two double-spaced pages indicating your reaction to the Lifecareer ethic.

2. Write a short paragraph noting the importance of the quantum definition of reality as it shows up in both professional and everyday life. Give examples. Also, comment on a commonly heard notion: "That's not realistic."

3. Illustrate how you would use at least one principle: (a) in everyday life; and (b) in a counseling session.

4. Name at least one health benefit of living Life-As-Career.

5. Track your intentions between class meetings using the following format, and report in your next class what you learned:

Intentions: Date Completed:

CHAPTER

4

Anna Miller-Tiedeman

Development, Decision Making, and the New (Quantum) Careering

Spotlight on Development

It takes considerable courage to move out of conformity and into the self-aware level of development. Congressman Elliot exemplifies that higher level. He did not ride the conforming wave of segregation hysteria. Elliott took a moderate position which in the 1960s proved difficult. Elliott fought for legislation enabling poor students to attend college, senior citizens to have Medicare, and to raise the minimum wage. He said at that time that one could not stay in Congress unless one voted against civil rights. But he voted for civil rights and other legislation for the disadvantaged. During his 1964 campaign, right-wing extremists led by the Ku Klux Klan went after Elliott and successfully thwarted his reelection. Two years later, he staked all his money on the Governor's race. It left him totally broke. He later said he regretted the debt, but not the cause. In 1994, Elliott received the first Kennedy Library Foundation Profile in Courage Award which came with a $25,000 stipend (Montgomery, 1990).

☐ Looking Ahead

Watch for the following important topics:

1. Why development became important to study

2. The Loevinger and Wessler model of ego development

3. Illustrations of development levels in everyday language

4. Reflections of development in current events

5. Important terms and concepts:

   a. Self-Protective

   b. Conforming

   c. Self-Aware

   d. Conscientious

Development, paradigms, and decision making all resemble a car engine in that all the parts work together to contribute to the functioning of the whole. A problem with any one of the parts weakens the entire system. However, development forms the foundation from which values emerge, which show up in your beliefs, and on which you make decisions. For instance, Congressman Elliott's stand on civil rights in the 1960s represents a higher level of development, one in which new ways of thinking could emerge, even though unpopular at the time. Elliott held the value of inclusivity and opportunity for those outside the power structure. His strongly held beliefs threaded themselves through his value system which directed his decision making. Even though Elliott's highly held values supported his beliefs, he ended up in economic disaster. However, his principles remained intact, causing him to say that he regretted the debt, but not the cause.

Development is a process characterized by stages that follow a progression growing into greater complexity as in self-organizing systems. Two aspects of self-organizing systems are (a) self-renewal—the renewing and recycling of components while maintaining the integrity of their overall structure; and (b) self-transcendence—reaching out creatively beyond physical and mental boundaries (Capra, 1982). Self-renewal is essential; self-transcendence a choice. Here's one example of such a choice.

Older Student: I'm interested in a clinical psychology degree.

Counselor: Let me tell you about the various kinds of foci, like trans-
                  formational psychology.

Older Student: No, don't. If I got involved in anything but mainline psy-
                  chology, I'd have to change. I like my life the way it is.

The choice is always present.

The Loevinger and Wessler (1970a, 1970b) model of ego development, like the New Careering model, is presented to invite practical application, not just academic discussion. Recognizing one's own developmental stage or level can lead to a change of mind, which shows up in the
language, and ordinarily translates into a behavior change. For instance, a
group walks away from a presentation. One person says, "What a boring
speaker." If the speaker did not appeal to you, it is tempting to fall into the
same thought pattern (paradigm) and say, "Yes, I thought so too." But
when you recognize that in the new physics you can not separate yourself
from what you observe, then you change your response to something like,
"That talk didn't work for me." In saying that, you take responsibility for
your perception. This moves the response from a Self-Protective stage of
development to the Self-Aware level. It also removes the violence from
the statement.

If you feel really brave, you might say to your friend, "No one is
boring, interesting, stimulating, or fantastic—it all depends on your values, your beliefs, your definition and, more importantly, your awareness
level. Ultimately, it's not so simple as just boring." This moves everyone
one step closer to a *kinder, gentler world.*

Two important notes: (a) This chapter does not deal with Loevinger
and Wessler's lower stage—Impulsive—or the top three stages and their
intervening level (the Conscientious stage, Individualistic level, Autonomous stage, and Integrated stage), as most functioning in this society hov-
ers around the Self-Protective and Conforming stages, and the Self-Aware
level of development; and (b) Miller-Tiedeman takes full responsibility for
the interpretation of the Loevinger and Wessler model of ego development as it plays out in real life.

Why Development?

Why development? Because development will help us individually and as
a society to grow up; it will make life more fun and less violent, and it will
help us more readily accept our own and other emerging visions that don't
conform.

Further, professionals may use their personal level of development, more than their techniques, to conform their clients to conventional reality. This can change when we learn how to bring development into our awareness potentially reducing verbal harshness and life-mission intrusion. In this chapter, Miller-Tiedeman used everyday situations to illuminate the aforementioned two stages and one level of development to help identify and potentially change both personal and professional responses.

Initially, the focus on development started when Miller-Tiedeman looked for ways to increase student interest in decision making, as many of the students felt they already knew about it. In other words, they thought, *been there, done that.* Never mind improvement. So, thinking that development might hold some answers, a deliberate search of related literature was made. The Loevinger and Wessler model of ego development surfaced as one that could be easily taught and, in addition, the learners could use it with each other in their everyday interactions.

The Loevinger and Wessler model (1970a, 1970b), composed of a hierarchy of stages and levels, describes personality development as shown in Table 4. 1.

As individuals move through the stages and levels of ego development, they tend to become more self-critical and more concerned about self in the broader context of others and events. It becomes easier to read the self in situations of the moment as one considers self-criticism a possibility. These stages reveal a moving away from selfish concerns and conforming tendencies, through the more self-critical condition involved in resolving concerns for self with others, and into an integrated stage similar in quality to that of Maslow's (1954) self-actualized person whose behavior is characterized by self-sufficiency, meaningfulness, playfulness, richness, simplicity, order, justice, completion, necessity, perfection, individuality, aliveness, beauty, goodness, and truth.

Loevinger and Wessler's stages of ego development overlap and differ depending on situation and circumstances. Thus, for example, one may use a Stage 2 response (the Self-Protective stage) in one situation and a Stage 4 response (the Conscientious stage) in another. Loevinger and Wessler assumed, as did Sullivan, Grant, and Grant (as cited in Loevinger & Wessler, 1970a, p. 15) "... that each person has some level of core functioning." A level where most of the responses on the sentence completion form, by which Loevinger and Wessler measure ego development, congregate.

The taking or non-taking of personal responsibility can be noted in the way an individual finishes a sentence, and the aggregate of these language responses translate into an ego-development level.

Loevinger and Wessler created their original ego-development scale from data collected on women only (1970a). However, in their study of

TABLE 4.1. Loevinger and Wessler's Ego Development Model

Presocial Stage (Infant)
Symbiotic Stage (Intimate)

1. **Impulsive Stage**

    Acting quickly without much thought. Individuals operating at this stage tend to class people as good or bad. "Good and bad at times are confused with nice-to-me versus mean-to-me" (Loevinger, 1976, p. 16). Present oriented.

2. **Self-Protective Stage**

    Fear of getting caught and blame are major themes. Avoids self-criticism.

3. **Conformist Stage**

    Uncritically accepts a group identity and obeys the rules because they constitute group-accepted rules.

3/4. **Self-Aware Level**

    Individuals at this stage see alternatives. They become aware of moments of nonconformity in that they break molds set by social norms from time to time.. This level represents the break-away point into higher awareness.

4. **Conscientious Stage**

    Individuals think in more complex terms: "trivial versus important; love versus lust; dependent versus independent, inner life versus outward appearances" (Loevinger, 1976, p. 21).

4/5. **Individualistic Level**

    Individuals experience a heightened sense of individuality at this level. On the other hand, the individual exhibits a stronger tolerance of both self and others. A strong self and strong empathy for others develops at this level.

5. **Autonomous Stage**

    In addition to respect for individuality, coping with conflicting inner needs and heightened toleration appears at this stage.

6. **Integrated**

    Maslow's self-actualized person emerges at this stage.

Adapted from J. Loevinger & R. Wessler, *Measuring Ego Development, 1.* San Francisco: Jossey-Bass, Inc., 1970a, pp. 10–11, and J. Loevinger, *Ego Development*, 1976.

boys and girls ages 9 to 18 (1970b), they reported that "a chi square test shows no significant difference of the TPR (total protocol rating) at the various age groups between boys and girls (p. 51)." Loevinger and Wesler also used this scale with over 500 boys and girls without noting any significant restraints on boys' development resulting from the scale's construction based on girls' data only.

How learners at various stages in ego development perceive the world and describe it to themselves mostly determines their actions. For instance, a student with a core functioning at the Self-Protective stage, will use language indicative of that level of development. When a teacher asks a student about late homework, the Self-Protective stage response might be, "The dog ate it" or "My sister tore it up." Additionally, the student might perceive himself or herself as picked on. Whereas a student at the Self-Aware level might respond, "Yes, I know it's consistently late, but something kept me from doing it, so I'd like to talk with you about it," or it could be as simple as taking responsibility without comment.

The Loevinger and Wessler theory proved teachable to both regular and learning disabled students as well as useful in peer teaching, with simplified stage and level definitions. By freezing a particular student comment while in conversation, it's possible to point out a stage or level of development right on the spot. This offers many teachable moments showing how development reveals itself in everyday situations. (See results of this study below.) When you start observing levels of development, you find them in all human interaction.

Study Results.   This study (Miller-Tiedeman, 1980) explored a curriculum model used by teachers in the classroom one day a week to stimulate psychological growth along with intellectual growth. Miller-Tiedeman hypothesized that increasing psychological growth using Loevinger and Wessler's model of ego development (1970a, 1970b, 1976) would increase change in appreciation of decision making and awareness of its power in shaping and designing one's life.

The results indicated that deliberate attention to personal development increased responses on the Loevinger and Wessler Ego Development Scale by one half a level. This result occured even with learning disabled students, and with ninth-graders as well as juniors and seniors in high school. In addition, the results held up when Miller-Tiedeman compared an experimental with a parallel control group. Finally, this result also appeared in a group of mixed grade levels who volunteered for a career future class. Since none of the other changes isolated in this study continued to be significant when control observations were deducted from experimental changes, the significant changes reported for the other variables must be treated with caution.

In summary, the study demonstrated that psychological growth, as measured by the Loevinger and Wessler scale of ego development, can be significantly increased when a psychological-education procedure is used one forty-minute period a week for a semester in conjunction with the teaching of English. In addition, it may significantly enhance critical thinking and reading skills as well (see Lesson Plan in Appendix B).

How Development Looks in Everyday Life

The Self-Protective Stage

Take one trip to any faculty lounge, in practically any school, anywhere in the world, and numerous examples of the blaming aspect of the Self-Protective stage of ego development will show up. The administration usually receives the blame from individual faculty members. And, if anyone chooses a Self-Aware level response, the group usually initiates its freeze response. This happens in church groups when members get dissatisfied with their pastor. They start projecting blame concerning what he or she is not doing which they think should be done or the reverse. Sometimes, this causes a split in the church with dissatisfied members breaking off to start their own church. Development bleeds into all life decisions one way or another even though few *pay attention* to it.

But ignoring a systemic problem reflects the American marketplace and its medical model, as many doctors treat symptoms rather than seeking root causes. For instance, many traditional doctors treat high cholesterol by prescribing cholesterol-lowering medication rather than working on cleansing the liver which, incidentally, alternative health care professionals usually attend to because cholesterol-lowering medication can make the liver sicker. That is why responsible doctors who prescribe cholesterol-lowering drugs usually order a blood test periodically to check for liver damage.

In schools, students often blame teachers for giving them bad grades. You find this also in gossip—someone blaming someone else for having said something. This occurs with high frequency in public education. Miller-Tiedeman experienced this in working with students who reported difficulty with teachers. If the student came alone to talk about the problem, he or she would often project blame onto the teacher. That usually changed when the teacher sat in on the conference.

In families, children play one parent against the other by not only projecting blame, but by suggesting that one parent said the child could do whatever the other parent objected to. In play, when something goes wrong, children frequently blame each other—all a part of growing up. But adults engage in the same kind of blame.

For instance, Newt Gingrich's (Lawrence, 1995) allegation that President Clinton snubbed him on the plane ride to Yitzhak Rabin's funeral. Newt wanted to talk about the budget and how to avoid a government shutdown and President Clinton did not oblige. Remember, both Gingrich and Clinton were on their way to pay their respects to one of the greatest peacemakers of the century. Each of us makes the decision we feel best suits the situation.

The "reader speaks" sections in most newspapers contain numerous examples of the Self-Protective stage of development, as the authors mostly project blame onto someone—either the president, the first lady, the city council, state government, entertainment industry. You name it, they blame it.

Then, young men who participate in creating a pregnancy often blame the young woman. For instance, a mother (Van Buren, 1995) reported the following example soon after discovering that a young woman her son had been dating turned up pregnant:

Son: She knew that I didn't want kids, yet she went and got herself pregnant.

Mother: You helped her get pregnant. Did you use any protection?

Son: No! That's left up to the dumb girl.

The above language reflects scant responsibility for behavior. That's typical for individuals speaking from the Self-Protective stage of development.

Nancy Reagan also checked in at the Self-Protective stage. Helmbreck (1989), in an opinion article commenting on Reagan's *My Turn*, said Nancy rationalized why she received so much blame. First, the "Popular Husband" theory. People liked her husband and did not like her. She said, "I think I served as a lightning rod." Her next projection was, "They hate me because I'm thin and wear nice clothes." She went on to blame her daughter, Patti, who, as she said, "failed to take advantage of opportunities open to her." Nancy blamed her busy schedule and her closeness to her husband, but took little responsibility herself.

Actor and movie director, Caroll O'Connor (The Associated Press, 1995) blamed drug pushers for his son's death. He said, "These dealers, they kill people" (p. A6). Drug dealers do not kill people any more than stress kills. They only make it possible for someone to make that choice. It might be argued that drug dealers often function on a higher level of development, as these people seldom become users. They've somehow figured out the killing part of drugs. This does not mean that they function all the time or even most of the time on a higher level. But for some unknown reason, they may in regard to drug use.

The Conforming Stage

Development in Action: Applying the Conforming Stage of Development (3) to Certification

The National Board for Certified Counselors' (1996) list of acceptable continuing education requirements reads like the graduate school catalog. For instance, counseling theory, human growth and development, and group dynamics were but a few of the topics listed. Further, for publication they offer a mere 20 contact hours within a five-year period. While Robert Waller wrote *Bridges of Madison County* (1992) in two weeks, the rest of us usually take more time on chapters and books. The failure of the NBCC to (a) open the categories to all learning that enhances the work of a professional; and (b) recognize writing as a professional maturation activity, best measured by quality rather than quantity, interferes with counselor growth and keeps counselors dumbed down to the Conforming stage of development.

The pain-pill manufacturers love the conforming public. Their product stops your awareness of the pain, but at a deeper level it can damage both the kidneys and the liver. It can also cause stomach bleeding. But that information along with a high cash return does not encourage manufacturers to educate the public. They prefer you stay good conforming customers, believing what they tell you.

Food manufacturers follow the lead of doctors and pain-pill manufacturers. They rush to offer the public convenience foods, most of which contain hydrogenated fat, a fat the body does not recognize, so it gets deposited into the arteries. This ends up contributing to an increasing number of expensive by-pass operations each year.

In recovery, not feeling well enough to do good food preparation, the public buys quick foods filled with hydrogenated fats and starts the whole cycle over again. But people stay in conformity for a variety of reasons including lack of awareness, ease, and comfort.

In Business 101 you learn it's all about profit, not health. Bottom lines do not usually grow by telling the truth, they survive on fears, hopes, and dreams, buttressed by low-level public awareness where it's easier to follow conventional wisdom (the Conforming stage). So, if you can sufficiently scare people or convince them of an instant fix, you can separate them from both their money and their health. Those at the Conforming stage of development fall prey, as they want to be in the group that follows popular trends. These people usually place utter trust in professionals.

Remember a few years back when the public became aware of Alar on apples and stopped buying them? The public reaction got the attention of the produce executives and things changed. Without public awareness, money will continue to drive the marketplace, not health. Corporate America in general, both large and small, considers the bottom line first, not the health of the consumer.

The tobacco industry provides a good example of that, and Jeffrey Weigand, the man who blew the whistle on the tobacco companies, showed us in real time why many choose not to move out of conformity. According to Bergman (1997), the tobacco industry relentlessly pursued Weigand and did not want to stop harassing him even after they worked out their agreement with the government. But the 24 state attorneys refused to sign off on the agreement until Brown & Williamson dropped its lawsuit against him. Even though you may not agree with the tobacco industry values, remember we all act in our own best interest, and tobacco sells even though it also kills.

Probably one of the best illustrations of the Conforming stage of development shows up in the abortion issue. Many in the anti-abortion group think they have heard from God and he (or she) said that abortion is wrong; therefore, everyone ought to abide by their truth. And those who go against it can find themselves dead, as Dr. David Dunn discovered when Michael F. Griffin shot him outside an abortion clinic (Kaczor, 1994). Those at the Conforming stage of development do not usually entertain exceptions and they act on their black and white views because they really do not see anything else.

Sometimes you cannot avoid the conformists even in death. Randy Shilts, a journalist who helped awaken the nation to the AIDS epidemic in his book, *And the Band Played On* (1987), died in 1994. A Kansas religious group threatened to picket his memorial services (Weise, 1994). They came and carried signs like "Shilts in Hell" and "Fags burn in hell." While you can say many things about the rights of the religious group to picket, at a deep level they suffer from a developmental deficit which has intolerance written all over it. That's how profoundly development plays in all our lives.

In 1992, the Southern Baptist Convention decided to banish two churches for accepting homosexuals (Cornell, 1992). Those churches did not conform to their Southern Baptist Convention, a group, along with other religious groups, that holds conformity in high priority. So the Convention threw them out.

The Self-Aware Level

Development in Action: Applying the Self-Aware Level (3/4) to Student and Teacher Interactions

Let the masters of the written word cling to their bodiless principles. Let them pronounce what is interesting and what is not, what is a poem and what is not, *what is a thesis and what is not* (italics added), what merits their grudging praise and what does not. For myself, I want another model. I want to hear this poem by this person on this muggy August morning under the pear tree. I want to know what it is doing in the life of her work, and in my life as well. I want to give her the courage to say the next hard thing, without fear of ridicule or expulsion if she strays across the borders of good taste, good sense, or good judgment demarcated by a tradition she had no part in forming. I want her to do the same for me. We can all nourish and strengthen one another by listening to one another very hard, "ask hard questions, too, send one another away to work again, and laugh in all the right places (Mairs, 1994, pp. 24–25).

Now let's look at the Baptist issue from the break-away point—the Self-Aware level. At this level, individuals see alternatives and exceptions. They start to accept, not necessarily approve, points of view instead of immediately taking a point of view. This ushers in the consideration of tolerance. In fact, some of the members of the Southern Baptist Convention in response to the banishment of churches accepting homosexuals, did object to their Convention's action.

They said, "We have seriously violated the autonomy of the local church" (Cornell, 1992, p. A8). They went on to say, "It's a major break in a wall which has protected one of the most vital principles of our heritage for 150 years" (p. A8). Notice the language used. They did not call the banishment weird, they took a higher ground. The Southern Baptists also apologized to the blacks for the way they had treated them over the years.

When Deepak Chopra, M.D., appeared on "The Oprah Winfrey Show," Winfrey asked him how he responded to those who thought him strange and weird. Chopra answered telling about his appointment to the Alternative Medicine Group of the National Institutes of Health, along with other similar appointments. He placed his response in the Self-Aware level, he did not resort to a Self-Protective response. As a result, he maintained peace and harmony which reduced the stress in his body and enhanced his immune system. All this by moving to a higher level of awareness.

A Self-Aware response to the abortion issues might look like this. "We know that you (anti-abortion advocates) believe you have the word from God stating that, 'abortion is wrong.' We honor your position, but we take a different view. We believe the choice rests between the woman, her circumstances, family, and her God." A higher level of development makes room for the views of others.

These are a but few examples of how development shows up in everyday life once you start looking for it—another quantum physics principle: You see what you look for, like the two young boys who received a box of manure. The optimist said, "Where there's manure, there must be a pony." The pessimist said, "This is only manure."

Weaving Development into the Fabric of the New Careering

All humans experience uncertainty, whether or not they take a traditional or process view of career. This means we all experience fear, some more than others. In traditional career, one guards against uncertainty allegedly by making it happen with effective, wise, and better decision making, usually about job, conforming to what has been. In process careering, embracing uncertainty along with outcomes that do not work acknowledges the holistic quality of life as an ever-changing design that requires a Self-Aware level of development. But in the struggle to unfold the calling, while acting from the Self-Aware level, there's a tendency to slip down the slope of conformity where common reality prevails and where it seems someone else has the answer that will make things easier. You know you're on a higher level when you *deliberately choose* to conform. Keep in mind no one functions completely on one level of development. We *yo-yo* up and down those levels, and with personal work, the core ultimately settles in at the higher level.

Those who live Life-As-Career trust their own thought, a Self-Aware-level behavior, which represents only a level increase beyond the Conforming stage of development. Individuals at this point tend to venture out into more things than would those who make decisions mostly at the Conforming stage. In other words, life's strategy—trial and error—comes into play. A feeling of aloneness and a need to find a new support group emerges. This happens without much effort when an individual follows his or her own career theory (story). This, in turn, brings forth inner wisdom and information about the next step toward personal life mission fulfillment. As Jane, a rehab counselor, said, "Bumping into other people, hearing how they work with their career theories, sharing their personal journey problems, interests, and concerns gave me a sense of comfort. I felt I again had a place" (personal communication with a client). C. S.

Lewis (1965) in his essay, "The Inner Ring," said this: "If in your working hours you make the work your end, you will presently find yourself all unawares inside the only circle in your profession that really matters" (p. 65).

This moving out of conformity resembles the lobster out-shelling. As the lobster grows, it sheds its shell and becomes vulnerable for several weeks. Then a new shell grows back and starts to harden, providing protection. That same defenseless feeling arises in moving out of conformity. But over time new protective layers form and harden. Even though very delicate and fragile in the beginning, the new shell offers the feeling of newness on which more and stronger layers will form.

But be aware, it does not happen overnight. Sometimes it seems it will never happen. But in time it comes together. In the interim, remember the biblical admonition, "To every thing there is a season and a time to every purpose under heaven." Or, you cannot push the river, it flows at its own rate.

Those who function mostly at the Conforming stage might think that living Life-As-Career is easy, but that's because they look through the lens of conformity and believe it works like all conforming activities—let someone teach you how to do it and go do it. "What's hard about that?" they ask. They overlook the personal work it takes to move up in development because conformity takes so little effort.

The ease with which someone can change his or her mind and attitude depends among other things on the level of personal development. For instance, those at the Conforming stage of development often cannot see beyond the status quo. He or she holds a rather black and white view of the world. This may make it difficult or even impossible to understand the New (Quantum) Careering because it departs from conventional career development wisdom. From another perspective, you might say that this individual's paradigm or model of the world screens out anything that does not follow his or her rules and regulations. Barker (1990) would call this *Paradigm Paralysis* (see Chapter 5 for more detail on paradigms). These individuals do not hear or see how the change works or that it could work better than what's already in place.

On the other hand, individuals functioning at the Self-Aware level of development tend to see alternatives and possibilities. They're more open and full of myriad possibilities. They experiment more and adventure into the unknown. They realize we do not live on the perfection planet, therefore, they do not obsess over getting it right. So they tend to venture out on thin ice more often in their life direction. Further, they can see, accept, and understand the perspective of those functioning at the Conforming stage of development even though they do not agree with it. They know you can have understanding without agreement or consensus.

Those who venture into the Self-Aware level invite change with both its positive and dispositive aspects. They also put their physiology somewhat at risk, as moving up in development increases stress and uses more physical and psychic energy. That's most likely why more people do not choose to move from their comfortable niche, it takes too much effort and energy. And we all prioritize our activities according to the value we attach to effort. This shows up in the market research (Teleshare 900, 1994); of the top five reasons, people buy: "(a) to make money; (b) to save money; (c) to save time; (d) to avoid effort; and (e) to get more comfort" (Section 1, p. 12).

Working to attain a higher level of development more often than not produces pain—of course, depending on the individual; while the Conforming stage of development resembles an old pair of jeans—it feels comfortable and good. So, individuals and businesses often take the position, *if it ain't broke, why fix it?* versus *if it ain't broke, break it.* The tobacco company, as mentioned in the above example, did the former while Weigand took the latter position.

Development and Shifting Paradigms

As long as you teach the familiar in any discipline, students will stumble less because they have a certain familiarity, like in the "old" math. But in the transition to the new math, they stumbled somewhat until the new math became regularized. That same thing happens in career development in moving from traditional to process careering. Some will love the change, some will hate it, and a group will fall in between. There will always be those who will fight for the status quo in any endeavor. But a major shift occurs when *talk about theory* gives way to seeing the *individual as a theory maker*. This shifts the focus from counseling to development and supports what may appear to the helping professional as idiosyncratic growth. Whether we like it or not, whether we choose it or not, growth is life's game; and, we can cooperate with the approaching forces and willingly participate or we can fight it, increasing our stress.

Pause a moment here to consider what the words counselor, therapist, and development really mean. This will show their usefulness in process careering. The term counseling means to counsel or advise, mutual consultation or deliberation (Costello, 1991). Therapist means a person trained in the treatment of disease, injury, or disability, either mental or physical. Development can be defined as, to uncover or unfold, to cause to pass or to advance from a lower to a higher stage as in function, structure ... to unfold gradually by natural processes. Therefore, those helping professionals midwifing individual life journeys are New Careering Developers, not necessarily counselors or therapists.

Counselors functioning at the Conforming stage of development offer mostly what *has been*, not what *can be*. This happens every day somewhere in the world, particularly with American-trained counselors. Reflect on this Southern California example. Joe met with James and Associates to see about signing up for a potential job after getting downsized. The woman who talked with him looked at his resume and said, "This is a lousy resume" (an example of a counselor *has-been* response). This comment had several effects. First, Joe's self-esteem immediately dropped. Second, for the remainder of the session he worried about the 200 resumes he had already mailed. Third, Joe's attention dropped to the point that afterwards he did not remember too much about the session. Finally, and perhaps more importantly, Joe experienced many days of depression, and his wife spent more time than she cared trying to pick up the pieces from this event.

Think about this situation in development terms. What do you think a higher level response might look like? How about, "I know you've worked on this a lot, but let me offer two or three suggestions." Joe might reply, "But I've sent out 200 resumes." The counselor might say something like, "Don't be concerned, just improve your resume and send out more. Life is about improvement, not getting it right. Move on and don't give it another thought." This type of response would validate the client's work, relax him, and open more psychological space for potential change. It would also show that the counselor knew alternative approaches to resume writing existed (an approach more on the Self-Aware level of development). In that way, the client's self-esteem stays intact. This would show the counselor understood process careering and one of its main propositions: Each individual has a career theory that works for him or her. And decisions made, whether about resume or some other life-direction problem, come from the best judgment of the client, given current experience. This means the professional acts to support the individual journey. He or she does not judge the actions the client takes, regardless of how much it varies with the counselor's professional paradigm. Few of these behaviors appear at the Conforming stage of development because they require the insight from the Self-Aware level.

Counselors at the Conforming stage, in general, do not:

- suggest that Life-Is-Career;

- tell their clients the story of our time;

- take readily to a new paradigm;

- encourage clients to explore many different perspectives and try different approaches to job hunting;

- acknowledge there are many ways to write a winning resume;

- relax clients about possibilities;

- help clients relax about their lives;

- focus on action taken;

- encourage setting intentions and scheduling;

- understand that job markets, like the cells in our bodies, change each moment.

To give this list a Self-Aware level spin, change its heading from *Counselors at the Conforming stage, in general, do not …* to *Counselors at the Self-Aware level do. …* That puts in plain sight how the developmental stage changes in language, which changes the action taken.

Going a step further, development matters in the New (Quantum) Careering, because not seeing options and exceptions, counselors often:

- adjust clients to what has been rather than inspire them to what could be;

- unwittingly model limitations which often come out of fears and personal issues;

- make judgments about client dreams—too quickly determining what they can or cannot do;

- bind clients to their (the counselor's) own cultural ignorance;

- press clients too quickly into something they could potentially do but are not quite ready to do;

- suggest testing because it offers the counselor a comfortable starting point;

- make suggestions that work from their (the counselor's) perspective but which throw the client into awkward circumstances, frequently shifting him or her away from what the he or she felt right to do.

The above represents an incomplete list, provided to stimulate discussion about development.

Development and the Four Societal Waves

In thinking about development, it's helpful to view it from the perspective of cultural shifts, starting with the agricultural era, which Toffler (1980) suggested "... began around 8000 BC and dominated the earth unchallenged until sometime around AD 1650-1750" (p. 14). He identified this period as the First Wave. Then the Second Wave picked up momentum and dominated until it crested in the early 1900s. Around 1955, white-collar workers outnumbered blue-collar for the first time, computers arrived on the scene doing more than before, commercial jets traveled the globe, the birth control pill was introduced along with other high impact innovations. During this time, the Third Wave grew and partially crested in the late '70s and early '80s, as do all waves eventually.

Then what Miller-Tiedeman calls the Fourth Wave (relieving Toffler of that responsibility), the Information Age took over, bolstered by computers. During this time, worker wages stagnated, CEO earnings grew, and workers found themselves caught in the downsizing stream resulting in multiple job connections and disconnections.

The Agricultural Era and Development

During the Agricultural era, the land provided the basis of economy, life, culture, family structure, and politics. Life organized around the village, and had divisions of labor, and, of course, various classes and castes. Birth determined one's position in life. Since land provided the foundation for all societal activities, war often served as a means to keep it. Those in power extracted conformity from the less powerful and acted in ways to protect their own space. Conformity afforded a tool to keep people in line. For instance, schooling was initiated to produce the kind of adults industrialism needed. As Toffler (1970) writes, "The problem was inordinately complex. How to pre-adapt children for a new world—a world of repetitive indoor toil, smoke, noise, machines, crowded living conditions, collective discipline, a world in which time was to be regulated, not by the cycle of sun and moon, but by the factory whistle and the *clock*" (p. 400).

The Self-Protective stage showed up in people's attempts to work through their oppression, which they did mostly by blaming those in power. At the Self-Protective level of development, people do not tend to see other options or other ways of being, and often think of themselves as victims of circumstances, which has validity in many instances. Even though conformity found its way into the life during the Agricultural Era, the Self-Protective stage more clearly fit the survival needs of that time (see Table 4.2).

Table 4.2 shows the possible parallels between development, the points of major societal transformation, and the career thought that grew from it. The Agricultural period has some correspondence with the Self-Protective stage of development; the Industrial Era with the Conforming stage from which traditional career grew and thrived; and the Information/Service span with the Self-Aware level.

The Industrial Era and Conformity

When individuals started to see they could work fewer hours and earn more money, they moved from the land to the factory. The Conforming stage of personal development fit the Industrial Period like a hand in a glove, as mass production and duplication were the name of the game. At this point, people were still very busy trying to survive and conformity made them feel more secure. Therefore, few questioned it.

It's easy to see how conformity took hold so quickly. At work, people were told what to do. The order of the day was steady work, decent pay, opportunities for advancement, vacation time, and fringe benefits—all supplied by the employer if the employees conformed to the rules. Individuals did not need to learn many new skills or do much thinking about income, as the employer both gave the orders and issued the pay. It was a conformist period, and it worked for both the employer and employee.

The Industrial Period and its accompanying conformist notions was influenced by the conventional scientific model of the day which, at that time, had been around for about 300 years. During that time, Newtonian physics held sway. It divided things into parts assuming the parts equaled the whole. "Throughout history we have drawn our conception of ourselves and our place in the universe from the current physical theory of the day," suggested Zohar (1990, p. 18). And the career development field did not escape this influence. Career counselors had their parts (resumes, job-search strategies, occupational theories, and the like) that they proposed made the whole. This lock-step thought and conformity made the industrial period a fairly rigid one. You can see this imprint in the theories presented in *Career Choice and Development* (Brown et al., 1990), where "the individual" is treated as a topic of discussion, where choice is not connected to a warm body, but finds itself in aggregate statistics and research methodologies; where theorists have not found a way to lighten up the science and look, if only briefly, into spirit.

In addition, career development theorists used males for most of their research (Super, 1957), as most women did not work outside the home. In addition, gender equity did not figure into the picture. Super (1957) said, "Adequate data on the career patterns of women are lacking" (p. 76). He

TABLE 4.2. A Likely Parallelism in Cultural and Personal
          Development

Integrated Stage

Maslow's self-actualized
   personality

Autonomous Stage

Respect for individuality

Conscientious Stage

Increased ability to see
   matters from other's
   point of view

Self-Aware Level	**INFORMATION/SERVICE ERA**
Break-away point from careering	New Careering (Lifecareer, Quantum careering, process careering
See alternatives and exceptions	
Aware of moving out of conformity	
Starts to see self differently	

┌───┐
│   │
│   **Paradigm-Shifting Point**   │
│   │
└───┘

Conforming Stage	**INDUSTRIAL ERA**
Uncritically accepts group identity	Tradition Career Job/External considerations and obeys rules.
Self-Protective Stage	**AGRICULTURE PERIOD**
Don't get caught major theme	
Blames others	
Opportunistic	

Developmental stages adapted from J. Loevinger & R. Wessler, *Measuring Ego Development, 1.* San Francisco: Jossey-Bass, Inc., 1970a. Parallelism—Miller-Tiedeman's construct.

went on to try to make sense out of female career patterns, in terms of work either outside or inside the home. Super said, "It is important to point out that woman's role as childbearer makes her the keystone of the home, and therefore gives homemaking a central place in her career" (p. 76). Mueller (as cited in Super, 1957) concluded that a figurative John may choose law, medicine, or engineering as a profession, but his counterpart Mary, "nine times out of ten, can see no further than her marriage. She wants a little job that will put her immediately in the company of men." The statements of both Super and Mueller reflect the cultural perspective on women's careers in the 1950s, one that glaringly excluded *personal journey and life mission* discussion. However, the latter seldom came up as a point of encouragement for either males or females; *the focus was on the job not the journey.*

This is not surprising when we realize that people at the Conforming stage of development, even theorists, tend to obey group-accepted rules and conventional wisdom, not necessarily because they fear punishment, but because they cannot see beyond the cognitive fences (paradigms) they constructed to make their identity. In addition, these people generally see life as mostly right or wrong, not as right and left (often called wrong). The conjunctions *or* and *and* make a big difference in life outcomes, stress, movement forward, learnings, to name a few. When we discount those things that do not bring positive outcomes, more than fifty percent of life gets excluded and that happens when right *or* wrong are treated as mutually exclusive. Whereas loving those things that work *and* learning from those that do not makes life a whole fabric. Those who disengage from the dispositive in life miss many economic and growth opportunities.

The Post-Industrial Era and Self-Awareness

As the Industrial Era faded into history, many skills, attitudes, and "how-to's" that worked well suddenly became obsolete. Then a paradigm shift into something totally new occurred: A shift away from products to information and service started calling forth a higher level of development from those who wanted to participate in this risk game, one that came without an operating manual. However, it did provide fertile ground for the New (Quantum) Careering to emerge.

But the story that parents had passed down from generation to generation—get a good education and you can find a good job—had less and less validity in reality. Everyone returned to ground zero as no road maps, information, or guidelines existed, even though many looked for ways to conform and get back into the flow again. But most discovered that previously learned rules had been shredded. One-size-fits-all had disappeared and custom designing advanced.

Today, new learnings appear almost every day. Making ends meet becomes ever more difficult. People who for years worked secure jobs now impatiently stand in unemployment lines. Some even join the ranks of the homeless; others work, but can afford food, not shelter. Further, more and more *families* get folded into the growing homeless group. As most try to find their way through the maze in this topsy-turvy world reorganized by technology and global movement of jobs, few know where to turn, even those who felt fairly secure in former years.

Most likely the New Careering paradigm, one without stages, levels, or otherwise measurable categories, will enjoy a long life because it responds to each individual's internal information which anchors the journey. This means familiar external markings disappear (those we've loved in conformity) and in their place arise shared stories which connect us to our deepest spirituality.

This dramatic and deepening Post-Industrial shift now forces many into new pathways necessitating new skills. Often this results in a reduced economic lifestyle which on the bright side holds promise for exploring the Self-Aware level of personal development.

The Beginning of a New Century

Today, horizons, both professional and personal expand and contract at dizzying rates. We peek through the cracks at this Self-Aware level and see that we ourselves are aware of being aware. That's a quantum leap from a lower to a higher energy level. Further, we see that many ways of looking at the world exist, that we no longer need to conform so much. This means we do not need to think alike; we can start to see and appreciate our individual differences. Championing uniqueness has been in our rhetoric for many years, but now we have to put our behavior where our rhetoric has been—a more difficult bridge to cross.

In addition, for the first time in the history of career development, we're invited to identify our personal career theory and its philosophy. This both scares and excites at the same time. It is not easy to take the first steps from that comfortable, conforming, fuzzy niche, with its definite views about how people should and should not be, how our life direction should and should not unfold. But we do it. We struggle, we fall down, we get up time and time again. But we know we'll overcome and arrive at a new place.

We step back and catch our breath and stand there in wonderment. Then we realize that maturing our career theory (continually revising and reviewing our story) and fine-tuning its philosophical aspects takes time, persistence, risk, and practice.

This vitally needed change in thinking compares to the one brought about by the voyages of Christopher Columbus. In the fifteenth century, most people believed the Earth was flat. They feared that Columbus, in sailing out to sea, would reach the edge of the Earth and fall off. However, Columbus, along with certain learned persons of his time, believed the Earth was round. Therefore, he felt confident he would reach his destination. While it took him eight years to gain the needed funding for his expedition, Queen Isabella of Spain eventually agreed to finance it. Columbus set out, intending to forge a new trade route to the Orient by sailing west. Instead, he reached the shores of a Native American world. This opened a whole new continent for exploration. At last, the mass perspective changed. They realized the Earth was round.

The Earth had always been round, but most people previously had no way to discover or confirm this. Similarly, many people today are unaware that life, not job, is their career, as social and economic conditions have not been right to help them discover this. When you engage the New Careering, you find the conditions right to move on to the higher levels of self-development by tuning into inner wisdom more and more frequently. This higher level of development can open a whole new world ready to be explored—a world that holds as much promise as the one found five centuries ago by Columbus.

We now stand at the crossroads, often feeling pushed into the Self-Aware level of development in order to maintain our personal economic bases. "How?" you ask. With work more difficult to secure, particularly work that will offer a lifestyle many have come to expect, more people now seek to find an entrepreneurial venture that feels right for them. This step into creating a work of your own, along with some kind of part-time outside work, will jump-start learning and offer more growth than most have experienced in working only one job, getting good at it, and easing on down the conveyor belt to a dependable monthly paycheck.

☐ Looking Back

1. Development anchors both professional and personal life.

2. A higher level development will open the door for a new spirituality that's free from bigotry and anchored in mercy and grace.

3. Stages and levels of development introduced in this chapter—Self-Protective, Conforming, and Self-Aware.

4. Parallels exist between development and the Agricultural, Industrial, and Post-Industrial periods in history.

5. Improvement in personal development will reverberate through all levels of life.

6. Each person can improve his or her level of development by knowing the stages and levels of development and practicing them in everyday life.

7. Counselors can help clients out of their fear of not doing things right (Conforming) by encouraging them to act at the higher level of development (Self-Aware) and do right things to advance their own growth.

☐ Discussion Questions

1. Discuss your impressions of the chapter.

2. Identify situations in your daily experience that reflect levels of development. Include both personal and professional.

3. What do you hear in your own language that identifies your level of development?

4. Discuss when you might find it useful to act at the Conforming stage of development.

5. Explain how the levels of development interrelate.

☐ Classroom/Group Exercises

Work in dyads using the following *"reader speaks"* articles, to identify the Self-Aware, Conforming, and Self-Protective levels of development. The language used will provide clues to the two stages and one level of development mentioned in this chapter. Try to ignore content and look for development. Make notes on your findings and share with the group later.

Example I

Killing Not the Same as Murder

"My religious convictions, and that of the majority of Americans, leave room for abortions. The law of this land says that abortions are legal.

"Why do fundamentalists insist on forcing the great majority to bow to their wishes? This is un-American.

"But, they say, they do this out of their religious convictions. I searched high and low for where the Bible forbids abortions. From the time of the canonization of the Christian Bible in 325 AD, to the middle of the 16th century, the church wrote nothing on abortions.

"It is true, they will have to say, that the Bible doesn't mention abortions, but it does state, 'Thou shalt not kill.' If this were true, you couldn't kill in self-defense or in defense of your loved ones. A police officer could not kill in pursuit of his duties. Our entire military would be helpless in the face of an enemy.

"The Bible says something entirely different. For thousands of years the Hebrew stem used was and is "r-ts-h" meaning "murder" and not "h-rg" which means "kill." 'Thou shalt not murder" is the correct translation.

"If a woman's health is in jeopardy from a bad pregnancy, she has a legal and moral right to defend herself. If the fetus within her is so malformed that it will not have a human existence and will destroy the mother's life, she is morally justified in having an abortion.

"If your daughter or your wife is raped, she has a right to protect herself and her life by an abortion. There is no logical, moral or legal bar to most abortions. Well-meaning but uninformed people help political demagogues create human misery" (Stillman, H., 1996, p. A6).

Example 2

"I tune into the Jim Romme and Tom Leykis radio shows daily. If someone has a dissenting view about either show, so be it; that's their entitled opinion. You people took offense as if I attacked you personally. How childish!

"C. J. Culp challenged me to prove a lie told by Rush, and I would never stoop low enough to tune into Rush's hatred, bigotry and Republican propaganda. But if I had a nickel for every lie Rush told, I'd probably be wealthy.

"The only time I listened to Rush was in my civics class during my senior year at San Pasqual High School when my teacher forced our class to watch Rush's television show. Isn't it amazing how you Republicans claim that the public school system is controlled by Democratic-run labor unions, while my class was force-fed heroics of Gingrich, Gramm and all Republicans, while all Democrats were contested to be nothing but your typical corrupt liberal.

"I'm still wondering why you label all who don't agree with you as a liberal" (Yerzyk, 1996, p. A9).

Example 3

"These dealers (drug), they kill people. They make a living giving people the means to kill themselves. He's as responsible for Hugh's (Hugh Edward O'Connor—Carroll O'Connor's son) death as anyone on Earth" (The Associated Press, p. A-6).

Example 4

Newt Gingrich's comment on Susan Smith's drowning of her two children. He said, "Susan Smith's drowning of her two children is a symptom of a sick society, curable by voting Republican" (Leo, 1994, p. B-5).

☐ Homework/Test Assignment

1. Choose a paragraph and rewrite to reflect a level of development opposite from how it reads.

2. Pick a topic you feel strongly about and write a paragraph about it using the Conforming and Self-Protective stages of development. Then rewrite the paragraph to reflect the Self-Aware level of development.

3. Listen for levels of development in the conversations you hear daily. Write them down for class discussion.

4. Identify situations in your work environment that reflect development.

5. Identify levels of development in your professional conversations.

6. Specify what you might need to change to move into the Self-Aware level of development.

7. If you took a quantum approach to development, how would you talk about it?

Anna Miller-Tiedeman

Paradigms, Development, Decision Making, and the New Careering

Spotlight on Paradigms

Gerry Spence, defense attorney of international renown and social philosopher, tells the story of working for 40 large corporations. In his home town, he represented a corporation in a case against one of the elderly residents. Gerry won. That evening, while standing in a supermarket line, Spence recognized the elderly man in front of him as the one who was involved in the litigation with the corporation Spence represented. The man turned around and spoke. Spence replied, "I am sorry about today." The old man, looked at him through his watery blue eyes, and said, "Mr. Spence, "You were only doing your job." Gerry helped the old man out with his groceries and went home. The next morning he woke and said to his wife, "You know, Imogene, I am working to keep honest people from getting justice." He then dressed, went down to his office and wrote 40 letters quitting his corporate clients. He now represents the smaller person. Gerry Spence made a major paradigm shift (Spence, 1985).

☐ Looking Ahead

Watch for the following important topics:

1. Types of paradigms
2. Advantages and disadvantages of paradigms
3. Personal cost of paradigms
4. The impact of paradigms on health
5. Important terms and concepts:
   a. Paradigm paralysis
   b. Intelligencing
   c. Paradigm Effect
   d. Paradigm Paradox
   e. Paradigm Pioneer
   f. Paradigm shift
   g. Lifecareer® Development
   h. World Views:
      1. Newtonian
      2. Quantum

Paradigm Reconsidered

A paradigm is a model we hold of the world. It's the way we explain aspects of reality. We arrive at those explanations through our assumptions. Other ways of defining paradigms are "conventions, pattern, methods, values, culture, routines, conventional wisdom, etiquette, traditions, customs, rituals, prejudices, compulsion, and dogma to name a few" (Barker, 1990b, p. 16).

Understanding paradigms offers the potential for better responses in conversation. Language exposes our paradigms quite readily. For instance, when someone labels anything weird or strange, you can bet something not in the individual's repertoire of behavior has happened—most likely something the individual does not do, and does not think anyone else should do.

---

*Lifecareer, Life-Is-Career, Career Compass and their derivatives are registered trademarks of Dr. Anna Miller-Tiedeman.

Multicultural problems often result from different paradigms. For example, the American paradigm is based on rugged individualism, the Asian one more upon group participation and helping each other. The Native American paradigm leans toward harmony with nature versus control over it. But hundreds, if not thousands, of cultural differences (paradigms) exist. Problems with cultural differences between two or more people occur mostly when individuals behave at the Conforming stage of development (for more detail on development, see Chapter 4), paradigmatically screening out those things that do not fit their model of how life should be. In other words, they do not tend to consider alternative viewpoints.

All kinds of paradigms shape our life—business, education, science, parenting, relationships, and family, to name a few. Awareness of paradigms has the potential to change lives, tolerance levels, as well as perception of others. It could help us recognize that we can have understanding without full agreement; and, put in place more tolerant behaviors.

Paradigms—Truth, Fiction, or Both?

Paradigms in Action: Federal Express

Frederick W. Smith, Founder of Federal Express, wrote a paper for an economics course proposing a new type of air freight service. Smith's professor pointed out the fallacy of Smith's reasoning, and marked it with a C grade (Longenecker & Moore, 1991). Where Smith was not stopped by the limited paradigm of his professor, others may be. That's why it's important to keep paradigms flexible.

One person's fiction may be another person's truth, an example of the paradigm effect (Barker, 1990a). It all depends on belief. For example, nineteenth-century Hungarian physician Ignaz Semmelweis (Broad & Wade, 1982) discovered that puerperal, or childbed fever, then causing typically 10 to 30% mortality in maternity hospitals throughout Europe, could be abolished. It only took a simple act of washing the hands in a chlorine solution before examining the mother. In his division of the obstetric clinic in Vienna where Semmelweis first tried out his idea, the mortality rate dropped from 18% to 1%. By 1848, Semmelweis was not losing a single woman to childbed fever. But this experimental evidence failed to convince his superiors at the hospital. Semmelweis's ability to see the new, represents his paradigm flexibility, and his superiors' paradigm rigidity.

Why did physicians and medical researchers ignore Semmelweis's theory as well as experimental evidence? Maybe they did not want to admit that each, with his own unwashed hands, had unwittingly sent many patients to their deaths. On the other hand, many of the physicians judged Semmelweis as not tactful, too strident in rhetoric, and his propaganda not sufficiently smooth and persuasive. In other words, he did not conform to the doctors' notions of how a physician should act (development comes in again in the *not-like-me* idea). On the other hand, few facts speak with greater emphasis and clarity than did his, but they were not sufficient to persuade physicians and medical researchers throughout Europe that their hands, which looked clean, served as a breeding ground for germs. The failure of other physicians to accept the new indicates the seductive nature of the old paradigm. Trapped in their old paradigm, they cannot change. Their failure to change, believing there was only one way of doing things, exemplifies paradigm paralysis.

Semmelweis, a paradigm pioneer, died on August 13, 1865. But the day before Semmelweis's death, Lister began to test the use of carbolic acid as an antiseptic agent. Once Lister won his battle, and Pasteur had persuaded the medical profession that germs did really exist, then, some thirty years later than necessary, the doctors understood the theory by which they could make sense of the facts that said for them to wash their hands before undertaking obstetric examinations (Broad & Wade, 1982).

When Paradigms Shift

Sometimes it takes a near death or potential suicide experience to change a belief system (paradigm). Buckminster Fuller—inventor, author, and anticipatory design scientist—in his early life was following everyone else's belief system (paradigm) in regard to what he should do. His last job for someone else was in business, in which he flopped miserably. He contemplated suicide, but as he put it:

> In 1927, at age thirty-two, finding myself a "throwaway," in the business world, I sought to use myself as my scientific "guinea pig" ... in a lifelong experiment designed to discover what—if anything—a healthy young male human of average size, experience, and capability with an economically dependent wife and newborn child, starting without capital or any kind of wealth, cash savings, account monies, credit, or university degree, could effectively do that could not be done by great nations or great private enterprise to improve the physical protection and support of all human lives (Fuller, 1981, p. 124).

Paradigms shift when we discover we can no longer tolerate the old belief system, as did Buckminster Fuller in the above example. However, Fuller's paradigm shift is the ultimate shift—away from what others thought he should do to what he knew he had to do as dictated by his own inner wisdom.

Paradigms do not shift sometimes because it is painful to let go of an old belief system. It's like discarding that old pair of well-worn shoes. Sometimes the shift is self-selected, which also has its cost. John Braine (1979), author of the best selling *Room at the Top* (1957), changed his paradigm from working in a library from 8 A.M. to 5 P.M., to going it on his own in order to write. Of this experience, Braine said that " Everything you get, you pay for" (1979, p. 71). So, it's not *if* you have to pay, it's *which price* do you want to pay. John Braine said, "I paid a high price for what I got, and as I grow older I have an idea that I may not have finished paying. ... However I won't complain. It has been worth it. Since I changed my life, I have lived every minute. Only the years before I made the change were wasted" (1979, p. 76). Of his life he said, "I didn't change my life because I wanted to be a success. I changed it because I wanted to earn my living by following my true vocation—writing" (1979, p. 76).

If your paradigm includes the idea that someone in authority knows best, you may give out information you wish later you had not. For instance, when you make a MasterCard or VISA card purchase, some merchants will ask for your social security number, phone number, and/or address. However, MasterCard and Visa do have a policy about extra information on charge slips. If a merchant refuses a sale because the consumer will not give additional information, the merchant could lose the privilege of accepting the credit-card charge slips. We can monitor our paradigms by stopping long enough to ask ourselves some questions. With more awareness, we can ask the merchant, "Why do you need that information?" Changing a belief system regarding a credit card may appear small and minor. However, when you learn to examine your smaller (credit card) paradigms (belief systems) then you are in a position to take on the larger ones, like your life direction belief system (paradigm).

General Paradigm Conditions

Barker (1990b) in *The Business of Paradigms: Discovering the Future Series, The Facilitator's Guide* lists the following paradigm conditions: (1) the paradigm effect; (2) paradigm flexibility; (3) the paradigm paradox; (4) paradigm pioneers; (5) the paradigm shift; (6) the paradigm shifter; and (7) paradigm paralysis (pp. i–iii).

The Paradigm Effect.   The *paradigm effect* on the positive side focuses our attention and helps us concentrate on what we think important. The paradigm effect enhances confidence in problem solving. But it also can block the vision to the future. Two examples come to mind: (a) women's suffrage; and (b) birth control for women.

Windle (1993), in her book *True Women* (1993), quoted from the *Journal of the Reconstruction Convention*, Austin, Texas, December 7, 1868, which recorded a vote against female suffrage, suggesting that every true woman would not want to mingle in the busy noise of election days. The document also suggested that, because they were mothers, they exerted far greater influence than they could at the voting booth. And finally, the committee opposed female suffrage because they believed that the right to vote " ... is a direct open insult to their sex by the implication that they are so unwomanly as to desire the privilege."

Margaret Sanger (Conway, 1992) founded and led the American birth control movement. She formed the American Birth Control League, which became a national lobby for birth control. This League later became the Planned Parenthood Federation of America. During the 1920s and 1930s Sanger smuggled European-made diaphragms into the U.S. She was indicted on nine counts for violating federal statues, all related to publishing a document about family limitation and sending it through the mail.

Knowing that if found guilty, she might be liable to forty-five years in the penitentiary, she decided to leave the country—a soul wrenching decision for a woman with a family—to avoid arrest, but she finally won the right to use the mail to send contraceptive materials to physicians. Sanger fought long and hard against the paradigms of most medical men of the day and the U. S. Postal Service, in order to help women secure the right to birth control. That fight broadened perception and saved the lives of thousands of women. Today, we take birth control for granted. But its history points out the destruction the paradigm effect can have on a society and on those who attempt to carry a cause forward.

Paradigm Flexibility.   Remember the rickety-card table story in the introduction? Bradley (1982) says that God throws down a card table and puzzle when we're born and says: "Okay, sort it out and when it's finished, you understand why you're here" (p. 14). Finishing the puzzles, we try to protect them against bumps and spills, in order to keep things stable and consistent with past experience. But when you practice *paradigm flexibility*, you expect your card table to get kicked every now and then. You even practice kicking it yourself so that when someone else bumps it, you're prepared to say, "Okay, time to consider something new."

The Paradigm Paradox.   A *paradigm paradox* comes from the paradigm effect. It may be responsible for our difficulty to change. When we find paradigms that are comfortable, like job security, we hold on even when the idea no longer works and even when evidence exists that it's counterproductive.

The Paradigm Pioneer. When you choose to change, you become a *paradigm pioneer*. These individuals move ahead even though the new paradigm does not prove they should be doing so. They have utter faith and trust it is right to do. They then find themselves in a paradigm shift—a new way of thinking about an old problem. For instance, from seeing ourselves as a nation to considering a global village. Paradigm shifts come about when old solutions to current problems no longer work. This may appear revolutionary, but it's only evolutionary, as life continually moves forward into greater complexity, as suggested by Prigogine (1980) in his theory of self-organizing systems.

The Paradigm Shifter. *Paradigm shifters* usually do not come from the inside, and most of them have difficulty with *the right way of doing things* as they can see better approaches. Very frequently they forge ahead disregarding the rules. This is where you see (if you have focused on your paradigm) personal development. Conformers do not usually engage in paradigm shifting, as they're too busy maintaining the status quo. In addition, because they do not see the benefit in the new, they do not move toward it. These people traditionally fight for the status quo and their decision making follows their belief system.

Paradigm Paralysis. *Paradigm paralysis* comes from the belief that only one way exists to do things, that there is no better way. We become blinded by the success of our old paradigms which keeps us invested in them. That's what made the Xerox invention hard to see. A successful copy system was already in place.

Scientific Paradigm Shifts

Paradigms in Action: Economics

In most beginning economics textbooks, the discipline is defined as "the study of scarce resources." Paul Zane Pilzer (1995), an economist, suggests that this totally contradicts the Judeo-Christian ethic. What kind of God would create a world where people get ahead by taking from someone else? The first people to question this system (paradigm) were the Alchemists. They felt they didn't have to go next door and kill their neighbor for gold. God would give them the ability to create wealth by mixing up chemicals and lead and mercury, with a lot of prayer. When you read their mix for making gold, it was 10% chemicals and 90% prayer. God would give them the ability to make wealth without taking it from someone else. They were not successful with gold, but they discovered pharmacy, metallurgy, chemistry, engineering—all the technologies that give us the unlimited resources we have today. If they had been successful in making gold it would have become worthless (Pilzer, 1995).

Capra (1982) suggested that before 1500, civilizations in both Europe and elsewhere held the organic view of the world characterized by interdependence of spiritual and material needs, with community needs coming ahead of personal needs. The authorities were Aristotle and the Church.

In the thirteenth century, Thomas Aquinas combined Aristotle's system of nature with Christian theology and ethics and established the view that remained unquestioned throughout the middle ages. The view found its meaning in both reason and faith and sought to understand the meaning and significance of things rather than prediction and control. Medieval scientists, in looking for their answers, gave the highest priorities to God, the human soul, and ethics.

In the sixteenth and seventeenth centuries, the notion of an organic and spiritual universe fell from grace. And, in its place, the world as a machine and the world-machine became the dominant metaphors. This development set the stage for revolutionary changes in physics and astronomy, culminating in the achievements of Copernicus, Galileo, and Newton, which lasted until the end of the nineteenth century when Maxwell's electrodynamics and Darwin's theory of evolution evolved concepts that clearly went beyond the Newtonian model, indicating that the universe consisted of far more complexity than either Descartes or Newton had imagined. Still, Newton's theory was believed to be correct in a narrowed domain of applicability.

The first three decades of the twentieth century brought about two developments in physics: relativity and quantum theory. These concepts shattered the principal concepts of the Cartesian worldview and Newtonian mechanics. This represented a quantum leap in worldview and a paradigm shift of dramatic proportion which still has not made its way into mainstream America, as did our first glimpse of the big blue marble suspended in space. At that instant, we saw the global village. This paradigm shift from a nation to a global village may represent the biggest paradigm shift of the century. As Neil Armstrong said on taking his first step on the moon, "That's one small step for a man, one giant leap for mankind" (Bartlett, 1980, p. 910). At that moment, we saw ourselves as one planet.

Joseph Campbell (1988) in his book, *The Power of Myth,* said:

The only myth worth thinking about in the immediate future will talk about the planet—not the city; not these people, but the planet, and everybody on it. This myth will deal with the maturation of the individual, from dependency through adulthood, through maturity, and then to the exit; and then how to relate to this society and how to relate this society to the world of nature and the cosmos. That's what the myths have all talked about and what this one's got to talk about. But this myth has to address the society of the planet. And until that gets going, you don't have anything (p. 32).

Health Paradigms

Dr. Bernard Lown, who wrote the introduction to *The Healing Heart* (Cousins, 1983), tells of a woman he saw when he was a young intern. The woman had a heart-valve problem, but nothing that kept her from functioning well at home and at work. Dr. Lown, as an intern, saw her, then her main-line doctor saw her. This doctor greeted her, checked her, and said, "This woman has TS" (p. 13). He then left. The woman had been in a low-grade congestive heart failure condition with some edema, but nothing life threatening. Nonetheless, she began to panic, her pulse went to 150, and she started hyperventilating. She quickly became ill. The young intern asked her what the problem was and she said, the doctor had said she had TS—terminal situation. Dr. Lown reassured the woman that TS did not mean terminal situation: it meant *tricuspid stenosis.* But the woman did not believe it and later that day she died. Her belief system just could not include the real meaning of TS (an example of paradigm paralysis). So belief systems can have power in a domain as important to humans as life maintenance itself.

Another woman, after undergoing two heart by-pass surgeries, traveled to a remote place in Alaska to help rebuild a missionary's home. She had to cook on a stove that stayed on all day, one that could not be turned up or down. So it took about two hours to prepare a meal, moving food from the warmer side of the stove to the hotter one. This was strenuous work. One of the women in the group said, "How can you do all that with your surgery?" "Easy," she answered, "I don't consider myself sick" (Pearl Miller, personal communication, May 1990). Her belief system (paradigm) did not include becoming an invalid because she had had by-pass surgery.

Outcomes tend to stay within the level of the individual's belief system and seldom rise above it.

Education Paradigms

Look at the people whose belief system includes college. They say such things as "I'm going to college—my parents would not have it any other way," or "I have to go back to school in order to get a job." These people live with the belief that they are supposed to go on to school. They usually do. Other people do not get the *college* message. Different paradigms for different reasons.

On the other hand, one individual may believe a college degree will make him or her more saleable in the job market, while another person believes it will make no difference. Who's right? Potentially both of them, as it may turn out they will both do well. But it may turn out the opposite for both; as each June, thousands of college graduates learn that their degrees do not necessarily land them jobs in their major, or even well-paying jobs commensurate with their training.

Then, for others, their vision means more than a degree. Steve Wozniak finished one year of college. His belief system did not include the social mantra *get a good education and find a good job*, so he dropped out and started working on the computer idea in his garage. That dedicated time led to the creation of the Apple Computer Company.

Those whose belief system (paradigm) includes the idea that life will inform them about what they should be doing seldom have major life direction problems. Yes, they have problems, but they trust life in totality to inform them. They do not press life for quick answers. They look at a variety of solutions. Why? Their paradigms are not prescriptive; therefore, they *cooperate with the approaching forces* while making the best decision in the moment. They know that, "To every thing there is a season, and a time to every purpose under heaven (Eccles. 3:1). They, therefore, do not break themselves against life's rocky shores.

Learning to identify personal belief systems (paradigms) helps create new memory. But first, you need to recognize when, in your language, a particular pattern of thinking manifests itself. Otherwise, it will continue. For that reason, many individuals ignore opportunity, and remain in old memory. This does not suggest jumping on all opportunity. It does propose leaping out of the old familiar rut more often, experimenting with creating new memories. Sometimes, this happens with something trivial but aggravating, like the problem an administrative assistant had with ridding his documents of double spaces after each sentence. He looked in his software manual to see what might cause this and found no answer. Then he realized that he was unconsciously adding the double spaces, a habit acquired in his earlier typing classes. When he became conscious of this, and worked to change his paradigm, he started breaking the double-space after each sentence habit. That shows just how illusive a paradigm can be and how, even though simple on recognition, it did not occur to him as a possibility. Increasing awareness, creating new memory, changes things.

Much of what goes on in job search comes from old memory or past experience. Go back in time to the 1970s. An advertising major graduated from college, sent out the traditional resume, and received nothing but rejection letters. So, he decided to make a video resume (new at that time). That act created new memory for him; and he did not remain prisoner to the paper resume. People who make new memory clearly understand the renewal aspect of life.

Financial Paradigms

Financial planning involves beliefs (paradigms). Some deem it important, others do not. For instance, Lois, at 64 years of age, carried no personal insurance, had done no financial planning, owned her home but that was all the potential cash she had. She suffered a heart attack and needed by-pass surgery, which amounted to about $60,000. After the surgery, she said, "I wish I had been more aware and looked more at financial planning." She went on to say, "I did not think about getting older; nor about having health problems; and I certainly did not think about dying. It was something that was too unpleasant to face." Different paradigms.

This woman lived in a time when financial planning did not top the list of things people discussed. Neither television nor radio aired advertisements about it. Few articles appeared in the newspapers concerning planning for retirement. Jobs were steady for the most part, and Social Security was seen as the retirement plan along with a company pension plan.

Today, however, the media carries endless advertisements about retirement planning. And only a small percentage of young people now put aside money for the future. For instance, Richard Hinman, a fourteen year old who lives in Roanoke, Virginia, wrote Marilyn Vos Savant (1997) who writes an "Ask Marilyn" column in *Parade Magazine*. He told her about his small lawn business which he does within his neighborhood. He mows lawns in the summer and shovels snow in the winter. However, he said, "Whether I get business depends on Mother Nature. If it doesn't snow, then I can't shovel snow; if it doesn't rain (or stop raining, for that matter), I can't mow lawns. What can I do during the rest of the time to make money? Also, how can I get more customers? I'm not looking for enough money to make a career out of this, and I'm not looking for just enough money to buy gum. I want enough *to be able to invest half* of it and still have enough to go to the movies and basketball games" (p. 7, italics added).

Young people like Richard know if they protect part of their income, even though they do not earn a lot, they can grow an investment, which they can use for more training and education later, a trip, buying a house, or just letting the money accumulate. Money buys independence and freedom. That's a different paradigm than one in which all incoming money is spent; and, in addition, credit cards are used to buy now and pay later. Belief systems can contribute to a wonderful life or a nightmare. It does not take money to change a belief (paradigm), just personal discipline and focused effort.

The following represent age-specific financial paradigms that describe many people:

Age 18–25:   I'm young, I do not have to worry about that now.

Age 26–40:   I'll think about that tomorrow.

Age 40–50:   It's too late to do anything about it.

More and more people now live well beyond age 65. Miller-Tiedeman's father lived 27 years beyond age 65.

Career Paradigms

Career paradigms represent beliefs we hold which get reflected in practice. As you can see in Table 5.1, the beliefs about traditional career and Lifecareer differ markedly, with the major difference being attention or non attention to the life principle of flow. These beliefs represent the major differences between traditional career and Lifecareer.

Summarizing Table 5.1 paradigms, when Life-Is-Career, the individual sees him or herself as a theory maker, as teller and developer of his or her own story which may or may not dovetail with those of current associates, friends, and family. He or she focuses on becoming that which he or she most deeply feels, and in this becoming creates a reality that supports growth into that new space which, though unfamiliar, feels right. While going through this valley and shadow of change, a deep understanding that the whole organizes the parts results in a profound cooperation with life—one where the individual realizes that his or her self is not lost, but merely continues to move into greater complexity and knowing, where inner trends dictate outer choices. The career is then played from personal knowledge and the individual realizes that he or she is making a life while making a living, which at the end of the twentieth century means exploring some kind of entrepreneurial venture.

While doing this, many stops and starts manifest along with many failures (or "left turns" in process careering), but out of all of this seeming chaos, great learnings both about the self and the self in work activity

TABLE 5.1. Traditional Career Versus Lifecareer Paradigms*

Traditional	Lifecareer
Job as career	Life-As-Career
Career theorists	Individual as theory maker
Trends and former paradigms guide	They understood life from personal experience
Focus on what you want to *do*	Focus on *becoming*
Common reality primary	Individual creates own reality
Parts organize the whole	Whole organizes the parts
Control of life	Cooperation with life
Self has to be found	Self cannot be lost
Interested in external trends	Interested in inner trends
Relies on other's opinions	Takes readings from inner wisdom
Plays career from conventional wisdom	Plays career from personal knowledge
Concerned mostly about work	Work seen as part of a balanced life
Focuses mostly on full-time work	Expands to include both getting a job and creating work
Needs to know before doing	Mostly learns while doing
Increased stress	Decreased stress
Major orientation: Job is career	Major orientation: Life is career
Discusses choosing a career	Lives a perspective
Career is made	Career is lived
Strong emphasis on plans and goals	Emphasis on setting intentions and organizing
Makes things happen	Cooperates with the approaching forces with thought
Self-concept	Self-conceiving
Focus on right or wise decision making	Values both right and left (often called wrong) decision making
Low trust in life	High trust in life
Suggests one has to "make it"	Acknowledges one has already "made it"

*These also show up as assumptive differences in Chapter 3.

emerges. Then, a far-reaching understanding comes into awareness: "I am living my career, not choosing it." So, the work becomes setting intentions, organizing and responding to earlier organizations and actions. Then, the value of cooperating with the approaching forces comes into awareness again, along with the value of thinking of life as a right and left matter, not a right and wrong one. Trust in life then streams forth, and the inner wisdom says, "You've made it. You're okay. You're a wonderful gift to life. Now bring people into your life who will reinforce that message and with whom you can return the encouragement." (See Chapter 3 for more discussion on selected Lifecareer paradigms.)

On the other hand, traditional career, a paradigm with its non-process rules and regulations, has been around close to a century. But in the mid 1980s, many counselors and helping professionals started to sense that the existing career development paradigms were not adequate. Table 5.2 represents a list of paradigms in need of change.

The traditional career assumptions counselors identified as needing change exemplify career mostly at the Conforming stage of development (see Chapter 4 for more detail on development) which usually follows conventional wisdom. Most of the work done adjusts clients to what has been, advises them on appropriate pathways, frequently using past history. Client dreams often have no history (like in the Federal Express dream) and this frequently makes for professional discomfort or discounting of its possibility. However, the counselors and helping professionals making the list (see Table 5.2) agreed that a significant group of helping professionals now goes against conventional wisdom and supports individual growth and expansion however that looks, and sometimes it is not pretty. In addition, no existing pathways may be obvious, but New Careering Development professionals trust life to unfold many possibilities for their clients, because these professionals know, through personal experience, that life provides those experiences for each of us.

It Is Possible To Help Someone

The counselors felt it more accurate to say that it is possible to support an individual as he or she lives through what is forming inside. Helping professionals create an environment—psychologically, emotionally, and spiritually— where the individual feels free enough to trust his or her own thought. Seeds of possibilities can be planted and supported, but the individual must tend and nurture those possibilities; otherwise, they will get tossed into the ever increasing high stack of *could have beens*. New Careering Developers support the natural unfolding of potential even though the individual may not recognize it. A major reason for creating the environ-

TABLE 5.2. Career Paradigms in Need of Change
(Not in order of importance, nor do they represent opposites)

It is possible to help someone.

There is a certain way to do things.

I'm responsible for solving my client's problems.

Clients do not know what to do.

Career is defined as work.

Planning is essential.

Doing nothing is doing nothing.

There is a direct path to getting what you want.

Society's norms are correct for the client.

There is a reality that works known as "let's be realistic."

Change is happening only with clients, not the counselor.

Counselors pour their wisdom on their clients, seldom acknowledging how much the client teaches them.

Certain way to help—information will solve it.

Individuals change careers.

Setting the right goal will get you on a conveyor belt that goes somewhere.

Procrastination is bad.

A reward will ensue if one does things right.

Linear is the best way to go—it's sure and certain.

The Self is lost and needs finding.

Practical must mean a technique or test or sure-fire advice.

Acts as if work career can be known ahead of experience.

Counseling will lead to positive outcomes.

Career is linear.

There's value in doing things right (versus doing the right things).

ment for growth comes from the fact that each individual has a reality that works for him or her, a reality not known to the helping professional.

Let's Be Realistic

This phrase has killed off many a dream, dissipated many an experience. For instance, a ninth grader wanted to travel the western United States with his mother. He talked with his teachers and many of them said, "no." They suggested that he would never catch up and he would lose so much by not attending class. This reflects paradigm paralysis, a belief that students' learning must be in class. However, his mother decided she wanted to take her son on this family trip. So, she talked with each of the teachers, and made arrangements for the assignments. The family left in December and returned in June. The student did not miss handing in an assignment. He took supervised tests, and ended up with an A average for the semester. That student went on to take all the math offered at the local university while still a high school student.

Reality plays itself out in student scheduling, that typically mundane activity. Consider a student with a math percentile of 30 who wants to sign up for Algebra. Professionals usually tell the student he or she won't do well in Algebra, based on past reality, rather than signing the student into Algebra and letting him or her discover that. Discovering your own reality offers practice in the skill of discernment; being told what you can and cannot do, directly affects self-esteem.

Both students and professionals can learn how to identify sentences that reflect a particular paradigm as well as developmental stages. Using this information offers a choice of response, but practice is the key word. Elbow (1981), in his book *Writing with Power*, discusses the similarities between developing your writing voice and learning to play a violin. He suggests that no matter how good a violin you have, it needs to be 'played in'—played long and vigorously—before it resonates well to all its frequencies" (p. 281). This sometimes takes weeks, sometimes months, but Elbow suggests that just as the clunkiest of violins can be played in and its repertoire of resonances broadened with practice, the writer, through practice, develops a strong writing voice. The same thing happens with paradigm and development identification. With practice, you can recognize it in the moment, your repertoire of responses automatically increases and the quality of information improves dramatically.

For many, shifting their career paradigm from job to life is not a walk in the park, as many still stroll the traditional career path (Conforming stage) where anything too different finds neither acceptance nor support. It is mostly about getting a good education and finding a good job, along with the notion that only theorists spin useful theories. Those two ideas anchor life direction in conventional wisdom, not individual intelligence.

But we need to remember intelligence stays busy working and figuring out what to do next. For example, in 1991, during Operation Desert Storm, Iraqi soldiers shut off the water, sewer, telephone, and food supplies in the U.S. Embassy (Masciola, 1991). However, one man, ignoring the fact that Kuwait is a desert, dug for water in the embassy yard and created a well that produced 200 gallons of water a minute. The staff said, "We may be the only people who ever dug a well in Kuwait and came up with water instead of oil" (p. B-1). They then figured out how to reconnect severed phone lines. Every time they had a problem, they sat down and came up with a solution. That's what intelligence is about. They even found some seeds, planted them, and had fresh greens on Thanksgiving Day. The Iraqis just could not disconnect the human intelligence in the embassy. So, a way to do most anything exists when we make up our minds to do it—even grow.

However, trying to shift your paradigm resembles drawing a line in the desert sand hoping a wind will not blow. Of course, it does blow, the tracks get covered, and you have to draw the line again, and again, and again, before enough understanding emerges to anchor the paradigm in place.

New Paradigms Help Us Reinvent Our Futures

As the end of the twentieth century approaches, many awaken to the ineffectiveness of old paradigms. For that spiritual journey to the higher self, we need a new language, new concepts, and new paradigms and new levels of personal development. Lifecareer represents one new perspective. Its propositions can be viewed as either a theory or a philosophy, depending on your perspective. It offers individuals a way to move out of conformity and closer to their higher selves. Therefore, Lifecareer explodes the notion that career is something out there in your future, to be chosen, planned, pursued, and reached. Career is. It is you, who you are, your Life. It is developing the capacity to be choiceful about your life, to be authentic, to be in deep touch with that mission that keeps moving you forward.

Our work, now and into the twenty-first century, starts with evaluating and eliminating those beliefs that pose a barrier to a new and even more expanded self, both for ourselves and our clients. Alternative non-talk therapies like structural bodywork and meditation can help identify and release old behavior and thought patterns that cannot be easily accessed otherwise (see Chapter 10 for more detail). We must remember that we provide the ceiling for our clients' growth. That is where development again appears. If we remain at the Conforming stage of development (usually associated with paradigm paralysis), we can not help our clients grow into a new level. Further, Conforming counselors see the rug being pulled from beneath them while those at the Self-Aware level (paradigm flexibility) learn to dance on a shifting carpet.

☐ Looking Back

1. Paradigms screen out what does not fit our model of the world and vice versa.

2. Decisions are made on information allowed in and sent out.

3. Many opportunities are lost due to narrow paradigms.

4. Paradigm conditions mentioned in the chapter: Paradigm paralysis, paradigm effect, paradigm paradox, paradigm shift, paradigm pioneer, paradigm shifter.

5. Paradigms impact all areas of life: Health, education, economics, science, sex, and all professional theories, to name a few.

6. Paradigm shifters risk loss of support group.

7. Seeing the big-blue marble in space perhaps, represents one of the biggest paradigm shifts in history.

8. Seeing life as the big career represents a paradigm shift.

☐ Discussion Questions

1. Why are paradigms important?

2. Offer one personal example where your paradigm made a difference in an outcome or an action.

3. What is your health paradigm?

4. What is your financial paradigm?

5. Discuss your life direction belief system (paradigm)? What do you exclude, or include?

6. What do you gain by recognizing your paradigms?

7. When an individual shakes his or her head from right to left, what does your paradigm suggest that means? When the head moves up and down, what does your paradigm suggest that means? (Answer in Appendix D.)

☐ Classroom/Group Exercises

1. Ask a student to go to the front of the class. Then ask him or her to tell you a little about his or her favorite interest. Then take turns rephrasing what the student said. Ask the student how close your interpretation comes to what he or she means. Can you notice when your interpretation is outside the student's paradigm?

2. Take the self-score survey on page 140 and share your impressions with the group.

☐ Work-Career Paradigm Survey

Below is a quiz that can give you a general idea of your level of career consciousness. Answer each statement by circling T (True) or F (False). Check your answers with those in Appendix C. Give yourself one point for each correct answer.

Now let's check out your work-career paradigm:

1. Job opportunities are related to the economy, to new technology, to an individual's ability, among other things. T F

2. People who develop a long-term career plan and stick to it will be more successful than those who do not. T F

3. It will be essential to develop skills in high technology in order to obtain a job in the future. T F

4. The best way to develop new job skills is to go to college. T F

5. Your feelings about your career contain accurate information for making decisions. T F

6. Some of the most valuable transferable job skills for the future will be communication, flexibility, and information management. T F

7. Your belief and values, more than anything else, influence your career path. T F

8. In the future, it will be necessary to become more of a specialist to ensure job security. T F

9. Everyone has a career.

10. What you encounter by chance is as important as what you plan. T F

☐ Homework/Test Assignment

1. Listen to people around you talk and try to identify their paradigms. For instance, identify the paradigm (beliefs) in the following excerpt:

   If you tell me (Eloise Anderson, director of California's Department of Social Services), 'I'm pregnant, and I've never worked,' I would say ... go talk to your family, talk to his family, but do not come to social services, because having a baby is not a crisis. That is a condition, and your behavior caused that.

2. Write two paragraphs on your interpretation of "it takes a village ... " At the end of the paragraph, list your own paradigms (beliefs).

Anna Miller-Tiedeman

Worldview, Decision Making, Paradigms, and Development— All One Fabric

Spotlight on Decision Making

Muhammad Yunus, after teaching college-level economics in Tennessee for several years, *decided* in 1972 to return to his homeland to help rebuild the nation. With his brand-new Ph.D., he started teaching elegant theories. After class, he walked outside and saw people dying due to starvation. He then placed his theories on hold and started talking with the village people. He met a woman who made bamboo stools. After talking with her he discovered she made the equivalent of two U. S. pennies a day. Why? Because she didn't have twenty cents to buy her own bamboo. She had to borrow money from a trader who imposed the condition that she had to sell her stools to him alone, at the price he decided. After considerable research, Yunus discovered that women entrepreneurs in general had problems getting just small loans like $2.00. They were victims of bankers who placed them in a box called poor, then *decided* they would not be good credit risks. They thought the poor simply would not pay their loans. The bankers then said, "Well, they are just fooling you. Soon they will take more money and not pay it back." Yunus gave the women more money and they repaid all of it. The local bankers then said, "Sure you can do it in one village. But if you do it in two villages, it won't work." So Yunus did it in two villages and it worked. Well, the bankers continued their skepticism and the success continued to happen. Yunus finally set up his own bank, The Grameen Bank. Today, his bank serves 36,000 villages in Bangladesh. The bank made loans to 2.1 million borrowers, 94% of whom are women. All this happened because Yunus refused to conform to the local notions about poor people (Yunus, 1997).

☐ Looking Ahead

Watch for the following important topics:

1. Decision making is natural to all life.

2. Worldview matters in decision making.

3. Problem solving at MIT.

4. Decision making and growth.

5. Exploring decision making using the quantum worldview.

6. The urge to grow and decision making.

7. Important concepts.

    (a) Decision making is natural to all living systems.

    (b) Improved decision making comes from practice and awareness.

Individuals, in complement with life, synergistically develop personal understanding of their decision making, noting those outcomes that work as well as those that do not. In so doing, they have the opportunity to holistically learn from their experience and make better decisions when appropriate. Understanding that each decision comes loaded with new informational possibilities lends encouragement to looking for those messages, as opposed to whether or not the decision is rational, non-rational, changeable, pliable, flexible, or suitable.

    Miller-Tiedeman, in talking with counselors around the USA and Canada usually asks two questions you might want to think about while you read this chapter. First, have you ever taken a class to improve your decision making? Second, would you take a class for that reason? Counselors' responses will appear at the end of the chapter.

This chapter suggests that a view which focuses mostly on wise, better, and best decisions quickly falls into dysfunction which has the potential of separating people from their experience, influences them to devalue those things that do not work, sets up stress in the body which kills off immune cells (Sapolsky, 1994), and, depending on the outcomes, can lower self esteem. Additionally, not feeling good about decisions has an eroding effect on motivation.

Decision Making Is Natural to All of Life

Our bodies provide the best evidence of the naturalness of decision making. Chopra (1989), suggested that six trillion chemical reactions occur every second—all without our help or decision-making instruction. Cells go in and out of existence, constantly replacing themselves without formal help. Electrons spread themselves out over possible futures and then make a decision without a formal cue (Zohar, 1990). Particles pop in and out of existence without human help. So, at the basic level of life, decision-making occurs most naturally, and in most cases, very effectively. As mentioned earlier, life works on the success scenario using trial and error. Life keeps what works and discards that which does not (Dulbecco, 1987). Humans tend to do that as well.

So, how did the field of career development stray so far from nature and holistic considerations, from what is easily observed about decision making not only by humans but by particles, electrons, and all living things? We might invoke the Fuerestein (1994) idea of "As above, so below" (p. 13), which translated to a professional field, might say *as with the leaders, so with its members.* This may provide a clue as to why a professional field fails to grow itself into a higher level of development. Often leaders and a number of professionals keep doing the same thing over and over again, somewhat like the medical doctors and their Newtonian approach to the body. But with increasing numbers of people using alternative medicine, the American Medical Association and many of its members are being forced to acknowledge alternative medicine, resulting in many doctors now retraining to incorporate some of these modern modalities into their practice. Change is seldom given a place; it makes its own place as the people make their decisions. Additionally, a shifting market can shift a paradigm rather rapidly, particularly for those following the money.

Worldview Matters in Decision Making

Separating good from bad decision making carries a Newtonian imprint. The Newtonian worldview permeates every aspect of our lives both personal and professional (see Chapters 3 and 7), and consequently our decision making. Early on, Newton's clock-like universe served as the blueprint of the day with separation as the motif. Decisions were made accordingly. These decisions ended up destroying the living cosmos of Greek and medieval times, one filled with purpose and intelligence, driven by the love of God for the benefit of humanity, because Newton reduced everything to the workings of a vast universal machine, dead, cold, lifeless, fragmented, and unconnected (Zohar, 1990).

Whether we know it or not, or even understand anything at all about science, we all wear the cloak of our scientific heritage. To grow ourselves out of the old worldview, whether personal or professional, we have to understand that a choice of worldview exists. At present, worldview education takes place mostly in the sciences, even though its outcomes bear on most of life. The success of the Newtonian worldview, deliberately constructed to separate things, e.g., the mind from the body, one person from another one, and professional disciplines from each other, shows up in our attitude (paradigm) toward worldview, "It's not relevant for our field or it's not practical."

Research and Decision Making.   When we research why people choose one occupation over another one, we Newtonianize decision making, thinking that one speck of time matters in the whole scheme of things. Research follows mostly in an effort to find out something that often translates into a decision to lay another discovered idea *on* a particular population. This sterile research adds neither heart nor spirit, nor does it take into account an ever shifting physiology and psychology that interacts with a moving environment and cosmos. Most research findings, of course, reflect group information, not an individual's perceived self because we mostly test via pencil-and-paper. Very few studies exist that use case study. Additionally, replication does not stand high on a list of values for student dissertations.

Theory Informs Decision Making.   Next examine counselor theory books. There you find theorists focusing on why and how people do things, which symbolizes a somewhat conventional career development theory approach. (In Chapter 2 and Appendix A these theories are summarized.) However, look closer and you find those theories hope to guide clients by going into the future, looking through the rear view mirror of logical positivism which places little value on truth derived from personal experience.

Holland's (1966) six-piece pizza-like representation of the occupational part of the work supposedly separates one type from each of the five other ones in his *wheel* of types—the realist type from the intellectual, the social type from the conventional one, the enterprising from the artistic personality, and so forth. Nevertheless, the major learning in any categorical inventory is separation and fitting your square peg into someone else's square hole. Multiple decisions follow with individuals frequently trying to get it right.

Practice and Decision Making.   Those studying in the helping professions learn these categories as separate boxes, use the inventory(s) that go along with them, and work with students to find which categories they best fit. The outcome? Helping professionals frequently teach people to match and fit into small categories (all parts of a whole), often failing to note that they could be a combination of all these categories and some yet to be invented—or, even more radically, something clients could invent.

Theories, current testing practice, and research—all presently bear the heavy imprint of a cold, lifeless, machine-like Newtonian universe. None of the traditional career theories, test results, or research can be integrated into a living, breathing, individual for *use in a Lifecareer developing*. They frequently reinforce the widely held notion that by getting the parts together an answer will be forthcoming, particularly in testing. This ignores the information within a particular decision that frequently becomes noticeable months and sometimes years hence.

Take this a step further and you find that theories and subsequent research spawned many decision-making programs from which flowed the fragmented idea that individuals should strive for sensible (You might want to ask, "in whose definition?") career decisions in an effort to make clients *good* decision makers. Most of these programs tend to ignore the value of imperfection and miscues, each of which provides enormous information for the next decision.

For instance, Alanis Morissette, a young Canadian singer and composer, won the 1991 Juno award (A jagged, 1997) as the year's best new female vocalist. Her next record was not a success so she started casting around for a new direction. This necessitated her moving away from home and stepping into major unfamiliarity. She collaborated with a parade of people but none of the people produced the kind of sound she wanted, but she learned. None of these nice, brilliant, or intuitive decisions seemed to happen. Sometimes it takes a myriad of what Buckminster Fuller would call left decisions (those that do not work out), before something starts to happen. In the meantime, it's important to feel good about the learning, otherwise the tendency is to give up. However, Alanis persevered and finally met her dream collaborator who understood her need to follow a *stream of consciousness*.

While Alanis's *stream of consciousness* related to music composition, those who follow their own career theory also follow a *stream of conscious-*

ness that often requires a lot of thrashing around in order to discern their niche. During this time, many decisions frequently do not work. But a playful interchange between those things that work with those which do not takes place.

On the other hand, if one does not value the action taken as opposed to the outcome, this can initiate stress with worry about making the right decision, having the right job, doing the right interview, or sending the right resume. Worry over something not in your control erases the joy of learning with and from life. It can introduce personal problems and issues never before experienced which, without professional help, could plague these individuals, at some level, for a lifetime. That's another legacy of the Newtonian worldview.

Problem Solving at MIT.   Now, hang your career development hat on the rack and step into the world of engineering where they take a more quantum approach to problem solving and decision making. They understand that few problems get solved through straight-line Newtonian thinking. But life is about trial and error, learning, correcting, and trying out new intuitions. "Biological species adapt by accumulating and reorganizing genetic specializations acquired from *prior lives* in other environments. Decision and systems theorists sometimes refer to these volumes of plausible answers as 'solution spaces,'" (p. 7) and trying to find a way through these volumes as 'searching' solutions space" (Hapgood, 1993).

Hapgood (1993) tells the story of Blanco, professor at the Massachusetts Institute of Technology who has designed a microstapler for eye surgery, a forklift truck, a stair-climbing wheelchair, and numerous other items. One day his niece asked him to design a music page turner. He thought it would take him about two weeks, but discovered that each of his notions left something unanswered. So, he decided to dump the whole idea as he had reached that stuck condition Pirsig (1974) referred to in his book *Zen and the Art of Motorcycle Maintenance*. Pirsig says that stuckness is the heart of the process, the place Zen Buddhists try to induce through koans, deep breathing, sitting still, and a host of other procedures. Just about anything you attempt can dump you into *stuck*, stripping confidence in your thought, your worldview, and your metaphysics, leaving you out in the desert without any notion of which way to go. Does this sound like a life direction problem?

The great designer Blanco had arrived at exactly *stuck* causing him to activate his self talk like, "I must be an idiot." "Why should I call myself an engineer if I can't solve this problem?" While *stuck*, his ego moved aside, and he experienced direct observation. As he manually turned the music pages, he observed what his finger was doing. "It wasn't ripping free from a turned page; it peeled free by rotating against the page" (p. 6). He continued to turn the pages and observe. Then voila! He got it. Peeling the page accomplished the turn. Hapgood reports that Blanco was not elated at his discovery because it came when he peeped out between fingers at the real world and remembered what he should not have forgotten: the difference between peeling and ripping. This did not constitute a new experience. Blanco realized that with every design of interest, you had to shred the ego and that trauma grows no less painful with each design.

Blanco speaks each year to MIT sophomores and tells them of the sacrifices they may have to make in their engineering profession. He holds the picture of a spiral, the pit of frustration, then proceeds to tell the group that they will be asked time and time again to throw themselves down that spiral. He says, "This doesn't just come with the territory, it is the territory" (p. 7).

Blanco might respond to the New Careering left turns (what some call wrong) by suggesting one needs to think up a completely wrong answer (but sincerely felt) approach to the problem, jump in, fail, and then do an autopsy. Each failure contains encrypted, somewhere on its body, directions for the next jump" (p. 8). Perhaps, "Try this next," "Buy a better battery." He goes on to say that "good engineering does not key on creativity, centering, grounding, inspiration, or lateral thinking, useful though they might be, but ... *of decoding the clever, even witty, messages solution space carves on the corpses of the ideas in which you believe with all your heart, and then building the road to the next message."* In other words, one thing leads to another. This also goes with Boole's reduction from absurdity. Do the most absurd thing and then work your way to what you want through successive approximations (as cited in Miller-Tiedeman, 1989).

Contrast the MIT and Boolean approach with Newtonian decision making and you discover they are light years apart. Once you find the solution, you may be able to use some of the Newtonian logic; however, this logic, in many instances today, does not represent a starting point.

But today, even with the lay writing about both the old and new science, many hold on to decision making as defined in traditional career. Here's where you encounter the power of paradigms (see Chapter 5 for more detail on paradigms) and an example of *paradigm paralysis* suggesting there's only one way to do things or a best way (Barker, 1990b). Then consider development, particularly the Conforming Stage (see Chapter 4) where things are done like they've always been done, where alternatives prove the exception and new thought unacceptable to those maintaining the status quo. At this point, the difficulty in changing decision making assumptions becomes readily apparent. Test it out. Ask yourself, how receptive would many leaders (yourself included) be to the suggestion that helping professionals consider training in Craniosacral work (a non-verbal therapy) so they could move from *assessment* and *talking* to working with individual energy fields that pose barriers to life direction, particularly for those choosing the journey?

Ask yourself, how quickly would you abandon ideas you have spent a professional life developing? It takes great courage and a solid desire to drop a half-century paradigm (see Chapter 7) in favor of something new. It's like leaving while you're ahead. But when you choose to move from the *Conforming Stage* of development and into the *Self-Aware Level* of development problems arise, as people tend to resist change whether of venue or mind (see Chapter 4 for more detail on development). But life ignores most of this and we all move on. In the process, we learn that personal development is a choice.

Decision Making and Growth

As much as growth and development get a popular nod in rhetoric, particularly among helping professionals, when taken seriously you discover little support exists for it. Put simply, "If you don't look like a duck or quack like a duck, then obviously you're not a duck." When you grow, change occurs and you see and act differently. For example, you may like a job for five years, then five years and one day later, it does not work. The job usually has not changed—you have. At this point, you look for something new and more compatible with your interests, values and beliefs and your evolving life mission.

The process of change often appears chaotic, not organized or presentable. (It functions like the particles in a Quantum universe, going and coming and changing form.) If anything, it appears seemingly messy and in that condition, people tend to back away. A colleague reported that when she had to quit her job to move to another state with her husband, she wanted to talk with her colleagues about this, but they tended to disappear from her life with the exception of one or two people.

Worldview in Action

A counselor educator: But this worldview notion is first of all not practical, and second, if it is, it's years ahead of where the field is.

A counselor replies: Would you entertain the possibility that the field of career development is 70 years behind the science of the day? If you do, you'd have to admit the field ought to change it's language to *catch up* rather than hide behind this *ahead* metaphor. In fact, Zohar (1990) suggested that the Newtonian science isn't even taught in main-line universities any more. Isn't it time for career development professionals to examine current theory and technique through the lens of Quantum physics philosophy?

Exploring Decision Making Using the Quantum Worldview

The worldview for human decision making of any kind, including career, comes from quantum physics philosophy. It works from a sense of a whole knowing that everything connects at every moment. Quantum physics came from "study of the subatomic realm, that invisible universe underlying, embedded in, and forming the fabric of everything around us" (Zukav, 1979, p. 45); and self-organizing systems theory (see Chapters 3 and 7 for more detail). The philosophical notions in Quantum physics and self-organizing systems theory provides many parallels helpful to healing our fragmented selves.

Quantum physics and self-organizing systems overlap and share identities, continually drawing themselves into larger wholes (Zohar, 1990). Without the quantum, self-organizing systems create nothing new, and vice versa. But both working together give us the growing, living world. When individuals make decisions, they use multiple information, both visible and invisible which continues to enfold, and unfold producing new information at each point like the quantum and self-organizing systems do (see Chapters 3 and 7 for more detail on the quantum principles).

Quantum physics is a physics of everyday life as suggested by Zohar (1990). It's a theory of wholeness, "All things and all moments touch each other at every point" (p. 34). This comes from non-local connections which make instantaneous contacts to the universe as a whole. You see this in the mind and body connection. In 1980 scientists found receptors for neurotransmitters in the immune system. Therefore, when you have a thought, it is instantly all over the body. It does not travel up and down the nervous system as previously thought. The body instantly mirrors every mental event (Chopra 1989).

Remember the electron, mentioned in Chapter 3, how it behaves when it intends (decides) to move from one orbit to another? It smears itself out over a large region of space, putting out temporary feelers towards its own future stability by trying out, all at once, all possible new orbits into which it might settle. These feelers are described as virtual transitions. However Bohm believed those virtual transitions often underlie many physical processes and, therefore, play more than a virtual role (Zohar, 1990).

On a human level, when in a quandary, we try out possible outcomes, (on the human level that is done one by one) selecting the decision that seems to match a sought outcome, like getting three job offers and imagining each one and how you might feel about them. These job tryouts frequently happen in nanoseconds, and become part of the woven fabric of life. And like the electrons, those virtual considerations remain a part of the Life-As-Career developing and from time to time underpin other considerations. In Chapter 12, Redekopp talks about the many decisions needed to get a lot of activities rolling that provides information to advance your vision. You don't think too much about the effectiveness of these decisions, instead you feel good and positive that you have made multiple decisions (see Chapter 12 for more detail).

Living life as process (quantum careering) requires multiple decisions, some matter in the moment, some later, some never. It requires feeling at home with all decisions, those that work as well as those that do not. Trial and error serve all of us well as we build our lives. Sometimes we err on purpose to learn quickly as did one woman CEO that Bennis (1983) interviewed in his study on leadership. Her style of leadership was to make as many mistakes as quickly as possible so she could learn the job faster. That is like starting with a completely wrong answer as Blanco suggested above. She treated miscues as possibilities, recognizing the power of the left or what some call *wrong* decision. While that style is not for everyone, it may be a good one to invoke

However, in Lifecareer® decision making (quantum careering) we recognize the unique patterns of individuals, each one free from style except the one dictated by his or her own career theory (developing story). That style cannot be dictated by research *by* or *on* another persons(s) because you can not infer anything certain from it for any one individual. That may be why classical (Newtonian) oriented career development professionals get nervous about the holistic, individual quality of Lifecareer decision making, and put their faith in decision making research. For instance, a recent study concluded that, "... individuals who make efficient, effective and wise career decisions, combine intuitive strengths with intellect or analytical thinking" (Kanchier, February 1997, p. 14). Wise in whose definition? Effective for whom? Combining of intuitive strengths with intellect or analytical thinking may occur but the quantum careering paradigm (Lifecareer), one built on probability, does not prescribe this. That paradigm does not tie career or any other kind of decision making to any one form, style, or get into what is effective or ineffective. The one deciding makes that determination, usually gleaned from using his or her Career Compass® (1982), a combination of experience, intelligence, and intuition which may or may not include analytical thinking. The Career Compass scans the entire body-mind-spirit-emotional landscape and from this information a gazillion potential choices emerge, both conscious and unconscious. The moment determines the choice and its history, the new choice(s).

New Careering Professionals need to adopt the physicists mindset. If something works, use it and work out the details later. Physicists put great

---

*Lifecareer, Life-Is-Career, Career Compass and their derivatives are registered trademarks of Dr. Anna Miller-Tiedeman.

faith in what works. In mediation, sometimes you do something contrary to the guidelines, but it works. What matters ultimately is not what someone else construes or what the research suggests, but what each of us needs in order to grow ourselves forward on a life mission that gives us that deep spiritual experience. Life at the micro level now tries to tell us when we cooperate with life, we can break the Newtonian stranglehold on our decision making which will unleash many wondrous and instructive experiences.

At the beginning of the chapter, Miller-Tiedeman noted that she had asked counselors two questions: (a) Have you ever taken a decision making class? And (b) Do you plan to take one? The answer was a resounding no to both questions. You might want to ask yourself another question then. "Why would I want to push for decision making instruction for public education students when I have neither taken nor plan to take a decision making class myself?" You might also want to ask yourself, "How do I make decisions and what about that process would be useful to those I work with?"

Miller-Tiedeman apologizes to all those students she worked with in decision making and career development, for passing on to them what she learned in graduate school, particularly the mantra about wise, better, and best decision making.

The Urge to Grow and Decision Making

A significant number of career development professionals have walked *through* that valley of change in their decision making thought but they do not tend to be the leaders. Nonetheless, these people help others do the same, as they recognize the importance of exploring a new worldview as they've personally experienced the deadening effects of the old worldview that killed off their creativity, separated them from their life mission and built a yawning fissure between them and their deep spirituality.

But these people know, as we all do, that if we step out of *conformity,* we grow and learn. We catch a glimpse of what can be. We pass that information among ourselves without the okay of the current leaders. We examine decision making, its current scientific foundation, and what it might look like coming from the philosophy of quantum physics. When we do that it becomes natural to abandon discussion about sharp-witted decision making and move to valuing all information encoded in any decision. This means moving to a worldview that has a basic assumption of connectedness, not separation. Then we can start to re-weave our lives with all the threads, not just the right and wise ones while we learn from the additional information that comes to us in each decision. To move in that direction, we educate ourselves about worldviews and the demands they make on us, separating us from our deeper selves. We can then choose which one we want to use as we make the journey to our personal knowing. Then we own an understanding of decision making we can use to empower our clients, family, and friends, an approach designed to build confidence and engender joy which most likely will increase motivation and help us all catch those winds of grace as we unfold our life journey.

☐ Looking Back

1. Breaking the stranglehold on Newtonian decision making requires understanding:

   a. decision making is natural to all living things,

   b. the difference between the Newtonian and quantum worldviews,

   c. former worldviews,

   d. the impact of world view on idea and personal development advance,

   e. the quantum perspective on decision making—a probability not a cause perspective.

2. Lower awareness accounts for part of the ignorance responsible for perpetuating the parts mentality: e.g., *a decision that results in a good education will lead to a good job.*

3. Worldview education has not historically been part of counselor preparation.

4. Maintenance of the status quo interferes with the capability of professionals interested in a different worldview to move forward developmentally.

5. Counselors talk a lot about growth and sometimes fail to note the loneliness of the experience.

6. Lifecareer opens us to our individual gifts and provides awareness of the importance of connecting up as we journey forward.

7. If something works, use it and learn from it, and like the physicists, work out the details later.

☐ Discussion Questions

1. Why is worldview important in decision making?

2. Share your impressions of trial and error as a way to approach your life direction.

3. How does maintaining the status quo interfere with changing the decision-making paradigm?

4. How does development relate to decision making?

5. What does growing mean to you?

6. Have you at any one time in your life decided to change some aspect of yourself? If so, could you share that experience? What kind of support helped you in that change?

☐ Classroom/Group Exercises

1. Form dyads and discuss your style of decision making by telling what you do and why it works for you.

2. Discuss the value of those decisions that did not work out.

3. Discuss the outcome of things that did not work and what that led you into.

4. If you've had a decision making course or class, share your impression of that experience.

5. Share your reactions to those decisions in your life that did not work out.

☐ Homework/Test Assignment

1. Interview several people in your community. Ask them to talk about their decision making. How they do it? What they find most useful?

2. Interview at least two professional people. Ask them if they've had formal decision making instruction or if they have attended a decision making class. Ask them to share their style of decision making and why it works for them.

3. Write a paper on why focusing on wise, better, or best decision making can be a dysfunctional approach. Comment on what you gain by loving all your decisions, particularly those that fail to materialize.

4. Read and write a review on pages 123-128 in *Critical Path*, "The Self-Disciplines of Buckminster Fuller," (pp. 123-128) and comment on the main theme in the pages assigned.

5. Read chapter 1, "Mutiny," pages 1-22 in James Michener's *The World Is My Home,* and report on Michener's decision making.

David V. Tiedeman

Stop, Look, Listen, and Allow for the New (Quantum) Careering

Spotlight on the Quantum

When you get to the level of atoms, the landscape is not one of solid objects moving around each other like partners in a dance, following predictable steps. Subatomic particles are separated by huge gaps, making every atom more than 99.9% empty space. This holds true for hydrogen atoms in the air, carbon atoms in wood tables, and all the "solid" atoms in our cells. Therefore, everything solid, including our bodies, is proportionately as empty as inter-galactic space (Chopra, 1989).

If you enlarged an atom to the size of Yankee stadium, it would be almost empty. The nucleus would be smaller than a baseball sitting out in center field. At the outer part, you would see tiny gnats buzzing about at a higher altitude than any pop fly Babe Ruth ever hit. And between the baseball and the gnats? Nothing. But this emptiness is the source of all being (Swimme, 1984).

☐ Looking Ahead

Watch for the following important topics:

1.   Important scientific revolutions

2.   Quantum physics and the New Careering

3.   Brief description of Newtonian mechanics and Quantum physics

4.   Differences between Newtonian and Quantum physics

5.   Copenhagen Interpretation

6.   Error as basic concept

7.   Non-local connections

Stop

"STOP, LOOK, LISTEN, AND ALLOW," mused the young professor as she thought about the topic she and David would discuss in the graduate lounge of Walden University, a perfect place to discuss the New Careering.

"David, let me use the mediation technique of mirroring to see if I understand the metaphors," the young professor said. "You wrote this chapter for those who care to STOP and to LOOK as they think their way into a new paradigm. This means collecting events and impressions, looking at emerging sensible patterns, and LISTENING to how our minds make sense of that to which we give attention and intelligence as we take life as it is. Then ALLOW other impressions to inform us as we construct our individual theories of self, society, life direction, science, logic, philosophy, religion and the like. Whatever evolves into truth for us is the outcome. That's where ALLOW comes in again to encourage the developing notions of each of us, to ALLOW us to experience the disorder of growing without judgment. To ALLOW good feelings about this process to flood through our bodies. To ALLOW us to celebrate the birth of our ever-expanding selves. Quantum careering can liberate us from the Newtonian box of ongoing evaluation of most experience. Am I right?"

"You're really on the point," replied David.

"Stop, Look, Listen, and Allow," the young professor rejoined. "It sure makes sense as four simple, powerful processes for useful learning. As life nudges us forward toward a process paradigm.

"Just think, while we sit leisurely looking, listening, and allowing our minds to open to something new, John Glenn bravely becomes the oldest astronaut to orbit the earth. Glenn seems to be taking it in stride as if he knows it's a snap to transition from Earth gravity to approximately zero gravity. That's the confidence we'll all develop as we transition from traditional career to quantum careering in the near future.

Look

Two Relevant Scientific Revolutions

In 1962, Kuhn published *The Structure of Scientific Revolutions*. The book caused a stir in the scientific community. True breadth and depth of scholarship increased.

Substance shifted to the novel but intriguing, and argument had the expected consistency. But scientists were not accustomed to thinking of nature's consistencies as *revolutionary*. Nevertheless, Kuhn's book over its 35-year history has had an important impact in many disciplines.

Kuhn's concept of "scientific revolution" provides context to the text developed here. Kuhn chose to use the histories of scientific advances big and powerful enough to have indelibly marked praxis worldwide in demonstrating that such changes are usually structural ones. They not alone come to pass; they also come to stay. The resulting models of such changes are called "paradigms."

This chapter will focus on two career-relevant scientific revolutions occurring in the twentieth century: (a) the transition of Newtonian mechanics into quantum mechanics; and (b) a parallel transition of career mechanics into quantum career process (Miller-Tiedeman & Tiedeman, 1983; Miller-Tiedeman, 1982, 1988, 1989, 1992a, 1992b). These two transitions presently coalesce. Personal transistioning from Newtonian to quantum mechanics serves as the necessary catalyst.

From Classical Physics to Quantum Mechanics. The transition from Newtonian to quantum mechanics started in a physical science that was older, further developed, and more disciplined than the career development field. However, career development grew up embedded in the Newtonian worldview. Its writings reflected that view until the Life-Is-

---

*Lifecareer, Life-Is-Career, Career Compass and their derivatives are registered trademarks of Dr. Anna Miller-Tiedeman.

Career® theory intruded with a focus on the individual as theory maker (Miller-Tiedeman & Tiedeman, 1983; Miller-Tiedeman, 1985, 1987, 1989, 1992). These two changes in theories will, beyond reasonable doubt, affect the quality of life in the first half of the twenty-first century. After all, the ongoing transition from a Newtonian physics (Zukav, 1979) to a quantum physics fundamentally changes the very cosmos in which humans believe they live. Little wonder that such changes transpire in those old devils of unfamiliarity, risk, anxiety, stress, and fear.

The paradigm shift from career mechanics to career process presently does not appear to have the head of steam and import that the shift from Newtonian to quantum mechanics had. However, signs indicate that a shift of that existential nature now waits in the wings of a universe theater ready to raise its curtain on a transition of the same order of magnitude.

The human career is one area in which such change is possible and wanted by some, needed by many. Such results can be achieved by citizens who master a process of self-counseling. Mastering that process requires personal understanding of the wonderful characteristic with which humans are endowed. We can be both conscious and *aware of being conscious*. This high-level activity (Koestler, 1964) requires familiarization, practice, and self mastery.

This chapter will facilitate the understanding of process careering through a dialogue with a young professor who exhibits a quantum intuition, and reaches for expanded understanding of what it's like to be more fully human. She senses the new and is willing to walk into unfamiliar territory to explore new ideas. She, like Karl Pribram, has the *courage to look foolish* in order to avoid knowing more and more about less and less. Could it be that career development would excite more professionals if they could step into the sandbox of exploration without the albatross of our degrees, credentials, and fears that often follows eminence? How long do you think it will take for us to treat our personal history and "herstory" with playfulness? Hold those answers as we move on to the Pond.

Discussing History at Walden University

The Deeper Roots of Traditional Career.   "Traditional careerists tend to see their roots within the vocational context," David said. But the scientific revolution on which today's career theory rests began with Nicholas Copernicus, whose heliocentric view of cosmic rotation overthrew the geocentric view of Ptolemy and the Bible, which represented the accepted dogma for more than a thousand years (Capra, 1982). Rene Descartes came along with his belief in the certainty of scientific knowledge. He even went so far as to conclude that nothing in the concept of body belongs to the mind and vice versa.

"Kepler derived laws of planetary motion, and Galileo performed experiments to discover laws of falling bodies. Newton combined those two and formulated the general laws of motion for all macroscopic objects in the solar system. He believed these laws confirmed the Cartesian view of nature.

"So, in the late 1700s, Sir Isaac Newton's method of investigation became the accepted scientific method for over a century. His mind and investigation of his hypotheses about the nature of gravity proved so successful that he held the scientific world in his mind's grasp for two centuries. Since we're near Concord at Walden, we might even say Newton 'fired the Mechanistic worldview shot heard round the world.' This worldview persists even into our twentieth century.

"With a 200-year backdrop of Newtonian physics, vocational guidance emerged in 1908 (Brewer, 1942). These two revolutions made deep inroads into human behavior and thought (see Table 7.1).

"In the early 1900s, the limits of Newtonian theory began appearing in atomic and sub-atomic experiments generally grouped as quantum mechanics (Capra 1982). Reconciliation was needed and a part of it was provided by the Copenhagen Interpretation, conceived by twelve physicists of genius. The Interpretation says, in effect, that it does not matter what quantum mechanics is about, the important thing is that it works (Zukav, 1979, p. 62).

"Einstein's General Theory of relativity ($E = mc^2$), where c represents the speed of light, proves to be one of the missing pieces of the needed theory of quantum mechanics. But Capra (1982) suggested, 'It was Heisenberg's great achievement to express the limitations of classical concepts in a precise mathematical form' (p. 79) known as the uncertainty principle. Niels Bohr provided a better understanding of the wave and particle picture, introducing the notion of complementarity. Abracadabra, quantum mechanics and general relativity relegated Newtonian mechanics to a special-case theory. At that time, the world literally changed in the perceptions of physicists, but few laypersons even 70 years later know the transformation or its important philosophical structure. Further, Zohar (1990) suggested that Newtonian physics is now considered so elementary that it is no longer taught in main-line universities."

Physics goes mainstream. "Then, what we today might call a quantum leap happened. In the beginning, instead of writing physics papers day after day, Capra (1975) started popularizing physics for the lay person. Zukav (1979) followed with his book, *The Dancing Wu Li Masters*, checking out his understandings with physicists. The popularity of these writings encouraged natural scientists in general to offer their views: Bohm (1980),

TABLE 7.1. Blazing the Science Trail

1543	Copernicus	Heliocentric view of cosmic rotation
1613	Descartes	Certainty of science and separation of mind and body. Nature as perfect governed by exact mathematical laws.
1609	Kepler	Laws of planetary motion
1609	Galileo	Laws of falling objects.
1620	Bacon	Set forth the empirical method of science
1687	Newton	Combined Kepler and Galileo and formed general laws of motion. Unified Bacon's systematic experimentation and Descartes mathematical analysis which led to the methodology upon which natural science rests.
1905	Einstein	Theory of relativity
1927	Heisenberg	Expressed limitations of classical concepts in mathematical form known as the uncertainty principle.
1927	Bohr	Complementarity principle
1927	The Copenhagen Interpretation	Physicists working with the new physics met in Brussels Belgium to address the question, "What is it that quantum mechanics describes." That answer became the Copenhagen Interpretation.

Prigogine (1980), Swimme (1984), Wolf (1981), and more recently, Hawking (1988, 1993). These books provide a solid core for a personal library on today's New Physics.

"This early splurge of books dovetailed with Miller-Tiedeman's discontent with career counseling assumptions and started her on the road to understanding what, if anything, the New Physics offered in parallels to life direction. It ended with her Lifecareer theory (also known as quantum careering and living life as process) and philosophy (Miller-Tiedeman & Tiedeman, 1983; Miller-Tiedeman, 1982, 1985, 1987, 1989, 1992).

"As you make your developmental leap (Miller-Tiedeman, 1996; Tiedeman, 1996) from a Newtonian to a quantum cosmology, never overlook your change from a supposedly stationery to a motion cosmos. The synergy (Fuller, 1981) of open collaboration during such growth, for benefit of all, will point us to a greater appreciation of potential and value in life."

Listen

"Well, as you might know, *growth* stands at the pinnacle of life's syllabus. Life keeps nudging its growth agenda forward (even when we don't listen) in the universe in individuals, in consciousness, and in social organizations (all this without a committee meeting). Life's main agenda is renewal which automatically pushes us forward."

"You're right," said the young professor, silent for half a minute. "Maybe that's life's way of kicking humanity out of conformity. Which raises another question. Doesn't taking on a quantum mindset unsettle your 50-year career in Newtonian research?" she asked.

A Personal Experience of Moving Ahead

"You bet it unsettles me. But only in the sense that I wish I knew then what I know now," David said a bit sadly. 'So much to do, so little time,' keeps flashing before my eyes.

"Read on and you'll see how I struggled with changing my paradigm. I share this information because it may provide courage to those brave souls who dare to cross the Newtonian bridge to quantum understanding. At this point, it takes Karl Pribram's notion of *the courage to look foolish* (Wilber, 1982) to support the start. If you don't step into the *new* periodically, you find yourself in high comfort and low learning, like we said earlier. Further, you might want to think about how easy it is to fall into the trap of staying with the familiar."

"Yes, I can see that," the young professor replied.

"I also share my paradigm change experience because it's part of the mandate in new paradigm research, that is, make clear where you are coming from in taking a particular view or embracing a particular idea, and, where appropriate, add experience to further explain the idea (Reason & Rowan, 1981). You see, in this approach, the quantum notion that the cosmos is a web of relationships with space-time coordinates depends on where observer and object are placed. In other words, ideas birth out of more than reviews of literature.

"But let's go on. Miller-Tiedeman has worked on this idea for 18 years. Even though we had numerous conversations, I only grasped the bottom line of the basic-trust core of Erik Erikson's (1959) psychosocial theory of identity formation when working to free myself from the Newtonian worldview. I then realized the importance of basic trust in any kind of personal change, particularly that of a worldview. I learned that too many differences between Newtonian and quantum theories exist to conceive of them as similar boxes fitting into one another from small to next larger to next larger, etc. But writing this chapter broke my reliance upon Newtonianism as the only paradigm for research.

"When I finally realized I simultaneously had to think revolutions in two theories, Career and quantum," David started, "I opted for simplicity in attack. I, therefore, decided to visit Walden Pond where Henry David Thoreau had in the nineteenth century so tellingly exemplified living attuned with nature, a core health outcome of today's Lifecareer theory/philosophy of going with, not against, the *flow* of life (Miller-Tiedeman & Tiedeman, 1983; Miller-Tiedeman, 1982, 1985, 1987, 1989, 1992).

Then I started to recognize the need to adopt quantum careering as the universe continues to move evolutionarily forward on Prigogine's (1980) *arrow of time* into the ever more comprehensive 'secrets' of the universe with which it teases and challenges humans to improve their quality of life on Earth" (Prigogine & Stengers, 1984).

The young professor then asked, "How did physics and career development come together? In a way they're unlikely bedfellows."

"Well, in the late 1970s, at an American Counseling Association convention in Las Vegas, Miller-Tiedeman and I had dinner with Tom Kubistant and Dick Carhart. Somewhere in the conversation, Kubistant mentioned *The Dancing Wu Li Masters*. This peaked Miller-Tiedeman's interest and Kubistant said he would send her a copy. He did and that marks Day 1 in the birth of the quantum careering idea.

"In the Spring of 1983, as President of the National Institute for the Advancement of Career Education, headquartered at the University of Southern California, I had the opportunity to showcase the quantum process theory (Miller-Tiedeman, 1983, 1988, 1989, 1992a, 1992b) at an Assembly to Advance Career. To support that quantum beginning, we invited Fritjof Capra (1983), physicist, as our keynote speaker along with Barbara Marx Hubbard and Robert Theobald.

The Birth of Quantum Careering

"After the 1983 Assembly, I worked with Miller-Tiedeman introducing Lifecareer to various groups. That experience led me to ask myself the following four questions: (a) What major characteristics do quantum physics and Lifecareer theory have in common? (b) How do citizens and their counselors go about using the parallelism of quantum and career theories? (c) Can one individual really change the cosmic views of another? And (d) By what mechanism do new wholes manifest in dissipating self-organizing systems?

"With regard to my first quandary, both quantum and Lifecareer theories are imbued with the same dynamic, universe energy which is complementary to matter via $E = mc^2$. Complementary energy and matter grows and dances (Zukav, 1979). Hence, quantum parallels include motion as primary, not holding fearfully to what is now working while wondering what will happen when things change. Change, like a movie camera, happens minute upon minute. And, as a specific energy configuration in universe energy, the Lifecareer theory is but one example of quantum energy.

"With regard to my second quandary, you've got to shake the logical positivistic notion, e.g., one that rejects all transcendental metaphysics, "... statements of fact being held to be more meaningful only if they have verifiable consequences ... and in statements of logic, mathematics" (Costello, 1991, p. 798) that a Newtonian paradigm is the only one worth considering. To do this, study process careering (Miller-Tiedeman, 1983, 1988, 1989, 1992); Reason and Rowan's (1981) new paradigm research; Capra's (1975, 1982) new physics ideas; Zukav's (1979) structure of quantum physics in non-mathematical terms; and Zohar's (1990) philosophy of quantum self.

"Also, talk with others about it. In either living process career, writing, or talking about it, you'll notice how easy it is to slip back into Newtonian thinking. When you catch yourself falling back into that mindset, you'll know you're on your way to changing your worldview. You'll also discover a new worldview doesn't spring full-blown like Minerva from Jupiter's forehead. It takes personal work. That separates those wanting quick fixes from those serious about change.

"With regard to my third quandary, it appeared that if I wanted to live the quantum process career (Lifecareer), I needed to start doing it. As my attitude toward process careering started to change, my worldview started to shift. I had to change my own attitude before I could have any hope of facilitating change in another's attitude. This points up the importance of living your own Life-As-Career. In that way, you develop your own content which you will use in helping others mature their life vision.

"My fourth quandary, my adopt-a-new-cosmos quandary, lasted six months during which I tried and revised theories, imposing them upon experience, and revising over and over again. For instance, with my old Newtonian paradigm well intact, I went into study for this discussion confident that I could derive new statistical techniques because I've done that!

(Rulon, Tiedeman, Tatsuoka, & Langmuir, 1967). I figured *experienced*-me would grasp quantum theory in a jiffy. Nothing was farther from the truth. That's how a Newtonian framework fools you. *Present Quantum Theory for laypersons is not about changing formulas, its about changing an attitude* (Capra, 1975), which then translates to experience. Quantum theory models the cosmos you must attitudinally assume.

"You have to realize that attitudes don't change or gel readily. So don't expect yourself or your students to become quantumites overnight. But if you both stick with it, you'll find a new worldview" which will bring incredible insights and newness.

"Why is a change of worldview difficult?" the young professor asked.

"Because it moves you into greater complexity. Self-organizing systems always generate new wholes out of the chaos of dissipating structures (the Newtonian worldview). This is the order out of chaos often referred to by Prigogine and Stengers (1984). The dissipative structures idea won Prigogine the Nobel Prize in 1977. It later became popularized as chaos theory."

We have to understand that the theory of self-organizing systems does not throw anyone into growth. It merely offers the opportunity to grow. This could be as simple as changing a response or a long-held behavior. It could also include evolutionary change which overtime changes one. In looking back you know something happened, but you didn't have the awareness of it happening in the moment. Like the universe as known to Prigogine (Lukas, 1980), we humans also trend toward more complexity even though sometimes we do it kicking and screaming as I did. But it's so much easier if you cooperate with the approaching forces while assessing the situation (Miller-Tiedeman, 1989).

"What do you think of all this?"

While what you say excites me, you must realize that quantum careering (Miller-Tiedeman & Tiedeman, 1983; Miller-Tiedeman, 1988, 1989, 1992; Tiedeman, 1996) now tries the doubts and self regards of leaders in career counseling. In addition, you bring those awakening to the precipices of unfamiliar change, after teasing them with the hoards of figurative gold that exist in the creativity released in embracing quantum principles. You show them leaps are necessary. But you do this using physics as context. David, you know that physics has been the course quite readily avoided by college students, even yourself."

"That's right," David said. "I was not attracted to physics, to say nothing of linking it to career. But I thought if Miller-Tiedeman found profound parallels, there must be something to it."

The young professor nodded, then replied, "I think I'm now on overload. So, I'll just cooperate with the approaching force of sleep. See you tomorrow."

Allow

The Graduate Lounge

David and the young professor met the next morning and David started: "It appears that to Lifecareer, you need to check your worldview as frequently as you check the gas gauge of your car. Ask yourself, 'do you believe that the parts equal their whole or do you assert that the whole organizes the parts and is more than the sum of its parts?' The former reflects Newtonian thinking; the latter quantum. If you don't get your worldviews sorted out like this, process living will elude you."

"David, I hear that you're hard to understand and this worldview thing sounds like part of that. In addition, you know we don't discuss worldview in career development. What does a worldview have to do with anything?"

"Well," David calmly replied, "your worldview reflects your beliefs and values which influence your decisions. Therefore, a worldview anchors your actions and behavior. Historically, the emphasis has been and still is on identifying skills, abilities, interests, then getting occupational information in order to match yourself to the "right job." Career is considered something you search for, lose, find, and go on to find a second, third, and fourth time. You see, career theory has been pretty much an outside job. Know it or not, traditionalists have the directionality of their effort 180 degrees out of phase, as the tendency is to dumb down clients; not intelligence them up.

"Supporting intelligence means accepting personal knowledge as the primary and best occupational information. On the other hand, you recognize the individual's intelligence will prompt him or her to gather any external secondary information needed. This approach indicates you understand how personal data for each of us changes momentarily as experience changes. That's why you need to check your worldview often using the question, 'Am I living process using my personal theory or am I hung up in the old Newtonian worldview, following traditional thinking that doesn't acknowledge me as a 'theory maker?' It's amazing how easy you can slip back into that old view without even noticing it."

Allowing With Points to View

With that stage setting, David restated his thesis and continued: "Two important career-relevant revolutions occurred during the Twentieth Century—quantum mechanics began replacing Newtonian mechanics in subatomic realms of energy, and process-career theory started displacing occupational selection in adolescent years. Quantum mechanics and Einstein's provision of his general theory of relativity, $E = mc^2$ linked both of these revolutions.

"Concerning quantum theory, twelve outstanding physicists met in Brussels, in the Summer of 1927, and agreed that quantum theory is about correlations in our experience. They further said, *'It doesn't matter what quantum mechanics is about. The important thing is that it works"* (Zukav, 1979, p. 62, italics added). These principles became known as the Copenhagen Interpretation. Zukav (1979) called this acceptance "one of the most important statements in the history of science" (p. 62). The rational part of our psyche began to merge again with our non-believing side. About thirty years later, physicists joined Einstein's general theory of relativity with quantum mechanics. They called the transformation matrix with that characteristic an "S" or scatter matrix. The 's-matrix' enabled physicists to reproduce fairly accurate paths into which several kinds of high-energy particles scattered upon encountering other high-energy particles.

"Concerning quantum careering, in 1983, Miller-Tiedeman introduced quantum careering to the career development field and it became known as the Lifecareer theory (Miller-Tiedeman & Tiedeman, 1983; Miller-Tiedeman, 1982, 1985, 1987, 1988, 1989, 1992a, 1992b). This led to the first attempt to integrate quantum physics and career and introduced the individual as a personal theory maker par excellence. This effort toward responsible self-direction needs encouragement, as the cross-over to quantum thinking will, in most instances, produce pain. But the elimination of the old handcuffs of Newtonian thought will bring new awareness and freedom.

"But David," noted the young professor, "quantum mechanics doesn't replace Newtonian mechanics?"

"That is right, quantum mechanics simply subordinates Newtonian mechanics into special-case theory. But in circumstances where Newtonian theory works, it is stunning, like getting us on the moon and onto Mars."

"David, it sounds to me like we need to help each other grow into quantum understanding because it's not easy, and support can ease the way," said the young professor. "As I remember the accommodation step in your decision-making paradigm (Tiedeman & O'Hara, 1963), the first stage would be *Induction*, where the idea gets tested knowing there's a lot to learn. When the individual starts to feel comfortable with quantum, this brings on the *Reformation phase* in which the reformer believes everyone should move in a certain direction. But after some meaningful personal experiences provide an actionable base, the reformer moves into *Reintegration*, realizing that everyone moves at the level of his or her own understanding which is constitutionally guaranteed American citizens."

"Crossing the bridge to quantum takes a lot of trust, perhaps way beyond Erik Erikson's (1959) notion of basic trust. But even more difficult is holding that trust, particularly when the majority isn't supporting it. This certainly makes it the *road less traveled*, doesn't it?"

"That's true," replied David, "But we need to recognize, as Prigogine (1980) demonstrates, that Life always moves into greater complexity. None of us have a choice about that. Our only choice is to ask ourselves, 'Do we try to understand the new and cooperate with it or do we remain in the backwaters?'"

The young professor hesitated, "I suppose quantum process refers to some of the presumed actions of electrons when physicists put an electron source into a linear accelerator and bombard the receptor with another electron source. As I understand it, under those conditions, physicists excite atoms so much that they eventually "leap" out of the nucleus ring in which they rotate when unexcited."

A graduate student at a nearby table broke into the conversation at this point and said, "Isn't that what the TV show *Quantum Leap*, does when the time traveler drops in and out of time periods?"

"Yes," said David. "Your question about the TV show illustrates how process is defined by different individuals. That's the old bugaboo of perception. But process speaks to each of us differently. Additionally, it veers from different meanings of process. That's a quantum characteristic just as leaping is also a quantum characteristic. But I didn't expect to get that illustration of 'process' so soon in our discussion. And that's another aspect of process, it continues to surprise us.

"While we're on the point, it's a good time to suggest recognizing quantum mechanics roots from two theories. One root will be the electron and sub-atomic phenomena of what is commonly called 'quantum theory.' The other root of quantum mechanics will be relativity theory. The resulting experiential 's-matrix' is the way scientists build, from stepping stone to stepping stones."

Upon saying, "relativity theory," another graduate student jumpted into the conversation.

"I know what relativity theory is," he said, "$E = mc^2$. Energy equals the product of mass times the square of c, the speed of light. Energy and mass are complementary. You can convert energy to mass and mass to energy."

"Wait a minute," David begged of the graduate student while trying to contain his surprise at the intensity and possible possession of many facts of relativity theory.

"With your more than average interest in quantum principles," David suggested, "why not plan a graduate forum to share your knowledge of the concepts I'll just skim in this discussion?"

"Yes, I'd enjoy sharing my knowledge of the atomic and subatomic worlds and relating it to life direction. That excites me."

Since the graduate student brought it up, David then offered short sound bites about relativity a little earlier than he planned. That's another characteristic of process. It dictates the content, but interestingly, all gets covered, but not in what we ordinarily call logical order. Process doesn't always cooperate with logic. That tends to frustrate us. That's when we sometimes break the flow to try to bend it back to logic. That's when we slip back down the slope of the Newtonian Worldview.

"Why is that?" asked the young graduate student. "Why can't we catch ourselves?"

David replied, "Because we're so used to doing it. It's what we call habit; and, habits don't change that easily.

"Further, human movement into subtle, causal, and spiritual realms in consciousness seems to hinge on worldview switch. In this regard Eastern Mysticism seems to have already advanced human being into such states of consciousness which are not commonly realized in our Western Culture" (Capra 1975, 1982; see Table 7.2).

David then complimented the young professor and the graduate students, "Since you all seem pretty well oriented to quantum theory as a

---

TABLE 7.2. Some Major Differences

Newtonian Physics	Quantum Mechanics
Can picture it	Cannot picture it
Based on ordinary sense perceptions	Based on behavior of sub-atomic particles and unobservable systems
Describes individual objects in space and their changes	Describes behavior of systems in time
Predicts events	Predicts probabilities
Assumes objectivity	Defines objectivity as subjectivity
Observe something without changing it	Observing something changes it
Claims absolute truth; the way nature really is	Claims only to correlate with experience

Adapted from G. Zukav, *The Dancing Wu Li Masters*, 1979, p. 66

whole, I have no intention of providing an elementary text on atomic physics. I will, however, with your concurrence, introduce several key quantum physics concepts because they offer compelling parallels from which we can learn to better understand our own approach and thinking.

"David," the young professor requested, "before you introduce those principles, please tell us a little about how this quantum thing came about."

David nodded and said, "Scientists and Nature got along pretty cooperatively in developing scientific understanding from the Renaissance to the twentieth century. Nature had given physical scientists a number of "yes" answers to their theory-guided inquiries about levers, inclined planes, pendulums, light, sound, heat, magnetism, gravity and the like. Various constants and several important ratios had been unified by using field concepts.

"As several of these fundamental constants and ratios were identified and satisfactorily stabilized, a new era of scientific activities set in. Higher level cognitive skills such as comparison, noting distinctions, attributing and verifying differences when possible—all found a friendly environment. These, of course, are elements of generalization. To humans, then, mind seems built on consciousness "blocks" such as: (1) data, idea, trial; (2) data, idea, trial at a higher level, etc. This is one procedure the successive mind uses in coming to understanding. Nature participates in such constructionist communications with humans. However, Nature is in no hurry to volunteer information. Humans, therefore, have to work for it; experiment, that is," continued David.

"But as you might guess, former centuries have not all been years of milk and honey for humans who elect, as R. Buckminster Fuller (1981) did, to pattern their lives on what they themselves come to know experientially, not on what they have been ordered to do. But truth strongly appeals to some humans despite the obstacles other humans erect to slow the sharing of advances.

"When the New Physics emerged, physical science had already dropped several soul-disturbing changes of view on the good burghers of Europe by the end of the Renaissance. For instance, it had been determined that Earth rotated about our sun, not the sun around the Earth. When Columbus wanted to make his expeditions to the New World, the masses cried, "The world is flat and he'll fall off." As we all know today, he didn't fall off nor did he discover a New World. The West Indians were already here. But, today, those changes in conventional cosmological grounds seem almost inconsequential. But they aren't so tranquil to people experiencing them while happening. Existential change is no bed of roses.

"In continuing to discover principle upon principle, specific by specific, physicists began to unfold the secrets of extant results which later revealed themselves as parts of a more general phenomenon. This is another illustration of life moving toward more complexity, as Prigogine (1980) presently contends. Life just won't stand still. It loves to grow irrespective of our inclinations that way. And the new physics is but one in an infinity of examples of how life continues to do that. The quantum and career process in consciousness union marks another example."

The first graduate student joined into the discussion of quantum processes. "I've been listening carefully," she started. "I've an intuition about unity. I'm probably wide of the mark, but the quantum process tolerates less than certainty, right?"

"A whole lot less than certainty. In fact, it's all uncertainty," replied David. "In shifting from an elemental to a quantum-relativistic view of mechanics and energy in universe, physicists had to move from only attending to elements to more inclusive attention to relationship in self-managed systems in general. And, importantly, the quantum paradigm includes experiential approximations, while Newtonian mechanics doesn't" (Capra, 1982).

The second graduate student then asked, "If physicists use experiential approximations, why don't we do the same about career? After all career is but another universe complimentary manifestation of energy and therefore subject to all universe concepts. That's what Miller-Tiedeman (1982, 1985, 1987, 1988, 1989, 1992a, 1992b; Miller-Tiedeman & Tiedeman, 1983) caught onto quicker than the rest of us."

"Even though quantum physics was discovered in the 1900s, it has not penetrated too deeply into many disciplines, not even career development," replied David. "In addition, there's something to Kuhn's (1970) notion that paradigms don't usually change at the top. They start at the edges in or the bottom up, as those at the top seem too invested in the old.

"You might think of it as Heifetz does in his book *Leadership Without Easy Answers* (1994). He maintains that good leadership means going to the balcony periodically and observing the action on the 'dance floor' below. In that sense Miller-Tiedeman did just that. She stepped to the career development balcony and started asking questions from the Quantum viewpoint.

"She was aided by her deep understanding that life's career is renewal, along with several other factors: (a) she read from the collective intelligence (that's another story) and places great confidence in it; (b) she learned from her experience; and (c) she listened to her inner wisdom and acted on the larger theoretical framework life pulled her toward. So, she didn't *decide* to write a process theory, *it evolved in her experience*. That's an important process understanding.

"Probably as important, she took the physics attitude she learned when Capra (1983) keynoted a 1983 Assembly to Advance Career. There, Capra told the group that physicists take a pragmatic attitude about any approach. When they have a certain theory that they think isn't quite sound, mathematically or otherwise, but it works, then they say, 'Well there must be something to it.' They then use the theory and work out the details later. And with many endorsements from groups and individuals, Miller-Tiedeman continues to work out the details."

The young professor then inquired, "How is it that a woman caught first early sight of quantum careering?"

David replied, "Well, you might know men tend more toward left-brained logic. They're more into explanation than experience. But more importantly, Lifecareer was her contribution and no one gets the opportunity to make anyone else's contribution. That's life's copyright on each of our missions. In that sense, there's no competition."

"Before we move on," the young professor suggested, "Let me note how the process of ideas jumping from mind to mind in local connections, again takes us over and encourages us to probe deeper. That's intelligence at work in consciousness. It doesn't abide by rules, it just keeps tumbling around and around like crystals in a kaleidoscope making new patterns time after time after time. It rather resembles what the electrons, photons, mesons, and nucleons do. They lead 'double lives as they are: now position; now momentum; now particles; now waves; now mass; now energy—all in response to each other and to the environment'" (Zohar, 1990, p. 98).

The first graduate student caught the rising feeling of understanding in the discussion, and willingly stopped being a stubborn Newtonian to contribute his growing understanding of quantum mechanics. "Quantum mechanics forms a dynamic whole. Quantum wholes are always greater than the sum of their parts. This is true in metal alloys and it's also true for groups. We're more together than we are apart. Only by putting the parts of a former whole into what may look like a virtual whole, as completed jig saw puzzles try to look, can you restore the pieces of a supposed whole into the semblance of a true whole. This is an important and difficult conceptual/perceptual change for any who will switch from the Newtonian paradigm to the quantum one. You must speak actively and tentatively in quantum if it is to work. But you're taught to speak passively and with certainty in the Newtonian framework if you want to do things right, forgetting about the higher level of doing right things creatively.

"Attitudes of a few about the nature of the universe and consciousness shifted as physicists attempted to gain more fundamental understanding of what their mathematics told them was necessary for a more adequate correspondence between their models and their observations. The search for more fundamental concepts persisted in physics in marked contrast to the habits we Newtonian career psychologists and counselors ordinarily exhibit of accepting the empirical with little or no thought into more far-reaching principles which unfold understanding, not mere satisfaction."

"Since Miller-Tiedeman introduced many of these principles to the Career Development field in 1983 and in subsequent publications (Miller-Tiedeman & Tiedeman, 1983; Miller-Tiedeman, 1982, 1985, 1987, 1988, 1989, 1992a, 1992b), said David, "I want to comment on one in particular and then on the principle of error. These are useful as you teach your University of Universe students about quantum careering. That way you help move these principles into more active use in our now so empirically-defined, Newtonian-based, career psychology. You can refer to Chapter 3 for more quantum principles.

Principle 1: In Logical Positivistic Science, Errors Are Basically Kept Minimal

"In both psychology and physics, measures are picked or constructed to minimize error but from different centers. In quantum mechanics, error is the seeming nuisance tolerated because one cannot predict with 100% accuracy. The uncertainty principle in physics awakens us to the fact that we are never going to predict with 100% accuracy: We cannot know everything; we cannot guide to any ultimate truth for another. On the other hand, the maximization of individual differences, as in psychometrics, separates individuals from their personal understanding, not from an ideal. By orienting thought to least errors around a group's average, psychometrics does not tell us anything about the individual's life journey. We need interpersonal data for that purpose but you do know something about life journey in physics, you know that all of physics is intrapersonal even though mostly theoretical."

The young professor then said, "Then the research will need to change, won't it?"

"Yes. Just notice some language of research—like dependent and independent variables. This assumes people can be reduced to a set of meaningful variables specifying persons and situations. When you elevate the individual to theory maker, those assumptions won't work. But the process remains the same. Reason and Rowan (1981) suggest that new paradigm research is a systematic approach to inquiry, a rigorous search for truth, which does not kill off all it touches. This new approach can be seen as a synthesis of naive inquiry and orthodox research.

"Another aspect of new paradigm research is making clear where one is coming from in taking a particular view. That is why I earlier shared a brief history of both science and the New Careering. Traditionally that is done by references to previous work. But Reason and Rowan (1981) consider it important to politics, current work, and relationships because it's a general way of being in the world. They suggest that acknowledging intellectual debt ought to go back even to ancient times, not just the last five years, which most computer search systems now offer. In literature reviews, however, new paradigm research works across disciplines incorporating works of philosophy, theology, history, literature, and multidisciplinary searches with the social sciences. 'We ought to watch that we don't fall in love with our numerics as they can be precise but not true. Statistical significance may have no human use and 'in human inquiry it is much better to be deeply interesting than accurately boring'" (p. xiv).

Principle 2: Non-Local Connections

"In the sub-atomic realm, changing the spin of a particle in Vancouver simultaneously counter-rotates a particle in Montreal, speaking figuratively, that is. Interestingly, the non-local connection seems to operate at a speed exceeding light.

"In career, we keep looking at what is. But every *what is* exists with a *what is not*. Furthermore *what is not* ordinarily possesses more powerful energies than *what is*, particularly when you consider that 99.9% of observable reality is invisible (Fuller, 1981). Similarly, we learn more from those things that don't work out than we do by the smooth flow of life. When we learn to take in all of life with interpretation and a modicum of judgment, we tune to the whole of our experience. Our intuitions serve as the non-local connections within incisive detail. When we give these non-local, intuitive connections opportunity to guide us, we find magical things can happen."

The second graduate student, with a worried look said, "This whole business of process scares me. I worry that we'll each start growing in different ways and directions and everything will fall apart."

The young professor hurriedly said, "You're forgetting about self-organizing systems. We may fall apart and decide our current group isn't for us. But then we turn around and surprisingly find a new group very friendly to our ideas. It seems we get tunnel vision thinking that the group we're in is the only group and nothing else exists. That's just where humanity currently stands in its evolution. But enough people now break out and find new groups and that courages the rest of us."

The first graduate student asked, "Why did you make 'courage' a verb?"

David replied, "Because when you start thinking motion and movement, many nouns metamorphose into verbs. Bohm (1980) has a chapter on the need for a new language. He knew this would buzz grammarians, but even they can't escape progress in understanding."

"That's enough for now," David said. "I'll conclude our discussion by looking back.

Toward Re-Integration

Stop and Look Back

"The quest for accuracy, flexibility, speed, wholeness, and more complexity in human/nature interactions intensified in the twentieth century. Humans brought science out of musty academic closets into the public domain. By century's end, science seemed as much at home in education of the public via radio and TV talk shows, educational programs, and entertainment as it was in schools and colleges. Politicians and commentators delight in telling who is leading whom in what kind of "scientific poll." Probability, DNA, the impossibility of having anything humans think they know being known with certainty, figure mightily in the recent life-or-death trial of an accused murderer who had been an outstanding football player.

"Economics, psychology, counseling presently get so specialized that citizens frequently can't cope with not knowing which pea of truth is under which of several thousands of shells the gods of chance shuffle under our noses. Fortunately, nature's self-correcting properties save humans when busted for gambling. "Ante-up, or quit" begins flashing in their minds, warning that more than money is now at stake—reputation, foolish use of credit, death, and little matters like that. Finally, some (the unaware ones) realize they play a losing game if playing against a large bank (and life is such a large bank) and play is of sufficiently long duration (and life has been around longer than any one of us) for the bank to win on size and endurance."

Listen and Notice Progress

"In similar vein, the 'bean counters' of banking are at present, quietly but openly, literally putting money out of circulation. Credit cards now name the money game and have practically become the 'coin of the realm.'

"America will downsize from Galbraith's affluent society into what I foresee a 'Junior Galbraith' may write: [The New America: The Credit Society]. In a credit society, banks and government will happily extend you their credit 'service' if putting your money to their profit requires granting you more credit. Banks and governments will know how each of us stands. Don't expect to know that yourself. Sure, banks and governments will reveal where they know you stand whenever asked. But neither you nor banks nor governments can adjust your account balances for the time lapse between their last entry and your last expenditure or payment request. That's the complementarity principle at work. You don't know or care what system the accountants use and they don't know what you have done in the last millionth of a second when you made your last electronic transfer to your Swiss bank account (that's the uncertainty principle).

"You don't have to tease yourself long and arduously with the discourse of these risks humans and nature accept as they make seemingly risky existential decisions before you undermine your confidence. So let's return to understanding how humans and nature learn to converse and cooperate."

Allow Quantum Careering

"The key to moving forward in life, whether in job or in general, is found by a cooperative relationship with life. The key to that improvement will be found in support of individual's unfoldments toward ever more perfect manifestations of themselves as atomic energy rather than as atomic particles (Bohm, 1980). This seems to be present conventional thinking of physicists. Energy is the most basic force in universe. Einstein's simple relationship between energy and particles, namely $E = mc^2$, where c equals the speed of light, governs the transformation of energy from one manifestation to the other and returns. The relationship is complementary, reciprocating.

"The change process inheres in the reciprocating relationship of energy and particles. That change process functions as a self-organizing system. Give yourself to that change process with understanding and you will not alone begin to know of self-organizing systems in general, you will also discern new means of understanding consciousness and spirit.

"This has been an exciting discussion. So many possible futures. And, I express deep gratitude to each of you. Your interest and thought impress me. I can well see how you all get on so well."

David admitted to himself the road had been long and tiring and uncertainty a constant companion while his new learning hadn't yet become familiar. That brought a silent chuckle to David as he thought, 'God must have loved ambiguity as he created so much of it.' But that's the oil in the wheel of life he concluded.

Au Revoir

At this juncture in my own quantum career, I join my faith with Anna Miller-Tiedeman and Dr. Lee Richmond, who has worked with us for a decade to leave for posterity what we three believe has endless life for those daring to appreciate the 99% invisible in the universe (Fuller, 1981).

We leave you with these good Irish wishes to accompany you on your personal journey to spirit in life:

As you walk courageously into your own quantum experience:

> May the road rise up to meet you
> as you consider yourself a theory maker.
>
> May the wind always be at your back
> as you reach for higher understanding.
>
> May the sun shine warm upon your face
> when you need support.
> The rains fall soft upon your fields
> when you need nourishment.
>
> And until we meet again,
> may God hold you in his all-encompassing
> quantum consciousness—
> today's ultimate state of oneness.

—Adapted from an old Irish poem

☐ Discussion Questions

1. After reading the chapter, what was your first thought?

2. What impressed you most?

3. What brought questions to your mind?

4. What do you want to know more about?

5. What relationship does the content have to your life?

☐ Classroom/Group Exercises

1. Choose a partner and talk about where you were aware that your focus on one thing caused you to miss other things (complementarity). A fairly common example is driving down the freeway and missing your exit because you had your focus on something else.

2. Change partners and discuss some common experiential examples of uncertainty? Downsizing would qualify in today's work environment.

3. With the same partner, discuss your view of *error* in life what some may call mistakes.

4. Form into triads, and work with the following Prigogine quote: "We are part of nature and nature is part of us. And, we can recognize ourselves by the descriptions we give to it." This means that whatever you see and like in your external environment, that is you. Whatever you do not like, well, that is you too.

   Example: You attend a lecture. Afterward, you say to your friend, "That was a boring lecturer." Your friend says, "It didn't work for me." Which of these responses recognizes self ownership?

☐ Homework Assignment

1. Not uncommon in the counseling field is the phrase "that's not realistic." In a two-page paper discuss reality in both Newtonian and Quantum terms.

2. Write a short paragraph detailing the importance of the quantum definition of reality as it is manifest in both professional and everyday life.

2

PRACTICING THE NEW CAREERING: THE *HOW* QUESTION

The New Careering builds its theoretical foundation on quantum physics, which assumes the whole is greater than the sum of the parts. So, the *how* looks quite different from that of traditional career. Two major differences that impact the *how* are (1) each person spins his or her own theory (from experience), and (2) he or she lives that theory. So, the New Careering is a lived not a chosen phenomenon which, of course, includes work. The order is reversed in the New Careering. The focus is on making a life while making a living, not just the latter. Therefore, the *how* is not so much *how to do* it as it is *how to undo* former career development notions, perceptions, paradigms, and attitudes that stand in the way of helping individuals recognize and find value in their individual theories, recognizing life as a partner in the life direction process. That is why paradigms and how you language your life direction challenge become so important in the New Careering. Think about the word "unfold." How many times have you heard it in your career development training? *Unfold* means to develop, to come forth slowly as the life process moves forward. How many times have you discussed the language of career development and its effect on both you and your client?

The *how* in the New Careering is more like that of a mediator listening first to the client's stories, following the dictates of the client's reality. So, a large part of the *how* of the New Careering becomes the unlearning of many 20th-Century career development ideas and theories that separated us from our wholeness, causing us to yearn for our deeper selves. When we get to that deeper place we will find a wealth of experienced-based information, including stories that will help those we interact with as well as our clients become more present in their bodies, reclaim their individual realities, and know the joy of the present moment.

CHAPTER

Anna Miller-Tiedeman

The New Careering (Lifecareer®) Practice

☐ **Part I**

Spotlight on Twenty-First-Century Career Counseling

By the year 2050, career development as we know it today may be totally irrelevant. Many issues we've fought over, preserved turf over, will fall into disuse and dysfunction. The market for tests and measurement in job choice will have declined, as children will mature vocationally with the help of their parents and the technology, and they won't ask questions like today's children do in regard to work. Many of them will have been entrepreneurial from a very young age. Some children will have written plays and books by the time they enter their teen years. Others will have invented needed items, and many others will be busy at work on inherent talents and gifts. They will be the generation better equipped to answer the question, "Why am I here?"

These children also will live life as career as a matter of course. They will wonder why we ever had to write about it as they will know it so well experientially. While we had to learn to dance on a shifting carpet, they will not notice the rug shifts, and will, therefore, dance with great skill and perhaps invent new ways to do it.

In the meantime, helping professionals will work with individuals and groups assisting them in understanding that life is a whole fabric even though the design keeps changing. These twenty-first-century professionals will reengineer career counseling, helping individuals honor their uniqueness. They will teach and offer personal examples of how to weed out the negative self-talk that stops many life directions from maturing. They will use their understanding of the New (Quantum) Careering to repair the breach caused by separating individuals from their basic instinctual selves. They will also know how to appropriately weave parts of traditional career in when necessary. But most of all, they will serve as *bridgers* who will say, "Come on across to the new. It's okay and I'll not only help you across, I'll be a support when you arrive. Because I, too, need that support and community."

But we are here and they are not yet here, so we'll work to build a bridge for them to walk across into the land of wholeness where they can unfold and offer their gifts to a growing world (Miller-Tiedeman, 1997).

☐ Looking Ahead

Watch for the following important topics:

1. Maturing individual career theories (re-visiting one's own story and re-visioning it)

2. Reengineering and the work environment

3. The job and the journey client

4. The electronic and new paper resume

5. The personal home page

6. On-line job search / a word about career testing

7. Focus on action taken

8. Encouragement and new possibilities groups

9. Portfolio career and career portfolios

10. Turning Lifecareer theory into practice for the job client

11. How paradigms and development surface in career counseling

Maturing Individual Career Theories
(Re-Visioning Personal Possibilities)

Prologue to Practice

When you live Life-As -Career, (either deliberately [journey] or randomly [job]) you cooperate with approaching forces while assessing the situation—a recurrent theme in this book. You make decisions, move on, learn more, make mistakes (or left turns) that provide additional information, then sometimes deliberately make left turns in order to learn faster. All this leads back to your own knowing, to that spiritual place in yourself where you connect, to that place so enchanting you can not help but return. Then you recognize you are on the journey.

This chapter divides into two parts: Part I deals with both the job and the journey client and Part II, turning theory into practice. Most people work throughout their lives, then at some point, the journey becomes more important. But it usually takes a higher level of personal development to recognize and embrace the journey, as it reflects the hero's journey Joseph Campbell writes about in *The Hero with a Thousand Faces*. The hero has more than his or her share of trials and tribulations, meets many tests, forms numerous alliances, and confronts enemies along the journey. All this culminates in the supreme ordeal. Everyone has an opportunity to choose the hero's journey, but not all will accept.

On the other hand, as work becomes more difficult to find, the job client will experience a fast forward in the direction of the journey. At that point he or she will find the sleeping genius that has been there all along. In the meantime, both the journey and job client need to generate an income. But several factors coalesce to make earning a living potentially more difficult.

The Reengineering Threat. Threatening income generation is the reengineering now starting to sweep corporate America. Jeremy Rifkin (1995), in his book *The End of Work: The Decline of the Global Labor Force and the Dawn of the Post-Market Era*, notes that "United States corporations are eliminating more than 2 million jobs annually" (p. 3). And while new jobs are being created, they tend to be in the lower bottom of the wage pyramid. Rifkin goes on to say that this trimming of jobs is not unique to the American economy. He cited Siemens, the German electronic and engineering giant, which has cut costs by 20 to 30% and eliminated more than 16,000 employees around the world.

Corporations in other countries presently follow this trend, swelling the ranks of the unemployed and underemployed (around 800 million) in

North America, Europe, and Japan. The young vent their frustration through antisocial behavior and older workers caught in this net of little possibility tend to feel trapped in social forces over which they have no control. As one woman with a master's degree in counseling put it, "We never dreamed that at age 62, we'd be going from job to job, just to keep our house and buy our medication."

As this book goes to print, corporations are substituting smart machines for human labor in most all occupational areas. When you consider that 75% of the labor force in many industrial nations work jobs that require little more than simple repetitive tasks, just think how vulnerable these jobs are to replacement by machine. In the United States, more than 90 million jobs in a labor force of 124 million would be at risk. And with current surveys showing that approximately 5% of the companies around the world have started to make this shift, massive unemployment in the future could result (Rifkin, 1995). Of course, Rifkin could be wrong in his judgment, but building an entrepreneurial safety net can soften the effect if he turns out right.

That provides an important reason why helping professionals need to educate clients about the many ways individuals earn income (see Table 8.1) ranging from entrepreneurship, considered a high-risk approach, to full-time work, noted as having a lower risk. However, in the twenty-first century, that idea may flip flop as the present lower risk occupations may become high risk due to their temporary nature.

The Global Economy.   Living in a global economy means young people will compete both internationally and nationally. For instance, many businesses now go to India for software engineers. Corporations have requested and were granted permission to bring in over 150,000 people from other countries to work American jobs, claiming that they could not find qualified Americans for this work. you may say, "Oh well, that's only 150,000, that's not much. It won't matter." Think again, as that's just the beginning of more individuals coming in for those cream jobs you would like either for yourself or your children.

Another example, Met Life now has a claims office in Ireland. That's more American jobs located somewhere else. Not only do American companies go abroad and recruit, they also take jobs out of the country, and this seriously affects work in America. This may seem distant and remote and not about your life when you read this. But like a small pebble thrown into a lake whose ripples go out to the end, the ripples from the globalization of work will ultimately impact all of us. Nothing happens in a vacuum.

Downsizing Forces.   Many people who planned for a secure future often end up on the streets or very close to being in that condition. Sally

TABLE 8.1. Work Alternative Hierarchy

High Risk
Entrepreneurship
Consulting
Contracting
Self-employment
Network marketing,
   selling utilities,
   phone services,
   and products such as
   as Amway, Shacklee,
   and similar ventures
	Values:	Risk, challenge, variety,
		flexibility, initiative, freedom

Moderate Risk Agent Talent pooling	Values:	Working with others, networking, advocating for another, selling, flexibility, initiative, freedom
Lower Risk Work sharing Job sharing Multi-tracking Full employment	Values:	Connection, stability, structure, following orders, hard money, regular income

Adapted from *Understanding Work Alternatives*, Centre for Career Development Innovation, 1994, p. 11.

and her husband John were well-educated people. Both had earned master's degrees, but both were forced onto the downsizing conveyor belt.

Then there's the research chemist who burned up in his cardboard shack in Los Angeles several years ago. I'm sure he didn't plan to be homeless. None of us wants to end up without the basic necessities. Contrary to conventional wisdom, that can happen even to the best in the society.

Jane attended college, majored in Accounting and graduated. She was hired by a prestigious firm and thought she had her future fairly well secured. Two years later, she feels uncertain about her continued employment due to a merger. Twenty years ago or maybe even ten, when you graduated from college, you could look forward to continued employment, but today's work world looks very different.

Education and Downsizing.   Many parents continue to push their children toward higher education on the basis of the Department of Labor statistics that the more education you get the more money you make. While true as a generality, specifically that argument falls apart. Downsizing can hit anyone anywhere regardless of age or educational level. Most every day the newspapers carry information about hundreds and often thousands of employees being downsized or from the company perspective "rightsized." You don't have to look too far to see how technology almost daily takes on a job once done by one person or numbers of people. According to Jeremy Rifkin, between 1979 and 1992, the Fortune 500 companies presented 4.4 million of their employees with pink slips. The handwriting on the wall now suggests that in the twenty-first century we could see the end of jobs as we know them today.

Looking in my neighborhood, three to four houses have gone up for sale due to loss of job. Some of these people had held their jobs for 20 years thinking they were secure, only to discover they're in the same position as they started out—unemployed.

Life, for its own reasons, placed human personal development in the economic arena. As each person works out his or her own economic future, the growth taking place will surpass anything present in today's education arena. Many paradigms will shift, personal pride will be forced aside, new work options will be considered (see Table 8.1), and new behaviors initiated—all of which will provide profound learning, personal and professional change.

New Careering (Lifecareer) Principles Revisted

Even through the job and journey client have been discussed in separate parts of the chapter, both face common challenges which the Lifecareer principles address. For that reason, we review three of the major principles for Lifecareer practice below (see checklist at end of this chapter).

Major Principle: Life-Is-Career

The three New (Quantum) Careering principles discussed in Chapter 3 are restated here for practice purposes. The first principle suggests that life is the big career and each person has a career theory which embodies that individual's beliefs and values which form the foundation for all decisions. Translating this to practice, the New Careering Developer wants to support the maturing career theory of each client with whom she or he works.

This happens when you:

- relax the client and support his or her present action;

- identify negative self-talk;
- actively listen and reframe the client's story to make sure you've heard it correctly;
- track negative, positive, and behavior-altering self-talk;
- track reoccurring ideas;
- identify bridge points;
- educate about the broader meaning of career;
- educate about the connectedness of all things including stress;
- educate about conscious breathing;
- tell the economic story of our time;
- check out financial status;
- check out health problems;
- assist the client in developing a short-term scenario; and
- introduce clients to the career portfolio.

Principle 8: Both Right Decisions and Left Decisions (Those Things That Do Not Work) Have Value

This is a necessary condition for maturing one's career theory and telling one's story.

You can identify the approach taken by:

- listening to client language;
- inferring a belief system based in the language;
- identifying values in language;
- tracking the decisions made as a result of beliefs and values; and
- listening for outcome admonishments and reinforcing action statements in the language.

Principle 1: The Self-Organizing Properties of Life Reduce the Necessity for Control

The litmus test for whether or not clients invoke a self-organizing philosophy is:

- high stress;

- working harder or smarter without much to show for it;

- working against the grain of life;

- not knowing when to let go;

- going after things that do not and most likely will not work;

- taking a make-it-happen approach;

- ignoring the things to which they feel attracted in favor of material gains; and

- language reflecting the Conforming stage of development.

Two Types of Clients—
The Job and the Journey Client

The Job Client

Most helping professionals see clients who experience a need for some kind of transition, whether changing jobs, changing major fields, or looking for a job as a result of downsizing. In this global economy, sometimes it takes anywhere from six months to two years to find work again, sometimes even longer. During that time, expenses continue which tend to result in high stress and frustration. Prolonged unemployment depresses individuals and decreases their self-esteem. All this mitigates against motivation, which connects to lethargy, dampening potential new ideas about work options. Further, the lack of connection to work also leaves the client without social interaction and without a feeling of belonging. Freud once observed that to love and to work forms a healthy foundation for life. The global economy now in the making threatens that foundation.

Remember the game of musical chairs where everyone walked around several chairs while the music played. Then when the music stopped, you grabbed a chair. But one slight problem—one person would be without a chair. Each round of the game, a chair would be removed until only one remained. At this moment, we're playing musical jobs so most job-hunters are not happy campers. Many feel they're up an industrial creek without an information and service paddle.

The financial reality is that most people cannot experience long-term unemployment—mortgages, and fixed expenses being what they are. Some have financial resources, but most do not and an urgent need continues, that of finding work. Recently, a potential client called and said something like, "I'm looking for someone to help me find a job I can work for the rest of my life and then retire from." While most people have more insight than that, a tendency still exists to deny that work as we have known it—permanent, full time, and long term—will not be as available as before (Barnet, 1993; Rifkin, 1995).

But that is then and we are here and now. So, what can we do, with clients and community groups to help buttress the psychology of those people thrown back into job hunting due to downsizing? In today's world, placing your qualifications before the eyes of thousands of employers all at the same time ranks as a number one priority. You do this by writing and filing an electronic resume.

The Electronic Resume.   A computer, not human eyes, scans your resume. Then OCR software converts it into editable ASCII text. If you use italic, script or other fancy fonts, underlining, or bold print, the OCR software will stumble. Garbled text then enters a potential employer's computer, which may or may not get cleaned up. So, keep it simple. Use a 12-point font (Times, Courier, or New Schoolbook). Avoid using all caps. And substitute the dash for the bulleted points. Finally, all information is typed flush with the left margin, which does not make it too eye appealing, but it works just fine for the computer (Kennedy & Morrow, 1994).

How Does an Electronic Resume Differ from a Paper One?   Electronic resumes use nouns called keywords, not action verbs as in the old resume. A keyword identifies special skills, job titles, awards received, schooling and/or degrees earned. Any noun makes a good keyword. The applicant with the most keywords wins. No kidding.

Another important difference—you can use your electronic resume as a paper resume, but the computer cannot read the old action-verb resume.

How Do You Write an Electronic Resume?   Start it like a regular resume with your name, address, phone number at the top. Remember, all information is typed flush with the left margin. Drop down two spaces and type keywords. According to Kennedy and Morrow (1994) the more keywords, the better your chances of selection, so spend time creating your keyword list.

A favorite format places a strength list after the keyword summary. You might include something like, "good people skills, communication skills, team player, leads by example." In other words, showcase your strengths. This list could help you during an interview.   The remainder of the resume presents standard information on your experience in chrono-logical order or by function using job title. When describing past experi-ence, avoid long text paragraphs, use bulleted points (instead of the dash) as in a list, because keywords do most of the work in the resume. Finally, add your education and/or awards (see Appendix C for sample).

How Long Should an Electronic Resume Be?   With the new elec-tronic resume, you can forget the "one page only" advice. A good rule of thumb might be, for a new graduate, one page; for most people, one to two pages; and for senior executives, two to three pages. But an electronic resume should probably never exceed four pages. When you finish your electronic resume, save a second copy on the computer. Use it for your paper resume to send out to selected employers. On this resume, add back in your bold or italic designations, as people, not computers, will read it.

Cover letters are useful if you're aiming for a top management job or responding to an ad. In your cover letter, do not repeat information in your resume.

Think Twice Before Sending Multiple Resumes to the Same Company.   With the improved applicant-tracking systems, multiple re-sumes can make you look confused. If you shape your resume for differ-ent jobs at the same company, you may look like different people and this could raise questions. So, send one resume per company whether elec-tronically or through the mail.

Electronic Resume Database Companies.   Some resume data com-panies charge anywhere from $10 to $75 per year to enter your resume in their data bank. A good rule—use the free data banks first, like E-Span (1-800-681-2901). However, before you do anything, go to the Internet and look up the on-line career centers to identify other places to file your re-sume. Military personnel can file their resume on the Department of De-fense Resume Service (DORS).

The New Paper Resume.   The new paper resume follows a similar format to the electronic resume. However, the format returns to an eye-appealing document that will be read by an individual. So, center the head-ing, bold up Experience and Education as headings. However, the short descriptions are maintained, not the long action-verb paragraphs. You can use a dash or a bullet with your short descriptions (see sample in Appen-dix C). In addition, the heading Keywords is changed to Key Information. Remember keywords are nouns and the one with most keywords wins

(Kennedy & Morrow, 1994). So, dedicate time to developing a good key-word list. Placing information at the top of the resume makes it even a quicker read than the old one-page action-verb resume. Key Information might look like the following:

Key Information

Management. Design Consultant. Writing. Assessment. Site Survey. Graphic Design. Floor Plans. Budget Manager. Quality Control. Testing and Evaluation. Technical Handbooks. BA Architecture. Assistant Architect New Mexico State University. Chief Drafter. Supervisor. Project Officer. Department Manager. Air Defense Controller. Operations Officer. Administration Officer. Training Officer. Technical Training Officer. Fiscal Officer. Senior Air Director. Top Gun. Weapons and Tactics Instructor. Navy Commendation. Air Force Commendation. National Defense. Commanding Generals Certificate of Commendation. Business Owner. Bookkeeper. Communications Specialist. Neuro-Linguistics Trainer. Certified Mediator. Software Testing.

A woman with twenty years of experience at the same company recently experienced downsizing within the company. Her Key Information list looked like this:

Case-Load Manager. Supervision. In-Service Training. San Diego Office Audit Coordinator. Alternative Dispute Resolution Program. Beginning and Advanced Supervisory Skills. Continuing Education. Certified Self-Insurance Plan Administrator. California Polytechnic University. Business Management.

The Personal Home Page.   If you want to put a new spin on a very old idea, take the advice of Jay Wilkerson in the Walden University Liaison Office at Indiana University. He reports that information technology students now design personal web pages. Many people think that home pages are just for businesses who sell items and services. While partially correct, remember your business is selling yourself. What better way to do this than through a home page that gets world exposure.

Here is Jay's suggestion: First build a home page. You can do it yourself or take a class at a local community college, business college, or four-year college, or hire someone to do it for you. If you have a friend with technical expertise, he or she may do that for a very reasonable fee. You also might ask a student in a Web Page Design class to use your page as his or her project.

After students activate their home page, they send a paper copy of it along with their resume to companies for which they want to work. They also invite the search committee to visit their home page for additional information. If you would like to visit one of those pages, use the following URL (address): http://www-slis.lib.indiana.edu//Students/resumes.html. Be sure to use a dash not a period after www and capitalize the S in "students."

On-Line Job Searching.   The possibilities for job search on line stretch to infinity. You need only go on the World-Wide Web, choose a search engine, and type "employment" and any descriptors you choose. Miller-Tiedeman chose Infoseek® and typed in "employment" and up came the *On-Line Career Center*, touted as The Internet's First and Foremost Career Center. They claim to have 451,827 bits of information. This Center has a database of employment ads, candidate resumes, and other career-related information available to the 20 million plus Internet users. The Center is available on Gopher, the World-Wide Web (WWW), Mosaic, WAIS, Infoseek®, and e-mail, in addition to traditional Usenet Newsgroups.

Among the things you can search are *Home Employment, Self-Employment Link Page, Links to Employment Sites and Pages, The Mother of All Employment and Jobs*, and *Official Job Center Mirror Site* where you can post your resume. The site also offers tips and examples. A *Federal Government Employment Opportunities Area*, a Canadian employment site, and an *About Australia—Employment Opportunities* site. You can search the world for jobs at this center.

Another link leads to the *Mother of All Employment and Jobs* (see Table 8.2); this site offers everything you might imagine, like, *Career Avenue*, a place where you can post your resume and search for a new jobs; *Build Your Future*, a searchable database of resumes for employers seeking employees; *Best Jobs in the USA Today*, services for job seekers and employers. You can post or read resumes, employment ads from *USA Today* and other media, job fair listings, career store, recruitment advertising, healthcare employment and more.

The Online Job Search Companion (Gonyea, 1995) provides information on how to do electronic career planning and job hunting, how to utilize electronic bulletin board systems, and contains an introduction to the *American Online Career Center*.

Online job search adds another level to the job finding process. Those not accessing jobs on computer frequently find themselves with less job possibilities. The Internet will change career planning in ways we cannot yet imagine.

Judy Kaplan Baron (personal communication, April 16, 1997), a nationally certified career counselor, now holds the position of Assistant Director of the American Online Career Center. How do you think she got that job? She merely logged on her server, checked out the career area

**Table 8.2 The Mother of All Employment and Jobs
(Partial List)**

B. F. Services: For those individuals looking for something new. You can browse through help-wanted ads or find out how to place your resume on the Internet.

Candidate Pool: Offers candidates to be hired without placement fees. Companies can receive unlimited resumes and have unlimited searches for one annual fee.

Capital Region Employment Network: Provides listings of resumes, jobs, company profiles, job fairs, and hosting services.

Career & Resume Management for the 21st: Professional career and resume services for job seekers, employers, recruiters, and related personnel.

Career Connector: Job search engine.

Career Exposure: Direct access to corporate job postings. Search for a job or research a company.

CareerAmerica: Employment center on the Web providing a job bank and resume bank.

CareerCity: Search the job data bases and submit your resume online.

CareerExchange: Searchable job/career database, covering a broad spectrum of professional employment opportunities. Free for job seekers.

Career Exposure: Search for a job, career opportunities, corporate membership.

Classified Employment Digest: Listing of hundreds of employers who hire those with a security clearance.

ConsultantSee Network: A free resource designed to help hiring managers looking for independent consultants, freelance professionals, and small businesses.

Contractors Direct: Free data base of contractors, freelancers, and self-employed people available for employment, contracts, or jobs. Employers can search for the skills they need.

Table 8.2 continues on page 194.

Table 8.2.   *Continued*

Drushim On-Line: Israeli job offers in the fields of hi-tech, medicine, and science.

Eagle Visions: National directory of police and fire safety employment.

Eastern and Central European Job Bank: A free resource for job seekers worldwide and for employers in Central and Eastern Europe.

ExeCon Information System: Large database of jobs in all industries and functions. Employment mailing lists. Free to job seekers.

FastWEB Classified: Tailored search of employment opportunities across the United States, available free to students.

Future Access Employment Guide: Add your resume or view resumes from all over the world for free.

London Careers:

Malaysia Online: Recruitment agency offering jobs in Malaysia.

Minnesota Jobs: Lists of technical and non-technical jobs and resumes in Minnesota. Access free with no registration.

Resume Canada: Post or view resumes free, post or view career opportunities free.

Work-Web: Local and national employment, resumes, jobs, colleges, training, and other information. Free to employers and job seekers.

WorkOnline Network Systems: Search for jobs in the United States and Canada.

and started answering on-line questions. She did not think much about that until she got an e-mail from the Director of the American Online Career Center who informed her she was doing his job. He then inquired about her background, they talked, and today she holds the position of Assistant Director.

In short, the Internet overflows with resume posting places and job opportunities. You only need a computer, a server to hook you to the Internet, and motivation.

On-line job hunting is exciting, fast, easy, and convenient. But encourage clients to play both sides of the job hunting street—get on the electronic wires and send resumes by mail.

International Job Search. Job hunters now compete in a world market, not just a national one. As mentioned earlier, companies like Metropolitan Life employ 150 workers in a village in County Cork, Ireland, to process claims from all over the world. These workers cost 30% less than American workers, and due to the scarcity of work in Ireland—with 1.1 million jobs and 3.5 million people—very little turnover results (Barnet, 1993).

The world is a rich pool of both professional and non-professional workers who will work for a fraction of a U.S. salary. So, while we helping professionals sit in our offices ticking off possible American job opportunities, American and multinational corporations are looking over the world market, the cheaper cost of labor, and deciding how they will play the job game with individuals. If this trend continues, work opportunities for American young people will continue to shrink if they look only in the United States. Thinking internationally will not occur overnight, but over time, it will.

We should, therefore, encourage students and young people to at least explore international work possibilities, which can be done on the Internet at most public libraries, or ask a friend who has a computer to help one go on line. In addition, young workers starting out have much to gain by working outside the United States.

A Word About Career Testing

Testing has its place and usefulness. The problem in the career field is overuse of testing to the point that individuals think a test will tell them what they should do. Most helping professionals know that is not true, but somehow what we do has had that effect. We need to change how we're using tests to counter that message.

Career tests work well in public education before students have much work and life experience. Tests often help students organize emerging interests. While students do request testing, many of these students fail to return for their results. But those who do find the information helpful. Career tests also help women returning to the world of work. It provides another piece of information for them.

On the other hand, if a client has at least five years of experience, testing may be unnecessary. By the end of the first session, the client will know whether or not testing will help. Also, most clients have a clear understanding of what they do not like and that can be as informing as knowing what you like to do. Many helping professionals have had the experience of seeing a client who requested testing to start with, but after the first session decided it was not necessary. The other side of the testing equation is money, as many helping professionals make substantial income from testing. So, to test or not to test connects to the helping professional's career theory and his or her need for income. Testing in the helping professions, like in the medical area, tend to be high income generators.

When career testing is used, look for a battery that, when combined, offers more information than any of its tests separately. For instance, the Career Occupational Preference System (COPS) (Educational & Industrial Testing Service [Edits], 1974/1982) surveys interests. The Career Orientation Placement & Evaluation Survey (COPES) (Knapp, R. & Knapp, L., 1977/1981), tests values important in work and other activities. The Career Ability Placement Survey (CAPS) (Educational and Industrial Training Service, 1976), in eight five-minute periods assesses four basic skills and four aptitudes. When scores from these three tests (all published by Edits) are used as scaled, and combined, you usually find one to three occupational areas where interests, abilities, and values match. This alignment provides a higher order information. Other sets of tests most likely exist that offer the *merge of information* arrangement. They deserve consideration as they tend to produce a higher quality of information.

Before going on to the journey client, Miller-Tiedeman offers an apology for any part she played in the overall impression now existing among many people that a test can tell them what they should do with their lives. Even though no helping professional Miller-Tiedeman knows admits to leaving this impression, it is there. Somewhere along the way, career counselors bear responsibility for that impression. And, perhaps an open apology might at least start trickling down to the person on the street, suggesting that no on knows what anyone else ought to do at any time, or anywhere, not even a test.

The Journey Client

The journey client follows his or her Career Compasss and constantly takes readings to inform his or her decisions. This does not ususaly include following trends and projections, however, he or she may find him- or herself in the flow of the trend simply because it aligns with the internal notions of what feels right next.

The job client works life from the outside in, and the journey client from the inside out. The journey client comes closest to asking the question, "Why am I here?" Certainly not just to eat and sleep and buy things. The job client is more concerned with making money to own things. This does not suggest that the journey client is not interested in things, gadgets, travel, and all the things money will buy. It simply means that material things do not top the priority list. Both job clients and journey clients work jobs unless they are independently rich, but their intentions about life differ, sometimes radically.

The journey client might take the following approach:

During childhood, I loved *teeter totters*. However, I didn't find the teeter totter of life direction as much fun until I recognized it as just that—a *teeter totter*. So when things become blurred, I know I'm on the down side of the *teeter totter*, and that somehow helps me through the maze of confusion. At this point, I try not to think too much about it. This does not suggest that I always know what to do or where I'm going. But I am quite comfortable with not knowing too much about what I'm doing. I just have utter confidence that what I am doing is right even if I am staring off into space, riding along Pacific Coast Highway, or wondering what to do next.

Even though I don't focus on *lack of direction*, I keep busy making contacts and collecting information because I know that I will eventually be informed. To focus on *lack* is to drain energy, and I need all the energy I can muster for the transition process.

Second, I have high respect for the intelligence in *Life* and the consciousness in all things. So, I keep unfolding my love affair with *Life* doing all I know to do and waiting for the wonderful surprises that arise as a result.

When I can't seem to get it together, I don't force it. I just let time pass and see what happens next and do whatever occurs to me. That may be making a list of my uncertainties, or talking with someone who can give me another perspective on things.

One major reason I can relax is that I know that *Life* is self-organizing, that I can trust it. Further, I know that *Life* is both a right and left proposition. If it doesn't go right, it will go left and therein will be the learning. Along with trusting *Life*, I know that *Life* works—not always the way I want it to, but it works.

Third, I only have a life direction problem when I think about it. Thought appears as both a gift and a curse. When I use my thought to support my creativity and activity, it feels like a gift. When I use it to *judge* my progress, it is a curse. This doesn't mean I don't give thought to life direction. I do. But if I can't get a cue, I don't *judge* that, I just take another step and wait for more information to come in. Sometimes the information comes quickly, and sometimes it takes months. Whatever the time frame, I don't judge that either.

When my life direction doesn't seem to make sense, I give it time and space. Because I know that when the timing is right, I always know what to do. I don't have to ask, "What do I do now?" It resembles love; you don't need to ask someone, "Am I in love now?" You know. The same holds true for life direction.

Fourth, I have learned that I can't leap-frog over the *uncertainty* and *waiting* period and go to *certainty* and *choice*. So, I don't use energy trying to do that. Furthermore, I now value the *thought fluctuations* that cause blurring of the focus, as I know that something new is in the making. And I don't try to immediately unravel it. I honor and value its process, even though at times it feels like "the valley of the shadow of death" as spoken about in the 23rd Psalm.

The *uncertainty* period has helped me see life direction as a *teeter totter;* sometimes it is up and sometimes down, and sometimes it just stands still. And whenever I take action it moves.

Fifth, I have learned that my life direction is in me and when the time is right, it always makes itself known to me. And when I need to talk with someone about it, I know that too.

Sixth, I have learned that unsolicited *Life* career advice is costly—both in time and in energy—and, at points, not too useful, simply because it is seldom within the rhythm of my experience and is inconsistent with my own personal knowledge.

Robyn Davidson (1980), in her book *Tracks*, describes her solo trek with camels across 1,700 miles of Australian outback. On return, she began sorting out all her experience and two important things emerged. They were: ... that you are as powerful and strong as you allow yourself to be ... that the most difficult part of any endeavor is taking the first step, making the first decision. Camel trips, as I suspected all along, and as I was about to have confirmed, do not begin or end, they merely change form."

So, my final learning is that life direction is always moving in and out of focus and, like camel trips, it doesn't end, it merely continues to change form. However, using my Career Compass—my experience, intelligence, and intuition—I can always get a reading for my next step and that leads to another, and another, and another. (Miller-Tiedeman, 1992)

The above story reflects t he following assumptions, as shown in Table 8.3:

TABLE 8.3. Assumptive Differences Between Lifecareer
(also known as the new careering and quantum careering)
and Traditional Career

Traditional Career	Lifecareer
Job is career; Major focus control	Life-Is-Career; Major principle flow
Career theorists make all theory	Individual as theory maker and story teller
Self-talk not a priority	Voice-activated positive self-talk a priority
Control of life	Cooperate with approaching forces in life
Parts equal the whole	Whole organizes the parts
Sets goals	Sets intentions
Know where you're going	Learn as you go
Self is lost	Self not lost but continually unfolds
External information primary	Internal information primary
Follows reality defined by experts	Individual creates own reality
Focus on doing	Focus on becoming
Plays career like a crap shoot	Plays career from personal knowledge
Relies heavily on other's opinions	Takes readings from experience, intelligence and intuition, factoring in other's opinions when appropriate
Work is major focus	Work is part of a balanced life
Heavy emphasis on first job, school to work transition	Not age determined
Mostly focused on getting a full-time job	Expands possibilities to include both getting a job and creating your own work
Focus on outcome	Focus on action
Ignores stress	Helps individuals consider stress as a career factor

Table continues on page 200.

TABLE 8.3. *Continued*

Traditional Career	Lifecareer
Focus on choosing a career	Acknowledges everyone has a career that s(he) lives each day
Self-concept theory discussion	Self-conceiving experienced
Focus on right or wise decision making	Values both right and left decisions with focus on learning that comes with those things that do not work out
Low trust in things working out	High trust in life even when it does not work
Making it defined with future tense	Acknowledges everyone makes it daily—present tense
Counselors are primary conveyors of life direction help using mostly talk and testing	Life direction done by people in all walks of life; with talk and non-talk modalities which include but is not limited to meditation, Conscious breathing, Cranio-Sacral work, structural body work, therapy, personal journal writing, yoga workshops, conferences, and the like—all of which assist in the process of constantly creating a future

1. Major principle—flow, cooperating with life while evaluating the situation;

2. Self-conceiving is paramount;

3. Learning is doing;

4. High trust in life;

5. Both right and left decisions provide important information;

6. Internal information primary;

7. Creating own reality, a high value;

8. Acknowledges personal theory as most useful.

Journey Clients Often Find That:

1. Many old friends no longer appeal.

2. Activities that seem routine lose their enchantment.

3. They start to pay more attention to food, particularly its quality.

4. All their material accumulations—closet contents and house in general—frequently start to feel cumbersome.

5. Reading becomes an important tool as they scan self-help books. Those authors become important journey companions.

6. It is useful to join study groups that discuss books of interest.

7. They start sensing their mission but cannot articulate it at the moment.

8. They connect with others on individual journeys but their journey is unique.

9. They love the journey. They recognize they are falling in love with their own potential.

10. They want to attend seminars and workshops that fill in a little more of the journey puzzle. They meet a lot of mew people, some of whom remain friends and others who do not. But they know if their paths need to cross again, they will; and, they need only cooperate with the approaching forces.

11. Some friends will invite them into their group. They weigh how that feels. They may think, "I may learn something new." Or maybe, "I'm there to serve someone else." Sometimes those connections work, other times they do not. But they provide the clarity they need for that stage of their development.

12. Sometimes their journey moves forward. Other times, it goes nowhere. It often feels like pushing water uphill. They experience rejection. They think that God has forgotten them. Yet, they find each morning fresh

with new possibility and they keep on working even though no one pays much attention. When they feel depleted, they treat themselves with rides in the country or a walk along the ocean, cups of coffee, a small shopping spree, or a new book they have long wanted. They do anything and everything that helps them take themselves and their journey more lightly.

In Summary

Journey clients tend to follow the principles of rhythm and timing, without trying to leap-frog past the frustration. Frequently they do not succeed, but they do take aim at flow. One of the difficulties with staying in the flow and in the presence of your experience comes from the pressure exerted from those who buy into the "make-it-happen" rhetoric. This does not suggest that those who go with the flow do not make things happen. They do. But the work they do in the now brings about results in a more natural way. From a biblical perspective you could talk about the Sermon on the Mount where Jesus said, "Take no thought for the morrow" (Matt. 6:25–34). This scripture encourages one to focus on today, which journey clients use to grow their futures. They have done today all within their control. They focus on the action taken and allow time for their efforts to show gain. In so doing, they end up with less stress, more joy and satisfaction, which makes for a better-functioning immune system.

Common Challenges of Both Job and Journey Clients

Negative Self-Talk

The job search problems do not differ much from life problems in that many reflect negative thinking, maybe because of the cultural taboo against holding yourself in high esteem. This kind of inculcation teaches individuals to come down on the side of *what they can't do* or *what won't work* rather than acknowledging their possibilities. This results in a focus on deficits or a feeling that they don't have permission to go for what they want. While it's ever so easy to tell someone to go for it, the psychological barriers that result make it sometimes almost impossible. These barriers result from programming done by teachers, ministers, parents, and friends (sometimes not deliberately) about what the individual can or can't do, what he or she is worth, and these memories stay forever in the psyche, even though buried deep, they do connect and either impede or enhance an individual's accomplishments. This need for permission doesn't reflect level of intelligence as much as stage of development. For instance, conformers (not a dispositive label, only a stage designation) don't tend to go against conventional wisdom.

Fear

Fear is a fact of life, particularly when it relates to income, which determines level of lifestyle. Fear works for us when it warns us of impending danger. However, it works against us outside of the help it provides for life-threatening situations. As mentioned earlier, our immune systems weren't constructed to handle mortgage, job or similar kinds of ongoing fear. Because fear stresses the immune system which in turn lowers our resistance and makes us susceptible to all kinds of physical problems.

Fear of ending up on the slag heap of life, often keeps us from fully expressing our true gifts. Many women fear becoming bag ladies. While both men and women fear not being able to support families. These fears are very real in a downsized environment and one in which available jobs frequently do not pay a living wage. A recent study surveyed present job openings in Oregon, Washington, Idaho, and Montana and found that 70% to 80% of those jobs did not pay a living wage without seeking public assistance (Krikorian, G., 1998).

Dodging the Pain of Income Generation

Many believe that knowing where they are going will save them from the chaotic job challenges facing many today. They subscribe to the notion that, "If you don't where you're going, you'll probably end up somewhere else." So, they spend enormous amounts of time planning and goal setting. Take seniors in high school. About one-third of them usually know their next step, one-third act like they know where they're going, and one-third out right don't know, but don't want to make that common knowledge. Why? Because the culture tends to support knowing where you're going even though most of us only have a slight consciousness of that because we stay busy with what life is bringing to us in the moment, most of which we don't have a choice about. All this suggests that, *even if you do know where you are going, you will most likely end up somewhere else.* That's why so many of us find ourselves in that place called *somewhere else.* And most of the time we don't even notice it because it is our life space at the moment.

Both the job and the journey client face many common challenges, but when the professional successfully deals with his or her negative self talk, fear and economic concerns, then a giant step has been taken toward helping clients do the same. Clients can then gently ease into the New Careering, loving life as it is and themselves as they are while keeping an eye out for improvement.

Turning Theory into Practice

In quantum physics a particle can be a wave and a wave can be a particle. It all depends on how the individual scientist chooses to view it. That holds true for the Lifecareer® theory. It can be either a theory or a philosophy. It all hinges on how the individual user chooses to apply it. In this section, Lifecareer will be applied as a philosophy which both the job and the journey client can use. For this practice section, Miller-Tiedeman selected the overarching theme in the New Careering—Life-Is-Career—along with Principle 1 and Principle 8 in the New Careering Model (see Chapter 3 for more detail on these principles) as they represent necessary beginning points for the New Careering.

Getting a Mindset That Life-Is-Career

This is necessary as many counselor education programs still define career as job, as does the *Random House Webster's College Dictionary* in its first definition, "an occupation or profession followed as one's life work," as do publishers of career development materials. The remaining definitions also suggest career as work, or job. So, little wonder that a need to reprogram in favor of life as the big career exists. While it sounds fairly simple on the surface, the application of it takes personal work, the degree of which varies on the openness and the development of the individual.

Here's How to Start.   You can gain a deeper understanding of life as the big career by reprogramming your psyche. Use the mirror technique to affirm aloud, "Life-Is-My-Career®." Claude Bristol (1985) elaborated on this idea in his book *The Magic of Believing*. During the 1930s depression, Bristol reclaimed his failing company by pasting slogans like "We're going to win," "We've got guts, let's prove it," on a mirror in the backroom of the office where his employees left their hats and coats. He then moved the mirrors to each person's desk. As a result, his salespeople tripled and quadrupled their incomes.

Lifecareer, Life-Is-Career, Career Compass, and their derivatives are registered trademarks of Dr. Anna Miller-Tiedeman.

The mirror technique, used regularly, can reduce all kinds of anxiety. Coaches use the power of positive affirmation to get the best performance. They know this has a powerful effect on the subconscious. In job search, it also lightens the waiting time. Here is how to do it. Stand in front of a mirror, breathe deeply three or four times until you feel a sense of power, strength, and determination. Next, look into your eyes and say, "Life-Is-Career. My job is to cooperate with life, update my resume, use it when necessary, review my financial situation, and make a Plan B" (or whatever works for you). The first day you may feel embarrassed talking to yourself in the mirror, but after several days, you'll get used to it. Doing this reprograms your subconscious that tends to say things like, "You probably won't get an interview." "Your resume is not strong enough," and you can fill in the blanks with other self-deprecating phrases.

Principle 1: Life Is Self-Organizing

Knowing this can help individuals manage fear of not finding work, fear of not having a good resume, fear of not having the right training, and fear of failing to compete. Believing that life organizes, the individual can let go, and fall back in the arms of life (or God, if you prefer). But this calls for high trust, more profound than Erikson's (1959) basic trust. From a development standpoint, basic trust comes in more at the Conforming stage; however, over-all trust in life during adverse circumstances demands a Self-Aware level of development which takes hard personal work to attain. However, if an individual has not mastered basic trust, the higher trust in life could be more difficult. Life moves forward without our permission, which is probably one reason it works, although sometimes not the way we want it to.

The theory of self-organizing systems can also be used as an affirmation ("Life is self-organizing, so I need only cooperate with its approaching forces"). Each of us epitomizes a self-organizing system. When relaxing into that system, comfortable interpretation happens and choices follow accordingly. The theory of self-organizing systems notes that all living organisms constantly engage in self-renewal with the opportunity to move beyond current boundaries. When individuals identify their self-organizing systems experience, they leap into life's flow effortlessly. With it comes a better-functioning immune system accruing many health benefits. Then living Life-As-Career becomes as easy as breathing.

Here Are Some Things to Do. When the resume is mailed, relinquish control. Remember that you've done all you can. This, too, requires personal work, as the inner critic is always present trying to tell you what you're not. When this happens, use the mirror technique again and tell yourself, "I'm a powerful and wonderful person. I've done all in my control." Say this twice a day in front of the mirror. When you get comfortable with this one, create your own personal affirmations.

Miller-Tiedeman used "I am a powerful and wonderful person" in a Career Theory class. The next day, one of her Asian students came in and said, "When you did that exercise, I thought it was rather contrived. But this morning when I woke up I realized I had to speak English for three hours. So, I affirmed myself and my capacity to do that, and it relieved my stress. I could not believe such a simple act could change how I felt this morning" (Student personal communication, Spring, 1984).

Principle 8: Life Goes Both Right and Left

Always has, always will. No amount of intervention will change that, as life was designed for learning, not perfection. But humans still stress themselves out trying to get it right. When you start appreciating the value of the right and left in life, you find it ranks up there with getting it right. Start believing that and new information will enter your life that will help you walk through your fear. Everything in life, those things that work and those that do not, provide new learnings for new possibilities and are primary to growing a future.

Neither the job client nor the journey client may like the outcome of his or her decisions. Nothing wrong with that. But if the individual berates him or herself for what he or she deems a bad decision, this sends a powerful message to the subconscious which places a drag on the energy available to live through the present life-direction problem.

On the other hand, if clients can learn to live in the minute, they will never meet a moment they cannot handle. They'll also experience less fear. Casting into the future or back into the past sets up most of the anxiety and dread we experience. The next time you feel fear, ask yourself, "Am I casting forward into the future, or is the feeling I'm experiencing resulting from something in the past?"

An important experience for Miller-Tiedeman happened in May 1990, when David (V. Tiedeman) was so sick he could hardly walk or talk. She did not know what to do. Then something said, "Take him to Scripps Hospital in emergency." She did not wait for the doctor to call. She acted in the *now* and it worked. When she sat through David's two major operations within four days, each moment worked. Living through David's 90-day intensive care situation with a report of "stable and holding," the *now* worked. At the end of this episode, she looked back and wondered how she survived that ordeal. Then she remembered that she stayed in the *now* and it worked. That holds true whether you're waiting for a call about an interview, or one telling you that you got the job, or you have wiped your data off your hard or zip drive.

Here Are Some More Things to Do.   Invoke the mirror technique again and affirm all your decisions. Say, "The *now* is my strength, the past or the future doesn't exist." Practice that sentence at least once a day. If you miss the mirror, affirm the same aloud to yourself as you drive. Never mind that others looking in your car will think that you're talking with yourself. If you forget it as you drive, affirm yourself in the shower or wherever you have some privacy. Consistency is the key.

The New Careering Professionals

In order to encourage clients to value life's major principle—flow—the helping professional must have some first-hand experience with it. And here is another place where the usefulness of paradigms shows up, as you cannot get to flow (a quantum principle) by using a parts mentality (a Newtonian notion). In other words, in process careering, the helping professional acknowledges he or she has no information, and will never have access to the client's internal information super-highway, his or her intuitions, or know the decisions the client needs to make, as is often assumed in traditional career. If the helping professional fails to recognize this, he or she will work counter to the client's flow: (a) by making suggestions that do not feel right to the client or (b) by sending non-verbal messages which dampen the client's momentary insights and understandings. The keyword is support. The professional supports the clients' notions regardless of how strange they sound, as no one of us knows a future outcome, but he or she does question the negative self-talk the client currently uses which slows down and, in some cases, stops progress toward a dream or vision.

Multiculturalism in Lifecareer

In process careering, the culture of the client does not become an issue, as the helping professional supports the client in her or his move forward; he or she does not try to adjust them to the professional's point of view, cultural or otherwise. In that sense, process counseling takes on some of the characteristics of mediation in that the helping professional does not make judgments, does not allow biases to enter the session, poses appropriate questions, and reframes client's story for clarity. Personal opinion has no place in this session but the professional can offer suggestions, options, choices, and alternatives if and when the client has exhausted his or her possibilities. Finally, the helping professional summarizes content and works toward an action plan written in the client's own words much like in mediation.

Language Matters

Of major importance is the language used in responding to the client. Remember the helping professional in Chapter 4 who took one look at a client's resume and said, "This is a lousy resume." According to the client's spouse, this one act killed off what could have been a good learning experience. In addition, it caused the spouse to have to spend an inordinate amount of time helping the client reconcile his *not good enough* feelings.

We should all remember that the day which makes a memory is never over. Everything we say to anyone is there for recall the remainder of his or her life. We also need to remember that we know very little about each other. We see a physical form, and we have an impression. Let us suppose that the judgment of the professional proves correct; it still remains important for the individual to make his or her own discovery as did Buckminster Fuller, the late inventor and anticipatory design scientist, in the following story.

At age 32 Fuller found himself "a 'throwaway' in the business world" (1981, p. 124) and almost committed suicide. He decided instead to do his own thinking, confining it to only experientially gained information, "and with the products of my own thinking and to articulate my own innate motivational integrity instead of trying to accommodate everyone else's opinions, credos, educational theories, romances, and mores, as I had in my earlier life" (p. 124). Fuller and many others (including those we know about who have made it and who have not, as well as those who do not receive media attention) used their individual career theories and philosophies. They refused to let others' paradigms and opinions limit them.

That is diametrically opposed to Brooks' (Brown, Brooks, & Associates, 1984) suggestion that, "Counselors use models or theories to help them define a client's problem, provide services to a client, formulate goals of counseling and assess results" (p. 337). This suggests that counselors look to a theory, not to a life, to help define a client's problem.

Honoring Individual Career Theory

The process professional works from the individual's career theory (life-direction notions and philosophies) not some theorist's idea. The work of the helping professional is to interface with the client in ways that empower his or her uniqueness and inclinations, even though that may run counter to what the professional deems appropriate. This does not suggest the professional must remain mute. To the contrary, the helping professional can work with the language the client uses to determine how his or her paradigms and self-talk presently hinder the client's progress. Also, when two people talk, something new happens that neither may have thought about previously. Just the act of talking brings in new information for both the helping professional and the client. In that sense, we teach each other.

From another perspective, the helping professional acts as midwife to the client's theory which will bring many new possibilities for him or her. In doing this, the client relaxes into his or her own space and life's possibilities; and, he or she may even feel exhilarated when something does not work out because he or she understands we do not live in a perfect world. Relieving this stress helps the client value and unfold his or her Life-As-Career in ways that increase self-esteem.

The Importance of Focusing on the Action Taken

First, it relieves stress as the individual tries to avoid the stress of how the job search, or whatever is attempted, will turn out. But that runs counter to conventional wisdom focused on outcome. A major overworked myth goes like this: If you get the right training, and/or education, everything will work out. This assumption does not square with how life works. This opens the door for negative self-talk which impacts the immune system immediately, paving the way for small to large physical problems.

The New Careering instead encourages clients to focus on their actions, a behavior which can buffer the disappointment encountered in rejection. Focusing on action supports self-esteem. For instance, when a client says, "I sent out 100 resumes and got 50 rejections," there is a high potential the client will feel down about it. However, when the client says, "I sent out 100 resumes, isn't that wonderful," he or she programs the body for a good feeling. You might address the law of averages here knowing that sending out 100 resumes just may garner you one or two invitations to apply, and you only need one job.

How Does God Fit into the New Careering (Lifecareer)

This question comes up in most every group. The answer is simple: however you want him (her) to fit. Lifecareer is a process, not a prescriptive theory. It recognizes that everyone embodies his or her own spirituality, so it remains a very personal matter.

The Work of New Careering Professionals

Helping professionals have always worked with groups, however, groups mentioned here focus on:

- providing an environment for individuals to share job challenges of one form or another;

- introducing a broader hierarchy of work (as shown in Table 8.1);

- facilitating the identification of negative and self-defeating phrases that impede self-progress, and offering exercises to extrude that language;

- introducing the idea of soft money (not a regular income, usually called multi-sourcing income) and the importance of money management as a safety net in an unsafe economic environment;

- working with individuals to help them organize what Faith Popcorn (1991) called a "kitchen cabinet" that meets on a regular basis to share progress, offer ideas and suggestions; and

- introducing the career portfolio.

The Encouragement and New Possibilities Group

Anyone looking for work, nationally or internationally, benefits potentially from a support group where he or she can share the results of the search, hear others' stories of both the up and down sides of their search experience, share their relaxation strategies, and just talk about how unemployment feels. Some may call this "sharing the misery," but study after study now shows the importance of group support in alleviating physical pain (Spiegel, 1989), reversing heart disease (Ornish, 1990), the longevity of cancer patients (Simonton, C. & Simonton, S., 1982), and the longing for community (results of a 1993 Harris poll, as cited in Leonard & Murphy, 1995).

Helping professionals could provide leadership in forming community groups to modulate the emotional pain of downsizing, generate new ideas, provide a feeling of belonging and support. This community group also could address self-employment and bring in guest speakers who now do that.

But paradigm paralyses of the professionals may keep this from happening as they may not believe the average individual can be self-employed. He or she will then not open the topic of self-employment for discussion. Instead, clients will revert to the common (conforming) notion that it takes an entrepreneurial person to work for himself or herself. While partially correct, this statement fails to appreciate the effectiveness of self-employment education along with an opportunity to process those ideas through personal experience.

Alternative Work Options

When individuals understand they can engage in self-employment on many different risk levels, as shown in Table 8.1, this opens up new possibilities. They can do this, in many instances, with little more than a business card and a calendar, until they find full-time work, or they can continue to do it after finding a full-time job. Introducing and supporting alternative work scenarios provides more options which makes a broader berth for client decision making.

Self-Talk: The Case of Joe

Joe is divorced and currently without work. He graduated from high school and worked about fifteen years as a roofer. He no longer feels safe on roofs and wants to do something else. Joe has no savings and no income at present, but he does draw unemployment insurance payments which will run out in six months. He needs work. His need for money is so paramount that money management would not enter, at this time, into the helping formula.

Joe and John, a career counselor, are neighbors. Both were working in their yards one day. John knew about Joe's work dilemma and wanted to help. The counselor, knowing how good Joe was with his hands, yard work, and roofing, asked, "Have you thought about handy work? You need only a business card and an ad in the local newspaper classifieds under Service Directory. Joe replied, "I have thought about that but I do not want to do that the rest of my life." The counselor said, "Nothing for any of us will last the rest of our lives." "Oh," replied Joe, "I did not think about it like that."

They worked a little more in the yard, then the counselor asked, "Have you considered applying at the local cellular phone companies? Joe replied, "Oh, everyone has a cellular phone." At this point the counselor said, "Joe, a big part of your failure to connect with work is in your head. Sure, a lot of people have cellular phones, but not near everyone. And, you're a good salesperson. It might be worth a try." "Okay," Joe replied. "I'll consider that."

The counselor finished his yard work and then said to Joe, "Why don't you come over and let me help you write the new paper resume? I'll also help you locate some places to send your resume." Joe, said, "That sounds great." He went to his truck and got his calendar and they made an appointment for the next Monday afternoon.

Very likely Joe can be coached into employment. He has all the right stuff, so to speak, but he needs someone to support him when his rejections come in and someone to help him move past the critic that shows up in his head. This provides an opportunity to (a) help Joe recognize that rejection is a part of life; and (b) to help Joe focus on his actions, not the outcome. Both of these attitudes can lower Joe's stress and increase his motivation, freeing up energy for new possibilities. Notice in this interaction, John did not mention Life-Is-Career specifically, but he worked with the Lifecareer assumptions (he knows them experientially) to help Joe move a little closer to employment and learn some new self-talk. John will help Joe talk about and activate new ways to move beyond *either/or* thinking into the *both/and* framework. For instance, Joe does not have to think only about being a handyman, he could do both handy work and hold a full-time job.

Pay attention to how Joe's self-talk stopped him from considering some potentially good leads. For instance, he turned down job possibilities that did not exactly suit him because, as he said it, "I don't want to work at that for the rest of my life." While many people know that nothing is forever, they tend to forget this when under financial stress. Then the self-deprecating talk takes over, dampening the individual's capacity to look for work. This kind of self-talk stops the flow of money into the bank account. Consequently, Joe loses financially each day. Joe's neighbor invited him to stop by from time to time to talk about his job-hunting progress and his feelings. Three weeks later Joe, a former roofer, got a job as a loan officer.

Job groups could do much toward helping individuals recognize counter-productive self-talk. This would improve their job-search situation, reduce stress, and enhance their immune systems (see Chapter 14 for more detail) freeing up more energy for creative approaches to finding a job.

Assumptions Reflected in Joe's Case:

1. All decisions in life are important.

2. Working with someone can help you identify energy patterns and speech patterns that keep you from fulfilling what you really want.

3. It's important to work with people who know how to help you mature your career theory (philosophies about your life direction) *while not interrupting the flow*.

4. The client can use intelligence to direct his or her own life and can do this very effectively.

Financial Management

Job groups could introduce topics like financial management in the form of simple budgeting. The less money you have to spend, the more important budgeting becomes. One client Miller-Tiedeman worked with said, "I don't have enough money to budget. We only have a $55,000 a year income." The story later revealed they had previously made $140,000 a year, so $55,000 to them seemed like nothing. It comes back to perception.

However, due to the soft nature of income, most everyone who works could benefit from a review of his or her financial status. Unfortunately, many people resist money management. Further, helping professionals seldom broach the financial management topic. After working in sales for a year, a young Greek immigrant wanted to try something different but he needed money to buy training, new software, and time to carry him through his job search.

When asked about his money-management skills, he replied, "I'm very good at knowing what I spend."

"How do you know this?" his counselor asked. "Do you keep records or do you guess at it?"

"Oh, I keep it in my head," he said.

So the counselor invited him to keep a written financial record for one month. At the end of the month, the client discovered that while he generally managed his money well, a good amount slipped through his fingers.

The record-keeping tactic produced another bonus for the salesman. He decided to research financial organizations for potential employment, and eventually took a job with a leading investment firm providing advice on personal investing. In his spare time, he helped people with money management and family budgeting. If fired or forced to quit, he is prepared to go it alone, he says.

The need for a financial safety net becomes clearer as radical changes—new technology, mergers, business failures, global movement of jobs—reshape where and how work is done. A choice exists: We either get a tight grip on personal finances, play the *What If* game, or experience the stress that shows up when regular income disappears.

You may wonder how financial management enters the life-direction picture. It's easy. When people encounter downsizing, financial position becomes paramount and dictates the length of time they can comfortably afford to job search. It becomes even more critical when a family or individual lives from paycheck to paycheck and has to find a job yesterday.

The New Careering Developer, with a quantum perspective, sees life as a web of relationships. Therefore, he or she sees how directly money connects to life direction and dictates what can happen vis-à-vis time for retraining, exploration of new possibilities, and financial resources available for retraining. Working with clients on financial management then is not off the mark for career counseling.

At this point, you see levels of development emerge. For instance, helping professionals at the Conforming stage of development may think money management should be left to the professional financial planners. This approach indicates the helping professional has eliminated those ideas that do not agree with how he or she sees the world—a good example of, "if you can't see it, you won't believe it."

Multi-Sourcing Income

According to the HayGroup (1988), career ownership and customization of life has been shifted to the individual and represents emerging forces. Career ownership means acting as your own organization even though you may work full-time for someone else. And the time may come when full-time turns into permanent part-time work. Then multi-sourcing income will kick in. And with the reengineering now going on in corporations and businesses, multi-sourcing income could come sooner rather than later for many people. A good helping professional works with individuals to set the stage for multi-sourcing income as humans need time to think about and get used to something different. Particularly something that threatens their economic base.

The Kitchen Cabinet

Job groups could also educate individuals on how to form what Faith Popcorn, in her book *The Popcorn Report* (1991), calls a *kitchen cabinet*. Think about the group as your personal board of directors. Ask people of different ages and interests to be on it. For instance, an attorney, a high-school graduate, a grandmother, two or three peers, a small-business owner, a corporate vice president if possible. With a speaker phone, you can have one of your board members in another city, or you can have the phone company set up a conference call between your home board (4 people) and your national board (4 people). This way, you access a much larger pool of intelligence.

In today's economy, linking up, sharing resources, and not reinventing the wheel may yield a better return. Besides, it is more fun to link up and work together.

In addition, we need to encourage individuals to work their contacts. Each of us has a different inner and extended (those people who come and go quickly in our life) circle of contacts. These contacts work both for and against us. Frequently, those extended contacts work better than the inner circle contacts, another one of life's surprises. But try to make use of all cues from both the inner and extended circles as well as all contacts from both volunteer and paid work situations. Then watch for life's surprises, those opportunities which bump into you bringing surprising outcomes. You never know where these may lead.

While everyone can soft network using the inner and extended circle of friends, it takes effort to hard network because it requires putting ourselves in situations for that to happen. Introverts find networking, hard or soft, somewhat more difficult to do. Extroverts, on the other hand, find it quite natural and fun, as they like working the room and linking up with all kinds of people.

But however you access your allies, remember we need each other and more comes from sharing intelligence. When we talk, interesting ideas occur to us that might not otherwise enter our minds. That provides another illustration of self-organizing systems: Ideas continue to move into greater complexity when given the opportunity. Many a project and book has been sketched on a napkin in a restaurant, a testament to the late Lewis Thomas (1980) notion that "The urge to form partnerships, to link up in collaborative arrangements is perhaps the oldest, and most fundamental force in nature" (p. 2).

Portfolio Career and the Career Portfolio

William Bridges, author of *Job Shift: How to Prosper in a Workplace Without Jobs* (1994) talks about the Portfolio Career. He suggests that those people who, (a) value controlling their own work schedule, (b) keeping different hours on different days, (c) making decisions about the nature of the work they take on, and (d) initiate independent projects are good matches for the Portfolio Career life. These people value change and variety and need multiple activities to maintain interest.

On the other hand, those who value stability, need structure, find their sociability at work, and like to rely on the traditional job, may not find it easy to engage in a Portfolio Career. However, in the interest of survival most people will need a Career Portfolio because permanent-temporary work will most likely abound.

Bridges also suggests that one in every four Americans now works in a contingency workforce—people on temporary or part-time assignments and those doing contract work. By the year 2000, the U.S. Bureau of Labor Statistics predicts that half the labor force will hold permanent-temporary jobs. This suggests that every American might want to rethink full-time work as the major way to earn money and consider the *working arrangement*, responding to what needs doing where, maybe for short units of time. The custom-made work career comes of age without our permission. Therefore the need to educate all workers, regardless of age, about their income options (see Table 8.1).

While business customizes its needs, the individual will slowly move toward temporary employment. The new *working arrangement* will support that shift. And since no one knows when he or she may fall into temporary status, a good strategy is to create a Career Portfolio as a safety-net precaution. A Career Portfolio also helps individuals get clearer about their past and rethink their futures.

You may wonder, "Why would a temporary employee need a portfolio?" Because of the tentative nature of their work, a portfolio showing and telling the experience they have gained will help them better present themselves to a new employer. Second, having a portfolio shows you care enough about your work life to organize it in ways that help the next employer know more about you. Third, you will know more about yourself as you develop your track record from job to job.

Those still working full-time jobs need portfolios in case their jobs get downsized. Everyone in the labor force, even high-level managers, are subject to downsizing in today's economic structure. Try putting a portfolio together after you have been downsized and you will wish you had done so when you had steady work with fewer economic and emotional issues. Downsizing, in the best of circumstances, causes considerable emotional upset, which often precludes even an interest in doing a portfolio.

Kimeldorf (1997), in his book *Portfolio Power*, tells and shows how to customize an individual portfolio. Specifically, how to

- Collect data for the portfolio's content;

- Analyze and prioritize that information;

- Plot your career intentions or changes using the portfolio;

- Customize your portfolio toward your own line of work; and

- Check the final product.

A Career Portfolio includes many things. Like anything of value, it takes effort and time to develop. But the rewards of seeing yourself in portfolio far outweigh the work involved in constructing it. Following are some of the things that Kimeldorf (1997) suggests:

1. Letters of recommendation. Get one each time you leave a job.

2. Index to contents.

3. Resume. Do a brief resume, an electronic resume, and a long version. One individual wrote a counseling resume and a writing resume. It all depends on your background and the kind of job you seek.

4. Book covers and table of contents from reports or manuals you have written.

5. Business brochure (if you have a small business) or brochure from agency where you worked, especially if your work or department is mentioned in the brochure or you helped design the brochure,

6. Copies of anything you have had a hand in writing.

7. Copy of something written about you.

8. News releases of any kind.

9. Customer satisfaction letters.

10. Three to five samples of work and experience, captured in graphics, pictures, or photocopies—never original items.

11. Accompany each work sample with a title and brief summary of the skills it represents. Leaving a lot of white space around the sample dramatizes it. Following are some examples of what might be included:

   - Employer evaluation.

   - Job description, duties, and responsibilities.

   - Indicators of one's quality of work, achievement or promoteability. For instance:

     - increased hours

     - increased responsibility (training or supervising others, more job duties)

- pay raises

- attendance record

- given improved or expanded job duties

- employee recognition awards, privileges, rewards

- demonstrating quality by a low error rate (few rejects, few returns)

- customer compliments or requests for one's personal service

- helping to increase production, more efficient procedures or services

- increased business, i.e., customers, income, sales, and/or requests

- If a writer, list writing experience, published articles, and your mastery of computer writing software.

If you work in the school setting, use *A Teacher's Guide to Creating Portfolios For Success in School, Work, and Life* (Kimeldorf, 1996) to help students start to learn about and design their portfolios.

In summary, job groups could play a major role in easing individuals into career ownership.

How Do Paradigms and Development Interface in the New Careering?

Simply, through the client's and the helping professional's language and attitude. For instance, a client might say, "I heard you shouldn't shotgun the employment market. So, I'm planning to send out resumes to five companies." A process response might be, "What do you think about trying both approaches?" This bypasses evaluation of either idea and allows the client to learn by experience.

A client may say, "I'd really like to go into computers, but someone told me it wasn't a growth industry." You can bypass that statement with, "Well, some people believe it is a growth industry, but others don't." Again the client can use his or her judgment about it. The helping professional who has attained a Self-Aware level of development knows that any notion about anything is only a perception and, in most cases, does not come close to the truth for any one person. Those helping professionals who function mostly at the Conforming stage tend to more readily buy into specific and limiting points of view. Put another way, the Self-Aware level professional has points to view; the Conforming stage professional has a point of view. Listen to your language the next time you work with someone, and you can identify rather quickly from what level of development you are speaking. In the beginning, tape your sessions and then listen back. This helps you check your language and hear your Conforming stage responses. You can then ask yourself, "Did my statements forward the client's idea or did they increase the client's uncertainty?" Getting in touch with your language takes time because conscious awareness is not present with each spoken word. This exercise makes a difference in the lives of people with whom you work and interact, particularly those who feel more uncertain.

Sometimes, and perhaps frequently, perceptions do not keep pace with change. Josh Billings, a twentieth-century humorist, said, "I believe when we stumble and fall, it is not our reasoning facilities that have failed us. It is what we know that just is not true." This happens more frequently to a helping professional who fails to grow himself or herself beyond the Conforming stage of development. Lack of a wider band of perception lays a glass ceiling beyond which the client cannot move. It thereby focuses clients' perceptions at the level of conventional wisdom, seldom freeing them to their own understandings.

If the client responds from the Conforming stage of development, at least in the life direction area, she or he may abandon important beliefs in favor of the professional's opinions, as they are supposed to know about these things. If the client comes from the Self-Aware level of development, he or she may hear the professional's notions but remain true to her or his own ideas about how things work.

Offering information on both sides of the question suggests a Self-Aware level of development that provides the client an opportunity to rethink his or her beliefs. The non-verbal energy that communicates attitude clearly indicates on which side the professional leans. This could weaken the resolve of uncertain clients if they read it as an opposing comment. The helping professional responding from the Self-Aware level of development—a level where exceptions and alternatives more easily come into awareness—does not tend to err in attitude or language. This lifts the glass ceiling for clients.

The transformation now taking place in our society will move humanity, with or without permission, from the Conforming stage to the Self-Aware level. This will happen through our economics and the breakdown of the occupational structure as we've known it. Already, technology now absorbs hundreds of jobs nationally and internationally. Those not subject to absorption, fast make their way around the globe. Work is no longer positioned within national boundaries. This makes it all the more important for humans to fast-forward themselves to the Self-Aware level of development. Because those who conform to the old rules and ideas are destined for economic hardship and stress beyond imagination. On the other hand, those who move willingly to the higher level of development will be the new pioneers. Many of them will find rough terrain, but they will eventually come out on the other side, but not without a lot of adventure, risk, and numerous learning experiences.

In the 1980s, many people in their 40s, 50s, and 60s found themselves in the middle of a major technological revolution. Many of these people retrained, retooled, and realigned themselves. Some made the transition rather painlessly, others became casualties. But all these people did the best they could and the best they knew; and as Abraham Lincoln once said, "I intend to keep doing the same until the end. If the end brings me out all right, what is said against me won't amount to anything. If the end brings me out wrong, ten angels swearing I was right would make no difference" (Bartlett, 1980, p. 524).

☐ Looking Back

1. Practice is dictated by the individual client's career theory, vision, and desires and holds more importance than any theory devised by any theorist.

2. Two types of clients stand out: The job-seeking client and the journey client.

3. The new resumes—electronic and paper—have different formats.

4. On-line job search provides a place to file resumes as well as carries job openings.

5. Job search is now an international consideration.

6. Focusing on action taken relieves the stress of outcome.

7. The new helping professional works with groups in identifying negative self-talk and turning it into a positive affirmation, educating about

financial management and soft money, understanding the value of support groups, and the necessity of creating a career portfolio.

8. The counselor's career theory, his or her paradigm, development, and values needs to remain secondary to those of the client.

9. Development and paradigms held by the helping professional dictate session outcome.

10. The client's theory as it comes through his or her story receives support and encouragement even though the counselor may believe she or he has a better idea about it.

11. New (Quantum) Careering touches all aspects of a life. Therefore, health and financial stability become appropriate check points.

12. Encouraging a client to own all of his or her decisions and value their learning aspects imprints wholeness.

☐ Discussion Questions

1. How do you see your own life direction? Is it oriented mostly toward job and things or is it toward the journey.

    Note: Answer honestly. These two designations (the job and journey) are merely two ways of being in the world, neither of which is better than the other. In other words, no socially acceptable answer to this question exists.

2. Which of the two types of clients (job or journey) appeal most to you? Why?

3. What is the difference between the journey and job client?

4. What is your reaction to the notion of global job competition?

5. If you have been in a support group, consider sharing your experience.

6. What do you gain by focusing on the action taken in most situations?

7. What is the difference between self-talk and ideational programming as done in cults? In churches? In schools?

8. How do you feel about living on what you might want to call soft money?

9. What would you have to do to live on soft money (not a regular monthly income)?

10. How important is it to help each individual do what he or she feels right to do?

11. How do you feel encouraging clients to do something you think may not work for them?

12. How do you deal with your own feelings, actions, and language at that point?

13. Where do development and paradigms enter into the counseling situation?

☐ Classroom/Group Exercises

1. Form an on-line career search group and report findings and procedures back to class.

2. List negative self-talk used by students, friends, parents, teachers, or minister/rabbi/or priest.

3. Discuss the effects of negative self-talk on motivation and self-esteem.

4. Form groups of two and set up a mock counseling session. Have the New Careering Check List in front of you. Tape your session. Then play back and determine how it worked. Where did you find yourself interfering with the client's ideas? Did you, by the inflection of your voice, convey something you now see was not useful?

5. Discuss self-talk you have heard your family, friends, and acquaintance talk about. If you feel comfortable doing so, share some of your own self-talk.

6. How does self-talk enhance or impede progress forward?

☐ Homework/Test Assignment

1. Listen to those around you and write down their self-talk. Share with the class in the next meeting.

2. If you have a computer and a server, use the World Wide Web and search employment.

3. Interview both a job client and journey client and talk with them about their experience and perceptions.

4. Interview someone about his or her self-talk.

5. Interview someone about his or her life. Ask if he or she ended up doing what s/he thought in high school s/he would do.

6. Update your resume to the new paper resume format and file it on line.

Checklist for the New Careering Practice

Major Principle. Life-Is-Career

____ Relax the client and support his or her present action.

____ Identify negative self-talk.

____ Actively listen and reframe client story to make sure you've heard it correctly.

____ Track negative, positive, and behavior change self-talk.

____ Track ideas that keep returning to the client.

____ Insert when appropriate the broader meaning of career.

____ Educate about the connectedness of all things including stress.

____ Show clients about conscious breathing.

____ Tell the economic story of our time.

____ Check out financial status.

____ Listen for health concerns.

____ Assist client in developing a manageable action list.

____ Introduce all clients to the career portfolio.

Principle 8. Life goes both right and left.

____ Listen to client language.

____ Infer belief system from the language used.

____ Identify values in language.

____ Listen for complaint and frustration about outcome.

____ Reinforce action taken.

Principle 1. Life is self-organizing. The following clues will alert you to whether or not the client believes that life is self-organizing:

____ High stress

____ Working harder and harder without much to show for it

____ Working against the grain of life

____ Not knowing when to cut loose

____ Going after things that do not and most likely will not work

____ Taking a make-it-happen approach

____ Ignoring things they're attracted to in favor of material gains

____ Using language indicative of the Conforming or Self-Protective stages of development

Anna Miller-Tiedeman
Jim Puplava

Money and the New Careering

Spotlight on Money Management

If you invest $2,000 a year (or $40 a week) for ten years at a 10% rate of return, starting when you're age twenty-one and stopping at age thirty, that $20,000 investment will have grown to over $985,000 in thirty-two years.

If you wait until age thirty-one to invest that same $2,000 a year for ten years at the rate of 10%, your $20,000 investment will be worth $400,000 by age 65.

If you wait until age forty-five to begin investing $2,000 a year for a full twenty-years, even if you don't retire at age sixty-five, you will have invested $42,000 and your investment will be worth approximately $140,810 (Godfrey, 1997). Retirement is not a function of age but of money and choice.

☐ Looking Ahead

Watch for the following important topics:

1. The importance of money in a soft economy

2. Universal principles—work, save, grow over time

3. Money management, development, and paradigms

4. The Godfrey financial categories

5. Interview with Jim Puplava, Financial Planner

6. Building a downsizing safety net

7. Values and money

8. College education or future financial security

9. Important ideas and concepts:

    a. Growing a secure financial future in a downsized environment

    b. Saving

    c. Money management

    d. Pooling resources

Eli Ginzberg and colleagues (1951) in their investigation of the un-employed in New York City in 1939 and 1940 said, "The studies of the unemployed made us aware of the significance of work in human life" (p. 10). The exchange of money for experience figures heavily in human life, its quality and perhaps its quantity. Today, as in the early 1900s, money anchors career. It always has and always will. And, most of us get money by working.

But the face of work changes almost daily. Many companies today link up with temporary agencies that provide the bulk of the workforce. A former client now works in a large corporation with over 500 employees, 400 of whom hold temporary status. This means they receive no company benefits. They don't know how long they will be employed, nor do they know if they can reconnect for another job after downsizing. This kind of uncertainty makes stressors much more stressful (Sapolsky, 1994), placing a heavier load on the immune system, killing off immune cells. These workers then find themselves more at risk for all kinds of physiological problems at a time when they need to be well to work and deal with their many challenges, both of a money and familial nature. Further, many don't have health insurance, which means out-of-pocket money for health care which the worker may or may not have. The stress from lack of work and money plays havoc with family relationships, setting the stage for breakup, abuse, and potential abandonment of family responsibility.

With these possibilities in mind, money management becomes a major challenge. While some people have always managed money well, most of us could use improvement in that area, particularly as stable work becomes less possible for many people. This may mean postponing an upgrade of your computer, using your old vacuum longer, or not eating out as often. All these decisions and others you can think of take discipline and monitoring of your monthly income.

This chapter cannot convey the potential pain, frustration, and aggravation awaiting those who don't turn their attention to money management in order to build a safety net. Anyone who works is a candidate for downsizing of a job, which could result in downsized savings. Therefore, this is a call for helping professionals who don't already address the money management problem, to at least start mentioning its importance—not for investment or retirement, or even for later change of life direction, but to help their clients cushion themselves against homelessness. Granted, behavior change doesn't happen overnight, nor do some people ever think ahead, but the helping professional can plant the seed of the benefits of saving, and then suggest several books like *Making the Most of Your Money* (Quinn, 1991), or *Your Money or Your Life?* (Dominguez & Robin, 1992). Then when the client hears the money-management idea again, or when he or she reads something related to it, that information may jump-start the client into action. Sometimes, it has to get real tough for the client; sometimes it even takes homelessness for money management to come to the top of the good-life priority list. Homelessness in all its dispositive aspects does have the potential to increase awareness, if only one that suggests it is not a good place to be.

Money Management, Development, and Paradigms

In most every chapter in this book, development and paradigms have surfaced, and this chapter is no exception. Habit serves all of us well, whether it pertains to money management or brushing our teeth. And we conform (see Chapter 4 for more detail on development) both to personal habits and to the habits of the culture which invites us to *wave the plastic (credit cards) and spend*. Some organizations even offer to extend credit for a year without payment. Advertisements by investment companies encourage hedging your bets in the stock market. So, we get a double message—spend and save.

Most people think they don't have much left to save and invest after they have bought what they think they need or want. So, the conforming behavior for many is spend. Self-denial is a more Self-Aware level behavior as it requires more thought. Many don't believe (paradigms) they make enough to save. This often has little to do with the amount made; it relates mostly to the perspective which informs the attitude. For instance, recall the client mentioned in Chapter 8 who had a $55,000 a year income and said, "I don't make enough money to do a budget." Take into consideration that the family formerly had an income of $140,000. In this case, it came down to perspective and perceived life style. Other clients could probably save 25% of that amount if they had it. When clients conform to the spend mentality in a culture that now boasts a $2 trillion consumer debt, when they believe they cannot get out from under debt, then they make decisions accordingly. These people then become our at risk homeless population.

While people make decisions for a myriad of reasons, if we could increase their level of personal development, (one level, not a full stage, beyond the Conforming stage in the Loevinger and Wessler categories, 1970a and 1970b) then an opportunity exists for a shift in belief which would tend to show up in their decision making and subsequently their behavior.

Neale Godfrey (1997), in her book *Making Change: A Woman's Guide to Designing Her Financial Future* suggests that women tend to feel intimidated and this creates fear and struggle with money issues. She notes that women fall into three financial categories. (While these suggestions were made for women, they work equally well for men, as some men fall into the same three categories.)

1. *Clueless.* She finds herself too busy to think about tomorrow.

2. *Traditionalist.* Traditional homemaker or career woman who still thinks the man takes care of the money. She equates love and trust, but she may learn better when her white knight rides off with a different princess on the back of his horse.

3. *Contemporary Classic.* Whether she stays home, works part or full time, she trusts herself financially and knows how to plan for the future.

Godfrey suggests turning your financial attitude around by thinking about it as you would cleaning out your sock drawer. She suggests setting aside five evenings and asking yourself key questions around money, (see Classroom/Group exercises at end of chapter) one chapter per evening. Whatever you come up with, work on them, but not all at once. That is like cleaning the entire house, not just your sock drawer. Then make a timetable of what you want to accomplish. For instance, curb spending right now. Create a budget by next week. Or get a will in the next month. Then think about saving enough money from your regular income to cover not only what you want to buy but what you want to save. And make sure you invest these savings shrewdly.

So, why hasn't money management figured strongly into career counseling? Perhaps for three reasons: (a) those seeking counseling have been somewhat higher on the economic scale; (b) jobs were once more readily available; and (c) financial planning was viewed as separate from career.

That judgment reflects how we learned to separate things into boxes, the remnants of a Newtonian worldview, when in fact everything flows into everything else as in the new quantum perspective. The office of the President of the United States is a prime example. He works in a multiplicity of arenas. But so do many CEOs and workers. For instance, financial planners frequently find themselves in the career counseling arena although they probably would not call it that. Jim Puplava, President of Puplava Financial Services, tells it this way:

> I have a client who is very disappointed about her son. She wants him to attend college but the son has decided to follow in his father's footsteps. The father is a foreman at a construction company that builds roads. He is in the union and he's got a wage where he's making close to $25 an hour. My client was so disappointed that her son wasn't going to college, and the son is saying, "I'm making $25 an hour, I'm out in the open, I love what I'm doing, I like working with my dad. If I follow this trade, when I work from journeyman to master craftsman, I'll make $45,000 a year." The son is saying, "Why should I trade that? I've got a job, and I like what I do."

Jim worked with his client to help her understand the importance of the trades in our culture and following one's passion. This came natural to Jim, as that represents the values he is instilling in his children, as in the following excerpts from an interview with Jim.

Miller-Tiedeman: Jim you have two sons and as a successful financial planner your children would not have to work while they're in school. So, I'm curious about how you counsel your sons about the future?

Jim: If you want any kind of financial future you have to save. So the number one idea I've instilled in them is saving, and they all do it. Second, I have made them work, even though they don't have to. This afternoon, my son will clean this building, including the bathrooms.

We do make enough income that my children would not have to work. But, if I don't instill that work idea in them, then what can they expect for themselves?

My oldest son worked here, and he didn't appreciate the job. So, last summer, we made him get a job at a restaurant called Rubio's, where he had to punch a clock, got pushed around, clean toilets, take people yelling at him. He later told me, "You know dad, that was the greatest eye-opener that I've ever gone through." I watched his responsibility and maturity make quantum leaps. Since he needed a car to go to work, we bought him one but he is paying for it. Each pay period he gives us so much for the car payment, the gas, and the insurance. Before this, he never knew how much it cost to own things. But now his buying decisions are tempered because he realizes how many hours of work he's going to have to put in to own the item or buy the service. So, we're trying to teach work and savings.

Third, we're encouraging him to do something he has a passion for, something he loves, not something his dad wants him to do like get a degree in finance and economics to come into the business.

Fourth has to do with my own attitude. If my sons would choose a trade, like electrician, it would not bother me whatsoever. I would not feel, nor would I make them feel they are a failure because they have not attended college. What is important to me is that they understand how economics and money works.

I'm now investing for one son. In fact, I have a $300 check to set up his first stock account. Working in the business, he comes in and cleans, and sees the stock machines, and he finds confirmation. We've got a group of companies that I'm going to sit down and talk to him about—each one of these companies and what they do—and he's going to make the decision of which stock we buy.

My son is seventeen and will be a senior in high school this fall. And he has been working since the eighth grade. That's the rule in my house. You get to be a kid until the eighth grade, then you get a job. They can still be a kid, but they have working responsibilities once they get into high school.

Let me say a little about what I'm teaching my children about money. I tell them that money is simply a medium of exchange that gives you the ability to do what you want to do. Obviously, people that have more money, can do a lot more things than people with less money. And so my whole concept of money is it facilitates something. It allows you to do things that you want to do. But without money, without saving money, you will never increase your own wealth. You will have limitations in terms of what you can achieve, unless, for example, you become a heart surgeon where your skills in an information society are so unique that you can demand whatever it is that you want for what it is that you do. And, unless you are in that unique profession or have that ability to become an entrepreneur, where you've got a great idea, like Bill Gates who dropped out of Harvard, or Tiger Woods who dropped out of Stanford. Steve Wozniak dropped out of college but had an idea about doing something, and it's not so much the education degree that allows you to do that. It's the application of human knowledge.

But getting back to money, you create wealth by building and saving. Let me give you an example from a recent film on China. They interviewed a man in the clothing business. During the reign of Mao Tse Tung in China you could only wear two colors, both in gray tones. After Mao died, things changed and this man figured out that women liked pretty dresses. So he saved his money working and he bought a sewing machine. And with that sewing machine, he was able to start making dresses. As he sold those dresses, demand increased because nobody had seen dresses in China. So, he saved more money, and bought a second sewing machine, and his wife began to sew. Now they had two sewing machines in operation to create dresses. The business continued to grow and revenues increased and soon he hired another person to work for him. He then bought another sewing machine.

After five years, he now operates one of the largest clothing factories, employing hundreds of people. He has taken that capital, and is now opening up restaurants, because restaurants were something that they didn't have readily available. But it all started with saving enough money to buy his first sewing machine. That principle works on most anything. For instance if you have one cow, it produces enough milk for your family and you have some left to sell. Selling the milk enables you to buy another cow. And that is the principle the man in China used when he bought his first sewing machine. The returns from that allowed him to grow his business. But again it is those principles of work, time, investment, and growth creating the wealth.

You can see these same principles in action if you take a look at one of the most successful stock market investors in history—Warren Buffet. This man doesn't even have a stock quote machine on his desk, and yet he is the second wealthiest man in the United States next to Bill Gates. Buffet bought into businesses he thought were good. He said, "The business is run in such a way that it is reinvesting, and saving capital, and expanding." Once he understood the concept and judged it to be a well-managed company and good business, he did nothing more than sit back and watch the business grow. That has turned Warren Buffet's net-worth into $21 billion. Now there is no other man on Wall Street that has been able, to the same extent he has, to apply that philosophy and build that kind of wealth. But the concept of building wealth is time and investment. Even though investors have come up with all different kinds of approaches to making money, it boils down to time plus savings. And this formula almost always equals success.

Miller-Tiedeman: Jim, how is downsizing affecting your clients?

Jim: I think what you're seeing today, in terms of financial planning and use of money, we're almost going back to grandfather's day, where you save to keep yourself liquid. I used to say that you needed three month's worth of living expenses in the bank. Today I tell a person one year. Because when you get downsized, it is much easier looking for a job when you have one year's worth of living expenses in the bank. That way you relieve yourself of the stress of big payments you can't meet.

I have a gentleman right now who works for a major insurance company that we use in estate planning. He was brought out here from Florida to represent southern California. His boss was promoted to the regional office in Irvine. Big, big promotion, bought a nice house in Irvine; two years later, they eliminated the entire Irvine branch. As the insurance company goes more toward automation, and the Internet, *he is seeing the writing on the wall.* He thinks he probably has three years left before he gets downsized. So, what is he doing?

He's upsizing his skills since he's going to come into this business. He will start with two things: (a) a marketing plan that he's going to develop over the next twelve months, and (b) a commitment to accumulating one year's living expenses in the bank. He stopped his 401K program, and he stopped his contributions for his daughter's education, because he's saying— I'm going to have to make this transition in the next 2–3 years, so, I better make plans now for that. He's also saying to himself, "I don't want to come on board and have all these bills with no money saved and have that pressure on myself." So, we're designing a plan for him to succeed by re-channeling his money *from stock investments to investments in himself.*

Miller-Tiedeman: You're talking about the universal principles of saving and growing an idea. Taking that a step further, everything grows with time.

Jim: Yes. And my client realizes this, if he has money in the bank and his wife continues to work, they'll have her salary. While it will take discipline to put that money in the bank, it will buy him *freedom of movement* to make his transition into a new profession without the burdens of heavy payments, without the burdens of the pressure to immediately become successful, because very rarely, if ever, does a business start out day-one successful. It is the same old formula—a lot of hard work, sweat and tears, and time.

Miller-Tiedeman: Think about work and savings and time and accumulation in the context of the permanent temporary jobs that now abound. It's not like you have a nice business with a client base and a steady income. I know stories like that exist, but many people are going to have to do something on their own. And that is going to take a lot more money, and it's going to probably water down what potentially could have been some savings.

Jim: The whole concept of planning today is much different if I compare it with my father's time when much of America moved off the farm and into the cities to work in industrial America. Many of those people spent 25 years on the Ford assembly line, had a level of income, union benefits, and some security.

Today, you're almost going back to the "pre-industrial era," where everyone was their own entrepreneur. For instance, you had the cabinet maker, the butcher, the blacksmith, and they worked at their house. And then suddenly we left the village or community and went to work in the city, many for big organizations. Well, if you look at all the down-sizing occurring today, you don't make the same assumptions when you get out of college. For instance, many of today's college graduates get married and start families, but they choose to rent, and build up their savings, rather than buy a house in suburbia. Why? Because they know if they don't save, when they get down-sized, they will get stuck with heavy car payments, and big house payments, and things like that. So, we're seeing a resurgence of pre-industrial entrepreneuring but for different reasons. In the exploding high-tech era, we might all end up entrepreneurs.

For instance, a client of mine was downsized from a major electronics company. He was skilled in setting up communications systems, and did some consulting for a lot of high-tech companies. Many of these high-tech companies didn't have the big bucks to pay him a big dollar, so they paid him a small fee and gave him company stock. Now, here is a guy down-sized five years ago who today has $8 million of a public company stock. His last fee was for a foreign government in Latin America that paid him $1 million up front.

This was a guy making $50 to $60 thousand a year five years ago as an engineer. He was an ordinary engineer. Nothing spectacular, no glittering credentials, but he was good at his job. So, he took his personal situation and said, "Hey, I want to do something and here's a opportunity niche. Some of the companies I deal with can't afford to buy the services of my company, but they might be able to hire me at a lesser fee." So, he was able to compete against the company who had recently laid him off because he priced his service in the ball park for the small companies.

Building a Downsizing Safety Net

Summarizing, Miller-Tiedeman continued. If you have a professional degree or similar experience, along with work experience in a company where you make contacts with outside businesses, as in the above Puplava example, then you stand light years ahead in this downsizing game. And many people today engage in that kind of business. But if you don't have that opportunity, what can you do?

First, think about connecting with a small group of like-minded friends and acquaintances who have a variety of skills. Something like Faith Popcorn's idea of the kitchen cabinet (see Chapters 3, 8, and 14). With diverse backgrounds, you each bring something different to the idea table. Next, set up weekly or semiweekly meetings. This is important as momentum builds. If you meet haphazardly, then you get haphazard outcomes. Brainstorm possible ideas. Assign research tasks to each person so when you meet again, you have more information with which to work. Remember the principles we've been talking about in this chapter—work, time, and investment. While you're researching, determine how much money (both time and currency) each person might be able to contribute to the start up idea. You can do something small that has the potential for great returns.

For instance, the Dacyczyns started *The Tightwad Gazette*, a monthly newsletter, with a 486 computer and worked from home. In addition, they saved $49,000 from a $30,000 annual income while supporting four children. That enabled them to purchase their dream home, a nineteenth-century farmhouse with an attached barn. So, you need to keep your eye on your money as well as on your next endeavor, which tends to cause you to make quantum leaps in development. The Dacyczyns' formula for success is "Produce a unique product that gets a lot of good publicity" (Tightwads ride recession, 1992, June, p. 54).

Learn While Employed.   Today, business trains the new entrepreneurs, not because they want to but that's how the precession effect works. The bee goes into the flower for honey, a little pollen rubs off on its wings, and when it enters the next flower, it cross-fertilizes, free of charge, and unintentionally. What people learn on the job, in many cases, will become an entrepreneurial endeavor. In that sense, business now serves as a training ground for their employees' future entrepreneurial activities.

Here's an example. Puplava wanted to have a system called "Lotus Notes" in his business. He called IBM and they told him it would cost 30 thousand to design the system. But he knew a woman who was downsized from another company. She gave him a quote for between $2,000 and $3,000. So, like the communications expert, she's competing with the big companies and will give Puplava the same type of system, adapted to his special needs. This woman started work when downsizing wasn't even an idea, but new workers have the jump now on the downsizing phenomenon. They can decide what they might want to do entrepreneurially, find a business that can teach those skills and work for the business long enough to save money and learn all they can, then go out on their own. The new permanent temporary workers will need to practice more self interest. But that is a principle business has practiced since its inception. On the other hand, when a business hires someone really wanting to learn, they have a better employee, and, if they treat him or her well, may hold that employee much longer.

Remember the engineer above who knew the small companies couldn't afford the services of his large corporate employer, and when downsized, this man went back and offered the service at a fee they could afford. In this way, we all serve each other unintentionally. But that's one of life's great designs.

Values and Money

Let's talk about attitudes toward money now. A fair number of helping professionals shun the talk of money, keep their budgets in their heads, and think they don't make enough money to invest. Their reply often is, "I'm not good at handling money" or "I'm more interested in helping people." They frequently see money as something separate from helping people. Where do you stand? Take a moment to check values from the following list (Givens, 1991) that are important to you. Then rank order the top 5.

___ Peace of mind

___ Security

___ Wealth

___ Good health

___ A close relationship with spouse/mate

___ A close relationship with children

___ Family (Spending time with parents or other relatives)

___ Meeting the "right" person

___ Meaningful job or career

___ Fame

___ Power

___ Free time

___ Happiness

___ Close relationship with God

___ Friendships

___ Retirement

___ Contributing time, knowledge, or money to others

___ Knowing important or famous people

___ Having your own business

___ Living to an old age

___ Personal passions—cars, houses, jewelry, etc.

___ Travel to exciting places

___ Sense of accomplishment

___ Respect from others—being thought a good person

___ Other

Notice that if you placed wealth at the top of this list, you can buy time and experience to either use or give away; thereby fulfilling many of the values on this list. Think about that and ask yourself if you need to adjust your money paradigm (see Chapter 5 for more detail on paradigms).

College Education or Future Financial Security

If you are saving for your children's education, here's another perspective. A very well-off family, the Days decided to invite their children to work and save for their college educations. The parents helped them find scholarships and loans.

They invested what they would have paid for the college education—$15,000 a year—in stocks and mutual funds, with a stipulation the children could not touch the money until they reach 40 years of age. They decided to give the bulk of their estate to charity, but they wanted their children to have security in their later years. They thought that when the children reached age 40, they would have enough maturity and life experience to handle the money well. The children were invited to contribute to that fund after they finished their education, if in fact they decided to go to college. This family realized that investing in education, while a good value, may not yield benefits in a nanosecond world. They had friends whose children had done fairly well, but nothing spectacular, and those children did not have much of a nest egg. So, they decided to focus on financial security in later years for their children, not the children's immediate education.

So, here's how their plan figures out financially. Given that a private education at some colleges would cost around $70,000 for four years, the parents invested $1,250 a month for each of the four years at 8% interest. This would yield $70,437. If that money were compounded at 8% interest for the next 20 years, it would yield $347,029. If their daughter Jane, after graduating college, decided to contribute $100 per month for twenty years, the amount would grow to $405,931.

But let's say at age 41 (the age of many graduate students), Jane looked at her life and said, "Hey, what I want to do is retire at age 55 with at least a million dollars. What do I need to invest to do that?" She could contribute $500 a month for the next 15 years and retire at age 55 with $1,575,894. And even with a 2% inflation, she would still have $978,581. This example represents the high end of income for college investing.

Another college costs $5,000 a year, and Joe's parents, since they didn't have much of an estate to leave him, decided to invest the money he would have received for college. They decided to start with $416 a month at 8% interest, over a four year period. This would accrue to $23,412. If Joe didn't make any more contributions for the next 20 years, and he let the money grow at compound interest, he would have $115,489.

On the other hand, if Joe decided to invest $100 a month for 20 years, the amount would grow to $174,391. But if at the end of 20 years, Joe said, "I want to retire at age 56. What do I need in order to do that with financial comfort?" Joe could invest $500 a month for 15 years. This would accrue to $749,716, and, with a 2% inflation, he would have $555,542 in today's dollars.

Money Management in Action

Sam, a physician, went to his financial adviser and said, "My son, Josh, is 10 years old. I have $25,000 to start an investment account for his college expenses. He may want to attend a private university, so I want growth with a minimum of risk." However, at age 18, Josh decided to attend a junior college. He then went on to a state university. In ten years, the fund grew to $125,000, and the college expenses have been paid by the interest and dividends.

An interesting aspect of this arrangement is that Josh doesn't know the account exists. Like most young men, Josh loves fast cars and has accumulated his share of speeding tickets. So, Sam intends to hold that account until he thinks his son has sufficient maturity to handle it. In the meantime, if the account is not touched, in forty years it would be worth 36 million. If Sam turns the account over to Josh, and he invests only $125 a month for the remaining 40 years, he could retire at age 62 with 56 million dollars, all of which started with a $25,000 investment.

In the present soft economy, many workers would love to have even $100,000 in the bank, not to mention a half million or even one million. While many parents will never accrue that kind of savings, they can help their children experience solid financial security in their later years. But to do this it takes thought, time, work, and disciplined living. In addition, the consciousness about preparing for the future is much higher today than even ten years ago because the need is presently starkly apparent.

☐ Looking Back

1.   Management of money is a top priority in a downsizing environment.

2. Money management or the lack thereof relates both to level of development and personal paradigms, among other things.

3. The principle of work, save and let your money grow offers more future possibilities.

4. Upsizing your skills, can help you bridge the downsizing gap.

5. Saving for potential downsizing possibilities provides a good safety net.

6. Grouping together to make a stronger unit makes sense, particularly when you have limited resources.

☐ Discussion Questions

1. What does money management and today's work scene have in common?

2. What benefits do good money managers experience?

3. How much money should you have in reserve in case you get downsized?

4. How many people in your circle of friends and acquaintances have been downsized?

5. Do you know whether or not they have or had sufficient funds to reinvent themselves either by buying training, returning to college, or starting up a small business?

6. Why is it difficult to tackle money management?

7. How can you help a client improve his or her money management skills?

8. How would you talk with a client about the importance of money management?

9. What books would you recommend?

10. What books have you read on the subject?

☐ Classroom/Group Exercises

1. Form groups of either two or three and discuss the importance of money management.

2. Over the semester or quarter, record your spending and share insights gained with your group.

    a. Note the level of difficulty you had in disciplining yourself to do it.

    b. Note the self-talk that came up, like "I know what I spend, why do I have to write it down?"

    c. Imagine how you would deal with a client who said similar things.

☐ Homework/Test Assignment

1. Visit a local university or clinic career center and ask if the helping professional discusses money issues with clients or educates them about money management.

2. Do the following money exercise and report back to the class: Select one question for each of five evenings and write down your answers.

    a. What things do I want to start doing about money that I've never done?

    b. What money habits do I want to change that I haven't changed?

    c. What things do I want to stop doing regarding money that I haven't stopped?

    d. What things do I want to say about money that I've never said?

    e. What things do I want to learn about money that I haven't learned?

3. Create a timetable for what you learned. Maybe starting with "Think before I spend." Maybe, buy a budget cash book. If you have a computer, buy a financial program.

10
CHAPTER

Anna Miller-Tiedeman
Laurie MacMenamin
Calvin Rich

Alternative Modalities for Uncovering Individual Life Mission

Spotlight on Alternative Ways to Grow

Each of us, counselors and clients alike, now stands at the threshold of incredible newness. Yes, it's scary, but it's also exciting. There will be many hits and bruises, more for some than others, but then the fresh wind blows and we marvel that we made it through the valley of the shadow of the death of growing ourselves to a new level of development.

Bach (1977) in his book *Illusions: The Adventures of a Reluctant Messiah* tells the story of the creatures at the bottom of the crystal river. One of the creatures grew tired of sameness and decided to let go and move to the top. His friends warned him how terrible it would be, warning that he would be bashed against rocks and perhaps killed, but he decided that would be better than being bored to death. So he let go. And sure enough he did get thrown against many a rough object, but he kept moving toward the top until one day he swam free. Then the creatures at the other end of the crystal river thought he had come to save them. He replied, "I saved myself, now you must save yourself." In a similar vein, we each have to work out our move to a higher level of development ourselves; the conforming road will not take us there.

☐ Looking Ahead

Watch for the following important topics:

1. Talk, whether therapy or counseling, will not likely provide clients with sufficient insight to grow themselves more deeply into their life mission.

2. Meditation offers positive physiological, psychological, spiritual and mental outcomes.

3. Structural body work helps release the issues in our tissues. Or as Joseph Heller, founder of Hellerwork, remarks later on in this chapter, "What is going on in your body is going on in your life."

Many hesitate to choose growth because of its chaotic, untidy nature. It's downright confusing at times; friends you thought you had somehow disappear with their conforming, polite excuses. You find yourself somewhat without a rudder. Having been taught you must be in control, you back away and postpone the pain of knowing that it's okay to float free without a direct path.

What they didn't tell you is that most everyone uses the float free technique in much of life, but that's the underground secret, as it must not show. We must always somehow appear in control. But the wise people in our society know that control kills both immune systems and dreams. But somehow, we don't let ourselves listen to that deep exquisite voice of life that would lead us into those things that mean the most to us, that we do best, and that produce joy in our hearts. Making money, making status, making ourselves suitable—all these preclude the wonderful magic of making a life while making a living and teasing out our deepest potential, which segues into a powerful spiritual journey. But many experiences exist to help you peel away the layers of cultural programming to get closer to your core, but they are mostly nonverbal and have little to do with skills, interests, abilities, aptitudes, vocational maturity, and self concept—many of the things with which traditional career appears most enchanted.

However, we have reached a time where we have to abandon intellect-only approaches to things. Additionally, we've done about all we can do at the Conforming stage of development. We're left with our noses against the Conforming wall. If we turn that wall into a veil we can see through and ultimately walk past, then we must start the journey to the Self-Aware level of development, which will lead us to our own deep knowing.

Those midwifing personal growth and development must experience these things for themselves before they can convincingly educate others about them. We need to be careful of recommending treatments we know little about. In that spirit, Miller-Tiedeman, having experienced structural bodywork, meditation, and Cranio-sacral therapy—all mostly non-talk therapies—recommends them as experiences that can help us move deeper into our own power, that free us from the psychopathology of the average (Maslow, 1954) and from our socially programmed hypnosis (Chopra, 1995).

While it's a time-protracted process, a deep sense of reward issues from even the smallest recognition of an old pattern having been dumped. Additionally, the more old patterns that we extrude, the more free our life direction flows, often into new channels—ones not thought about or even dreamed of. All things being equal, old archetypes we hold in our bodies probably impact life direction much more than skill deficit.

The two modalities discussed in this chapter are (a) Hellerwork and (b) Meditation. Educating clients about these therapies makes it more likely that they will use them, along with other available growth-enhancing therapies that you, the reader, have experienced. If you want to use either or both of these modalities, check out the Internet for more information about them.

Hellerwork[1]

Hellerwork, founded by Joseph Heller, combines structural bodywork, guided dialogue and movement awareness to improve function, balance and well-being in the body. All kinds of people use structural bodywork: those wanting to reduce stress that they experience on their job, those coming for help with physical conditions, those wanting better body presentation, those who are working to mature their life vision, and those who would like better rapport with their bodies in general. Companies use neck and shoulder bodywork to reduce stress of employees. When stress is reduced, more focus is possible. Miller-Tiedeman used structural bodywork once a week to help her through the stress of David's (V. Tiedeman) 112 days of hospitalization in 1990. So, structural bodywork finds its way into many lives for a variety of reasons.

Hellerwork works with the individual to match body structure with inner personality and bring integration and integrity to the body. The work is based on the guiding principle that balancing the body structure and

---

[1]By Laurie MacMenamin, a registered Hellerwork practitioner.

reestablishing natural movement and expression reveals the innate whole-ness of the individual. The root word of integrity, *integer*, means whole. Wholeness is revealed when we are in balanced relationship with body, mind, and spirit. It's about recognizing our habitual and unconscious pat-terns that no longer support our growth, and discovering and developing new habits that will.

Hellerwork embraces a more active role with the client than does traditional massage. One way clients interact with their practitioner may be with dialogue, not trivial in nature but a respectful exploration of them-selves and their life experiences. Clients are given supportive attention to discover and express their truths. They frequently move around the room or work area to practice new movement patterns including sitting, stand-ing, and walking. They learn to feel the difference between how they have moved in the past and how they can move more fluidly.

The body mirrors who and how we are. It also reflects our life expe-riences at the physical, emotional, mental, and spiritual levels and how they have shaped us. It reveals how we have chosen to respond to all those life experiences. But much of the time, awareness of our many life choices remains dim. Joseph Heller maintains that the continued explora-tion of the body, in greater and greater depth, illuminates and brings into focus the awareness of one's self (Heller & Henkin, 1991).

Emotion reflects energy in motion, a complete structure with a be-ginning, a middle, and an end. If we recognize and allow for this energy to move with its natural rhythm and structure, it will complete itself. Other-wise, it gets stuck in our body and *we carry our issues in our tissues*. This tension commonly shows up in the body as tension, strain and/or pain in the face, neck, and back. These symptoms frequently bring people to see a bodyworker. Many of us suppress our expression of ourselves because of society's narrow and confining limits that allow little leeway for comple-tion of emotions. Some phrases that are common in our culture are, "big boys don't cry," "tough up," and "girls don't do that." We also have some ideas regarding when and where expression of emotions may or may not be appropriate. This results in holding back both positive and dispositive feelings. When there is confusion or lack of experience about our respon-sibility or appropriateness to express ourselves, we often hold back the tension or joy we feel.

To give you a feel for this, John, an accountant, wanted to see life line up like his figures in a column, neat and tidy. But life didn't work like that and John had difficulty fitting the pieces together. In addition, he was working the last few days of a job he knew would not continue, and he was the only remaining employee. He worked knowing that soon he would receive his pink slip, not if but when. As a result, he lived with enormous unpredictability and had difficulty dancing on the shifting rug of employment. He held a lot of concern about what he could do versus his capability.

His presenting complaint was pain in his neck and shoulders. He felt old and uncomfortable in his body. He was wearing out and he was not willing to accept that. John had expressed an initial concern about the look of his body and going to interviews. With a sunken chest and a rigidity due to loss of stability, he felt that communicated to the interviewer and he wanted to change that. He knew he did not express himself well, both in speech and in posture, particularly as he considered his need to interview for new job positions.

Often, due to physical or emotional trauma, continuous stress, or lack of balanced movement, body tissue changes from being elastic and flexible to being stiff and rigid. This rigidity is sometimes mistakenly accepted as an irreversible condition of aging. John wanted to set the stage for the second half of his life that was different from the way it was currently going. John was very rigid in his torso, and his spine was extremely tight. His body image was of a sunken chest and rounded shoulders and back.

John voiced a concern that life felt more out of control. He tightened up his body to gain a sense of control. Many of my clients do this thinking it will bring them more control and hence, stability. An example of this is that drunk drivers usually don't experience much injury because they're so much more relaxed. People who tense up on collision often experience far more serious injury. A different example comes from the martial arts. When your opponent strikes you, you are less stable when you harden your stance. The optimum approach is to allow the body to receive the strike, move with it, and then send back a response. But John couldn't relax sufficiently to flow with his situation. He didn't handle the flow principle well. In other words, he continually broke himself against the rocky realities of his work life.

John went through the series of eleven Hellerwork sessions. Each session addressed a specific area of his body and embraced a particular theme pertinent for the section. For example, the second section and theme is "Standing on Your Own Two Feet." The work focuses primarily on the feet and legs. Dialogue may involve discovering how the client determines his foundation in life, how he stands up for himself, how he "thinks on his feet," etc. The discussion is never limited to the theme, but it is a starting point for deeper understanding.

The process follows an ordered sequence; organizing the body in relation to gravity introduces change to a more functional way of being. Upon completion of the eleven sessions—having utilized structural bodywork, guided dialogue, and movement education—John attained many of the goals and expectations that he put forth at the beginning. He felt less anxious and more relaxed about life. He also felt more peace of mind and more energy in his body. He recognized his ability to be relaxed in interviews and cope with feelings of uncertainty. He felt more at ease. Initially, he had felt that he had a mind/body split, but the Hellerwork process helped him to unify these two.

After the series, his chest opened up and could expand comfortably with breath. The bodywork assisted him to produce better stability and a more balanced posture by bringing his legs soundly under his body. His spine's flexibility increased, hence it became more comfortable to live with. Discovering a more flexible back bone translated into a greater feeling of stability and flexibility to John's life in general. He could then relax and lean into the wind without feeling a loss of control.

Joseph Heller said Hellerwork brings excellence with ease. "We work, we play, we love for the ecstacy of the excellence that comes with ease.... The challenge that life presents and that integrative bodywork addresses is that such excellence and the concomitant experience of joy can be available in everyday life" (Heller & Henkin, 1991, p. 232).

Joseph Heller, Founder of Hellerwork, Comments

McMenamin's above description of Hellerwork does it justice. She aptly brings out the fact that our bodies are expressions of our whole selves and therefore reflect all the stresses and imbalances present in our lives. One of the hardest things for clients to admit initially is that whatever is going on in their bodies is a sign of something going on in their lives. We keep wanting to separate the physical from the mental, emotional, and spiritual aspects of ourselves. But in my experience such separation is often akin to self-deception. When people are ready to see all their parts as representing the whole, they generally move forward rapidly.

The other thing I want to emphasize is that the most intelligent use of Hellerwork is as preventive maintenance rather than as a fix-it procedure. When it comes to cars, we know that preventive maintenance works better than waiting for a breakdown. The same holds true for our bodies.

The Meditation Experience[2]

"Wait a minute! I have an idea."

When you say this people wait for you to express your idea. After all, it's normal for each of us to have a spark of an idea and need time for it to

---

[2]By Calvin Rich.

take shape. But why is this so? Perhaps it's because this phenomenon, this intuition before precise understanding, is a fundamental aspect of who we are. It may, at the very least, serve as an example of how your self began, not in the physical sense but in the psychological/characterlogical sense.

You have some idea of your self, of who you are, but you may feel that the idea hasn't really taken shape. When asked who you are, you probably respond by naming one of the major roles you play in life. That may be your career role, your role as parent or child, or one of the other roles you play in life. However, if you're like most of us, at one time or another you've asked yourself, "Who am I? Right to my very core, who am I?"

Going beyond your self, finding that intuited spark of Self and raising it to the level of conscious understanding can seem an impossible task. This can lead to a sense of disconnection. You think you're the adjectives, but you also sense you're something more. Making the connection between the two, making life your career, can often seem as elusive as finding that pot of gold at the end of the rainbow.

In reality, you're both self and Self. As self, you're a pattern of personality characteristics that have been shaped by interactions with family, friends, culture and the greater world. As Self, you were born "I"—that unique individual whom you sense yourself to be but just can't seem to pin down.

Here, I use the term Self in the same sense as Jung used it. Jung "... preferred the term *Self*, which has the advantage of being a Western concept that with some extension corresponds closely to the Eastern notion of the Self as the divine core of one's being" (Odajnyk, 1993, pp. 18–19). This section is about a path that may help you in your quest to make clear the divine core of your true Self. For it's only then, only from an understanding of Self that you can experience the true meaning of Lifecareer.

Going Backward to Go Forward

Psychologically, each of us begins as a spark. Like the spark caused by striking two pieces of flint together, it can ignite a fire for good, evil, or any of the gradients in between; it all depends on what happens after the spark has been struck. Unlike fire, however, what happens to you after your psychological birth can be reversed all the way back to the original spark.

It's important to remember that every spark is unique. This means that experiencing the characteristics of the spark of Self is difficult—but not impossible. It requires effort coupled with discipline and a certain amount of objective awareness that comes with practice and determination. This is the combination that makes your spark a coherent, brilliant light.

Meditation is a way of discovering your Self. It is a method of going backwards through your life, as though your life is a tunnel the walls of which are constructed by the molding and shaping that has led to your current sense of self. Examining the walls as you pass backward through your tunnel will reveal much about your self. Revealing the attributes of the self releases their hold over you. Then, you will leave the tunnel and be in the presence of the spark of Self. Finally, using the deep wisdom that comes from knowledge of self, you will be able to guide the spark of Self to more fully live life as the big career.

Life Equipped with an Automatic Transmission

What is meditation and how does it work? There are many books written on the subject, most tell you how to meditate. It isn't my intention to repeat what others have so ably written. What I have found lacking are books in which meditators actually share some of their experiences with others. This, for what it's worth, is what I want to do here.

There is a difference between what we experience during meditation and what I call the Meditation Experience. Some of the details of what we experience are deeply personal and very, very private. Some of these experiences are unique to each of us, and make up the complexes which result from the fact that our lives have been molded and shaped by others. It is important to find ways of working through our complexes so that psychic energy is freed up for the Meditation Experience. Other experiences are more general and can be shared because they are felt by most of us. First, let me give you a few examples of this last type of experience.

Those of us who are over fifty may remember when cars came with standard transmissions. Driving required a certain vigilance because we often needed to shift gears. When automatic transmissions became common, we found that driving was easier—less thrilling, perhaps, but easier. So much of our life is lived as though we had an automatic transmission. When I first started meditating, I began to notice this. I found that much of my time was spent in thought, not in meditating. My mind would begin to wander, and I'd have to bring myself back to my meditation. My thinking mode seemed so automatic.

Then I began to examine my thoughts. At first, I felt conflicted. Was the examination of thoughts the opposite of meditating? Wasn't I caught chasing my own tail? I wasn't meditating when my mind wandered, but I didn't think I was meditating while I was examining my thoughts either. Ouch! There seemed to be no way out.

Actually, I discovered that the thoughts I was having weren't very important to my life. I was so accustomed to thinking, that I believed it was impossible to live without my thoughts. They were with me especially during mundane, routine tasks such as eating, getting dressed, or taking a shower. In fact, I became aware that too much time was being spent in thought and not enough feeling deeply connected to my life. I began to realize that I was driving through my tunnel of life with an automatic transmission. I needed to downshift and take a closer look at the tunnel in which I was living.

What I've left out here is the content of my thoughts—my plans, fantasies, and daydreams. These are very private. What I eventually experienced as I became aware of my thinking is something that happens to most of us after meditating for months. It is the Meditation Experience.

Did I *Really* Eat Breakfast?

During meditation, there are periods called "dives." Dives happen when you begin to go deeply into meditation. They are often accompanied by feelings of joy, peace, and deep relaxation. They eventually lead to a state of ecstasy.

When I started meditating, I did so for 20 minutes in the morning and afternoon. During my sessions, I would occasionally check my clock to see how much time I had left. However, I began to notice that this checking was almost always before a dive. In others words, something in me sensed a letting go, a diving into a deeper part of me. By interrupting my meditation, I was sabotaging my breaking free from my thoughts. What I didn't realize at the time was that my self was feeling threatened with abandonment.

At first, I was bothered by the idea that I was actually impeding my own growth. In order to understand this, I felt I had to state it: "I want to look at the clock, but I know that this is a way of remaining in my thinking mode." Then I began to understand that I was judging myself—something that is a familiar pattern for most of us. With that understanding came an acceptance of the impulse to check the clock, which led to not checking the clock, which led to discovering more impulses beneath other thoughts.

As I began to reveal the impulses that led to thinking, I found that thinking had less and less appeal. I began to apply this to my everyday activities. By being aware of the impulse that led to a thought, I found that I could make even routine activities objects of awareness. As a result, life became more meaningful.

Breakfast, for example, became an eating activity, not something I did automatically while planning my day. As I started to *really* eat breakfast, I began to take control of my nutrition. I started by shopping at the local organic food market.

Getting dressed took on new meaning as I began to experience it more deeply. I felt my arms going into the sleeves of my shirt, or my legs going into my pants leg. Walking, even walking up and down stairs, became a Meditation Experience as I felt the movement of my body. Greater body awareness meant that I started to do more physical exercise.

By going deeper into my daily activities and becoming more aware of how I led my life, I freed up more and more psychic energy—energy which had been wasted in meaningless thinking. Over time, I began to feel that my daily life was a Meditation Experience. More psychic energy meant more joy, freedom, and choice. The freed psychic energy made work less stressful because I wasn't fighting with myself trying to make life and work fit into ideas I had in the tunnel of my mind.

This led to an examination of how I got into the tunnel in the first place. I was releasing the grip that outside expectations had over me. By freeing myself from old patterns of behavior, I was developing a deeper awareness of my self. Gradually, I began to feel more authentic. My actions were actions based on truth, not on the expectations of others in my past. I began to take more control of my life. I began to shift my own gears. This left me open to even more profound experiences.

The Four Levels of Soul

Life for me *became* a Meditation Experience. I went deeper and deeper into life and got more and more out of it. During meditation itself, I came to feel changes in four areas of my life. Two I've mentioned above are the mental and physical, and the other two are the emotional and the spiritual. As I lived in the Meditation Experience, I found that my thinking happened in response to necessity, and was not the result of old tapes running in my head. I also became more physically relaxed. My emotional responses became more authentic (I stood up for my self more), and I began to have spiritual experiences. These four areas have been referred to in several of the mystical paths as the Four Souls (Cooper, 1994).

The Physical Soul.   The Mental Soul and how I dealt with it is fairly well described above. During meditation, I also became aware of physical tensions which I'd lived with for much of my life. Through awareness of this Physical Soul, I was able to simply relax certain parts of my body which felt tense. I noticed tension between my eyes, in my hands, thighs and abdomen, and as I became aware of them I simply relaxed them without judgment. In some cases the causes of these tensions became known to me; in some, I had no idea why I was tense. But the mere fact of letting go built up a pattern which carried over into the Meditation Experience of my daily life. As I became more physically aware, I became better able to monitor my body's movements and actions. I built on this by learning to do walking meditations, which I found very pleasant.

The Emotional Soul. Emotional releases during meditation can be dangerous. Deep-seated wounds can suddenly flare up in ways that can be overwhelming. It is best to see a competent therapist if you begin to feel overwhelmed by experiences you have during meditation. However, allowing emotional releases during meditation that are not threatening can be therapeutic. At times I experienced very strong releases of raw emotions. Afterwards, I felt cleansed. These releases should be approached with caution. For me, they deepened my trust in myself and in my feelings.

The last Soul is where I met my Self.

The Spiritual Soul. The Spiritual Soul is the realm of Self. There are two aspects of this, the Personal Self and the Transpersonal Self. The Transpersonal Self is Nothingness, Enlightenment, Ayn Sof, the Tao, or any of the many other words which have been used to try to name the Nameless. I'll not attempt to describe this. Instead, I will leave that up to the Masters of the various wisdom paths.

However, the Personal Self, which I refer to here as Self, is the core from which we live Lifecareer. When the Physical Soul enters into a period of sustained relaxation and tensions are, whenever appropriate, controllable, when the Emotional Soul has been cleansed and the Mental Soul is brought into a state of peace, then the spark of Self is released into the Spiritual Soul. The only thing remaining is to give the Self the freedom of expression it craves. By working through to the deepest levels of the Four Souls, by living the Meditation Experience, Lifecareer becomes the most natural, effortless experience there can be.

A Final Note

The self does not give up easily. It works hard to cling to its old patterns, and fears abandonment. It is important to understand that the freed psychic energy does not cause the self to disappear, but it becomes transformed into Self. In other words, self gets transformed into Self. This transformation is the aim of most of the world's wisdom teachings. What we do with this transformation is what is truly important. We are here on Earth for a purpose. By seeing our life as a process and unfoldment, we more readily come to experience that purpose.

☐ Looking Back

1. Hellerwork is a combination of structural bodywork, invited dialogue, and movement awareness.

2. A Hellerwork practitioner strives to help the individual bring integation and integrity to the body.

3. The body mirrors each individual's issues.

4. Structural bodywork helps in further unfolding our life direction, but it is not a fix-it or quick fix.

5. Hellerwork acknowledges life's process of healing.

6. Meditation helps with the integration of body, mind, emotion, and spirit.

7. Each person experiences meditation differently. That is why it is difficult to explain.

8. The four levels of soul are: mental, physical, emotional, and spiritual.

☐ Discussion Questions

1. What most impressed you in this chapter?

2. How do you feel about the idea that the mind and the body are connected?

☐ Classroom/Group Exercises

1. Divide into dyads and discuss your experience of structural bodywork. If you have not had that experience, share your impression, pro or con, about it.

2. Do you do any kind of meditation? If so, share your thoughts about the benefits you felt. Also, has meditation made a difference in your mental, physical, emotional, and/or spiritual life?

☐ Homework Assignments

1. Scan Herbert Benson's book, *The Relaxation Response*, and report his findings to the class.

2. Interview someone who has had structural bodywork or does meditation and report his or her experience.

3. Read Chopra's (1987) *Creative Health: How to Wake Up the Body's Intelligence* and report on his notion of the mind/body connection.

11

Hal A. Lingerman

Pythagorean Assessment: An Assessment Paradigm for Process Careering

Spotlight on a Larger Assessment Paradigm

Each life is a moving mosaic, created from our individual desires and our deeper resonance with the *Calling*. In the midst of what we may want, the unlimited Life of an infinite Presence is living out itself through us. So, we exist in the midst of a much larger creative process, which we can gradually begin to sense and align ourselves with, or we can choose to fight the natural process of our life. *Our greatest sense of fulfillment comes when we learn more about how to go with the flow and make our finest contribution.* A growing sense of our *calling* opens our consciousness to our true vocation and the jobs available to us that genuinely allow us to express our most authentic identity and real life work.

The teachings of Pythagoras, a master philosopher and mathematician of ancient Greece, and the writings of his followers suggest the existence of a dynamic energy field or spectrum, which feeds us and offers us an inclusive perspective or "window" through which we can view larger potential opportunities in the midst of the approaching forces of our lifetime. Such a viewing helps us to balance our personal desires with our larger needs. Pythagorean assessment helps us to identify our deepest intentions; it teaches us how to express our highest consciousness more clearly through the filter of our temperament. Such a tool gives us important clues about how to let the larger Presence of Life live itself through us as we discover our larger vocation and become creative instruments in a larger life design: "... the great cosmic pattern {is} a model to be imitated on earth—a sentiment that is epitomized in the maxim 'As above, so below'" (Feuerstein, 1994, p. 13).

☐ Looking Ahead

Watch for the following important topics:

1. Living our life harmoniously and letting the one Life express itself through us.

2. Going with the flow and not fighting Life.

3. Viewing the NINE great power streams of energy, suggested by Pythagoras, and their currents and themes:

   a. New ideas and entrepreneurial possibilities

   b. Connection, collaboration and partnership

   c. Creative self-expression

   d. Accomplishments of work and labor

   e. Newness and diversification

   f. Contribution to the family, group, and community

   g. Inner connection with the Creator

   h. The will to power and righteousness

   i. Compassionate service to all living beings

4. Important terms and concepts:

   a. Flow and harmony

   b. Calling

   c. Connection

   d. Interconnection

   e. Newness and diversification

  f. Compassionate service and synthesis

  g. Giving and helping: being an instrument of Life

  h. Life mosaic

6. Important contributors:

  a. Pythagoras and his students

  b. H. A. Lingerman's many clients through the years

Living Our Life Harmoniously and Letting the One Life Express Itself Through Us

Each person's lifetime is a new opportunity to create a more beautiful mosaic of desires, intentions, and responses to the great *Calling*. To make the most of our journey, it is helpful to gain increasing perspective and perception about ourselves and where life is leading us. Each of us has our own *calling* to complete. Our true work and the formation of our own unique life mosaic arises out of our *calling*. Our *calling* is to identify and to make the best of our own patterns and possibilities, while sharing and wishing all others well on their life path: no comparison, no competition, no complaints! "... in the series of (successive) earth lives, the soul can regress or advance, depending upon whether it surrenders itself to the lower or to its divine nature" (Schuré, 1961, p. 342).

  Each job adds colorful pieces to our evolving life mosaic; different cycles activate different opportunities, which can later become useful in completing a total life design. All that we do, feel, and think eventually integrates into the pattern of a larger totality and become part of the ways we celebrate our essential selves. Our most joy-filled works happen when our intentions connect with our *calling*. In union we feel the flow of life moving through us: our existence and daily rounds become a happening.

Going With the Flow and Not Fighting Life. We move in the creative tension of our personal desires and an invitation to a larger destiny. As we live our life, the *calling* is living itself through us. In the midst of our own intentions, new horizons filled with creative opportunities surround us. When what we want harmonizes and integrates with what we need, a greater good can occur. In the larger picture, it may be wiser "to release the lesser for the greater." Remaining alert, yet not forcing our own way upon the universe, we allow larger possibilities to appear. Such gifts and graces always become visible on the journey, in many cases after the fact. Living in rapport with the *calling* releases our deepest creative gifts and motivation.

Eventually, we will recognize that the more we can go with our intuitive flow to move in the direction where we sense the energies are leading us, our highest vocation begins to emerge. Without being either impulsive or passive, we live more in rhythms of cooperation and co-creativity with our life mission. Such an attitude brings joy, deep peace, and increasing vitality and power, freeing us to discover our highest potentials. We may not always know in the moment what the best decision or outcome for us might be, but as we try to check in with our "gut feelings" and listen to our inward leadings, while looking clearly at the perspective before us, the most beneficial results for all will eventually happen. That is what this book is all about: learning to listen, to feel, to think and to act.

How can we develop greater sensitivity to go where the energies of life are leading us, thus avoiding "fighting life"? Pythagoras of Crotona, a master philosopher and mathematician of ancient Greece, who may even have studied with the Buddha, was very finely attuned to these higher frequencies of existence. Pythagoras taught a basic "outer" mathematics and an "inner" science of numbers, which can suggest the movement of energies taking place in each person's lifetime. One of his students said that Pythagoras could "read the ripples on the water," or sense the direction of life's energies according to the corresponding movements of the heavens. Pythagoras discovered in the music of the octave the most harmonious proportions of sounds, which suggest a larger music of the spheres. Likewise, Pythagoras believed that such beautiful celestial music, sounding through the universe, also can be embodied in each person's daily life. In this sense, each of us IS music, always refining itself in harmony with the great Word, waiting to be played and heard in its larger entirety. Our responses to the great *calling* create music describing the unique beauty and mystery of ourselves connecting with all living beings, our relationships, and a deep longing to express unspoken feelings, impressions, and the love in our hearts: to become all that we truly were created to be. "Above all other sciences or parts of the mathematics, however, the followers of Pythagoras esteemed the doctrine of Numbers, which they believed to have been revealed to (humankind) by the celestial deities" (Oliver, 1975, p. 14).

The Nine Universal Energies

Pythagoras and his students describe the interplay of each person's consciousness and temperament resonating with individual purpose through the currents of Divinity. This process of moving in the vibrations of Divinity is called NUMBER. NUMBER honors the uniqueness of each person's *calling* and suggests an open, inclusive energy paradigm: a dynamic spectrum containing NINE major universal energies which stimulate and feed every person's life path. No one of these paths is superior to another. According to our consciousness, tendencies, and temperament, each of us draws continuously upon these diverse streams of cosmic power, thereby making our choices, selecting our array of inspiration, and thus continuously creating new designs and harmonies in the spiral of expanding life. Pythagoras is reputed to have said, "... true happiness consists in knowledge of the perfection of the numbers of the soul" (Guthrie, 1988, p. 33).

The nine Pythagorean streams of energy include all the essential ingredients necessary for everyone to create his or her life mosaic on Earth. They may be briefly summarized as follows: (1) New Ideas and Possibilities; (2) Connection, Collaboration and Partnership; (3) Creative Self-Expression; (4) Accomplishments from Work and Labor; (5) Newness and Diversification; (6) Contribution to the Family, Group, and Community; (7) Inner Connection with the Creator; (8) The Will to Power and Righteousness; and (9) Compassionate Service To All Living Beings. These dynamic reservoirs of energy help us to feel the many different nuances of our life path. They provide the essential themes necessary for us to use in creating our life mosaic (Lingerman, 1992).

How we contact, combine, integrate, and synthesize these energies expresses our creative identity in varied proportions through our behaviors, feelings, thoughts, intentions, and intuitive, soulful responses. These responses are like many colorful threads interweaving and forming the moving quilt of our continuous life journey. "Few people are conscious of the degree to which names and numbers influence all human communication and progress" (Jordan, 1965, p. vii).

The nine power streams (1 through 9) suggested by Pythagoras can be observed in the following descriptions:

The First Power Stream: New Ideas and Possibilities

This is a stream of cosmic power that quickens and catalyzes our mind with archetypes and ideas for the future. (See Figure 11.1 for a description of each power stream.) When we make contact with this energy, through discussions, study, taking classes, etc., we tend to think bigger, conceiving an "impossible dream," and are willing to take risks to make something happen which has not previously appeared. Every breakthrough begins with a pioneer idea: the new concept which is on the "cutting edge" between abstraction and visible concreteness. New ideas and education motivate us to advance in our consciousness and our work. Without mental challenge, it is often difficult to find incentive, and life tends to stall in the ruts of appetite and creature comforts. We reach a critical stage in our *calling* when we move beyond mere physical and emotional concerns to welcome the challenges of continuous learning.

The Second Power Stream: Connection, Collaboration, and Partnership

Collaborative Partnership moves from discovering a new idea to sharing partnership through the heart and feelings. When one hoards an idea or tries to use life's gifts and resources just for oneself, the person becomes too polarized, too dry and brittle, lacking fluidity needed to commune with someone else regularly (Schimmel, 1993, p. 46). A person stays more receptive, pliable, and fluid, more alert and dynamic, by agreeing to become vulnerable—by learning how to connect with others through emotional intimacy. If we are unable to trust, come close, share ourselves and take someone into our heart, life will eventually leave us alone and separated; we will feel more isolated, suspicious, cynical, heartless, and withered.

Our willingness to become open enough to feel our own feelings and share them sympathetically with someone else expands our hearts, our soul, our strength, and our mind. In close relationship we learn patience and humility; we reshape our life according to what is needed in the moment: We experience the give and take of deep bonding. Relationship teaches us how to listen, care for, and be interested in someone else ahead of ourselves. Learning to sense the needs of others, sometimes just "being there," or responding in whatever ways we can be helpful, we will find a new assignment opening for us, a different kind of "employment" in our *calling*—a need for the sweetness of our heartspace ahead of any tasks, knowledge, or solutions.

The Third Power Stream: Creative Self-Expression

This energy source stimulates us to use our imagination and inspiration to add beauty to our life mosaic. The energy focuses through our feelings and creativity. It is important to contribute something beautiful and poignant to life; the creative arts move us as humans to feel the depth of life's joys and sorrows. An important part of our *calling* is to leave our work and our relationships more lovely than when we arrived. Our contacts with beautiful music, paintings, sculpture, poetry, literature, drama, dance, songs, etc., open our hearts to exhilaration and often lift us out of the more mundane and predictable drudgery of the daily arena to see the miracle in our midst.

As new ideas provide our mind with arrows lighting the future, and close relationships open our heart, so our own inspiration and imagination grow new flowers in our garden, enriching the soil of our creativity wherever we go. Whatever work we may be doing, we can always cultivate greater joy, beauty, and color. These qualities put us in closer touch with the flow of our creative process; they open our hearts to the marvels of Nature, and they link us with the mysterious Muse: the bringer of vision and delight.

The Fourth Power Stream: Accomplishment from Work and Labor

This energy vibration helps us satisfy our need for productivity and excellence in our work. It is important to see definite progress in what we do. It is discouraging and depleting to keep doing the same task over and over or to make dedicated efforts which go nowhere and yield no tangible results. We often work hard just to maintain ourselves, but there is a natural need in us to achieve and to surpass ourselves. Our natural talents can be cultivated by organizing our tasks, planning according to specific intentions, and acquiring skills, so that our gifts can find concrete expression and purpose through definite expertise.

When we tune into better ways to plan a project or accomplish our intentions, we build a stronger foundation for our work to yield definite results, leading to a visible cornerstone. Somewhere in all of us the desire to be useful and to make a significant contribution exists. By applying ourselves to the task each day, with eagerness and thoroughness, and by doing our best, we will see progress, and our abilities will demonstrate increasing excellence and usefulness.

The Fifth Power Stream: Newness and Diversification

Part of our life mosaic will always contain the visible results of our desire to dig in, do better, and labor with love. And sometimes, learning how to change direction and go with the flow helps us to laugh and be amazed; we are more willing to hang loose, change quickly, and move in new directions. Life demands spontaneity, quick adjustment, and good humor. Many addictions and appetites find release in diversification, variety, exercise, and sudden movement. Loud laughter, especially at ourselves and our predictions, makes our *calling* clearer and our life mosaic richer.

Inspiration teaches us how to respond to the unpredictability of the journey. Despite all of our efforts to plan our work and relationships, surprises and sudden changes often occur to break us out of assumptions, rigidity, and narrowness. The processes of life are often larger than our limited view and our pre-planning. While intentions shift, goals and timelines change. When the unexpected happens and invades our space, flexibility, humor and diversification help us to step lightly, adjust, and move forward. Learning how to change direction and *cooperate with life* helps us to laugh and to be amazed.

The Sixth Power Stream: Contribution to the Family, Group, and Community

Becoming a part of the community provides a source of energy that helps us to value our family, friends, and the larger neighborhood. Cultivating and appreciating our friendships is a vitally important part of our *calling*. Besides being able to share intimacies with "our significant other," we add to our mosaic by loving and being loved by many friends. Our *calling* begins by putting us into a certain family, often with relatives who may be challenging to us. Our family and friends may know our strengths and, even more, our weaknesses. This enables them to more easily "push our buttons," often triggering deep memories and strong emotional responses. As we face our issues and move to harmonize our family ties, a larger group and community of friends frequently opens to us.

We learn how to enlarge our friendships by being a better friend to others, by valuing and appreciating others, and working with them as a team. Friends who know how to support and nurture each other form a powerful group that builds sweetness and strength like a honeycomb, in order to accomplish a project, to gather in fellowship, to serve others with needs, or to perform together for entertainment. Every friend we make and add to our life mosaic is like a beautiful candle, helping to warm our journey, brightening our way as we move toward the completion of our life mission.

The Seventh Power Stream: Inner Connection with the Creator

The *Creator* energy stream activates our soul and intuitive mind. This source of inspiration and spiritual power often makes its presence known in times when we are alone and quiet. We usually experience those mysterious pockets of time when alone. Then we often find ourselves turning inward, feeling peaceful and reflective, or desperate in our solitude. At length, through the stillness, the timeless Presence in some way makes Itself known, perhaps through the nearness of departed friends, in a breeze or a fragrance, a bird's song or a whisper, our Guardian Angel, or other beings of Light who serve the Eternal Way.

We are continuously blessed and nurtured in ways both visible and invisible. To know that Divinity always accompanies us, in its countless dimensions, awakens our awareness of a deep inner connection with all life and the Source of all Goodness. To keep mindful of the abiding Presence of the One who made us helps us live in the awareness of a continuous *calling*, filling our lives with generosity and grace. Often, in the open spaces between difficult assignments, we experience a "time-out" of Spirit, which we can use to re-connect our consciousness with the infinite Love that supports our journey.

We gather strength and inner wisdom from knowing how to draw back periodically in order to re-align our energies and prepare for our return to the arena of our earthly journey. In so doing, we can take heart that even as we seek direction for our next task or job on the path of our *calling*, something wonderful and necessary awaits in the wings for us.

The Eighth Power Stream: The Will to Power and Righteousness

This energy stream teaches us how to wield the authority that is given to us in ways that empower others. A part of our *calling* will inevitably put us in charge of making decisions that affect other lives, property, or situations.

Whatever our work may be, we will need to learn how to be a just and fair manager; we will need to learn how to follow through on our efforts to realize a successful completion, and we will have to stand up for the rights of ourselves and others. At times, life will require us to step forward, take the lead, and make the final decision; in other situations we may feel powerless to bring about the outcome that we might prefer. How to use power and wealth wisely and to know when to step in and when to step back in the Name of the greater Power—when to speak and when to remain silent, are complementary rhythms that are an important part of everyone's *calling*.

The Ninth Power Stream: Compassionate Service to All Living Beings

This energy stream completes the Pythagorean spectrum and paradigm for balanced careering. In the midst of all human striving, our greatest work and the real essence of our *calling*, is to serve the Highest that we know. To render and surrender our loving service and compassion for all living beings highlights our greatest gift along many turns in the labyrinth of a lifetime.

Love and self-giving are what ultimately connect us most closely to our fellow human beings, the animals, and higher dimensions of nature, and to our Creator, whose own immensity of Love and care for us reaches far beyond our comprehension.

After all agreements and differences, we remain one; interwoven and moving in a cosmic quilt creating its increasingly intricate design. All ages, cultures, faiths, persons, lives, and relationships ultimately interconnect: one world, one universal family of humankind, ascending the ladder of infinite life. All *callings* link somehow. When we help another's life to advance, we advance. When we cause hurt to another life, we hurt ourselves.

Why Are We Here?

Ultimately, we will find our greatest work and fulfillment in addressing the needs of many others in our midst and showing kindness where kindness is absent. In this way our life path may pass through many different jobs and assignments, with a variety of outcomes—some personally pleasing, some not; we can give only the best of ourselves wherever our feet may walk, in ways that matter far more than how much money we make, what position we hold, or how famous we may seem to be in the eyes of the world.

When our time comes to cross over into the greater ongoing, after all our jobs are over, questions will be asked. Among them will be these three: "How much did you love?", "How much did you learn?", and "How much did you give?" How we answer these three questions will be mirrored back to us as we see and feel the contents of this lifetime pass before us, and infinite Love will show us how much our careering resonated with our deeper *calling*.

For your current resume, consider your life experience. All experiences have been valuable; your efforts not wasted. But how much does your job really fulfill you? Remember, it and all past experiences connect in some way with a soulful sense of your larger *calling*. Only you can know for sure!

For what are we really here? What we give is worth much more than what we make. What we are learning is likely to replace quickly what we thought we knew. Each life we touch deeply continues to vibrate in our heart. Expressing the beautiful reminds us that we come from joy, and our life is given to us to be enjoyed. By finding ways to contribute to the larger good, we find our place and sink a root. We feel less irritation and more good humor when we can keep dancing and laughing free in the midst of chaos and uncertainty. Our friends help us experience loving and being loved. When the company leaves, and we sit quietly in the silence, the abiding Presence of our greatest Friend fills our room, and we know that we are never alone.

When we have made all the money we can count, own every stock and toy, and hold the highest imaginable position of power, what else is there except to feed the hungry, clothe the naked, and house the homeless, while encouraging them and sharing with those in need ways to better their condition! Give and it will be given to you in the fullest measure possible; share yourself, and you will never be lonely; wear out to become new. Keep empty, and you will keep being refilled. Complete the circle and continue climbing life's spiral.

Light your torch of new ideas, send out every valentine waiting in the chambers of your heart; give colorful bouquets from your garden of delights; continue to make beautiful music. Contribute where you can; make a difference! Bubble with laughter like a fountain; keep juggling life's circus of surprises. Value and appreciate your friends: show affection and tell them how much you love them. Take some time to be with yourself; get to know yourself and be good to yourself the way the Creator is good to you. Count your blessings but never at others' expense.

When you cannot control the person or the pain, keep close and bring hope; continue to love through hurt and loss; remember that we all are forever alive and growing; know that we will meet again. The veil is thin; a door is always open to you. Until then, run your course with joy and embrace every moment! Complete with grace all that you have been given to do. Celebrate the carnival and wave to others on the carousel. Enjoy ALL your rides! Your life is the greatest gift you will ever receive.

The Case of Jennie

One of the many clients who has benefited from the nine Pythagorean power streams is Jennie. This young woman in her mid-twenties came for a counseling session and a Pythagorean life path overview. Using the spectrum of living harmonies (see the wheel in Figure 11.1) and talking with Jennie, it became clear that she faced a major conflict between her perception of her life and that of her dad, who saw her through his eyes. Her dad wanted his daughter to go into a profession that repeated his own: law and politics(primarily 6 and 8). Jennie, however, felt a strong inclination to become a body worker and an airline stewardess. She identified strongly with Pythagorean power streams of initiative, creativity, travel and service to a large cultural diversity. She also expressed a unique spiritual depth and a love of God that motivated everything she did (1, 3, 5, 7, 9). One

Hal A. Lingerman

Figure 11.1. A Spectrum of Living Harmonies

could say that in this case her father represented the even power streams (2, 4, 6, 8) representing the more conventional energies; Jennie's real joy came through the power streams that are listed as "odd." Even though father and daughter loved each other deeply, the conflict arose from a misunderstanding of each other and the father's projection for his daughter's life and future.

As Jennie became more sensitive to her own leadings and to her right to live her own life according to her perception of her deeper calling, she was better able to stand up to her father with love and a firm resolve, rather than continuing the yelling matches that formerly had dominated the father-daughter relationship. I might also add that since it is important for each individual to activate ALL the NINE power streams within oneself, in order to be more completely expressive, one person who may seem quite different from another may eventually become a good ally or complement. We can learn from difference; even though we choose to remain uniquely who we are becoming on our own life path. We can use the abilities and creative talents of others to activate very different parts within ourselves. And since we are all ultimately created and alive in the One Creator of all life, so at a deep level, we are all a part of each other. Jennie realized that her life path was quite different from her father's. And her father, who naturally wanted the best for his daughter, tried to share and impose on Jennie "his" best, not "her" best. As Jennie and her dad shared their ideas and feelings, it also became clear that the father as a boy had never been permitted to activate and express his deepest dreams: to be a sailor and an explorer. *Ultimately, therefore, the most we can do for a person whom we love is to share our journey through our own example and to try to identify the dreams and talents of the other and open doors in those directions that we notice.* Ultimately, we all express a fascinating mixture of odd (1, 3, 5, 7, 9) and even (2, 4, 6, 8) energies. These combinations fluctuate continuously throughout the different cycles of our lives.

☐ Looking Back

1. The Pythagorean assessment offers a different approach to life direction, which honors the uniqueness of each individual's life path and the cycles of one's journey. The Pythagorean approach is not a "pigeon-holing" or "labeling" system which diagnoses or "captures" a person. It is free from useless competition, comparison or complaint.

2. Nine primary energies suggest nine basic power streams that are universal and available in every person's life:

1. The First Power Stream: Initiative

2. The Second Pathway: Close Relationship

3. The Third Pathway: Artistic Creativity

4. The Fourth Pathway: Achievement

5. The Fifth Pathway: Freedom and Life Experience

6. The Sixth Pathway: Sociability

7. The Seventh Pathway: Inner Wisdom

8. The Eighth Pathway: The Will to Power

9. The Ninth Pathway: Humanitarian Service

3. Why Are We Here? The Pythagorean spectrum of living harmonies activates different dimensions of awareness and possibilities for our life. It provides an open and visionary paradigm which describes inclusively many valuable ingredients for our life. These potentials form a non-confining model for wellness that is useful and practically accessible to everyone. No two persons can ever share exactly the same "style" or way of expressing who they are, what gifts only they can contribute in their own individual ways, and what they came to earth to complete—their calling or highest purpose and, ultimately, the fulfillment of their destiny.

☐ Discussion Questions

1. Using the Pythagorean wheel (A Spectrum of Living Harmonies), discuss the different power streams identified 1 through 9. Notice how each of these nine power streams focuses energy through different parts of ourselves: i.e., the body, emotions, mind, will, and intuitive thoughts and feelings.

2. Mention a particular friend or historical figure who you think embodies each of the nine power streams. For instance, Einstein strongly embodied the power stream 7—scientific research and interior intuitive thinking.

3. Identify three out of the nine power streams that seems to be the strongest at this time of your life. For example, 2—strong interest in

intimate and close relationships, 4—preference for structure, organization, productivity, and concrete achievement.

4. Which of the nine power streams were strongest in your parents? How much of the variety of power streams that you are currently expressing is "yours" and how much may be an "absorption" or "carry over" from childhood and upbringing? How much do we ever become who we truly are vs. what we have absorbed from others around us?

5. Select each of the nine power streams, one at a time, and describe how this energy stream is currently active in your life.

6. What are you doing at this time in your life to activate and expand the nine different power streams?

7. How and which of the different power streams are most active in your life today vs. how (and which ones) were active ten years ago?

☐ Classroom/Group Exercises

1. Have each student share with the group one of the nine power streams and how he/she is expressing this energy in particular relationships, activities, interests, etc.

2. Have each student share the experiences and memories of an individual who has strongly embodied at least one of the Pythagorean nine power streams.

3. Let students share a power stream that they may feel to be currently "weak" or inexpressive in their life. Call for suggestions from other students about how to activate and expand this energy stream which is more "buried or undeveloped in themselves.

4. Using all the students in the group, create a color wheel that describes or pictures the blend of energies that the class brings to the class. Find new ways to share in creative synthesis the energies that are present.

☐ Homework Assignment

Take any two persons whom you have observed in relationship. Describe the relationship in terms of the nine Pythagorean energy streams, especially as each partner expresses these streams in the following areas: finances, decision-making process, overcoming boredom or stagnancy, adventure and intimacy. Where are the partners similar, complementarily opposite and completely different?

12

Dave E. Redekopp
Barrie Day

Canadian Innovations in Career Development

Spotlight on Canadian Innovations

In the book *Engage Your Life* (Centre for Career Development Innovation, 1993), in the "Allies and Access" section, there's a scene on main street in the evening. The townspeople gather in front of the Saloon. Our hero mounts his horse. Miss Ellie steps out of the crowd and offers help. But our hero says, "Mighty nice of ya to offer to help me, Ma'am. But if I stay, I'll be leaning on you and your Pa. I ain't never been beholden to no one and I ain't gonna start now. I gotta ride this road alone" (p. 18).

Our hero tips his hat and rides out of town. While on the range, he runs into David Redekopp and Barrie Day, who tell him about following your heart, the vision, and the need for partners.

☐ Looking Ahead

Watch for the following important topics:

1. Five important messages in Canadian Career Development:

    a.   Change is constant

    b.   Follow your heart

    c.   Focus on the journey

    d.   Stay learning

    e.   Be an ally

2.   The Engage system

3.   Important terms and concepts:

    a.   Career building

    b.   Preferred future

    c.   Serendipity

    d.   Work dynamic

    e.   Work search (vs. job search)

    f.   Vision

This chapter introduces recent "Canadian" ideas and practices in career development. Of course, the notions in this chapter are not exclusively Canadian; only the authors are! We, like many others, have come to view career development as a complex, dynamic, often chaotic process. It defies traditional planning processes that assume an unchanging planner who sets and reaches long-term goals in a predictable world of work. Economic changes in Canada, the rest of North America, and around the globe have forced us to question the very basics of our field: "planning," "goal setting," "decision making," "occupational choice," and "assessment" need revisiting from a very different perspective, one in which chaos, rather than organization, becomes primary.

Five Important Messages in Canadian Career Development

Our reexamination of career development in a world of downsizing, flattened organizations, global competition, instant information exchange, environmental concern, and rapidly accelerating technological innovations, led us and others[1] to develop five messages that encapsulate our approach to career development:

1. Change is constant.

2. Follow your heart.

3. Focus on the journey.

4. Stay learning.

5. Be an ally.

We explain these messages in this chapter. Interspersed with our explanations are descriptions of tools, techniques, and strategies that we have developed to help people live these messages.

Change Is Constant

Change is and always has been a reality. Change is particularly important to career development due to the speed with which it now occurs and because of the way it directly affects the world of work. The most significant areas of rapid change include technology, globalization, demographics, environment, and the workplace. Information about change is plentiful, so we will focus on only some career development implications of change here.

Defining/Capturing the Labor Market Is Impossible: The Labor Market Is Becoming a Moving "Work Dynamic."   The labor market is in flux. New occupations emerge at a rapid rate (the last U.S. census identified more than 40,000); many occupations are changing quickly and some are disappearing. Also, a considerable amount of work presently available holds no occupational title. This new work takes its form from tasks required for the duration of a project; when the project ends, so does the work. Emerging work alternatives like consulting, contracting, and multi-tracking (see Table 8.1) are further changing the labor market by blurring the distinctions between "supply" and "demand." Employees of a company more frequently step out of the company to form their own organizations that subcontract back to the original company. Formerly "supply," these employees become "demand" and "supply" almost overnight.

---

[1]These messages were created by many Canadian career development specialists and validated by Pat Butter, Donna Davidson, Carol Durnford, Aryeh Gitterman, Helen Hackett, Tracy Lamb, John McCormick, Marnie Robb, and Michelle Tocher.

We have chosen to label the context in which work occurs as the "work dynamic" rather than the "labor market." This term allows us and our clients to appreciate the changing nature of work and to recognize better the important but unpaid efforts of individuals (e.g., parenting, volunteering, engaging in hobbies).

Occupations Are Moving Targets, and Therefore "Occupational Choice" Is Not a Very Useful Activity.

Clearly, few occupations are presently stable in number or structure. The direct implication of this is that "occupational choice" is unnecessary and perhaps counterproductive. Still, high school students across Canada are being encouraged to "decide what they are going to be" before graduation. We know, however, that their occupational choice may not exist by the time they train for it. Alternatively, their choice may be so different in structure that they will no longer want it. We also see how rigidly young people stick to these goals even in the face of direct evidence that the original target has moved. Graduates of law schools who insist on calling themselves "lawyers" even when no law position may be available, rather than seeing themselves as involved in law within a broader context; graduates of general undergraduate degree programs who see themselves as unemployable because the degree did not lead to a specific occupational title; unemployed nurses who cannot see that they are in the broader area of "health care" and therefore sit waiting for nonexistent hospital positions—these are the types of individuals who have been actively hurt by the insistence on occupational choice. (Miller-Tiedeman note: These examples illustrate the Newtonian "sum of the parts equal the whole" paradigm.)

We encourage both young and old clients never to choose what they "are going to be." We help them develop a broad-based vision (see the next message, "follow your heart") that includes concerns of lifestyle, work, relationships, leisure, and community. This vision becomes the "north star" for their day-to-day decision making (see the "focus on the journey" message).

Job Search Is Becoming Less Useful Than "Work Search."

As a variety of work alternatives partially replace the full-time job, it becomes much more important to teach individuals "work search" strategies rather than "job search" strategies. Although the two strategies overlap, we find that the language change helps individuals better understand the work dynamic and manage their way within it. Seeing themselves as searchers of work, individuals can more easily look beyond traditional want ads, beyond formal application procedures and beyond the ever more rare 40-hour week with full benefits job.

Some Sectors of the Economy Change Less Quickly Than Specific Occupations and Therefore They May Be Better Targets for Workers than Occupations.   For work searches to be manageable, searchers need to have some way to filter out the myriad of unlikely options and focus on the likely ones. However, we have encouraged them not to choose occupational targets, so where does direction come from? First, the vision they have created helps set parameters around their search (more on this later). Second, we encourage individuals to think about sectors of the economy (e.g., logistics, retail services, manufacturing) rather than occupations when managing their career paths. For example, we encourage forestry officers to think "forestry," "environment," "logistics" or all three sectors of the economy; doctors to think of the "health care" sector; aspiring rock and roll (or rap or whatever is current) musicians to think of the "entertainment" sector; and truck drivers to think of the "logistics" sector. Usually, hundreds of doors open for individuals when they move away from occupational titles and move toward a career path within an economic sector.

Long-Term Goals Are Becoming Impractical.   Change is constant in all areas of life, not just work. All long-term goals are therefore becoming suspect, whether they pertain to occupational choices or lifestyle choices. We believe that long-term goals need to be either abandoned or held very tentatively. A combination of a strong vision (which is also long-term but is not goal-specific) and flexible short-term goals can replace long-term goals. (See Chapter 8 for more on intentions.)

Short-Term Goals Need Revisiting: We Must Account for Serendipity.   Even short-term goals need to be tentative in a changing world. As we pursue these goals, other opportunities often present themselves. If bound too closely to goals, individuals miss these opportunities. *Serendipity, the act of discovering something useful while one is pursuing something else, is key to the process of career development.*

Career Planning Is Not as Useful as "Career Building."   In a world of serendipity, tentative short-term goals, no long-term goals, and continual decision-making, it no longer makes much sense to talk about "career planning." Planning assumes specific goals and objectives plus clear activities by which to reach them. Career planning, then, implies a broad range of long-term goals. We feel the term "career building" better addresses the actual activities of individuals as they take control of their lives: They are building on their previous life/work activities and are doing so with a direction in mind. However, they are not following a blueprint that specifies outcomes. Instead, they are drafting and re-drafting the blueprint as they go (a quantum careering approach).

Individuals Change Too!   All the talk of constant world change sometimes prevents individuals from seeing that they change, too. Most conventional career development tools focus on what seems unchanging about individuals (e.g., personality, aptitude, interests), and this has led our field often to ignore how individuals change (even fully recognizing the efforts of theorists such as John Krumboltz, Donald Super, David Tiedeman, and many others).

Follow Your Heart

In a world of constant change, people need something stable on which to base intentions and decisions. When individuals realize that occupations are moving targets, they sometimes feel lost. We encourage individuals to get their bearings by following their hearts. The "heart" is the set of core values, beliefs, and interests that provide meaning and motivation to one's life. We define these components as follows:

> *Values* are fundamentally important concerns. Values form the bedrock of motivation, morals, and meaning. Examples of values include family, independence, freedom, justice, people, and nature.

> *Beliefs* (paradigms) are central conceptions about oneself and the world. This set of ideas or worldviews strongly influences behavior, particularly behavior related to values. Beliefs inform individuals regarding the best ways to live their values. (See Chapter 5 for more detail on paradigms.)

> *Interests* are areas of enjoyment. These areas may also be valued, but often they are not. For example, an individual may work with computers and programming because it is fun to do so, but the individual may not find the work to be particularly important.

Unlike the labor market, the set of values, beliefs, and interests that form the heart is moderately stable. The heart's components will change in priority over the years, but the core parts of the heart will remain fairly stable. By following their hearts, individuals move toward a way of life that allows them to do what is important to them (values) and what is enjoyable for them (interests) in ways that allow them to perceive success in doing so (beliefs).

Working With the Heart.   From a career counseling perspective, simply recognizing one's values, beliefs, and interests is insufficient for the purposes of daily decision making. We need a forward-looking orientation that allows individuals to see the heart fulfilled in the future. We therefore have individuals create visions of a preferred future, visions that include lifestyle, work, leisure, relationship, and material concerns. These visions provide a focus to the heart, serving to make tangible the heart's components.[2]

A vision of a preferred future that is consistent with one's heart becomes a "north star" for all decision making. A vision sets direction without locking in any specific goals or destinations. It allows the individual to move toward a more meaningful and satisfactory life without attempting to tie that life to a specific occupation or work area. It also provides some stability to the individual, even fully recognizing modifications to the vision over the years.

An example may clarify what we mean by the heart, a vision, and the relationship between the two. One of our colleagues, Kris Magnusson (1990), University of Calgary, was approached by an 18-year-old male client for career counseling. Kris asked the young man, whom we will call John, to describe his dream of the future, the life that would be lived in the best of all worlds. John responded with little hesitation: "My dream is to play center position for an NHL (National Hockey League) team." John had tied his dream to an occupational title, like "professional hockey player." Kris, sensing that others had denigrated John's dream in the past, encouraged him to continue—"Wow, you must be a great skater! Tell me more." John responded with "Actually, I don't skate at all now; I damaged my knees a few years ago." Rather than immediately searching for a "realistic" occupational title to shoot for, Kris asked John to describe his dream as if he were an NHL hockey player. Kris listened between the lines and recorded John's values (e.g., athletics, health), beliefs (e.g., "Competition builds character." "Team outcomes are more important than individual outcomes."), and interests (e.g., athletics, traveling). Kris also recorded the dream itself—John's ideal lifestyle, relationships, and activities. After summarizing what he had heard and verifying his interpretations, Kris pointed out that it was quite achievable for John to live out a large portion of his vision. He just needed to move away from being stuck with the occupational title "professional hockey player." After some discussion and brainstorming, Kris gave John homework involving talking to individuals in the hockey world about their work and related work. To make a long

---

[2]More often than not, we engage in a reverse process in which the individual first creates a vision of a preferred future and then discovers from that vision his or her values, interests, and beliefs.

story short, John's exploration led him to physiotherapy training. This eventually led him to a physiotherapist position for a hockey team one notch below the NHL. This was not John's initial vision, but his current life and work capture a host of his values, beliefs, and interests.

In our view, Kris' main achievement here was to keep John's dream alive while disentangling the dream from an occupational destination. John was stuck because he confused an occupational title with a vision of the future. When John could see the components of his vision without the label of an occupation, it became much easier for him to see how his life could move in the direction of his dream. It also became easier for John to see that "life" and "career" are not separate, that work integrates with all life concerns. Finally, it became possible for John to move away from linear career planning ("I'm going to be a professional hockey player") to developmental career building ("I'm going to make day-to-day decisions that take me a little closer to my vision and keep open doors toward my vision").

It is also worth noting that Kris helped John *describe* his heart; he did not attempt to *categorize* John's heart. There was no effort on Kris' part to label John as an RSI (from the *Self-Directed Search,* Holland, 1977), an ENTJ (from the *Myers-Briggs Type Indicator,* Briggs & Meyers, 1983), or a type of any kind. We have found that this type of labeling often prevents rather than enhances self-analysis because individuals often stop at their label when examining themselves.[3] The other difficulty with labels of this type is that they can prevent exploration of the work dynamic because they are usually linked with specific occupations. Although counselors attempt to educate them otherwise, individuals become seduced by the sample occupations that go with their label. This seduction often prevents them from truly examining a wide range of work possibilities. Finally, another difficulty with labels is the implication that personal change is unlikely. Although we believe the heart is stable, we also believe that *personal change is possible and probable.* For these reasons, we parallel Kris' attempt to describe our clients' hearts rather than classify them.

"Follow your heart" is not simply a romantic prescription. "Follow your heart" is a means by which people can make decisions about their lives that will reliably lead them toward a more meaningful and satisfying future. The traditional alternative, "follow the labor market," is simply not viable for the host of reasons described in the earlier part of this chapter.

"Follow your heart" is also not a whimsical prescription; it does not mean "follow your every whim." Although the heart includes those things

---

[3]This is not to say that all psychometric or even personality assessments are therefore useless. For many individuals, they are a useful starting point for self-analysis. However, we usually choose not to score tests that we give to arrive at a label; we simply use the individual's answers to items as a starting point for discussion and portfolio development.

that bring sheer enjoyment (interests), the inclusion of values and core beliefs ensures that the individual is not living simply for the moment without regard to the future. In other words, the heart incorporates meaning and enjoyment. For example, Dave, one of the authors, repaired vending machines for a living for several years. Not only did this pay the bills through the university years, it was very enjoyable work. Dave loves driving, tinkering with mechanical/electrical things, meeting a variety of people, and working independently. In fact, from a sheer "interest" point of view, vending repair suits Dave almost perfectly. However, from a value perspective, vending repair had little to offer. Dave's current work in career development, which in many ways is not as "interesting" as vending repair, fulfills a larger part of Dave's heart.

A central part of following one's heart is to clarify its components. We spend a considerable amount of time with individuals helping them to identify and differentiate their values, beliefs, and interests. Of course, we do not challenge people's values or existing interests (imagine trying to convince a client that he or she should not value the environment nor be interested in hiking!), or certain beliefs (e.g., we would not challenge a client's belief in God). However, some of the individual's beliefs should be challenged. Distinguishing between those that we should challenge and those that we should not is a central issue in career counseling. Our approach has been to *challenge beliefs that reduce the individual's ability to perceive or use options that may lead toward the vision*. These beliefs can be either about self or about the world.

Examples of beliefs about self that we would challenge include the following:

- "I'm not smart enough to go back to school."

- "I'll lose my integrity if I cut my hair for a job interview."

- "I'll never be able to use a computer."

- "I need security too much to ever do contract work."

- "I'm a nurse; all I can do is be a nurse."

Examples of beliefs about the world we would challenge include:

- "Experts can predict which jobs and how many jobs will be created fairly accurately."

- "I need to choose an occupation or I will be aimless and a failure."

- "There is a single occupation that is right for me."

- "I should stay away from occupations for which statistics show no openings."

- "Finishing school is pointless; there are no jobs out there."

These beliefs have the potential to close doors that lead to the vision and are therefore worth challenging. Also worth challenging are less obvious "spin-off beliefs" that emerge from beliefs that probably should not be challenged. For example, the career counselor has no business challenging, "I believe in a Christian God." However, this belief can lead to spin-off beliefs that may be barriers, such as "I can't work in a company owned by non-Christians." We might challenge the latter belief, not to try to prove the individual wrong, but to ensure the individual has thoroughly reviewed a belief that imposes large limits on options.

Earlier we mentioned that we do not challenge existing interests. We do, however, challenge nonexistent interests occasionally. For example, we may confront an individual who informs us that "I detest computers; I have no interest in them." Again, we do so when we perceive that the lack of interest or a negative interest may close doors in the future. We would double-check with the individual who hates computers that he or she has actually used a computer. Interests emerge from experience, and individuals are often uninterested in activities in which they have no experience. We therefore challenge avoidance of activities when lack of experience may be causing fear or resistance. This is particularly true in areas of marketing, sales, and entrepreneurship. In a world full of alternatives to full-time employment, enjoying these activities (and being good at them!) is helpful. We see many clients who automatically dismiss anything hinting of entrepreneurship because of both beliefs they have about entrepreneurship and other work alternatives, and lack of experience in entrepreneurial activities.

Again, we do not challenge values. We help individuals identify their values and perhaps note how they may have changed in priority over the years and how they may change in priority in the future (e.g., an individual planning to have children can expect values around security and family to rise in priority when the first child arrives, if not before). We also help individuals rediscover their values when they feel discouraged or insecure. We find that reminding individuals of their values, having them recognize how they currently fulfill those values, and help them see how they are moving toward greater fulfillment of their values provides them with feelings of greater comfort and stability as well as greater motivation.

One more central component to following one's heart toward a personal vision remains—helping individuals believe in themselves, trust in themselves, and be true to themselves. This component demands the best career development practitioners have to offer when providing assistance. *Many individuals today no longer trust themselves and their hearts;* their dreams have been denigrated by others, their experiences have beaten them down or their relationships have been destructive. Even when helped to identify their values, beliefs, and interests, these individuals do not trust themselves sufficiently to follow their hearts. They want to be true to themselves, but fear keeps them following the labor market ("I just want a job"), following the advice of their friends ("Just find some work that's secure"), or following the prescriptions of mass media ("There are no jobs out there, so consider yourself lucky if you find anything"). There are no easy solutions to helping individuals trust themselves (in fact, most of this book and Miller-Tiedeman's previous work (1988, 1989, 1992a, 1992b), is dedicated to helping individuals trust themselves and the Lifecareer process). These individuals need constant reminders to challenge their beliefs ("I'm no good; my dreams are not worthy"), continuous support and encouragement, and a host of small successes to give them evidence that they are capable of doing what they want to do.

Focus on the Journey

In days gone by, one could sacrifice today knowing that tomorrow would bring a better and brighter future. In a world of endless change, one does not know with certainty that today's sacrifices will pay off tomorrow. As a consequence, following one's heart needs to be a daily occurrence as well as a long-range strategy. Each day can fulfill some of one's values, beliefs, and interests; each day also can lead to a more fulfilling future. Focusing on the journey means stopping to smell the roses as one moves toward a vision.

One of the first steps in focusing on the journey is to help individuals create a self-portrait or portfolio of their current assets. We have them identify their skills, knowledge, attitudes, experiences/activities, relationships, material assets, and financial assets. In doing so, we hope to achieve a number of outcomes with the individual:

- greater understanding of his or her assets

- experiencing higher levels of confidence and esteem simply by understanding his or her range of assets

- understanding additional assets needed to move toward the vision

- understanding next steps required to move toward the vision

Although the review of assets is a look in the rearview mirror, it brings the individual up to the here and now (precisely where the journey begins!). The person can then focus his or her energy on "now" and "next." This frees the person to more clearly see what the future may offer.

We then help the person recognize that *every decision is a career decision*. Every decision along the journey has the potential to move the person closer to the vision (thereby making the journey more meaningful with each step) or further away from the vision. Another way of putting this—*There is no need to ever make the Big Decision*! The individual does not have to "decide what I'm going to be" in this changing economy. Focusing on the journey means being conscious of all the little day-to-day decisions and juggling these to keep open pathways toward the vision. Focusing on the journey also means that making little decisions does not force one to commit to long-term decisions. We strongly encourage individuals to make decisions that get a number of balls rolling in their lives (e.g., taking courses, working on consulting/contractual projects, exploring work opportunities, volunteering) without feeling like they have to commit to keeping any of these balls rolling.

For example, we worked with a teacher who was reasonably satisfied with teaching but who was very interested in being an agent in his province for certain artists from other provinces. This teacher was struggling with the question/decision, "Should I quit teaching and jump into the art world?" This jump into a new line of work was a risky one given his obligations to his family (e.g., mortgage payments). After participating in an instructional workshop of ours (we did not participate in counseling this individual), he recognized that this big decision was not necessary. He went to his school principal in the middle of our workshop and asked for a temporary 80% position instead of his full-time position (the principal, faced with budget cuts, was ecstatic with this voluntary reduction). He then arranged to begin representing artists with his newly created free time. This man kept two significant balls rolling in his life, both of which had meaning and contributed to his vision, without feeling compelled to permanently commit to either option. No big decision was necessary (even without making any money as an art agent, his income changed little by the 20% reduction in his teaching position, simply due to his drop into a lower tax bracket).

The little decisions, the ones that get a number of things going in the individual's life, help individuals acquire experiences that inform their next decisions. The teacher/art agent put himself in a position to explore an option he had always dreamed about and to do so in a safe way. He took no huge risks, but gained many insights by *experiencing* this option rather than simply *researching* it. This teacher began to *live* his vision (albeit not all of his vision) rather than to just plan for it.

Once the individual has a few things on the go, we help the person build scenarios of possible futures for each rolling ball. We borrowed the idea of scenario-building from industry. Several big corporations use scenario-building to project best, worst, and middle-of-the-road situations. This gives the corporations parameters within which to make further decisions. Similarly with individuals, *scenario-building* gives them the chance to mentally experience worst/middle/best futures. Much like Einstein's thought experiments, scenarios help individuals see the possible consequences of their own decisions in relationship to possible factors in the world.

We also work with individuals to help them live one of Gelatt's (1989) paradoxical principles, "be focused and flexible." Focusing on the journey requires both movement toward short-term goals (e.g., for us, getting this chapter in on time) and openness to opportunities along the way (e.g., in writing this chapter, coming up with a number of ideas that may lead to a book of its own). We spend a considerable amount of time assisting individuals to recognize the importance of sheer chance in their lives, and to recognize how chance leads to serendipity (discovering something important when one is searching for something else). Serendipity plays a key positive role in the lives of those who are open to seeing it, and serendipitous opportunities can be increased in a number of ways:

1. Keep individuals informed of what one is doing and what one wants to accomplish (see the "Be an Ally" section). Chance encounters with individuals often turn into serendipitous meetings when individuals are willing and able to communicate their needs.

2. Keep track of ideas, regardless of how disconnected they seem to be from other ideas. Individuals often discard important ideas because they do not see the ideas as important, they do not have the resources to do anything with the ideas or they believe that the ideas are incomplete. We encourage individuals to keep track of any and all ideas because: (a) seemingly unimportant ideas may be important in the future; (b) the resources needed to do something with the ideas may be just around the corner; or (c) another idea or set of ideas may come along that, combined with

an apparently incomplete idea, may lead to some very useful outcomes

Chance is not converted into serendipity randomly; serendipity visits those who are ready with ideas and open to new ones.

3. Take risks. Someone once said that a rut is simply a very long grave. Focusing on the journey sometimes requires that individuals peek above the walls of the ruts in which they occasionally find themselves, examine other possible paths and climb out of their ruts to try something new. Trying something new is what risk-taking is all about, and it is key to setting the stage for serendipitous discoveries.

4. Assume serendipity is waiting around the corner. Quite simply, it is more useful to be optimistic than pessimistic about the future. By assuming that serendipity awaits nearby, individuals are more likely to spot it, be ready for it, and do something about it when it emerges.

5. View "mistakes" and bad news as opportunities. As Miller-Tiedeman points out elsewhere in this book, and in *How NOT to Make It ... And Succeed* (1989), it is more useful to see "right" and "left" rather than "right" and "wrong." "Mistakes" are often prerequisite to serendipity (e.g., the mistake that resulted in a glue that would not stick properly led to the enormously popular *Post-It Note*®). Even when they do not lead to serendipitous events, they almost always can be used as learning opportunities.

Focusing on the journey is perhaps the most difficult message for individuals to live out (fortunately, it is the message to which Miller-Tiedeman's writings pay the most attention). It is difficult because *there are no rules* to follow; no step-by-step instructions to follow. By focusing on the journey we stay aware of and open to needs, feelings, perceptions, values, interests, and beliefs as they emerge, wax, and wane. It is also about comparing all this self-information to changes in one's immediate context—changes in relationships, work situations, and lifestyle opportunities. Balancing this open and immediate awareness with a sense of direction toward a preferred future can be difficult when bills are due, deadlines have been passed, relationships are tense, and the future seems bleak. However, this difficulty also makes "focus on the journey" an exceedingly important message.

Stay Learning

In a world of never-ending change, continual learning names the games. However, the obviousness of the message does not guarantee that individuals have the motivation, tools, or strategies by which they can take control of their learning. Nor does it guarantee that individuals understand the changes that affect their learning. Some of these changes are:

- Flattened organizations. The flattening of North America's organizations has resulted in fewer supervisors/managers. Individuals can no longer rely on their supervisors to identify their learning needs, plan appropriate training, and deliver it when needed. Supervisors simply do not have the time or energy to do these tasks well.

- Team management. In the effort to reduce management costs, many organizations have moved to self-managed teams. Team members supervise themselves and provide assistance to one another. Again, the individual cannot rely on someone else to point out what he or she needs to learn and to provide the necessary training.

- Work alternatives. The greatest growth in work has been and will continue to be in small businesses, self-employment, consulting, and contracting. Individuals choosing these alternatives cannot rely on anyone but themselves to ensure that learning needs and learning strategies are implemented appropriately.

- Rapid change. In many work areas, change happens so rapidly that there is no time to develop and deliver formal training programs–change is so quick that the programs can be obsolete before they are delivered. Individuals therefore need to keep up with changes without relying on traditional training systems.

- Smaller budgets. Global competition has resulted in many employers being increasingly concerned about the bottom line. Training budgets are often among the first to be eliminated when employers look to cut costs. Again, individuals need to find ways to look after their own learning in this case.

- Increased specialization. The age of the "knowledge worker" brings with it a context in which workers are often more knowledgeable in specialized areas than their supervisors. Their supervisors are therefore unable to determine, predict, or meet their learning needs.

- Increased demands for individuals to add value to the organization. Due to many of the above conditions, workers are increasingly being asked to determine for themselves how they contribute to an organization. Decision-making around value-adding activities no longer rests with the employers and managers. Adding value—whether it is through increasing sales, decreasing costs, increasing customers, or retaining customers—almost always requires learning (conversely, learning usually results in added value for the learner and the organization).

All of the above indicates that individuals must take charge of their own "stay learning" strategies. As a general process, we recommend that individuals go through the following processes, adapted from a learning-to-learn model we call CONDUCT.

1. Develop/clarify their visions. (See the section "follow your heart" for a description of this.)

2. Understand their current position relative to their vision. (See the "focus on the journey" section for a description.)

3. Identify needs (gaps between current position and vision). Individuals need to be able to pinpoint their needs, particularly those related to learning. These needs include:

   a. long-term learning needs that directly relate to vision;

   b. long-term learning needs that may create opportunities and open doors;

   c. short-term specific skills, knowledge, and attitudes required to perform one's current roles; and

   d. short-term generic competencies that will increase transferability, even if not directly related to one's vision.

4. Set short-term learning goals. Individuals need ways to make decisions about the short-term that will move them toward their visions while being meaningful in the immediate. They also need to be flexible with these goals (see the "focus on the journey" section).

5. Learn new skills/knowledge/attitudes. Individuals need strategies and tactics for acquiring competencies they currently do not hold. These include:

   a. formal instruction (i.e., courses/workshops);

   b. self-help-directed learning (e.g., reading);

   c. self-help—trial and error learning (i.e., systematic self-directed attempts at learning); and

   d. tutoring (e.g., having a co-worker or supervisor provide instruction).

   Part of this requires determining how best to learn a specific competency or process, how best to make use of the learning strategy that has been selected, and how to ensure that some follow-through happens after the initial learning takes place.

6. Entrench or "own" acquired competencies. After individuals have acquired new skills, they need ways to use these skills so that they do not just fade away. This includes getting help from supervisors and/or co-workers. In particular, when individuals try new competencies, they need descriptive feedback (rather than judgmental feedback) that will enable them to analyze and modify their own performance.

7. Enhance or "build" acquired competencies. Once individuals become reasonably competent at newly acquired competencies, they need to work on enhancing these competencies to make them their own. Enhancement strategies may include self-supervision, specialty workshops/seminars, specialty books/journals/magazines, etc. Mentors can be helpful here as well. Therefore, individuals require skills and attendant processes that will help them identify potential mentors, select mentors, inform mentors of their needs, give feedback to mentors and end mentor/protégé relationships.

8. Elaborate on or "challenge" existing competencies. To get really good at something, individuals need to find ways to create their own competence by experimenting, teaching, coaching, and/or supervising.

9. Identify learning defenses and methods for overcoming these defenses. People defend against the sources of learning, the con-

tent of learning, and the delivery of learning. Some of these defenses are listed below:

a. Defending against learning because of sources

- do not like the personality of the source, therefore do not learn from the source;

- do not like the source because of stereotypes (e.g., race, gender, culture), therefore dismiss the source;

- do not like the source because of credentials or lack thereof, therefore dismiss the source; or

- do not like the status (e.g., subordinate, younger) of the source, therefore dismiss the source.

b. Defending against learning because of the content

- message is contrary to beliefs;

- message, if followed, will cause more work; or

- message, if followed, shows previous practices were incorrect, inappropriate or inadequate.

c. Defending against learning because of the delivery of the message

- past experience with the delivery method (e.g., classroom instruction) has been negative; or

- beliefs about delivery methods (e.g., "you can't really learn anything from a TV show").

The above aims at consciously putting learning in the context of career development and to help the learner take charge of his or her learning experiences. When connected to one's vision, learning becomes meaningful; when driven by one's own motivations, learning becomes effective.

The Engage System. We have implemented these ideas and strategies with young people (ages 14 through 24) within a system of workshops and products called *Engage. Engage* includes a two-day workshop for youth plus print products for youth, their teachers, and parents, all focused on helping youth take charge of their own career development and learning. *Engage* teaches at-risk youth, in a highly interactive manner, the five messages described in this chapter. The pivotal feature seems to be the realization among youth that their lives are *theirs* and no one else's; that although they may not be able to control/manage their lives, they can direct their lives better than anyone else can.

Be an Ally

Tapping into the new work dynamic requires the full use of current and future relationships. In creating an audience or market for services and products, in finding emotional support for life/work challenges, in learning new things, individuals will have to depend on others. Success in life and work will always be enhanced by relationships in which individuals give and receive.

Abundance.   The work dynamic becomes more complex every day. People who believe that opportunities are becoming scarce, and that any time they can gain an advantage over others will be of benefit, will have a difficult time in establishing solid relationships. This belief in scarcity will lead to conflict and, ultimately, to the disappearance of precious resources. The building of mutual support through the sharing of ideas, information, and talent (valuing or believing in abundance) will open additional opportunities—personally and in the world of work.

Guiding Principles of Building Relationships.   Organizations now respond to the need for efficiency by contracting out unproductive work. This work will be available through contracts, consulting, talent pool participation or part-time employment. The degree to which individuals can take advantage of such opportunities will depend on how well-connected they are to people that can alert them to the potential of contracting to organizations.

Building relationships requires a great deal of attention. The mindless collection of names and addresses, business cards, and portfolios will not be of great benefit. Building relationships involves trust: Does the individual exhibit the trust necessary in a supportive manner? Will this individual share information and knowledge with you if required? Do you relate to this person in a trustworthy way? Relationships also require mutual confidence: each person seeing a mutual interconnection with the other. The process of building successful relationships requires a great deal of time and effort. It is not a spontaneous act.

Relationships are reciprocal. Individuals who spend time and energy supporting you, assisting you in marketing your products or services, or opening doors for you will desire the same effort in return.

The sun now rises on wholeness, spirituality, connectedness to the heart, and opens the way for enormous wealth of unused human intelligence and resourcefulness. "Our hero rides back into town with a new vision and excitement. Therefore, the sky glows with possibility. The towns-people gather. Miss Ellie mounts her horse to ride out with Our Hero. He says, 'Mighty nice of ya to offer to help me, Ma'am. I'm beholden to you.' They ride off together guided by the north star of vision" (Centre for Career Development, 1993, p. 18).

☐ Discussion Questions

1. What did you like in this chapter?

2. Which parts resonate with your experience?

3. How does this Canadian approach differ from the American approach? Discuss this from your own high school experience and that of your children.

4. What do you think is the most important concept or group of concepts?

5. Which concepts could you use in your professional work or with your children and their friends?

6. How would the approach taken in this chapter change, in some way, American youth?

☐ Classroom/Group Exercises

1. Divide into groups of three and plan a mini skit using concepts from this chapter.

2. Designate one in your group as a client and another as a helping professional with the third person observing. Ask the client to pose a life

direction challenge to the helping professional who will use some of the concepts in this chapter, along with information from Chapter 9, to help the client. Do a 5 to 10 minute session. Then ask the observer to use the checklist provided in Appendix D to note what the helping professional did to help the client through his or her challenge which will be instrumental in maturing his or her vision. Remember, the exercise is offered for learning, not to grade someone according to what he or she did right or wrong. Wrong doesn't exist in the process careering vocabulary.

a. After the session, ask the client:

    1. What helped and what hindered your understanding?

    2. What attitude or non-verbal message (body language or otherwise) from the helping professional helped or hindered?

b. Check out any other comments.

c. Then ask the helping professional:

    1. How did you feel about the interchange?

2. Could you stay within the client's framework?

3. Did you work from the client's agenda?

4. Did you try to change a client impression?

5. Were you conscious of bringing in your own comments as opposed to sticking with the client's thoughts?

6. Did you educate, when appropriate, about potential approaches that your client might want to try on for size?

7. Did you find yourself slipping into the traditional approach to career?

8. Did you challenge negative beliefs?

☐ Homework Assignment

1. Ask a friend, co-worker, or family member about his or her thoughts about the future. Then using the content from both this chapter and Chapter 9, ask your subject if he or she would like for you to do one session with him or her to demonstrate the ideas you have learned.

2. Write a two-page, double-spaced paper on how you might use the ideas in this chapter in your own life and/or your professional life.

Lee Joyce Richmond

Learning About and Teaching Lifecareer®

Spotlight on Teaching Lifecareer

Had I not come to view "career" as "life" (or, to be more exact, my life as career) several years ago, I would probably be a very unhappy/demanding/turned-off person by now. Following are a few things I have learned about life/career:

1. Money is far from the most important thing in life/career. On the contrary, it can be a trap, impede growth, become a (false) goal, and create the illusion of security.

2. Nothing lasts forever, least of all the feeling of being alive/growing/learning in a job. When that feeling goes, it's time to move on.

3. The postponed life is not worth living—i.e., living for the next coffee break, vacation, raise, retirement, death. To be open and alive in the present, to experience the present as fully as possible, and to make my own sense of it is how I try to live my life/career.

Lifecareer, Life-Is-Career, Career Compass and their derivatives are registered trademarks of Dr. Anna Miller-Tiedeman.

4. I am not alone, no matter where I am in life/career. Right now I'm over-worked and underpaid, like millions of others. I'm scared to make a move, like thousands of others. I'm not sure what I want to do next, like most people. But I have come this far, and when the right time comes, I will know what to do in order to go further.

5. The most important things in my life/career are, in order of importance, love, friendship, art, and nature.

—Dorothy Meckel, Ed.D.
Freelance Editor

☐ Looking Ahead

Watch for the following important topics:

1. Learning about Lifecareer.

2. Teaching Lifecareer and learning from the students.

3. Choosing Lifecareer learning from social context.

Pick up the daily news in any large American city. The local head-lines are likely to read something like this: "Young drug runner shot in head by crazed user." "ABC corporation rifs fifty managers." "Young mother holds three jobs to support family." There is a story behind each of these incidents reported in the paper, and each story demonstrates the need for career counselors and other helping professionals. Nevertheless, the course in career development remains one of the most disliked courses in counselor education programs. Perhaps this is because, all too often, teachers of this course stress a worn out prescriptive model that serves little purpose in a world characterized by continuous change.

This chapter is about teaching career development according to a new model—Lifecareer. This model provides a fluid paradigm offering students *process rather than prescription*. And, it encourages involvement and innovation as a means of self-instruction. It is, therefore, exciting to both teachers and students. This chapter contains three parts: (a) Learning Lifecareer from Anna Miller-Tiedeman; (b) teaching Lifecareer; and (c) choosing Lifecareer in the context of the times in which we live.

I have been teaching Lifecareer for the past ten years, both to pastoral counseling and school counseling graduate students at Loyola College in Maryland, and also to career specialists and other managers of the United States Postal Service. In each instance, it has been an adventure, one that I am pleased to share with you.

Learning About Lifecareer ...
From Anna Miller-Tiedeman

Life-Is-Career! Career is process (Miller-Tiedeman, 1982, 1985, 1989, 1992). Look through a kaleidoscope and see the beautiful patterns the colored shapes make. As one turns the instrument, the patterns change and present to the viewer visual patterns that delight. So it is with us when we use our intelligence, experience, and intuition—our Career Compass, so to speak—to see the patterns that we make through our daily being and becoming that defines our journey through life.

In Lifecareer theory, no external structures are imposed on a person, chance is interpreted as an opportunity being offered, and choices can always be made. Why? Because life works! A remarkable synergy exists in the universe whereby life unremittingly works for each of us, always for our potential good when we open our eyes to the connectedness of things: the persons, places, and events that comprise each individual's history and future.

Therefore, helping professionals ought to empower people to see these connections and help them understand that they make a pattern that describes how life works for each person being counseled. Counselors also should encourage clients to act, often in the face of an uncertainty that can never be fully eliminated. Helping professionals should teach clients that only by acting can one know what steps to take next.

Life consists of a sequence of actions, each potentially based on a decision. When we teach students to examine decision-making in the light of Lifecareer theory, we teach them that decisions are neither right nor wrong, but opportunities to move in right or left. Instead of being fearful, students are then free to view decision-making as an exciting opportunity. As counselors, they can communicate to clients the notion that choices can be altered, or even reversed. With this in mind, clients can move more easily through life's twists and turns and around its corners.

To understand Lifecareer, there are a few principles from the new science that students need to embrace (Miller-Tiedeman, 1989). One such principle is that of wholeness. The whole organizes the parts and is capable of continually doing so. Earlier, you learned about Don Bradley's notion of the rickety card-table that goes something like this: When we are born, a shaky-legged, rickety card table is set up in front of us. A huge puzzle is placed upon it. Most people take until mid-life to build it, and many of us spend the rest of our lives protecting it, for the pieces represent the way we believe our lives should be, and the meaning that our lives should have. However, life experience often shakes the table and knocks it over. All too frequently, people try desperately to protect the arrangement of the puzzle pieces because they do not realize that the whole is capable of rearranging the parts into something more beautiful or more fitting than that which presently exists.

Another principle undergirding Lifecareer process theory is that of complementarity (Miller-Tiedeman, 1989). Prior to the atomic age, the quest of physicists was to find the building blocks of matter. Modern physics tells us that, at the sub-atomic level, entities are not separate realities, but complementary aspects of the same reality. A particle and a wave are complementary aspects of the same thing. All matter can be converted to energy, and vice versa.

In Lifecareer theory, this principle is very important. Simply stated, this principle asserts that all things in the universe have their complements. Each complement is essential to the other, but both cannot be observed nor measured at the same time.

Both red and blue exist on the color spectrum. To some degree, they exist in each other, although we do not see one in the other. A thing is red or blue to us. What is limited is our power of observation. In fact, opposites are actually complements existing together. For instance, we see things as either mass or energy because only one can be measured at a time. However, the entire material world is both. As previously stated, a thing that is both a particle and a wave, however, appears to us as either one or the other, depending on what we are looking for and how we view it. The psychiatrist Carl Jung taught us that introversion and extroversion, male and female, yin and yang, are complementary. In career development, complementarity plays out personally. The more one specifically searches in one direction for opportunity, the less one sees opportunity in other directions.

Flowing from the complementarity principle is another, also essential to Lifecareer theory. It is the principle of uncertainty (Miller-Tiedeman, 1989). This principle, named after its observer, Heisenberg, states that the more focus that is placed on one complement, the less can be known of the other. Nothing can ever be measured (or known) exactly. In terms of Lifecareer, this means that the more one focuses on one possibility in life, the less one can know of others. This is not good or bad; it simply is.

In terms of Lifecareer theory, finding and preserving careers cannot be understood objectively according to prefixed models. Only the context of a person's subjective life experience makes his or her career activity understandable. Objectivity is not possible. Einstein demonstrated that we are a part of all that we observe.

Though we are connected to all others in "an intricate web of relationships" (Miller-Tiedeman, 1989, p. 86), no one else can define us. The principle of connectedness applied to Lifecareer simply tells us that each experience we have is a part of, not apart from, the whole of the life journey; nor can we separate ourselves totally from the others with whom we live and the circumstances in which we live.

Lastly, the work of chemist Ilya Prigogine (1980) calls our attention to the fact that all things are in a state of flux. Everything cycles through dissipation and reorganization.

The more fixed a system becomes, the more its propensity for instability. In Lifecareer, sudden shifts and changes in one's job, even in one's life, are to be expected and can be viewed positively. Permanence or security in anything is an illusion and contradicts the way life works.

However, Lifecareer is optimistic. Its basic premises are positive. "Life works, not always the way you want it to, but it works" (Miller-Tiedeman, 1989, p. 13). Despite the absence of a predictable linear path, there is clearly direction on the journey. And this direction can be discerned by using one's Career Compass—one's experience, intuition, and intelligence—to discern this direction (Miller-Tiedeman, 1989, p. 213). This is to say that one's career counselor is his or her own "inner voice." Everyone can "fuller" (do what you love) which essentially means to do that which brings joy and gives meaning (Miller-Tiedeman, 1989). To make things happen, one sets intentions, follows one's Career Compass, and remembers that there are no right and wrong turns in life, but simply right and left ones.

I learned the above things from Anna Miller-Tiedeman and subsequently discussed them with David V. Tiedeman. Since meeting them and reading Anna's works, I have been both learning and teaching Lifecareer. The rest of what I know, I have learned from my students and from the experience of teaching them.

Teaching Lifecareer ... Learning From Students

As process theory, Lifecareer is best taught to students and learned from them through experience and story. This section contains stories and experiences from my life and my students' lives that illustrate some of the principles and basic premises of the new careering paradigm.

Remember the rickety card-table story mentioned earlier? This story illustrates wholeness, uncertainty, dissipation, and self-organization. When my students have read or have heard this story, they often have had an "ah-ha" experience. This has helped them view their world in a new way. They recognized how Einstein had to kick over the Newtonian card table and rearrange the pieces of the universe puzzle in order to understand it in a new way. They understood that the picture of universe energy, the relationship of mass to energy and energy to mass, was a new portrayal of something always there, but never before seen. What was always there was now viewed differently.

From this story, students learned that what we see depends, in part, on the lens through which we look—our perceptual optic. This notion has profound implications for helping professionals. How we and our clients see our respective "worlds" depends on how we look at them. If we think ourselves to be victims of others, or of circumstances, perhaps a change of lens, a new optic, a kicking over of our card tables, can change our view of self, of others, and of circumstances. We don't have to be victims of the world we see, but rather we can be victors based on how we see the world.

I was conducting a demonstration counseling session for students with a middle-aged pastoral counseling student of mine. She is an example of a person who kicked over her card table. Her husband had died when he was young, and she tenaciously held to the money which she had received from his life insurance. She also held tightly to the remains of a small estate left to her by her parents. Her goal was to join with some of her fellow students who, upon graduation, were forming a group practice. She wanted to buy into the practice, but she was afraid to invest her funds lest she lose her "security."

We talked for a while about where she had gotten the idea that security resides in holding on to dollars. She told me that she was carefully taught by her parents that the most important thing in life was to save for a "rainy day." She added that this is what her parents had done in their lives. "They hoarded their money and they lived and died miserably," she said. My student then paused for a moment and, with eyes opened wide, she exclaimed, "I don't want to live like that!" She then talked about how she wanted a fulfilled, rather than a miserable, life. Then she uttered the statement that shook her card table. "Perhaps," she said, "my security can reside in me and in my skills rather than in my money." In saying this, she began to look at life through a different lens. She was ready to become a victor. She was busy reorganizing her belief about the way things should be. She could rid herself of the harmful "parent" inside.

A story that illustrates the principle of complementarity for students is that of my own son. For as long as I can remember, he had wanted to be a lawyer. He spoke of this dream in elementary school, secondary school, and college. So interested was he in becoming a lawyer, that he looked at nothing else. In college, he majored in political science and, when he was accepted into a first-rate law school, both of us rejoiced. At the end of his fifth week in school, he came to me and said, "Mom, I want to quit." Trapped into his single vision regarding law and, unlike any good counselor that I have ever heard, I replied, "Quit, what do you mean, quit?" Disgusted, he spelled "Q. U. I. T., Mom, I want out. I liked the lawyers that I saw on TV. I liked the drama of law, I didn't like the reality. There are too many books for me. I don't want it."

Still trapped with the vision that a career in law equalled happiness for my son, I begged him to stay in school until after Thanksgiving. He told me that if he did this, I would lose all the money that I had paid for his tuition. Nevertheless, I begged him to stay in school because I thought that he had not given himself enough time. Despite his protestations that his intention to quit law school was well thought out, I prevailed. He stayed in school until after Thanksgiving. Then he quit. And I lost all of my money.

What happened next further illustrates the complementarity principle. What my son enjoyed about law was a life of action that involved working with people. When he turned from looking at law to looking in another direction—and this time he looked all around—he finally settled on business. Today, he owns a fabric store and a fabrication factory. In his work, he now has all of the action that he has ever desired, and the people in his world range from the woman making curtains to world class designers and drapers of offices and hotels. Only by kicking over the card table that held his childhood ideas about his life's work could my son rearrange the pieces of his life into a picture more fitting for his adulthood.

As previously stated, when one concentrates on a specific aspect of a complement, one misses other aspects—complementarity! And since one cannot focus on all aspects at the same time, one can never be certain—this produces uncertainty! But that keeps life interesting.

I learned from graduate students that the fluidness of Lifecareer process theory perplexes them temporarily, but when they "bumble and fumble" with it, they rejoice to hear that, in Lifecareer theory, bumbling and fumbling is viewed positively. Miller-Tiedeman (1989) reminds us of the bumble-bee who, with pollen on wing, cross-fertilizes flowers. The students then recognize that life is continual flux and change and, at this point of recognition, the fluidness of process is freeing to them.

Students laugh when I tell them the story of my youngest daughter, who bumbled and fumbled the entire summer after she graduated from college, under the approving gaze of Dr. Miller-Tiedeman, much to my consternation.

The story is as follows. Jessica had graduated cum laude from the University of Maryland in May. Prior to receiving her undergraduate degree in speech and hearing, she had applied to the seven top graduate schools in her field in the United States. Lucky for her, she was accepted by all seven. At about the same time, she had acquired a boyfriend who had been recently discharged from the U.S. Marine Corps. My daughter neither answered her acceptance letters nor went to work. Her boyfriend also remained jobless. The two of them "vegged out" day by day at my swimming pool. Nothing short of my throwing them out of the house would get either of them to budge, and I did not want to ask my daughter to leave her home.

Now, it so happened that I was coordinating the graduate program in counseling and human development at The Johns Hopkins University at that time. I had earlier invited David Tiedeman and Anna Miller-Tiedeman to teach summer school at Hopkins, and they had agreed to do it. I told my daughter, Jessica, that though I was dismayed that she had not taken any action toward selecting a graduate school or getting a summer job, I would, nevertheless, allow her to stay at home and "do nothing" as long as she took Anna and David's course on career development. This she did, and one summer day in the middle of the afternoon, after what I knew was a consultation with her teacher—Anna—my daughter came home smiling like the proverbial Cheshire cat. Thinking that she had finally made a decision about school and/or work, I asked my daughter why she seemed so happy. She told me that Dr. Miller-Tiedeman had validated her by encouraging her to continue to bumble and fumble for a longer time. Fit to be tied, I confronted Dr. Miller-Tiedeman myself, only to hear her advise me to leave my daughter alone. She thought that Jessica needed time to decide what she wanted to do.

Reluctantly, I followed Miller-Tiedeman's advice, but it wasn't easy. Then, early in the first week of September, my daughter told me that she had written to the appropriate people at all seven out-of-state graduate schools. She told them that she was not going to attend. She also told me that she got a part-time job selling women's better dresses in a local department store. And, she had enrolled in the graduate program in speech and hearing at Loyola College. She would live at home and go to school. By the way, her boyfriend also got a job.

I telephoned Anna in California to tell her that I then knew that she was correct in her advice to me about my daughter. Anna was not surprised. Today, both my daughter and her boyfriend are married but not to each other. Jessica now has earned her Master's degree plus thirty more graduate hours in her field. For the past six years, she has worked as a speech therapist. As for me, well I am glad she took the time she needed to bumble and fumble.

Every time I tell this story to my graduate students, someone thanks me. Many of my students, about a third of them in pastoral counseling, are over 40 years of age. They identify because they are at their wits' ends with similar experiences with their own sons or daughters. Younger students in their twenties also identify and wish their parents would "understand."

Students and their professors need to experience that, to practice Lifecareer, one needs to develop "the courage to look foolish." Rather than listen to the demands or constraints of others, one follows one's inner call. No one on the outside can tell one what the real world is like, though people sometimes live as if there were a real world and a phony one. Counselors, however, need to know how the way life is at any time for any person is the real world for him or for her. Children often hear the injunction, "Wait 'til you get into the real world," as if they were living in an unreal one. Reality for a child, as well as for an adult, is simply one's experience of it.

I was once approached by a writer from *Reader's Digest*. He was composing an article about how parents should help their children prepare for a future in the real world—the world of work. The writer assumed that, as a teacher of career counseling, I would tell him how parents could give their children good advice about choosing college majors which would lead to jobs.

The interview was a flop. I vastly disappointed the author because I told him that no college major guarantees anything in the world of work. I also told him that no advice from parents could assure that their children would even stay in school. Lastly, I said that parents would do well to avoid trying to save their children from bumbling and fumbling through college because their children's experiences, both positive and negative, are all that they have to serve them in the world. I added that the world of the students is a different reality, vastly different from that of parents—and equally real.

Oftentimes, readiness signals go off within us. These signals tell us when we are ready to change our reality. This is what happened to a man in my Pastoral Counseling class. He gave up a six figure salary and an executive position in a large corporation in order to follow his heart's desire and become a counselor. When his readiness signal alerted him, he had the courage to look foolish, and the wisdom not to suffer from his ulcers anymore.

People who live Life-As-Career are employed by life. They may be out of a job, but never out of career. When I tell students about this Miller-Tiedeman notion, they argue that however lofty sounding, life doesn't feed the poor. People need money. The unemployed poor need jobs.

Students will say, "This Lifecareer philosophy may be fine for the wealthy, but the poor can't afford to bumble and fumble." I ask, "Will you give those who need more, less? Help them use their Career Compass (their experience, intelligence, and intuition) to get their immediate needs met. Use all traditional and non-traditional sources that you know in order to help them seek and find work. However, do not make the mistake of thinking Lifecareer theory is not for them when it is, in fact, tailor-made for them."

Lifecareer emphasizes "self-conceiving" (Miller-Tiedeman, 1989) rather than "self-concept" (Super, 1957). Self-concept theory is self-limiting in that it is tied to the present. It translates in terms of how I see myself now, at a specific point in time. Self-conceiving is far less limiting, ongoing, moving, and flowing into each moment.

The Disney Corporation coined the saying, "If you can dream it, you can do it." This slogan exemplifies self-conceiving. When one dreams, one is not limited by present circumstances. The counselor's task is to help people see themselves more broadly, more deeply, more fully, and to help them find ways of living their dream. Whether one does this by continuing one's education and thereby acquiring new knowledge, or by geographic moves, or by using talents perhaps unvalued by peers, matters little. What is important is that one expand one's sights and follow one's inner dictates. To empower clients to do this is the counselor's most important task.

Almost twenty years ago, I was asked to teach a career development class to male prisoners in the Maryland State Penitentiary who were about a year from "getting out" on work release. Most of the people in the small class were cat-burglar types with three to five repeated offenses. My prisoner students were not terribly excited about learning traditional career development. Finally, I stopped being the teacher and became the learner. I asked, "Why do you continue to rob homes when you know you'll eventually wind up back in here?" The answer was simple. "Robbing homes is what we do." Certainly, their answer to my question fit with traditional self-concept theory. Then I asked a very different kind of question. "What," I asked, "are the skills you use in robbing homes?" They looked surprised. It was as if no one had ever asked them that question before. After several moments, they told me about skills and abilities they used in robbing homes. It was using their skills that excited them. Stealth, discrimination, hand-eye coordination, intelligence, and speed were the skills they used. They also enjoyed using their knowledge of merchandise the marketplace demands.

The prisoner-students and I began to talk about how their skills and knowledge could be utilized in other occupations. Each person imaged what he or she might look like, and feel like, in some of these occupations. Self-conceiving!

As all of this was going on, interest in the course grew. When the time came for the program to end, and for me to take leave of the prisoners, they presented me with a gift covered with ersatz wrapping. The gift was a psychology book that my students had stolen from the prison library.

Perhaps this story about prisoners was not the ideal story to tell my counselor education students about the importance of self-conceiving and of imaging self in a new role. But it worked! As a result, I have seen one student set intentions and acquire a pilot's license. I have seen another set intentions and take a 100-mile bike hike. A third student set her intentions to write and publish a novel, and she did. Each person succeeded because he or she first dreamed that he or she could do the desired task, imaged it in totality, set intentions, and then, inch by inch, acted.

My career development students in the pastoral counseling program taught me that they gravitate to Lifecareer theory for yet another reason. Traditional career theory focuses on self. In traditional career theory, social context is used for only two reasons—to predict or suggest proper choices for particular outcomes, and to add to one's understanding how one arrived where one is. Lifecareer is concerned with social well being, with social forces that unify humankind. Lifecareer, then, describes the path each individual leaves behind, but it also portrays the procession and progression of humanity through history, sometimes struggling on the path toward unity in an ever more global society. Life works!

When I first started teaching the career development course to pastoral counseling students, they hated it. Students preparing to be school counselors did not like the course much either, but at least school counselors saw the relevance of career guidance to young people. They understood the importance of a course in career development and career counseling for their futures as counselors. They could relate career choice to the total educational effort. Pastoral counselors in training viewed themselves as mental health counselors and therapists and, as such, they could not see the relevance of career development to the world of mental health or to the area of spirituality. With the exception of approximately one-third of my most perceptive students, my first career development and decision-making classes with the pastoral counseling group were a disaster.

Gradually, I began to bring in to the course more of Lifecareer, the concept of fullering, doing the work one loves. I also introduced the topic of dissipative structures—losing old ways of being and forming new ones. These notions began to coincide with the process theology courses that many of the pastoral counseling students had taken in the past. The students liked the idea of finding one's own way by letting go rather than finding one's way and then letting go. It seemed familiar. To these students, this idea was similar to taking a leap of faith. Additionally, pastoral counseling students also resonated to the notion that each person is his or her own career theorist. There is no one theory that can be applied to everyone—only the process is similar. How the process plays out is individual. The Career Compass is within, just as the Kingdom of Heaven is within. Lastly, Lifecareer's emphasis on the connectedness of all humanity appeared as manna in the desert to this group of students who were trying to connect career development to spirituality.

Lifecareer provides a link between spirituality and career development. When my students and I realized this, we did everything we could to strengthen that link. We compared the career journey to a spiritual journey using Lifecareer philosophy. We also compared the career journey to the journey of Moses and the Hebrew people through the desert to the Promised Land. We also compared it to St. Paul's sea voyages through the Mediterranean with winds of change and through the shoals of discontent. We recognized that career development specialists, career counselors, and other helping professionals use the word "abilities" in the same way that religious people use the word "gifts." Other words also are analogous: "Discernment" is synonymous with "decision-making"; "fruits" and "outcomes" are the same thing. Vocation was to be called one's meaningful work in the universe.

After teaching Lifecareer theory twice using story and experience, my career counseling theory classes began to fill. I began to realize that it was the Lifecareer philosophy that was attracting students—students who now found career development at least digestible, if not actually tasteful.

Once students' careers were connected with purpose lived out, it was easy for the students to connect career to mental health and well being, and also to connect it to spirituality. They began to "fuller," to live with joy. To live with joy, to work, and to love and to laugh, is to be connected to others and to recognize one is connected! This is ultimate health and ultimate spirituality. With this realization, Lifecareer theory links career counseling and mental health counseling. The whole organizes the parts!

Only one question remains. How do you teach this stuff? Anna Miller-Tiedeman, in addition to this book, has written a philosophy book (1989), a theory book (1988), and a practice book (1992). Much that is in this chapter comes from those books. The three books, and the one you are now reading, can be used as texts, and students enjoy reading them. Furthermore, I borrowed from Anna the technique of having students keep a diary about themselves. Throughout the course, students write about what they are learning about careers and about themselves. These student journals all have a common title: "I'm Nobody But Myself." Partially, by means of this diary, students take ownership, each one of his or her own Lifecareer.

Now, all of my graduate career counseling students study Lifecareer, whether they are in school counseling, mental health counseling, or pastoral counseling. Lifecareer is an individual process, and it allows each student to do his or her own thing with it. It is learned through text and story, through teaching and modeling, but Lifecareer is mostly learned through doing. How do you teach Lifecareer? You teach it by joining your students in living it, and by living it with gusto!

Choosing Lifecareer ... Learning From Social Context

From broad social context, and from the counseling profession itself, the time is right for Lifecareer. One can learn from the past, but today the past cannot provide knowledge sufficient for the future. Perhaps it never did. One reads in Deuteronomy, " ... I have set before you life and death, blessing and curse; therefore choose life ... " (Deut. 30:19). To choose life always means to choose growth, which often constitutes a move away from the security of old knowledge and old ways. A system receives signals when the time has come to change direction. If the system does not heed the signals, it will die; if it does respond to them, it will change and grow and live. It may even live more fully, more abundantly.

The living, growing system never senses the whole of its future when it changes. It just trusts and lets go, and allows new experience to change it, trusting in its certitude that knowing will come with action. To grow or die is the challenge.

The challenges to the profession of career counseling today are mammoth, and they press from both without and within. Externally, our world is changing rapidly. Wars that were once fought on battlefields are passé, but there is increasing violence on the street. This is, in part, because the socio-economic conditions in which people work are changing, and the media frequently flags the haves and have nots.

Furthermore, objectivism and logical positivism have no place in a post-modern world. Even as more and more people utilize science and technology, so more and more people become disillusioned with their capacity to truly improve their quality of life in a way that is globally meaningful. After all, some say, it was aerospace technology that led to global warming, aerosol sprays that led to the hole in the ozone layer, and high technology that led to insufficient cradle-to-grave work for would-be workers in first world countries.

Thirdly, there is a boom in America of the spirituality of the general public wanting to move beyond the material toward a quest for meaning. This is evidenced by the multitude of books on the market that refer to caring for the spirit, the populist movement that shook a kingdom in its sympathy for Princess Diana, and the millions who memorialized the work of Mother Theresa, while at the same time castigating the American corporation for perpetrating *justa*s (justa clerk, justa word processor) instead of valuing the worker and letting the worker know it. The strength of this silent public outcry has been felt so profoundly in the marketplace that even the very fist of American industry is softening.

From within the career counseling profession, there are also signals that we must change. Student apathy and downright boredom in some career courses (frequently cited in professional journals) might suggest that old theories that hide behind status positions may have lost their relevance to students who have studied process theory not only in physics and chemistry, but in philosophy and theology as well. If, theologically, people are co-creators of the universe, as Fox (1995) and Soelle and Cloyes (1984) have suggested, do they not have the same responsibility and challenge with their own Lifecareers.

Furthermore, the multicultural nature of modern life argues for new counseling paradigms that put process above product, emphasize stories rather than scores, and affirm the client's own expertise in making meaning out of personal experience.

If counseling is to exist in the future, the idea that getting a life of worth is more important than getting a job, will be the focus of future helping professionals in general and career counselors in particular. The self is the seat, not only of body and mind, but of spirit as well; and it is through spirit (synonymous with breath, wind, or energy) that self is defined by the actions we take in life.

The teaching and learning of Lifecareer in the counseling curriculum is a social imperative. For the profession, it is a case of grow or die. The societal signals have already been given.

☐ Looking Back

1. Life-Is-Career and a process we all experience.

2. Life works, not always the way we want it to, but it works, even in teaching.

3. Lifecareer notions parallel the new science and can be used in everyday life.

4. You learn best about your own life process through telling your story and listening to the stories of others.

☐ Discussion Questions

1. How did this chapter impress you? What worked for you and what did not?

2. Do you believe that you have to be a science major to understand quantum physics?

3. What aspect of the chapter resonated most with your experience?

☐ Classroom/Group Exercises

1. Form dyads and relate parts of your life story to the ideas presented in the chapter.

2. How would you teach Lifecareer?

3. Take one of the ideas and make a mini lesson-plan, then share with the group.

☐ Homework Assignment

1. Talk with at least two friends or family members about this chapter. Record their responses and share with the class.

2. Use one or two of these ideas on situations that will come up before you return to class. Report to the class what happened.

3. Design a lesson plan to teach any of the concepts in this chapter or in the book.

3

LIVING THE NEW CAREERING: THE *WHY* QUESTION

Put very simply, improved health occurs when we don't break ourselves against life too often. That's a very important *why* in the New Careering. The unhealthy outcomes of maybe getting your round peg into a matching round hole; choosing a career; losing a career; looking for first, second, and third careers—all of this outer focus on a career that you may or may not have—encouraged Miller-Tiedeman to seriously look at traditional career and ask several questions:

- Does traditional career development harmonize with life?

- Does it encourage people to appreciate their *now*? If not, is there a tendency to spend too much time out there in the future?

- Does traditional career support the unfolding life? Or is it about money, finding the hot trends, setting goals, making life happen, trying to force mainline career theories to fit life?

- And, finally, what effect is all this having on health?

You only have to watch secondary and college students fret about finding a career, or work with adults searching for a noble purpose with little success to observe the stress involved.

Miller-Tiedeman believes that life-direction frustration is a learned response to the myth that individuals can control their lives irrespective of life's agenda. Thus, too many people continue to break themselves against life time and time again, which in the long run tends to depress the immune system in ways mentioned throughout this book.

Finally, if you are living your own process, connecting when necessary while loving life as it is and yourself as you are, with an eye out for improvement, then your body is receiving positive cues that support your immune system. This frees up more energy for career creativity. This results in improved health, a very important *why* in considering the New Careering.

CHAPTER

Anna Miller-Tiedeman

Health Benefits of the New Careering

Spotlight on Health

Consider these statistics from Northwestern Mutual Life, the American Institute of Stress, and the American Psychological Association (Cryer, 1996):

- Disabling stress has doubled over the last six years.

- 72% of American workers experience frequent stress-related physical or mental conditions that greatly increase health care costs.

- Depression has doubled with every generation since the 1920s.

- One million people per day are absent from work due to stress-related disorders.

- One in three Americans seriously thought about quitting work in 1990 because of job stress, and one in three expects to "burn out" on the job in the near future.

- If that weren't enough—a landmark 20-year study conducted by the University of London concluded that unmanaged reactions to stress were a more dangerous risk factor for cancer and heart disease than either cigarette smoking or eating high cholesterol foods.

☐ Looking Ahead

Watch for the following important topics:

1. Everything connects to everything else in life, and stress is no exception.

2. Stress kills off immune cells.

3. Trying to support a lifestyle often produces high stress.

4. Asking yourself financial questions and taking corrective action can lower your vulnerability to a downsized situation.

5. Social support networks can reduce stress.

6. Interference with life mission can increase stress.

7. Suggestions for reducing stress.

8. Important concepts:

   a. Interconnectedness

   b. Stress recognition

Health and Life Direction Intricately Intertwine

Health and the New (Quantum) Careering—what do they have in common? Nothing, if you take a Newtonian perspective (presumed separateness). But, everything, when you take the quantum worldview that suggests life is a web of relationships. David Bohm (1980), author of *Wholeness and the Implicate Order*, might call it unfolding and enfolding of all things in the universe. He called this "undivided wholeness in flowing movement" (p. 11). Things form and dissolve in the flow, some recur and persist in a more or less stable way, others become imperceptible.

The flow is everything impinging on the aggregate or the whole kit and caboodle.

Furthermore, if your paradigm does not include health as a part of life direction, then you won't see it. (See Chapter 5 for more detail on paradigms.) Then think in terms of development. At the Conforming stage individuals tend to carry forward what has been, those at the Self-Aware level frequently look for the new to augment the existing. (See Chapter 4 for more detail on development.) So, traditional ideas tend to appeal more to conformers while both traditional and alternative notions attract those with a higher level of awareness.

Everything Is Connected to Everything Else

Deepak Chopra, in his PBS lecture "Everyday Reality" (1995), explained that "a quadrillion atoms have circulated through your body that have circulated through the body of every living species. Think of a tree in Africa, a peasant in China, and you have in your physical body raw materials that were floating there three weeks ago."

Milani and Smith (1985), in *Rotational Physics: The Principles of Energy*, contend that "For every (re)action occurring in nature, some change in either mass or energy occurs" (p. 143) even when there's no perceivable change. They went on to say that both internal and external forces co-create change which ultimately affects all that is. Atkinson and McCraty (1996) found that recalling an angry episode, as short as five minutes, can suppress the immune system for as much as six hours. The opposite is also true. Positive feelings boost the immune system; and, even if we get sick, we recover more quickly and recoup lost energy (Cryer, 1995). Cryer said that attitudes that boost the immune system tend to create a harmonious and more productive workplace. A software group at Motorola initiated monthly meetings to acknowledge accomplishments. As a result, they saw patent applications rise, work dilemmas being solved faster, and more teamwork and unity among the workers (Internet info). Many businesses now see how connected appreciation and praise relate to the bottom line.

Therefore, it is not a leap of faith to believe that life direction and health connect in profound ways; this connection often remain imperceptible until, like a tire tread worn thin, it breaks and the result becomes visible. We get mentally, physically, and spiritually ill, then spend the remainder of life wondering why we failed to fulfill our mission; why life turned out opposite to our plan; why, having done all the right things, the promised reward somehow failed to materialize. Frequently, in trying to be something we are not, we discover much of life has passed us by; why we hate our jobs, and the list goes on.

Technically speaking, it appears that immune suppression occurs via glucocorticoids because they halt the formation of new lymphocytes (those white blood cells that protect us from invaders) in the thymus. In addition, "glucocorticoids cause lymphocytes to be yanked out of circulation;" (Sapolsky, 1994, p. 139) and, these glutocorticoids can kill the lymphocytes. Sapolsky said, "This occurs through a mechanism cell biologists are wild about: glucocorticoids can enter a lymphocyte and cause it to synthesize a suicide protein that chops the DNA in the lymphocyte into thousands of tiny pieces: (Then the lymphocyte is dead as a doorknob since you need DNA to generate the proteins that keep you in business)" (p. 139).

Stress plays a role in the diseases that develop over time, like heart disease and cancer and other cerebrovascular disorders. And these are the diseases most prevalent now. Sapolsky (1994), in his book *Why Zebras Don't Get Ulcers*, identified three kinds of stress: (a) survival stress, which includes worry about predators, starvation, or bodily harm; (b) chronic stress, due to drought, famine, or earthquakes, or having to wander several miles each day for food; and (c) psychological and social stress.

The body will organize to handle the first two types of stress, but the third type is a rather recent invention. Research now suggests that stress-related diseases show up because we use our bodies for psychological and social stress when they were built to respond to acute physical emergencies, not for months-on-end worry about mortgages, relationships, promotions, downsizing, job security, and the like.

A stressor upsets the balance in the body; but the anticipation of a happening also can do the same damage. For instance, pretend someone asked you to keynote a particular meeting. You may experience that stress numerous times, not just at the keynote. Why? As you practice and envision the audience, your body reacts indicating the body received a message. So, when you feel that tinge of nervousness, then your body reacts by suppressing digestion, depressing growth, decreasing sex drive and putting reproduction on hold, and arresting immune activity. With sustained stress, we do not recognize pain quickly, but aspects of memory improve. The stress response does what it's supposed to do. Heart rate, blood pressure, and breathing all increases to deliver nutrients and oxygen faster to take care of the emergency (Sapolsky, 1994).

If you constantly invoke the stress mechanism, you don't store surplus energy. This results in fatigue and susceptibility to disease. Further, constant stress does not allow the body to work on long-term building projects as it stays in emergency mode. In short, stress increases your risk of getting diseases that make you sick and overwhelm your defenses if you are already sick. *However, stress not only suppresses the immune system but stress disassembles it, shrinking tissues and destroying cells.* That's serious in the long run; and, when your body breaks down, it's often too late to fix what, in many instances, could have been prevented (Sapolsky, 1994; emphasis added).

When you live Life-As-Career you use the stress response more for its original intention—handling acute emergencies—because you invoke cooperation, not confrontative nor combative behaviors, in an effort to control life. By so doing, you build your body's immunity because it does not get killed off as often nor work with inferior cells. You may, if you insist on control, win the external battle but lose the internal war. You also learn the more we cooperate with life, the kinder we treat our immune systems. This translates into fewer colds, headaches, and other minor ailments, not to mention the big ones.

Health and Work

When you live on the fast track of money and possessions you frequently end up working to support those things. This can increase stress. When you do not design a spending plan with the event of a possible downsizing in mind, your stress jumps. The fear of job loss, or actual job loss, traumatizes and stresses the body. Dr. Deepak Chopra, in *Creating Health* (1991), said, "When a person's under chronic stress, production of the body's natural killer cells, called T-lymphocytes and macrophages, seems to be inhibited" (p. 61). This supports Sapolsky's notion about the relationship of stress to immune function.

Stopping to think, ask questions, and discuss family economics has the potential to decrease stress. For instance, asking what if ...

- my job is eliminated?

- my job is relocated internationally?

- My company merges with another one and I lose my job?

- I haven't considered the possibility of a downsizing event?

This brings other questions like:

- What would I do financially if I got laid off?

You then ask how can I modify my spending habits to prepare for possible job loss or other time off I may want to take?

Talking and thinking about future possibilities, particularly one as potentially imminent as downsizing, can markedly reduce stress.

The current downsizing qualifies as a major stressor for many Americans, even those who consider themselves fairly well off financially. With no certain knowledge of how and when they might reconnect for work, they end up front runners for major stress. Unpredictability brings on stress that increases the glucocorticoid level and, as noted above, the glucocorticoids kill off immune cells. It's been found that rats who hear a warning bell before each electric shock have fewer ulcers. The rats who receive no warning always feel they're a half second away from the shock and, therefore, have difficulty relaxing; and, on the physical level, the glucocorticoids shoot up. Another experiment shows a similar result. When rats are given the same amount of food in an hour as rats fed on a schedule, but get it randomly and less predictably, up go the glucocorticoid levels (Sapolsky 1994).

So, in addition to being out of work, many Americans have stress going through the roof, which makes them prime candidates for all kinds of ailments. However, *"It is never really the case that stress makes you sick, or increases your risk of being sick. Stress increases your risk of getting diseases that make you sick, or if you have such a disease, stress increases the risk of your defenses being overwhelmed by the disease"* (Sapolsky, 1994, p. 17, italics added).

Health and Group Support

Social support networks are very important in life and, more specifically, in life direction. Sapolsky (1994), in his research with baboons, found that male baboons with lots of friends, playing with the kids and having frequent nonsexual grooming bouts with the females, had lower glucocorticoid concentrations than males of the same general rank lacking these outlets (p. 185). This means that fewer immune cells get killed off. For humans, any kind of physical contact—holding hands, and the like—lowers cardiovascular responses to stress. It's also been found to lower cholesterol levels.

In a downsized environment, it's particularly important to stay connected with friends and family. As mentioned earlier, forming another group (and by now you know Miller-Tiedeman likes this idea; see Chapters 3, 8, and 9), such as Faith Popcorn's "kitchen cabinet," would offer a second level of support. You'll recall that Popcorn suggested approaching eight or ten of the smartest people you know. If you're a psychologist, approach someone you know who works in packaged goods, maybe your neighbor who teaches history. Mix ages, educational levels, and personalities. Tell them what life direction problems you're having. Have each one come up with five to ten ideas. Don't hesitate to listen and ask questions. This could become a group that works on different problems that arise for other members. We each have only a piece of the puzzle, therefore, we are more together than we are apart. Popcorn (1991) suggested that too many of us wake up in the middle of the night feeling alone and afraid of what's coming. "We'd all be better off facing the future together, collaborating in the light of day (p. 14).

Health and Life Mission

The purpose of life is not what to do after you are educated, but what to do in opening up your powers of understanding your potential as a human being. When this natural urge is blocked, stress results and the individual finds himself or herself going from pillar to post in an effort to find some small spark of that light which feeds his or her soul because it represents a calling.

Parents often unknowingly kill off the natural urge of children to move toward that which beckons or will fulfill them, when they insist their children do a certain thing, like train for a particular profession and/ or attend college. They want to save their children from some of the things they experienced. They frequently see higher education as a route to more and greater income along with greater security. However, blocking of the natural unfoldment of children and adult children sets up enormous stress in the child's body and may account for some of the physical problems children encounter which frequently carry over into adult life.

Counselors and other helping professionals often unconsciously increase stress in the people with whom they work by moving them toward trends and discouraging personal inclinations. For instance, a student transfers into a new school and goes to the counselor to schedule classes. The student requests an algebra class, but the counselor looks at the test scores in the student's folder and sees a 30th percentile in math. He or she decides the student couldn't do algebra and tells the student that he or she should sign up for General Math. The student doesn't want that but goes along. The counselor takes the position that all students who score in the 30th percentile cannot do algebra, rather than letting the student discover the outcome. It's been shown in many instances that students in the 30th percentile in math can and do pass algebra, maybe not at the A level, but they can frequently do C work. When students make the determination of level of difficulty, then they're not left regretting what might have been; self esteem remains intact, as they don't have the feeling the counselor didn't think they were smart enough to take algebra; and stress in this once instance has not been exacerbated.

In counseling adults, frequently counselors and other helping professionals will make judgments about what the client can and can't accomplish. No one knows that about anyone else.

Suggestions for Reducing Stress

Choose Interpretation Over Judgment

Living Life-As-Career® offers the opportunity to choose interpretation over judgment. Interpreting experience can reduce stress, increase motivation, and produce more joy and happiness. In short, choice can change response patterns, which can improve over-all health. In addition, the attention on growing your life frees up psychological space for new work and life ideas to come in. Then you discover you have time to discern and grow your personal career theory. You do this by making decisions, assessing what worked and what did not, making space to think about how you felt about selected decisions, and looking at the pattern of past decisions to see what you can learn. All this takes time and needs quiet contemplation, as Joseph Campbell, in his book *The Power of Myth* (1988), maintained:

> You must have a room, or a certain hour or so a day, where you don't know what was in the newspapers that morning, you don't know who your friends are, you don't know what you owe anybody, you don't know what anybody owes to you. This is a place where you can simply experience and bring forth what you are and what you might be. This is the place of creative incubation. At first you may find that nothing happens there. But if you have a sacred place and use it, something eventually will happen (p. 92).

Campbell went on to write that this sacred place does for us what the plains did for the hunter. For him, the whole world was a sacred place. But modern day life has become so hectic, so economic, and so detail oriented that as you get older, the momentary demands are so great that you hardly know where you are or what you intended to do. This may mean you live a good part of your life out of your body, in the future, or in the past, but not too often in the *now*.

In your sacred place you at least get the opportunity to return to your own wonder and knowing (Miller-Tiedeman, 1992b). It's in this place that you get in touch with your inner career voice. Your inner career voice serves as the engine of your Lifecareer.

The Freeze-Frame® Technique

A popular notion has it that the brain dictates body functions, and the heart receives orders, serving as an unintelligent pump. But the Institute

---

Lifecareer, Life-Is-Career, Career Compass, and their derivatives are registered trademarks of Dr. Anna Miller-Tiedeman.
Freeze-Frame® is a registered trademark of the Institute of HeartMath.

of HeartMath has published research showing that the heart affects how we perceive. When the heart rhythms are smooth, they empower reaction speeds and decision-making, when jagged and irregular, they slow brain reaction and impair decision-making ability. But the good news is that individuals can learn to consciously control these rhythms. Bruce Cryer, Vice President of HeartMath suggests that we cannot change many external things, but we can change how we perceive them. That is consistent with Ellis' (1979) notion that it is not what happens to us that causes us problems, it is how we think about (perceive) those events. Ellis used the A-B-C method: A represents the activating event; B, the perception of it (belief); and C, the individual's reaction (consequence).

In psychology, researchers tend to ask people questions or give them paper and pencil tests to determine change. But the Institute of HeartMath in Boulder Creek, Co., went to the heart of the matter—heart rhythms—to determine if their Freeze-Frame stress intervention (not management) technique worked. Doc Childre, President of HeartMath LLC, led a team that researched and developed the Freeze-Frame Technique. They measured beat-to-beat changes in heart rhythms before and after the simple, self-induced Freeze-Frame technique. Individuals feeling stressed were asked to consciously focus warm, caring feelings around the heart. Before the individual used the Freeze-Frame technique, the heart rhythms were jagged and chaotic, but after the Freeze-Frame, they became smooth. Further experiments showed the effect of Freeze-Framing on several measures studied. "Heart Rate Variability, Pulse Transit Time and Respiration were all measured before and after Freeze-Frame. After the Freeze-Frame experience, the different oscillating rhythms actually became frequency locked—totally in sync" (entrainment) (p. 2).

You can learn to use the Freeze-Frame technique from the book, *Freeze-Frame: One-Minute Stress Management* (Childre, 1998). Here is a condensed version of the steps:

1. Recognize that you are experiencing stress.

2. Freeze the feeling and take time out. Then shift your attention away from your racing mind and emotions and toward the area around your heart. Visualize your breath moving through your heart. Stay focused for 10 seconds or more.

3. Recall a pleasant, wonderful, fun feeling or time in your life, then re-experience it.

4. Now using your intuition, frame a heart-intelligent response to the stressor. Ask your heart, "What would be a more efficient re-

sponse to the situation, one that will minimize future stress?'
(McCraty, 1995, p. 1)

5. Listen for your heart's answer.

The wonderful part of this technique—you can use it on the spot.
You don't have to wait until you go home to do something.

☐ Looking Back

1. Life direction and health are irrevocably linked.

2. Building a financial safety net can lower stress.

3. Group support, whether family or friends or both, is essential when
   things in your life fall apart.

4. Allowing someone to interfere with what you think you should do
   sets up stress.

5. Interpret your experience, but let go of judgment.

6. Use the Freeze-Frame technique the moment you recognize a stressful feeling.

☐ Discussion Questions

1. What did you learn from this chapter?

2. Share a stressful situation in your life and tell how you handled it.

3. Discuss the importance of understanding the stress and immune system connection.

4. Share how you recognize you are under stress, what you do about it,
   in the minute or later.

☐ Classroom/Group Exercises

1. Form dyads and discuss your own experience of stress.

2. Try to identify physical conditions you think have been brought on by stress.

3. Share information about any kind of alternative health care you participate in that you think helps relieve your stress. For instance, structural bodywork, meditation, cranio-sacral work reflexology.

☐ Homework Assignment

1. Try out the above suggestions between now and the next class meeting. Interpret but don't judge your experience.

2. Try out the Freeze-Frame technique, and report your results to the class. Interview several people (consider inviting them for a cup of tea or coffee) and ask them what they do to relieve stress. In return, you may want to share with them what you have learned about how stress depresses the immune system as well as telling them about the Freeze-Frame technique.

Anna Miller-Tiedeman

After All Is Said and Done

Humanity will find its way and will learn appropriate lessons. The New Careering is but one approach that will help many enter transformation and then continue on that wonderful journey into potential kept hidden by our conveyor-belt, job-oriented culture. Jobs will remain important, but humans were meant to do more than make money and buy things. We're seeing the transformation from the material, to the journey into spirituality, as we enter the twenty-first century, even in our professional books (Bloch & Richmond, 1997).

Three important principles put forth in this text—Life-Is-Career®, life is self organizing, and life teaches us by letting us learn from our left turns (often called wrong) and experience joy in those things that work—all three will help individuals throughout the coming centuries, not because they're in this book, but because they represent timeless and self-evident principles, written about in many ways from the beginning of time. Most religions in some way speak about these principles, and philosophers and poets have written about them. However, the time was not right for those ideas to move to the cellular level where we could become conscious enough to start acting on them. So, we broke ourselves against life time and time again. But that is how we presently grow ourselves to a higher level of development, a place where we can expand our paradigm, and a place

---

Lifecareer, Life-Is-Career, Career Compass and their derivatives are registered trademarks of Dr. Anna Miller Tiedeman.

where our decision-making can help us recognize and navigate around potential hazards. Cooperating with the approaching forces while assessing the situation then becomes as easy as breathing, as does loving life as it is and loving ourselves as we are, doing the best we can and moving on while forgiving ourselves for our miscues.

At this point, inner wisdom takes on more meaning. Put in computer terms, we start to scan our inner e-mail that arrives daily from our internal information super-highway. No server breakdowns here, only an overloaded mailbox due to so many unread messages. When we clear our inner e-mail, we then start to sense the web of connections—that life is really easier than we thought, that it doesn't knock on our door each day asking for direction, that we really can trust it, that career is here, now, who you are, your life. That we get it by living it.

Reynolds (1984), in his book *Playing Ball on Running Water*, writes of a young prince, who at a very early age, was suddenly faced with becoming king, owing to his father's serious illness. The prospect caused the young prince to panic. He told everyone he wasn't ready. He thought, if his mother were alive, she could assume the throne. Then he wondered why his sisters couldn't.

Two days before the coronation, the young prince suddenly locked himself in his room. He refused to come out. The ailing king summoned the grand wizard to his bedside and told him to solve the problem.

That night at suppertime, the grand wizard knocked on the prince's door. He was told to go away. But the wizard persisted. "I have a dynastic pill for you to take with your meal," he said. "You cannot reign without taking this dynastic pill."

The prince said that he had never heard of such a thing. But the grand wizard told him where the bottle containing the pill was located. He advised him to read the instructions carefully before taking it.

The prince found the bottle. He picked it up and read the label. It said, "Dynastic Pill." The label indicated that the pill was personally prepared by each monarch for his royal successor. The prince opened the bottle and saw the piece of paper bearing the instructions. As he began to read them, he suddenly started to daydream about the coronation banquet. He could see himself standing regally at the head table, toasting the people of his kingdom—poised, confident, fully a king.

Two days later, the royal coronation took place. All who attended talked about the splendid bearing of the young king. They speculated he would be another in a long line of wise monarchs.

After the excitement of the day had died down, the prince, now a king, returned to his chamber to finish reading the note he had found in the bottle. It said:

For you, my son. No man is ever ready for such authority as this. No man begins by feeling like a king. You become a king by being one. In time, you will wear your crown as comfortably as anyone has. There is no magic in the pill. It is made of the bitterest herbs. The instructions are to hold it in your mouth until you grow used to the bitterness. Then, when you have conquered it, when the pill has completely dissolved, you may swallow it. That's all.

Your loving father (p. 137).

The individual who can similarly overcome the bitter taste of self doubt, and continue to be guided by his or her experience, intelligence, and intuition will also be rewarded with confidence and growth. The Lifecareer theory will then serve as a port of confidence that the individual may or may not need to return to periodically for support. But the individual will soon realize that his or her inner wisdom (personal career theory) has been there all long, that his or her story provides the guiding light to navigate this thing called life.

APPENDICES

☐ Appendix A. Vocational Theories Summarized
By Anna Miller-Tiedeman
and Eileen McCarthy[1]

Frank Parsons–Law

In the nineteenth and twentieth centuries, science entered its third era. The natural sciences success with highly structured observation, reasoning, and investigation impressed psychologists and they started adopting Descartes' logic and Newton's mathematics and the direct querying of nature "untouched by uncontrolled human being" as much as possible. The philosophy of logical positivism and the science of behaviorism took hold in psychology. Differential psychology and its handmaiden, psychometrics, followed almost naturally, just in time to attract Parsons' quest for matching persons to traits and jobs. Trait and factor logic and instrumentation underlies all career theories grounded in advising clients concerning choices of education, job, occupation, vocation, and/or career.

Brown (Brown et al., 1990) notes that researchers who reviewed trait and factor theory somewhat agree about its propositions and assumptions. He paraphrased Klein and Wein's conclusions as follows:

1. Each individual has a set of traits that can be measured reliably and validly.

2. Occupations require certain expertises (traits) for success, and a worker with wide-ranging characteristics can be successful in a given job.

3. Occupational choice is a rather straightforward process, and matching is possible.

David V. Tiedeman and Anna Miller-Tiedeman express their deep appreciation to Eileen McCarthy, who interned with the Lifecareer Group in Vista, California. Her dedication and untiring effort at a critical time of need shall remain in our hearts. Thank you, Eileen.

4. The closer the match between personal characteristics and job requirements, the greater the likelihood of success (i.e., productivity and satisfaction).

Frank Parsons spearheaded the vocational guidance movement because he
was deeply concerned about the exploitation of workers by the industrial leaders.
Parsons advocated what has defined the field of vocational choice for half a century: (a) personal analysis; (b) job analysis; and (c) a scientific matching and advising of the two. The scientific matching allegedly optimized satisfaction of worker
with job.

The Miller and Form Career Pattern Study–Sociology

Miller and Form (1951), laid down one of the best known studies of career patterns focusing on various work periods of men in a small but selected sample.
Their classifications were:

1. The stable career pattern. Going from school or college to a particular
   job and not changing jobs.

2. The conventional career pattern. The socially expected job progression
   that leads to a stable job.

3. The unstable career pattern. Returning to a trial job after experiencing
   a stable career pattern.

4. The single career pattern. Starting first jobs.

5. The disestablished career pattern. Returning to a temporary job after
   working a stable one.

6. The multiple-trial career pattern. Changes jobs frequently and fails to
   establish himself or herself in a career.

Stability was defined as remaining more than three years on a given job
which reflected a high degree of occupational security. Further, the "stable and
conventional might be regarded as reflecting a high degree of occupational security" (p. 713). The unstable, single trial, disestablished, and multiple-trial patterns
tended to include a high degree of occupational insecurity. Today, the words "stable
and permanent" do not necessarily describe work. Now the discussion points to
permanent-temporary assignments, and no occupation escapes the possibility of
the twentieth-century version of instability (downsizing).

Donald Super–Psychology

The Miller and Form study launched Super's (1957) career pattern study. (New
career development professionals might want to note that Donald Super found his
start in the field of sociology with Miller and Form's work, and his later work from
economics relying on Eli Ginzberg's vocational choice as process. So, Donald Super, like Miller-Tiedeman, stepped outside of vocational psychology to build a life

work. Vocational psychology is not a field with a knowledge base sufficient enough to study the growth of the whole person. People are more than data provided in group studies.)

Donald E. Super stayed with the Miller and Form career patterns for men, dropping the single trial and disestablished from his consideration. But for women, he added the double-track career pattern, and the interrupted career pattern as shown below:

1. The stable homemaking career pattern. Women who marry after schooling with no significant work experience (work, as in "outside the home").

2. The conventional career pattern. Working full time after schooling for several months to several years, marrying, and becoming full-time homemakers.

3. The stable working career pattern. Women who start out working thinking they will work until they marry. Frequently this turns into a long-term engagement with work.

4. The double-track career pattern. Women who complete their education and combine work with marriage and a family.

5. The interrupted career pattern. Working before marriage, quitting to have and raise a family, then returning to work.

6. The unstable career pattern. Working outside the home, marriage, homemaking, working, and returning to full-time homemaking. Work becomes something she does to fill economic and personal needs.

7. The multiple-trial career pattern. Trying out a lot of work situations, but seldom settling on one long enough to establish herself.

A large part of Super's work focuses on developing a self-concept. It appears self-concept emerges from exploration of self in the home and at work, then on the exploration in school, exploration in part-time work resulting in various aspirations.

Important to Super's thought remains his idea that a self-concept must be developed. Look definitionally at this and you discover Super describes normal child development with a high interest in how this happens. This suggests that he observes what happens in different situations. This approach tells you little about the individual, and for all observers know, their data may be totally invalid. But that reflects a 300-year-old Newtonian mindset where the observer looked at the subject, totally unaware that he or she could not separate himself or herself from that observation. But this perspective remains the academic standard.

The separation of observer from the observed shows up again in Super's Life-Span, Life-Space idea. Following, find his propositions:

1. Each individual comes with a set of unique possibilities.

2. Each individual's capabilities qualifies him or her for various occupations.

3. Occupations require varying levels of expertise and thereby attract a variety of individuals.

4. Time changes everything including self-concepts.

5. Change may be seen as a sequence of Growth, Exploration, Establishment, Maintenance, and Disengagement. Between each of these stages is a mini-cycle with its individual challenges.

6. Career pattern of any one individual links closely with such things as background, mental ability, education, skills, personality (needs values, interests, and self-concepts), and career maturity as well as given opportunities.

7. Success in any one of the stages depends on individual readiness.

8. Career maturity refers to where the individual places along the continuum between Growth and Disengagement.

9. Development takes place partly through maturing different aspects in the individual and partly by reality testing and in self-concepts.

10. Career development process is " ... that of developing and implementing occupational self-concepts" (Brown et al., 1996, p. 125).

The remaining four propositions deal with work satisfaction and life satisfaction, and point to work and occupation as a focus for personality organization.

Super's career rainbow is reminiscent of the bell curve; it points to interesting averages, and in Super's schema, stages, and roles, at various ages. But ask yourself, "where is the personal information, or the heart beat of what it takes to mature a life vision?" Also, ask yourself how the vocational maturity concept has impacted your life.

Eli Ginzberg: Occupational Choice–Economics

In the latter 1930s, Ginzberg and colleagues (1951) conducted several empirical studies in economics and group behavior, aimed at studying the "interplay between significant changes in the economic environment and the behavior of large groups" (p. 11). They first studied coal miners of South Wales and reported their findings in *Grass on the Slag Heaps: The Story of the Welsh Miners*. The second and more elaborate investigation based on case studies of the unemployed in New York City in 1929 and 1940, was published in *The Unemployed*. These investigations sought to determine what adds to or detracts from the efficiency with which individuals use their own resources and how society uses its human resources. From *The Unemployed* it was found we learn from contrast. "We learn from unemployment the true significance of work" (p. 10). Unemployment brings to conscious awareness very quickly the essential nature of work and quality of life.

Earlier investigations turned up a significant number of variables that operate in the choice process, and, further, that important variables react on each other. But no theory had discovered the principles of these interactions. Ginzberg et al. (1951) went on to say that no theory existed which gave a convincing description of the strategic variables themselves. So, the Ginzberg group decided to do small empirical studies each aimed at a specific and important variable. Four variables were selected: (a) reality factors—social and economic forces which determine the environment into one is born; (b) educational impact on choice; (c) emotional factors in occupational choice; and (d) factors leading to atypical patterns of decision-making.

Lazarsfeld (1931), in his *Jugend und Beruf* (Youth and Occupation), reviewed a large number of empirical studies done by European investigators. He concluded those studies reflected a major methodological error in that they had asked the Why question ("Why do you want to enter a particular occupation?" This elicited simple responses like, "I want to do what my father does," or "I want to make a lot of money") instead of the How question—how the individual came to make decisions that led to particular choices. This change in the question from *why* to *how* led to the first study of the *process* of choosing. Lazarsfeld took a genetic approach and initiated several studies. The adaptation of the genetic approach to a study of occupational choice assumes that analyses of the intellectual and emotional life of the child will reveal developmental sequences though they may not be as apparent as in physical maturation.

Professor Super reviewed the American literature, particularly investigations of two decades, to determine what light might be thrown on the role of parents and other key people in the choice process, the relation of occupational choice to personality structure, and the relation of goal and value changes to occupational choices. In addition, Super looked at the extent to which individuals considered reality factors. Specifically, did they have job opportunity information? To what extent did work satisfaction matter, as distinct from income and opportunity for advancement?

Super's review found that no integrative factors were present, and, in addition, some findings were contradictory. For instance, one study showed that boys tended to enter their father's occupations, while another one showed that pattern was the exception, not the rule. Another investigator held that occupational choice was mostly dictated by social and environmental factors, while another stressed the emotional determinants. Most of the studies analyzed the relationships of particular factors such as family background, age, or sex. These studies proved nonuseful in securing testable results. Ginzberg et al. (1951) concluded that, "It had been impossible to build a general theory of occupational choice out of the findings of our own empirical investigations" (p. 17), and little was added by the literature review.

The Ginzberg group, who had the support of vocational counseling experts, thought that a great waste of individual and social resources occurs due to how individuals reach decisions about their occupations, how they fail to make the most of their own capacities, and fail to take full advantage of the educational opportunities and other social resources offered them. Thus, the Ginzberg group wanted to understand how occupational choices were made in the hopes that this knowledge would reduce the waste that occurred (p. 17).

Ginzberg and his group were ahead of their time, as they included women in their study of occupational choice, along with separated male military personnel. Ten psychoanalysts who reviewed the case histories of five patients who recently completed training and were working, and individuals who planned to enter the ministry were also participants in Ginzberg's research. The major conclusion from the findings is that occupational choice is a developmental process—not a single decision, but a series of decisions made over a period of years. Each step in the process relates to those which precede and follow it.

"The basic elements in our theory of occupational choice, then, are three: it is a process; the process is largely irreversible; compromise is an essential aspect of every choice" (p. 186). Ginzberg et al. divided occupational choice into three periods: (a) fantasy, (b) tentativeness, and (c) realistic.

Anne Roe–Psychology

Roe's theoretical interest focused on personality theory and occupational classification and how these might be integrated. She looked at the range of occupations, and "their relationship to individual differences in backgrounds, physical and psychological variables and experiences" (Roe & Lunneborg, 1990). Roe stated that her interest in occupation and personality theory had nothing to do with career development, as she knew nothing of such studies until she wrote *The Psychology of Occupations* (1956). She therefore formulated the theory without concern for practical application. This provides a pointed illustration of process careering. Roe did not plan to write a career development theory. She merely followed her interest and it evolved as happens in all our lives, with or without our permission.

Roe used Maslow's (1954) hierarchy of needs, which was seminal to her study of occupation and personality because occupation had a relationship to need satisfaction.

Following is Maslow's Hierarchy of Needs, listed in the usual order of potency:

1. Physiological needs

2. Safety needs

3. Belongingness and love

4. Importance, respect, self-esteem, independence

5. Information

6. Understanding

7. Beauty

8. Self-actualization

Roe pointed out that occupation stands as one of the most necessary in satisfying a larger number of needs.

She then devised an eight-group and six-level classification of occupations (see Table A-1). The eight groups indicate the primary focus of activity in the occupations, and are as follows:

1. Service: Primarily working with people, serving and attending to a variety of needs.

2. Business Contact: While people contact remains important, it is focused more on persuasion than on helping, where the persuader profits from his or her action.

3. Organization: Primarily concerned with commercial and government activities. People contact more formal.

4. Technology: Mostly deals with things, as in production and movement of commodities and utilities. People interactions of little importance.

5. Outdoor: Concerned with conservation, preservation, gathering of crops, water resource management, and animal husbandry to offer a flavor of this grouping.

6. Science: Deals mostly with scientific theory and its application in various circumstances.

7. General Culture: Preservation and transmission of the general cultural notions. Interest in human activities versus individual people.

8. Arts and Entertainment: Creative artists of all kinds. Focus is on individual, group, and the public.

Occupations in the above eight groups fan out through six levels based on responsibility and demonstrated skill, as shown below. These also follow, for the most part, education. For instance, one rarely finds a high school graduate working in the professional occupations. The six levels are as follows:

Professional and Managerial #1: Top creators, administrators, and professionals who work independently with considerable responsibility. They are usually policy makers with a high level of education, usually a doctorate. However, Miller-Tiedeman would also place a sports figure like Michael Jordan, Oprah Winfrey, Janet Reno, heart surgeons, and medical doctors in general in this category.

Professional and Managerial #2: There exists only a slight difference between this level and the first level. This level indicates less significant responsibilities, policy interpreting (not making), and education above the bachelor's degree level, but below the doctorate level.

Semiprofessional and Small Business: Less responsibility for others, mostly policy interpretation for self, not others, with a high school or technical school education or equivalent.

Skilled: Occupations requiring apprenticeships, special training, or experience.

Semiskilled: Requires low-level training and or experience. Workers follow orders of someone else with little responsibility.

Unskilled: Usually entry-level occupations with simple, repetitive tasks.

Further, Roe's theory includes five propositions concerning interests and needs. They are:

1. Genetic inheritance limits potential of the individual.

2. How individuals develop directly bears on their general cultural background, and their family's socioeconomic class.

TABLE A-1. Two-Way Classification of Occupations[1]

Level	I. Service	II. Business Contact	III. Organization	IV. Technology	V. Outdoor	VI. Science	VII. General Cultural	VIII. Arts and Entertainment
1	Personal therapists Social work supervisors Counselors	Promoters	U.S. President and Cabinet Industrial tycoons International bankers	Inventive geniuses Consulting or chief engineers Ships' commanders	Consulting specialists	Research scientists University, college faculties Medical specialists Museum curators	Supreme Court Justices University, college faculties Prophets/Scholars	Creative artists Performers, great Teachers, university equivalent Museum curators
2	Social workers Occupational therapists Probation, truant officers (with training)	Promoters Public relations counselors	Certified public accountants Business government executives Union officials Brokers, average	Applied scientists Factory managers Ships' officers Engineers	Applied scientists Landowners and operators, large Landscape architects	Scientists, semi-independant Nurses Pharmacists Veterinarians	Editors Teachers, high school and elementary	Athletes Art critics Designers Music arrangers
3	YMCA officials Detectives, police sergeants Welfare workers City inspectors	Salesmen: auto, bond, insurance, etc. Dealers, retail and wholesale Confidence men	Accountants, average Employment managers Owners, catering, dry-cleaning, etc.	Aviators Contractors Foremen (DOT I) Radio operators	County agents Farm owners Forest rangers Fish, game wardens	Technicians, medical, X-ray, museum Weather observers Chiropractors	Justices of the peace Radio announcers Reporters Librarians	Ad writers Designers Interior decorators Showmen
4	Barbers Chefs Practical nurses Policemen	Auctioneers Buyers (DOT I) House canvassers Interviewers, poll	Cashiers Clerks, credit, express, etc. Foremen, warehouse Salesclerks	Blacksmiths Electricians Foremen (DOT II) Mechanics, average	Laboratory testers, dairy products, etc. Miners Oil well drillers	Technical assistants	Law clerks	Advertising artists Decorators, window, etc. Photographers Racing car drivers
5	Taxi drivers General house-workers Waiters City firemen	Peddlers	Clerks, file, stock, etc. Notaries Runners Typists	Bulldozer operators Deliverymen Smelter workers Truck drivers	Gardeners Farm tenants Teamsters, cow-punchers Miner's helpers	Veterinary hospital attendants		Illustrators, greeting cards Showcard writers Stagehands
6	Chambermaids Hospital attendants Elevator operators Watchmen		Messenger boys	Helpers Laborers Wrappers Yardmen	Dairy hands Farm laborers Lumberjacks	Nontechnical helpers in scientific orgnization		

[1]From *The Psychology of Occupations*. New York: Wiley.

3. The pattern of an individual's development links to his or her experiences and the direction of his or her involuntary attention. This relates to the relationship between personality and perception and how early.

4. The amount of energy directed toward specific activities indicates interest.

5. The amount of drive toward accomplishment reflects intensity of needs and their satisfaction.

Roe also hypothesized a relationship between occupational choice and parent–child relations. She devised a Parent–Child Relations Questionnaire (PCR I) based on classification reported here. "Analysis of questionnaire results gave three factors. Two—Loving Rejecting (LR) and Casual-Demanding (CD)—were bipolar, and one—Overt Attention (O)—was unipolar. Only factors LR and O were assumed to affect person orientation" (Roe & Lunneborg, 1990, p. 78).

Edward S. Bordin–Psychology

Bordin (1990) used the tree metaphor for the structure of his theory, to suggest that there exists root assumptions which grow into specific propositions. He postulated that the both personality in work and career somehow roots in play. Play and work could be seen as two sides of the same coin. Following find Borden's seven propositions:

Proposition 1. All people seek the experience of joy, in all aspects of life which relates to their sense of wholeness.

Proposition 2. How individuals integrate work and play depend on their developmental history, effort, and motivation.

Proposition 3. Individual lives reflect a stream of career decisions made to gain a better fit between the self and work. Bordin suggests a key to understanding individual turning points in a career path is a better understanding of what the self seeks at that point in time.

Proposition 4. A useful mapping of occupations for intrinsic motives will be one that " ... captures life-styles or character styles and stimulates or is receptive to developmental conceptions" (Bordin, 1990, p. 115).

Proposition 5. Roots of personal aspects of career development are usually found in early development.

Proposition 6. Each individual seeks to integrate aspects of father and mother with elements unique to self.

Proposition 7. Problems at decision points may link to self-dissatisfaction.

John Holland–Psychology

John Holland's contribution grew out of his work as a counseling and clinical psychologist. This lead to his development of the *Self-Directed Search* (1977). Holland's inventory assesses personality through occupational titles, not hypotheses (Crites, 1969).

Holland began harvesting and sharing the fruits of his personality/occupation study in the mid-fifties. The 1950s were exciting years in the occupational environment of career development research. Just prior to World War II, Super (1942) had worked out a concept of vocational adjustment and started a union of occupational choice and occupational adjustment. Parsons' Proposition 2 contained the seed of such a union which extended guidance of an educational and vocational nature from early educational decisions on to a first occupational choice, and advising into continuing multiple occupational choosing and advising. Although "career" did not find its explicit way into vocational guidance usage at that time, the concept has been around ever since Parsons spread the jelly of matching and advising on to the bread of occupational environments liberally enough to have started a movement which spread rapidly in an economy moving primarily from an agricultural era into an industrial one

The expansion of Holland's theory over the years has left his basic relationship of matched personality and occupational environments intact. His suppositions hold up well in a plethora of circumstances. In addition, "Holland intends his theory to explain the everyday questions people ask about their careers, especially regarding the career decisions they must make" (Brown et al., 1990, p. 39). This statement has probably added to the popularity of Holland's theory, which is very much in use today. Through this theory, one will see parallel sets of ideas applied both to people and to environments. Holland views one's vocational interests as an aspect of one's personality. Since a person takes his/her personality to the work place, Holland built his theory (1966) around the links in types (typology) connecting the two. He classified people and environments as one of the following types:

Realistic. This groups tends toward mechanical and technical ability.

Investigative. These individuals are mostly scientifically oriented with aptitudes in both math and research. They are analytical, curious, scholarly, and open with broad interests.

Artistic. Those in this category are generally drawn to creative endeavors in writing music, sculpting, painting, photography, and the like. These individuals live creatively and frequently see life as a living art.

Social. These individuals have a tendency toward extroversion, helping, and have a genuine interest in the social fabric of society.

Enterprising. These types like working on their own, like the challenge of building something for themselves. They also like the connection and networking that goes along with building a business. Many of these types see their life as a private business tin into which they invest. They tend to like autonomy and going ahead (a higher level of development), as opposed to conforming to what someone else wants them to do. They tend not to score high on following

TABLE A-2. Personality Types and Salient Characteristics[1]

	Realistic	Investigative	Artistic	Social	Enterprising	Conventional
Traits	Hardheaded Unassuming Practical Dogmatic Natural Uninsightful	Analytical Intellectual Curious Scholarly Open Broad interests	Open Nonconforming Imaginative Intuitive Sensitive Creative	Agreeable Friendly Understanding Sociable Persuasive Extroverted	Extroverted Dominant Adventurous Enthusiastic Power-seeking Energetic	Conforming Conservative Unimaginative Inhibited Practical-minded Methodical
Life goals	Inventing apparatus or equipment Becoming outstanding athlete	Inventing valuable product Theoretical contribution to science	Becoming famous in performing arts Publishing stories Original painting Musical composition	Helping others Making sacrifices for others Competent teacher or therapist	Being community leader Expert in finance and commerce Being well-liked and well-dressed	Expert in finance and commerce Producing a lot of work
Values	Freedom Intellectual Ambitious Self-controlled Docility	Intellectual Logical Ambitious Wisdom	Equality Imaginative Courageous World of	Equality Self-respect Helpful Forgiving	Freedom Ambitious (–) Forgiving (–) Helpful	(–) Imaginative (–) Forgiving
Identifications	Thomas Edison Admiral Byrd	Madame Curie Charles Darwin	T.S. Eliot Pablo Picasso	Jane Addams Albert Schweitzer	Henry Ford Andrew Carnegie	Bernard Baruch John D. Rockefeller
Aptitudes and competencies	Technical	Scientific	Arts	Social and educational Leadership and sales Interpersonal	Leadership and sales Social and educational Business and interpersonal	Business and clerical
Self-ratings	Mechanical ability	Math ability Research ability	Artistic ability	—	—	Clerical ability
Most competent in	Mechanics	Science	Art	Human relations	Leadership	Business

[1] Adapted and reproduced by special permission of the Publisher, Psychological Assessment Resources, Inc., Odessa, FL 33556, from the *Self-Directed Search Professional User's Guide* by John L. Holland, Ph.D., et al. Copyright 1985, 1994, by PAR, Inc. Further reproduction is prohibited without permission from PAR, Inc.

rules and obeying policies. They tend to play the role of the movers and shakers in the society.

Conventional. Those gravitating toward this category really like to conform. They tend to lack high imagination and they enjoy routine work. They also tend to be high producers and take joy in ordering life.(See Table A.2 for more information.)

Holland's theory extrapolates the above six primary types into subtypes, thus bringing about profiles that are called three-letter codes. These codes have rudimentary, not full, relationship to results from multiple discriminant analysis which is a more straight forward way to address questions pertinent to the amount of information gained by different analyses.

Table A.2 shows the descriptors usually associated with the six Holland types.

Both Holland and Roe succeeded in deriving a valid system for predicting occupational membership using conventional psychometric logic. (See McLaughlin and Tiedeman, 1974, in Chapter 2 for more detail.)

David V. Tiedeman–Education

Differentiation and Integration form the engine of the Tiedeman career decision-making theory. Differentiation distinguishes a specific difference; parts are separated from wholes. Differentiation is only important when combined with other distinctions. Closure results when differentiated parts are integrated properly. Both processes are necessary in attaining rational solutions to problems encountered by the processes of differentiation and integration at work. Often differentiation is caused by a problem. The paradigm represents the process of reaching a rational decision in solving such problems as work.

Basic formulations undergirding Tiedeman's theoretical constructs.

1. "Career development is conceived as the process of fashioning a vocational identity through differentiation and integration of the personality as one confronts the problem of work in living" (Tiedeman & O'Hara, 1963, p. v).

2. Since individuals tend toward goal orientation, the study of career development is the study of the ends and means individuals use to pursue those goals. Tiedeman admits he has no definitive theory about the origin of career goals, just a concatenation of relevant ideas.

3. Career development includes the following elements:

   a. Biological constitution of the person.

   b. Psychological make-up of the person.

   c. Society or subculture as a source of identification.

4. Career development and personality development are cut from the same cloth, with origins from the outside looking in, the inside looking out, or both. It depends on the paradigm from which one looks. This rests on the assumption that while differentiation and integration proceeds in the realm specifically

concerned with career choice, a process of differentiation and integration in the realm of personality development that is related to career development also exists.

5. Career development is part of the psychosocial process of forming an ego identity. Erikson's ego identity is the central construct in Tiedeman and O'Hara's career development constructs.

6. It is possible to choose educational and vocational goals on a rational basis. The individual does not have to be impulsive; he is free to choose; and the delaying mechanism in individuals allows time to weigh the alternatives.

I. Aspects of Anticipation or Preoccupation.   Exploration, Crystallization, Choice, and Clarification are aspects of anticipation in which differentiation and integration work continually as the decision process unfolds and re-folds.

1. Exploration is characterized by random behavior. Goals are considered in imagination. Differentiated alternatives are considered; perceived alternatives depend on prior experience, degree of dissatisfaction, and help given in attacking the problem.

    The individual creates cognitive structures within a psychological field relating to goals and consequences. Often these fields are transitory and today's downsizing accelerates these relationships.

2. Crystallization is the process of comparing sets or alternatives in solving the problem. As the individual compares advantages and disadvantages and imagines consequences, the value of alternatives can be assessed. This stage results in stabilization of thought for this process of valuing, which gives order to the forming fields. Each alternative becomes well defined in the process of differentiation and integration.

3. Choice and/or decision follow readily upon crystallization. This goal now serves to orient the behavior system, which becomes more and more integrated. The growing certainty of the choice affects the motive power of the goal. Many factors influence the person's ability to feel comfortable with his/her decision and his/her pursuit of the complexity of solution. Freedom and clarity in living the repeatedly defined goal are a result.

4. Clarification of the decision takes place as the person rethinks his/her decision. Doubt is likely to arise if the expected situation does not begin immediately. As new information is discovered the decision is clarified even more.

II. Aspects of implementation or adjustment start when imagination meets reality.

1. Induction produces an interaction of the person's field and goal with society's field and goal. The person usually orients himself/herself in attaining a goal in a receptive capacity, but the person must detect some acceptance of his/her uniqueness by others. Identification takes place as the goal and field of the person become part of the social system's region. This is a process of assimilation as the individual futher perfects definition of goal and field.

2.   Reformation works into this process of change as the group acknowledges the membership and success of the person. The orientation changes from receptive to assertive. With a strong sense of self, the person sets out to improve the group. This produces modification of the group goal and field.

3.   Integration is a condition of dynamic equilibrium. As convictions of the new members are asserted, the older members react, causing compromise. If the new member can accept compromise, he can appreciate himself as part of the larger field. The individual and group strive together for a common goal.

Additional Clarification of Tiedeman's Career Decision-Making Theory.   Tiedeman further clarifies the probelm solving process by the following points:

1.   Each step is intended to represent a distinction or change in the psychological condition of the person.

2.   The steps may occur simultaneously.

3.   The change from one step to another is neither instantaneous nor irreversible.

4.   Differentiation and integration are a part of each of life's problems, which can be experienced singly or together. The condition of one differentiation can effect other differentiations or prior integrations.

5.   The organization of self-in-situation takes place during differentiation and integration. Through this continued organization of self-in-situation, career identity is formulated.

6.   Career development ordinarily occurs within the context of several decisions, which may overlap. Here is an example of an embryo physician as a freshman in college. Notice she is in different stages in solving related problems:

   a.   integration of high school curriculum

   b.   reformation regarding college choice

   c.   induction regarding college course

   d.   clarification regarding medical school

   e.   exploration regarding place to practice medicine

7.   The aim of educational and vocational counseling is to enhance the operation of reason. The counselor hopes to show each person that his decisions are links in a means–end chain. Ergo, counseling is didactic.

Ego Identity and Career Development.   Tiedeman continues to show the relation between personality and career development. The construct of ego-identity is central. The evolution of ego-identity is as process (a) of successively more complex differentiation of attitude of self-in-world, and (b) of search for integration through identification and acceptance. Tiedeman attempts to show how Erikson's crises effect career development. For brevity, this will not be clarified.

Tiedeman attempts to show how time serves as a limiting factor to career development. His model includes the lifetime of the person. The biological aspects of the individual are considered important: He must learn to live within biological limits and to meet his own needs. Tiedeman accepts Maslow's hierarchy of needs.

Cultural and Social Expectations also Influence Time Occupancy. The individual must learn to live within the expectancies or "premises of structures in interaction: of American society. Selected propositions are:

1. The key to becoming in American culture is the assumption of personal responsibility or independence.

2. One becomes independent only as he achieves independent status within definite roles in society.

3. The striving for independence results in interpersonal problems, which are handled in the differentiation-integration process.

4. The problem of identity formation is to integrate the press for independence appearing as real problems.

5. The evolving ego-identity or cognitive map is strongly influenced by the staging of work and study in America. These produce the necessity for a series of choices.

6. There are times when the position choice must occur and other times when it can occur. The first type is defined by external forces

7. Vocationally relevant position choices are

   a. part-time employment while in school and afterwards;

   b. junior-high subject choice;

   c. high school subject choice;

   d. college selection;

   e. program of study in college;

   f. graduate school selection;

   g. program of study in graduate school;

   h. armed forces potential;

   i. choosing a specialty in the armed forces;

   j. first full-time work;

   k. job search resulting from current job dissatisfaction; and

   l. retirement.

8. The culture provides a fairly definite age at which each of these problems begins.

9. Retirement shows some of the above propositions for some Americans. But there still remains conviction in America to the effect that "you can't go home again." Once identity shifts, because of the somewhat rigid cultural paradigm, making a new identity, for some, is too big a mountain to climb.

Bandura–Psychology

A major thesis of Bandura's social learning theory is this: "Except for elementary reflexes, people are not equipped with inborn repertoires of behavior. They must learn them" (Bandura, 1977, p. 16). Learning results from positive and dispositive effects of action taken. Bandura suggested that responses teach, in that they offer information, serve as motivators, and strengthen responses automatically. Learning by consequences requires detailed attention to the following functions:

1. Informative. People notice effects of responses, develop hypotheses vis-à-vis appropriate responses.

2. Motivational. Past experience creates expectations of future possibilities.

3. Reinforcing. Reinforcement informs and motivates. " ... 'Response Strengthening' is at best a metaphor" (Bandura, 1977, p. 21).

Individuals learn through observation and modeling, so learning is modulated by four component processes.

1. Attentional Processes. Learning cannot happen unless individuals "attend to, and perceive accurately, the significant features of the modeled behavior" (Bandura, 1977, p. 24). Important are observers' characteristics, features of the modeled activities, and structural arrangement of the interactions. However, the associational patterns stand out as dominant. Individuals with whom we associate often determine the types of behavior observed and therefore learned.

The media provides us with boundless models, both positive and dispositive. The speed of learning through modeling is partially determined by individual need and past experience.

2. Retention Processes. Learning by observation is determined by how much information the individual can retain. Observational learning relies on two systems: (a) imaginal, and (b) verbal. Certain stimuli return memory of external events. With repeated exposure, modeling stimuli make enduring, retrievable images. For instance, when you're introduced to someone you see again and again, the name brings the vision of the person. But without the opportunity for repeated interactions, the name and the face often fade.

Most behavior is regulated by verbal coding. For instance, details of a route traveled can be learned, retained, and later, the visual information can be converted into a verbal code describing the route. In addition to symbolic coding, rehearsal aids memory. Athletes make good use of this by practicing visually.

3. Motor Reproduction Processes. Behavioral reproduction happens when one organizes responses spatially and temporally in accordance with modeled patterns. This behavior can be separated into (a) cognitive organization of responses, (b) initiation, (c) monitoring, and (d) refinement based on feedback.

4. Motivational Processes. Since people do not use everything they learn, Bandura distinguished between acquisition and performance. Normally individuals use learning that leads to positive outcomes.

Antecedent Determinants. Since certain regularities exist, knowledge of conditional relationships enables one to predict outcomes with varying accuracy. Effective functioning requires a certain amount of probable consequences. Lacking these, unproductive behavior often results. Humans both respond to and interpret stimuli.

Consequent Determinants. Behavior, for the most part, gets regulated by consequences. Things that do not work usually are dropped, while others that work are retained. Individuals respond from an aggregate of information, not particularly to each moment of feedback as they process and synthesize over long periods of time. Some individuals pattern faster than others.

Extrinsic and intrinsic incentives reinforce behavior. With extrinsic reinforcement, the consequences are externally produced, as with working and receiving a paycheck. When the paycheck stops, the work usually ceases. Intrinsic reinforcement has three types of arrangements between behavior and consequences: (a) the consequences originate externally but relate to behavior—for instance, stepping out of the rain reduces wetness; (b) behavior produces naturally occurring consequences internal to the organism—for example, repetitive performance creates fatigue, and relaxation exercises relieve tension; and (c) self-reinforcement occurs when the evaluative consequences are internally generated and satisfied according to individual values.

Cognitive Control. Cognitive factors partially determine what will be perceived, what lasting effects will result, and how the information will be organized for future use.

Reciprocal Determinism. The social learning view suggests that psychological functioning is a continuous, reciprocal interchange between personal, behavioral, and environmentally determined limits, with interdependence as a keyword. A distinction is made between the potential environment, which is allegedly the same for all animals, and the actual environment, which depends upon behavior.

Discussion also proceeds on the reciprocal influence and the exercise of self-direction, and the limits of social control. Topics include personal freedom, and the traditional freedom versus determinism argument, as well as individual and social safeguards. In general, social learning theory explains human behavior in terms of reciprocity between cognitive, behavioral, and environmental determinants. Reciprocal determinism suggests each human's capacity to influence his or her destiny both positive and dispositive.

John D. Krumboltz–Psychology

Mitchell and Krumboltz (1990) approach career decision making as a sub-system of Bandura's (1977) superordinate general system of social learning rooted in reinforcement and classical behaviorism. Mitchell and Krumboltz thus cast empowerment of an individual's career decision making as a learned matter and its reciprocal learnings as empowering the individual's career decision making.

Although the social learning theory recognizes humans as intelligent problem solvers who control their environments to suit their own purposes and needs, this principle needs the limitations of humans' alleged environmental control.

Instrumentally (Richards, 1955) Mitchell and Krumboltz commit their work in vocational guidance to a learning framework consisting of three major types of learning: instrumental, associative, and vicarious. Each type is described and exemplified as reinforcement and classical behaviorism expect.

The theory addresses questions of why people enter particular educational programs or occupations and why they change at selected points in their lives. The theory also examines the impact of such factors as genetic predispositions, environmental conditions and events, learning experiences, and cognitive, emotional, and performance responses and skills. Four factors theoretically influence the career decision-making path:

1.   Genetic endowment and special abilities;

2.   Environmental conditions and events;

3.   Learning experiences;

4.   Task approach skills.

Both Krumboltz and Bordin agree that vocational interests derive from self. Take care though. Bordin specifies his formulation in a psychodynamic paradigm: vocational interests derive from self-concept. Mitchell and Krumboltz, on the other hand, put their derivation of principle in a behavioral paradigm; vocational interests are then self-observational generalizations.

Interests which are important in career decision making are a result of self-observation generalizations. Task-approach skills are used in the process of career decision making. These skills are the sum total of the previous experiences and observations.

Mitchell and Krumboltz stated that this model operates regardless of the individual's race, gender, or ethnic background. It is suggested that more research is needed in determining the relevancy of some of the task-approach skills, particularly those involved in decision making. Another area of future research would be investigating ways of helping people to identify inaccuracies in self and world observations. Krumboltz's Career Belief Inventory meets this need but research is needed on effective uses.

The interventions in this theory focus clearly on skills that can be used to examine and assess the self-observations and worldview generalizations that relate to one's values. The interventions focus on task approach skills. Since career decision making is a lifelong process, Mitchell and Krumbalt (1990) suggest that this set of skills can be employed throughout one's life. Positively reinforcing events have been found to highly benefit the client in making career choices.

Blau and Duncan–Sociology

Blau and Duncan (1967) analyzed the American occupational structure using a representative sample of over 20,000 American men between the ages of 20 and 64. The study analyzed the patterns of occupational mobility, conditions, and consequences in order to explain part of the stratification system in the United States. They hoped to provide information that might impact policy. For instance, they looked at the effect of education and other factors on occupational opportunity.

The authors did not set an objective to build a stratification theory, but they did intend to place their findings into a theoretical framework and suggest theoretical interpretations. In regard to social mobility, Sorokin (as cited in Blau & Duncan, 1967) indicated that vertical movement of individuals goes on continually, but without knowledge of how it is taking place and the characteristics of the process. He said too much speculation was taking place with too few facts. He called for a *saner method* of collecting facts and data. Blau and Duncan (1967) reported that after World War II, this challenge was taken up.

In regard to patterns of occupational movement, they found two class boundaries, which divided the American occupational structure into three classes (a) white-collar, (b) blue-collar, and (c) farm. When the sons of farmers moved into the city, they could not compete for the white-collar jobs and usually ended up working as laborers. On the other hand, some of the sons of white-collar workers were disinclined to move into manual work, and, in some instances, took lower-paying jobs in order to stay with white-collar work. Socioeconomic status figured significantly in occupation.

Blau and Duncan (1967) do what sociologists do, they research and comment on people in groups because sociologists study people in groups. Even though psychology purportedly deals with individual behavior, many researchers use the sociological model of studying people in groups, and report findings that apply to groups when this information has little connection with individual behavior. In this sense, the research could be seen as socio-psychological in orientation. That approach imprinted heavily in career development theory and research, buttressed by the long-held and respected Newtonian deterministic worldview, and logical positivism.

Douglas T. Hall–Business

Hall (1990), who studied career development in organizations, defined career as "a sequence of work-related experiences and attitudes that occur over the span of a person's work life" (p. 422). Hall suggested that organizational career development theory deals more with life-long work experiences, while vocational psychology focuses more on high school and college students. However, Super did look at some mid- and late-career issues. In general, vocational psychologists focus more on young workers and students, while organizational career researchers focus on working adults.

According to Hall (1990) the study of organizational careers grew out of Kurt Lewin's field theory (1951), The Chicago School of Sociology, and political science notions.

Lewin (1951) suggested that the person's behavior (b) comes from the person and the environment (e). This contrasted Freud and other biologically oriented psychologists, suggesting that inborn or early socialized differences accounted for most human behavior. Lewin introduced the idea of the interaction of the individual with the environment. He also suggested that various things occupy the life space, such as roles—key involvements that collectively represent the person's total life but which are separated by different boundaries. The person's life takes on a series of transactions with individuals and institutions over the life span. Lewin is attributed the distinction of introducing the first of the holistic models to deal with the whole person. This contrasted with other models that dealt with slices of life.

Lewin was also the first to deal with adult behavior over time in institutional settings. He was particularly interested in how people change as a result of their experience.

The Chicago School of Sociology, on the other hand, suggested that one could not develop formal theory without understanding the detail of everyday social life. The varied social settings in Chicago in the 1920s served as a laborator of this study.

W. I. Thomas and colleagues used life histories to study social events causative to why individuals assumed certain social roles. Like Lewin, Thomas tried to understand how individuals perceived their lives and how they constructed reality. Thomas focused on on the social role, Lewin on the person.

Hall (1990) notes that Everett C. Hughes (1958) is reported to have first used the term *career* in relation to formal institutions. He defined career as any social role or facet of a person's life. Hughes studied people in a wide variety of occupations, making the distinction between the objective career (a series of positions or offices the person holds as seen by others) and the subjective career (view of the individual's perspective). Viewing both the inner and outer world provided useful information about the connection between individuals and organizations.

The political science view moved away from the psychological approach as a few political scientists took as their focus administrative practices that tended to control individual careers. They offered another dimension of insight on how organizations impacted individuals in the long run.

These approaches laid the foundation for the emergence of organizational behavior. Several books were written (Argyris, 1957; March & Simon, 1958; McGregor, 1960) to address how psychologically healthy individuals and the goals of the organization can be successfully integrated. Schein (1973) also contributed to the research on organizational socialization. He applied studies of brainwashing and attitude change done by the Chinese during the Korean War to management development. He found that many of the processes used to affect change in dispositive situations can be applied to the process used by organizations to socialize their members.

This stream of former contributions led to Hall's Psychological Success theory. He focused on identity and psychological success and how they relate over time in the career. Identity lies at the heart of how the person perceives him- or herself in relation to significant others in the social environment. Self-esteem drives the individual. People do things that enhance self-esteem and avoid things that diminish it.

In summary, the various perspectives carved out by the above scholars points to the New Physics concept of Complimentarity, simply stated in philosophical terms: when you focus on one thing, you miss all the rest, then uncertainty is introduced. It is also a good illustration of how no one of us carries all the information necessary to make a final judgment about anything. This sets up a perpetual necessity of needing each other. In addition, it shows the importance of brailleing the literature in order to bring together those impressions that help us form our own notions about what works and doesn't work in life and why. This sometimes shows up as a life work, and at times in a work life, which leads us to the importance of knowing our roots, then forging ahead to carve out a direction specific to what we came to do. But, as pointed out in Ecclesiastes, we can't leap-frog faster than how life prefers to unfold, because everything has its season and time.

☐ Appendix B. Personal/Social Skills Lesson By Sharon Smith and Clinton Smith

Objectives

Area: Personal Development

Student Behavior: Identification

Conditions: Concept identification

Performance Criteria: With 90% accuracy

Teaching using two levels of personal development: Self-Protective and Conforming

Strategies for Promoting Generalization of Personal Development:

1. Student will be taught development using examples from their own experience, newspaper, magazine, television, or Internet.

    Summary: This strategy will encourage conceptual learning using examples of the Self-Protective and Conforming stages of development. The content (the two stages of development) will be presented, discussed, student questioning encouraged, feedback given, and materials used from the above media sources to help students apply thinking skills to identify the two stages of development.

2. Self- and group monitoring of language to identify stages of personal development.

    Summary: The students will have first acquired the definitions of the Self-Protective and Conforming stages of personal development. Self- and peer monitoring will occur after students demonstrate fluency in identification of the stages. The identification will show the student can apply and generalize the concepts to everyday situations. A student who can identify his or her own tendencies has the potential, through language, to move to a higher stage/level of personal development. This can ultimately help students avoid the slippery slope of conflict which can translate into a smoother transition into normal life activities.

    Curriculum Area Addressed: Language Arts

    General Level of Interest: High

Materials: Each group will receive two cards: One with "Self-Protective" and one with "Conforming" written on it. The teacher will provide several written examples to start the discussion and identification process.

Procedure:

1. The teacher will:

   a. introduce personal development, and give examples of how and why it is useful in all life situations;

   b. introduce the Self-Protective level of development and give specific examples;

   c. ask students to identify and write examples from their experience; and

   d. supervise students as they identify the self-protective level in each other's language

2. The procedure followed in (1) will be used to teach the Conforming stage of personal development.

   a. Strengths of procedure: Students will learn the language of personal development. This can produce better relationships for them at school, home, church, and any other place where people gather in groups. This means they can potentially experience less stress which means a more fully functioning immune system (Sapolsky, 1994) which often translates into higher motivation.

   b. Weaknesses of procedure: While most students tend to learn the two levels of development in their behavior and can identify it in the behavior of others, some students, for a variety of reasons, may learn less.

   c. Evaluation: The students will be tested using Performance Assessment. They will each receive two cards, one with "Self-Protective" and one with "Conforming" written on it. The students will also receive eight cards, four with Self-Protective and four with Conforming-stage examples. The students will sort the examples and place them under either the Self-Protective or Conforming stage of development.

☐ Appendix C. Resumes

Electronic Resume Sample

John Going Places
1825 Breeze Lane – Somewhere, CA 92027
1-800-000-0000 – 760.123.4567 – Phone and fax

KEY WORDS

Director/Sales & Marketing, Western Operations Manager, National Accounts Manager, Territory Manager, Management by Objective, Salesperson of the Year – Four Years, Trade Show Host, Seminar Leader, Industrial Safety Eyewear, Vision Screening Services, Telemarketing Design, Support Staff Training, Small Business Training, Patient Services, Specialized & Market Research, Success Sharing Program for Optometrists, Product Planning, Budget Management, New Sales Administration Procedures, Annual Forecasts, Safety Program Design & Implementation, Safety Management in Arizona and California, Municipal & National Agreements Implementation, Dollar Volumes to $100K in First Year, Security Services, Safety Planning, Personnel Review Responsibility, Employer/Patient Forms Designer (Spanish and Vietnamese Translations), Creative Forms for Accurate Order Processing, Trained the Trainers, Health Insurance Sales/Individual and Business, Coe College, Bachelor of Arts, Political Science, Teaching Certificate, Xerox Sales Training School, Par Club Award, Palomar Community College, USMC Officers Candidate School, PC Computer, Microsoft Word, Excel, Telemar, Lotus Notes.

Strengths include:

Self-starter	High energy level
Outstanding people skills	Above average leader
Efficiency oriented	Problem solver
First-rate written and oral communication	Excellent public speaker
Exceptional organizer	Team player
Teaching/training	Loves the challenge
Intellectually involved in current events	Information oriented
Diplomatically aggressive	New product introduction

Experience:

June 1997 to October 1997 – Director/Sales and Marketing – Occupational Vision Services

• Developed new industrial safety eyewear programs/accounts
• Developed vision screening accounts in both United States and Mexico
• Developed new programs to increase sales and profitability

January 1997 to April 1997 – Territory Manager – Bausch & Lomb (Continued from Polymer Technology Company)

• Responsible for building contact lens solutions & accessory products

July 1995 to January 1997 – Territory Manager – Polymer Technology Company (Division of Bausch & Lomb)

- Responsible for increasing market share/usage, and sales of Rigid Gas Permeable Contact Lenses and solutions
- Increased dollar volumes for Boston® contact lens sales

March 1993 to June 1995 – Division Manager – Heard/Bristow Optical Companies

- Responsible for two facility sites' operation, management of industrial sales of prescription and non-prescription safety eyewear. Responsibilities in Arizona and California
- Product planning, market research, budgets
- Developed new sales administration procedures, policies, and aids
- Sales projections and annual forecasts
- Maintained an industrial and optical distributor customer base
- Developed and administered telemarketing program
- Developed plans for and implemented municipal agreements
- Sold protective eyewear and accessories
- Increased dollar volume from a zero dollar base to over $100K in one calendar year

October 1992 to March 1993 – Telemarketing for Temporary Services

May 1992 to October 1992 – Field Sales – Pearle Vision, Inc.

- Responsible for sales in Southern California and Arizona
- Sold optical services to retailers, optometrists, and ophthalmologists
- Set up prospective franchisees, prospective new stores to provide Pearle Vision Products and Services

August 1990 to May 1992 – Independent Contractor – Vista, CA

- Developed customer base in residential consumer goods and public medical insurance along with industrial safety and security services, and safety planning to various size industrial locations

August 1980 to August 1990 – Sales Representative, Sales Trainer, and National Accounts Sales Manager, Western Operations and Sales Manager – Titmus Optical

- Responsible for two facility sites' operation
- Managed budgets and sales force
- Trained sales people
- Engaged in product planning and market research
- Developed new annual sales administration procedures, policies, and aids
- Forecasted annual increases, conducted annual personnel reviews
- Maintained an industrial and optical distributor customer base
- Generated plans for and implemented national agreements
- Increased dollar volume annually at a rate of nearly 50%
- Created a telemarketing program that included staff training for national accounts

June 1977 to August 1980 – Sales Representative – American Optical Corporation

- Represented and sold protective eyewear and industrial safety equipment
- Attended trade shows
- Planned seminars
- Managed budgets and engaged in forecasts
- Assistant Regional Sales Trainer

April 1976 to June 1977 – Sales Representative – Bausch & Lomb Corporation

- Sold soft contact lenses
- Hosted trade shows and seminars
- September 1973 to April 1976 – Sales Representative – Xerox Corporation
- Sold and leased entire line of duplicators, copiers, facsimiles, and accompanying supplies
- Trained sales people
- Forecasts of future possibilities

June 1972 to September 1973 – Sales Representative – Blue Cross/Blue Shield of Iowa

- Sold health insurance—individuals and small business enrollments
- Increased enrollment from 50% to 85% of territory in one year

Education:

- John Smith College, Bachelor of Arts Degree, Political Science, Teacher Certificate, Cedar Rapids, IA
- San Jose Community College, San Marcos, CA
- Xerox Sales Training School, Ft. Lauderdale, FL
- United States Marine Corps, Officers Candidate School

Honors:

- Par Club – Xerox – 100% of sales objective
- Salesperson of the Year for four years
- Increased enrollment from 50% to 85% of territory in one year

References: Available upon request

New Paper Resume Sample

Jane Going Places
1825 Breeze Lane – Somewhere, CA 92027
1-800-000-0000 – 70.123.4567 – Phone and fax

KEY INFORMATION

Director/Sales & Marketing, Western Operations Manager, National Accounts Manager, Territory Manager, Management by Objective, Salesperson of the Year – Four Years, Trade Show Host, Seminar Leader, Industrial Safety Eyewear, Vision Screening Services, Telemarketing Design, Support Staff Training, Small Business Training, Patient Services, Specialized & Market Research, Success Sharing Program for Optometrists, Product Planning, Budget Management, New Sales Administration Procedures, Annual Forecasts, Safety Program Design & Implementation, Safety Management in Arizona and California, Municipal & National Agreements Implementation, Dollar Volumes to $100K in First Year, Security Services, Safety Planning, Personnel Review Responsibility, Employer/Patient Forms Designer (Spanish and Vietnamese Translations), Creative Forms for Accurate Order Processing, Trained the Trainers, Health Insurance Sales/Individual and Business, Coe College, Bachelor of Arts, Political Science, Teaching Certificate, Xerox Sales Training School, Par Club Award, Palomar Community College, USMC Officers Candidate School, PC Computer, Microsoft Word, Excel, Telemar, Lotus Notes.

Strengths include:

Self-starter	High energy level
Outstanding people skills	Above average leader
Efficiency oriented	Problem solver
First-rate written and oral communication	Excellent public speaker
Exceptional organizer	Team player
Teaching/training	Loves the challenge
Intellectually involved in current events	Information oriented
Diplomatically aggressive	New product introduction

Experience:

June 1997 to October 1997 – Director/Sales and Marketing – Occupational Vision Services

- Developed new industrial safety eyewear programs/accounts
- Developed vision screening accounts in both United States and Mexico
- Developed new programs to increase sales and profitability

January 1997 to April 1997 – Territory Manager – Bausch & Lomb (Continued from Polymer Technology Company)

- Responsible for building contact lens solutions & accessory products

July 1995 to January 1997 – Territory Manager – Polymer Technology Company (Division of Bausch & Lomb)

- Responsible for increasing market share/usage, and sales of Rigid Gas Permeable Contact Lenses and solutions
- Increased dollar volumes for Boston® contact lens sales

March 1993 to June 1995 – Division Manager – Heard/Bristow Optical Companies

- Responsible for two facility sites' operation, management of industrial sales of prescription and non-prescription safety eyewear. Responsibilities in Arizona and California
- Product planning, market research, budgets
- Developed new sales administration procedures, policies, and aids
- Sales projections and annual forecasts
- Maintained an industrial and optical distributor customer base
- Developed and administered telemarketing program
- Developed plans for and implemented municipal agreements
- Sold protective eyewear and accessories
- Increased dollar volume from a zero dollar base to over $100K in one calendar year

October 1992 to March 1993 – Telemarketing for Temporary Services

May 1992 to October 1992 – Field Sales – Pearle Vision, Inc.

- Responsible for sales in Southern California and Arizona
- Sold optical services to retailers, optometrists, and ophthalmologists
- Set up prospective franchisees, prospective new stores to provide Pearle Vision Products and Services

August 1990 to May 1992 – Independent Contractor – Vista, CA

- Developed customer base in residential consumer goods and public medical insurance along with industrial safety and security services, and safety planning to various size industrial locations

August 1980 to August 1990 – Sales Representative, Sales Trainer, and National Accounts Sales Manager, Western Operations and Sales Manager – Titmus Optical

- Responsible for two facility sites' operation
- Managed budgets and sales force
- Trained sales people
- Engaged in product planning and market research
- Developed new annual sales administration procedures, policies, and aids
- Forecasted annual increases, conducted annual personnel reviews
- Maintained an industrial and optical distributor customer base
- Generated plans for and implemented national agreements
- Increased dollar volume annually at a rate of nearly 50%
- Created a telemarketing program that included staff training for national accounts

June 1977 to August 1980 – Sales Representative – American Optical Corporation

- Represented and sold protective eyewear and industrial safety equipment
- Attended trade shows
- Planned seminars
- Managed budgets and engaged in forecasts
- Assistant Regional Sales Trainer

April 1976 to June 1977 – Sales Representative – Bausch & Lomb Corporation

- Sold soft contact lenses
- Hosted trade shows and seminars
- September 1973 to April 1976 – Sales Representative – Xerox Corporation
- Sold and leased entire line of duplicators, copiers, facsimiles, and accompanying supplies
- Trained sales people
- Forecasts of future possibilities

June 1972 to September 1973 – Sales Representative – Blue Cross/Blue Shield of Iowa

- Sold health insurance—individuals and small business enrollments
- Increased enrollment from 50% to 85% of territory in one year

Education:

- John Smith College, Bachelor of Arts Degree, Political Science, Teacher Certificate, Cedar Rapids, IA
- San Jose Community College, San Marcos, CA
- Xerox Sales Training School, Ft. Lauderdale, FL
- United States Marine Corps, Officers Candidate School

Honors:

- Par Club – Xerox – 100% of sales objective
- Salesperson of the Year for four years
- Increased enrollment from 50% to 85% of territory in one year

References: Available upon request

☐ Appendix D. Work-Career Paradigm Survey Key

6   You're trying out life on your own terms.

4–6   You're on the verge.

1–3   You're flirting with the idea.

A total of seven points or more indicates that you are now ready to apply the Lifecareer concepts.

Answer to Head Moving Question:

It means the person is merely moving his or her head right to left, or up and down. The usual interpretation suggests that right and left head movement means no, while up and down movement means yes. Interpretation is everything.

REFERENCES

A jagged pill to swallow. (1997, May 4). *The Edmonton Sunday Sun: Sunday Express*, pp. 4–5.

After the war, the time of the teen-ager. (1995, May 7). *The New York Times*, p. 4-E.

Associated Press. (1995, March 30). Alleged dealer held after actor's son kills himself. *The Desert Sun*, A-6.

Bach, R. (1977). *Illusions: The adventures of a reluctant messiah*. New York: Dell.

Bandura, A. (1977). *Social learning theory*. Englewood Cliffs, NJ: Prentice-Hall.

Barker, J. (1990). *The business of paradigms: Discovering the future, facilitators' guide*. Burnsville, MN: Charthouse International Learning Corporation. (Video of the same title available.)

Barnet, R. J. (1993, September). The end of jobs. *Harper's Magazine, 287*(1720), 47–52.

Bartlett, J. (1980). *Bartlett's familiar quotations*. Boston: Little, Brown.

Beck, D. (Speaker). (1995). *Health, wellness, and the brain*. San Diego, CA: Questhaven Retreat.

Beck, D., & Beck, J. (1987). *The pleasure connection: How endorphins affect our health and happiness*. San Marcos, CA: Synthesis Press.

Bennis, W. (1983). *Interview* (video). Los Angeles: University of Southern California.

Benson, H. (1975). *The relaxation response*. New York: William Morrow.

Bergman, L. (1997, August 4). Risks and reporting: The view from behind the camera. *Commonwealth, 91*, 2–8.

Blau, P. M., & Duncan., O. D. (1967). *The American occupational structure*. New York: John Wiley & Sons.

Bloch, D., & Richmond, L. J. (Eds.). (1997). *Connections between spirit and work in career development*. Palo Alto, CA: Davies-Black Publishing.

Bohm, D. (1980). *Wholeness and the implicate order*. London: Routledge & Kegan Paul.

Bolles, R. (1974/1994). *What color is your parachute? A practical manual for job-hunters and career changers*. Berkeley, CA: Ten Speed Press.

Bordin, E. S. (1990). Psychodynamic model of career choice and satisfaction. In D. Brown, L. Brooks, & Associates (Eds.), Career choice and development (2nd ed., pp. 102–144). San Francisco: Jossey-Bass.

Bradbury, R. (1962). *Something wicked this way comes*. New York: Simon & Schuster.

Bradley, D. (1982, November). On board. *Motor Boating and Sailing 150*(5), 14.

Braine, J. (1957). *Room at the top*. Boston: Houghton Mifflin.

Braine, J. (1979). Starting afresh. *Quest, 3*, 71–76.

Brewer, J. M. (1942). *History of vocational guidance: Origins and early development*. New York: Harper & Row.

Bridges, W. (1994). *Job shift: How to prosper in a workplace without jobs*. New York: Tarcher/Putnam.

Briggs, K. C., & Myers, I. B. (1983). *Myers-Briggs type indicator*. Palo Alto, CA: Consulting Psychologists Press.

Bristol, C. (1985). *The magic of believing*. New York: Simon & Schuster.

Broad, W., & Wade, N. (1982). *Betrayers of the truth: Fraud and deceit in the halls of science*. New York: Simon & Schuster.

Brooks, L. (1984). Career counseling methods and practice. In D. Brown, L. Brooks, & Associates (Eds.), *Career choice and development* (pp. 337–354). San Francisco: Jossey-Bass.

Brown, D. (1996). Brown's values-based, holistic model of career and life-role choices and satisfaction. In D. Brown, L. Brooks, & Associates (Eds.), *Career choice and development* (3rd ed., pp. 337–372). San Francisco: Jossey-Bass.

Brown, D., Brooks, L., & Associates (Eds.). (1984). *Career choice and development*. San Francisco: Jossey-Bass.

Brown, D., Brooks, L., & Associates (Eds.). (1990). *Career choice and development* (2nd ed.). San Francisco: Jossey-Bass.

Brown, D., Brooks, L., & Associates (Eds.). (1996). *Career choice and development* (3rd ed.). San Francisco: Jossey-Bass.

Buehler, C. (1933). *Der menschliche Lebenslauf als psychologisches. Problem.* (The human life course as a psychological subject). Leipzig: Hirzel.

Campbell, J. (1988). *The power of myth*. New York: Doubleday.

Capra, F. (1975). *The tao of physics: An exploration of the parallels between modern physics and eastern mysticism*. Boulder, CO: Shambhala.

Capra, F. (1982). *The turning point: Science, society, and the rising culture*. New York: Simon & Schuster.

Capra, F. (1983). The turning point. In C. Lynch, A. Miller-Tiedeman, & D. V. Tiedeman (Eds.), *Proceedings of the 1983 Assembly to Advance Career*. Lifecareer Foundation, Vista, CA.

Centre for Career Development Innovation. (1993). *Engage your life*. Edmonton, Alberta: Author.

Childre, D. L. (1998). *Freeze-Frame*™. Boulder Creek, CA: Planetary Publishers.

Chopra, D. (1989). *Quantum healing*. New York: Bantam Books.

Chopra, D. (1991). *Creating health: How to wake up the body's intelligence*. Boston: Houghton Mifflin.

Chopra, D. (1995). *Everyday reality* (audio cassette). San Diego, CA: Public Broadcasting System.

Conway, J. K. (Ed.). (1992). *Written by herself. Autobiographies of American women: An anthology*. New York: Vintage Books.

Cooper, R. D. (1994). *The mystical Kabbalah* (audio cassette). Boulder, CO: Sounds True.

Cornell, G. W. (1992, June 11). Ouster of Baptist congregations concerns dissenters. *The Herald Dispatch*.

Costello, R. (Ed.). (1992). *Random House/Webster's college dictionary*. New York: Random House.

Courion, J. (Speaker). (1997). *Storywork and mediation*. Malibu, CA: Pepperdine University.

Courtland, L. F. (1976). A visit to Idreas Shaw. In L. Lewin (Ed.), *Elephant in the dark* (pp. 82–99). New York: E.P. Dutton.

Cousins, N. (1983). *Healing heart*. New York: Avon Books.

Covey, S. (Speaker). (1997). *Address to the Commonwealth Club in San Francisco*. San Diego, CA: KFSD.

Crites, J. (1969). *Vocational psychology*. New York: McGraw-Hill.

Critser, G. (1996, June). Oh how happy we'll be. *Harper's Magazine*, 39–48.

Cryer, S. (1995). Published scientific study shows significant stress reduction using "Freeze-Frame"™ technique. HeartMath™ Institute Web Site: www.heartmath.org.

Csikszentmihalyi, M. (1990). *Flow: The psychology of optimal experience.* New York: Harper Perennial.

Dacher, E. (1997, Summer). Healing values: What matters in healthcare. *IONS: Noetic Sciences Review, 42,* 10–15, 49–51.

Davidson, R. (1980). *Tracks.* New York: Pantheon Books.

Dominguez, J. Robin, V. (1992). *Your money or your life?* New York: Viking.

Dulbecco, R. (1987). *The design of life.* Montreal, Ontario: McGill University Press.

Educational & Industrial Testing Service. *Career occupational preference system.* San Diego, CA: Author.

Educational & Industrial Testing Service. (1976). *Career ability placement survey.* San Diego, CA: Author.

Elbow, P. (1981). *Writing with power: Techniques for mastering the writing process.* New York: Oxford University Press.

Ellis, A. (1979). *Rational emotive therapy for alcoholics and substance abusers.* New York: Van Nostrand Reinhold.

Emmett, J. D., & Harkins, A. M. (1997, September). StoryTech: Exploring the use of a narrative technique for training career counselors. *Counselor Education and Supervision, 37,* 60–73.

Erikson, E. H. (1959). Identity and the life cycle: Selected papers. In *Psychological issues* 1.1: New York: International Universities Press.

Estes, C. P. (1990). *Women who run with the wolves* (audio cassette). Boulder, CO: Sounds True Audio.

Estes, C. P. (1992). *Women who run with the wolves.* New York: Ballantine Books.

Ferguson, M. (1980). *The Aquarian conspiracy.* Los Angeles: Tarcher.

Ferris, T. (1985, November 20). *The creation of the universe. NOVA* TV program, PBS.

Feuerstein, G. (1994). *Spirituality by the numbers.* New York: Tarcher/Putnam.

Field, S. (Interview). (1996, December 23). *Inside the Actor's Studio.* Bravo TV program, Bravo Network.

Flanagan, J. C. (1947). The aviation psychology program in the Army Air Forces. *AAF Aviation psychology program research report, No. 1.* Washington, DC: Government Printing Office.

Forbes Magazine. (1997, June 16). Cover, and pp. 12, 157.

Foundation for Inner Peace. (1975). *A course in miracles.* Glenn Ellen, CA: Author.

Fox, M. (1995). *The reinvention of work.* San Francisco: Harper.

Fromm, E. (1964). *The heart of man.* New York: Harper & Row.

Fuller, B. (1981). *Critical path.* New York: St. Martin's Press.

Fynn. (1974). *Mister God, this is Anna.* New York: Ballantine Books.

Geer, C. T. (1997, June 16). Your shadow career. *Forbes, 159,* 12, 156–168.

Gelatt, H. B. (1989). Positive uncertainty: A new decision-making framework for counseling. *Journal of Counseling Psychology, 36,* 2, 252–256.

Ginzberg, E., Ginsburg, S. W., Axelrad, S., & Herma, J. L. (1951). *Occupational choice: An approach to a general theory.* New York: Columbia University Press.

Givens, C. J. (1991). *Charles J. Givens financial library.* Altamonte Springs, FL: Charles J. Givens Organization.

Godfrey, N. (1997). *Making change: A woman's guide to designing her financial future.* New York: Simon & Schuster.

Gonyea, J. C. (1995). *The on-line job search companion: A complete guide to hundreds of career planning and job hunting resources available via your computer.* New York: McGraw-Hill.

Gubernick, L., & Ebeling, A. (1997, June 16). I got my degree through e-mail. *Forbes, 159,* 84–92.

Guthrie, K. S. (1988). *The Pythagorean sourcebook and library.* Grand Rapids, MI: Phanes Press.

Gysbers, N. (circa 1975). *Life-career development.* Xerox.

Hall, D. T. (1990). Career development theory in organizations. In D. Brown, L. Brooks, & Associates (Eds.), *Career choice and development* (2nd ed., pp. 422–454). San Francisco: Jossey-Bass.

Hapgood, F. (1993). *Up the infinite corridor: MIT and the technical imagination.* New York: Addison-Wesley.

Hawking, S. (1988). *A brief history of time: From the big bang to black holes.* New York: Bantam Books.

Hawking, S. (1993). *Black holes and baby universes and other essays.* New York: Bantam Books.

HayGroup, The. (1988, May). *1988 environmental scan: People and pay in the '90s.* Stamford, CT: Author.

Heifetz, R. (1994). *Leadership without easy answers.* Cambridge, MA: Belknap Press.

Heller, J., & Henkin, W. A. (1991). *Bodywise.* Oakland, CA: Bookpeople.

Helmbreck, V. (1989, November 1). Mrs. Reagan's self-portrait not pretty. *The Herald Dispatch,* p. A-6.

Heppner, R. P. (Ed.). (1997, July). School to work transition. *The Counseling Psychologist, 25*(3).

Hofstadter, D. R. (1979). *Goedel, Escher, Bach: An eternal golden braid.* New York: Vintage Books.

Holland, J. L. (1966). *The psychology of vocational choice: A theory of personality types and environmental models.* New York: Ginn.

Holland, J. L. (1977). *The self-directed search.* Palo Alto, CA: Consulting Psychologist Press.

Holy Bible (The). (1976). New York: Thomas Nelson.

Horney, K. (1942). *Self-analysis.* New York: Norton.

Huang, A. (1973). *Embrace tiger: Return to mountain.* Berkeley, CA: Celestial Arts.

Jordan, J. (1973). *Numerology: The romance of your name.* Santa Barbara, CA: J.F. Rowny.

Kaczor, B. (1994, February 21). Abortion doctor slaying trial to begin. *Times Advocate,* p. A-6.

Kanchier, C. (1997, February). Using intuition for career decision making. *Counseling Today, 39,* 14, 16.

Kaplan, G. (1994, July 29–August 4). The mountain paradise that was Mahler's hell. *The European.*

Kelley, T. L. (1940, July). *Talents and tasks: Their use in conjunction with a democracy.* Cambridge, MA: Harvard Education Papers.

Kennedy, J. L. (1996, April 16). *A local author fair. North County chapter.* Fullerton, CA: California Association for Counseling & Development.

Kennedy, J. L., & Morrow, T. J. (1994). *Electronic resume revolution: Create a winning resume for the new world of job seeking.* New York: John Wiley & Sons.

Kimeldorf, M. (1996). *Creating portfolios for success in school, work, and life, Teacher's Guide and Student Workbook.* Minneapolis, MN: Free Spirit.

Kimeldorf, M. (1997). *Portfolio power: The new way to showcase all your job skills and experiences.* Princeton, NJ: Peterson's.

Knapp, R. R., & Knapp, L. (1977/1981). *Career orientation placement & evaluation survey.* San Diego, CA: Educational & Industrial Testing Service.

Koestler, A. (1964). *The act of creation: A study of the conscious and unconscious in science and art.* New York: Dell.

Kottler, J. (1997, April). Finding your own truth. *Counseling Today.*

Krikorian, G. (1999, January 10). Living wage hard to find in northwest. *Los Angeles Times,* p. A-12.

Krumboltz, J., & Ranieri, A. (1996). Learn, earn, and yearn. In R. Feller & G. Walz (Eds.), *Career transitions in turbulent times.* Greensboro, NC: ERIC/CASS Publications.

Kuhn, T. S. (1970). *The structure of scientific revolutions.* Chicago: University Chicago Press.

Landers, A. (1996, April 14). Elderly mom finds fiancee, stuns kids. *North County Times*, p. A-6.

Lao Tsu. (1972). *Tao te ching* (G. F. Feng & J. English, Trans.). New York: Vintage Books.

Lawrence, J. (1995, November 16). House leader says snub led to shutdown. *Times Advocate*, p. l.

Lazarsfeld, P. F. (1931). *Jugen und beruf* (Youth and occupation). Jena, Austria: G. Fischer.

Leishman, K. (May 1980). Interview with Lewis Thomas. Like other animals, we go around creating whatever reality we perceive. *Quest*.

Lent, R. W., Brown, S. D., & Hackett, G. (1996). Career development from a social cognitive perspective. In D. Brown, L. Brooks, & Associates (Eds.), *Career choice and development* (3rd ed., pp. 373–421). San Francisco: Jossey-Bass.

Leo, J. (1994, December 12). After Gingrich shoots from lip, send in the rhetoric coach. *Times Advocate*, p. B-5.

Leonard, G., & Murphy, M. (1995). *The life we are given.* New York: Tarcher/Putnam.

Levine, B. (1998, October 29). After 36 years, she's still aiming for the stars. *Los Angeles Times*, p. E-2.

Lewin, K. (1951). *Field theory in social science.* New York: Harper & Row.

Lewis, C. S. (1965). *The weight of glory and other addresses.* Grand Rapids, MI: Eerdman's.

Lingerman, H. A. (1992). *Living your destiny.* York Beach, ME: Samuel Weiser.

Lingerman, H. A. (1992/1994). *The book of numerology.* York Beach, ME: Samuel Weiser.

Loevinger, J. (1976). *Ego development.* San Francisco: Jossey-Bass.

Loevinger, J., & Wessler, R. (1970a). *Measuring ego development. 1.* San Francisco: Jossey-Bass.

Loevinger, J., & Wessler, R. (1970b). *Measuring ego development. 2.* San Francisco: Jossey-Bass.

Longenecker, J. G., & Moore, C. W. (1991). *Small business management: An entrepreneurial emphasis.* Cincinnati: South-Western Publishing.

Lukas, M. (1980). The world according to Ilya Prigogine. *Quest,* 80.

Magnusson, K. (1990). *An introduction to career counseling.* Edmonton, Alberta: Life-Role Development Group.

Mairs, N. (1994). *Voice lessons: On becoming a woman writer.* Boston: Beacon Press.

Masciola, C. (1991, January 16). Yankee ingenuity held the embassy. *Times Advocate,* pp. B1, B2.

Maslow, A. (1954). *Motivation and personality.* New York: Harper.

Maslow, A. (1968). *Toward a psychology of being.* New York: Van Nostrand Reinhold.

May, R. (1976). *The courage to create.* New York: Bantam Books.

McCraty, R. (1995). Published scientific study shows significant stress reduction using "Freeze Frame®" technique. Institute of HeartMath Web site: www.heartmath.org.

McGregor, D. (1960). *The human side of enterprise.* New York: McGraw-Hill.

McLaughlin, D. H., & Tiedeman, D. V. (1974). Eleven-year career stability and change as reflected in project talent data through the Flanagan, Holland, and Roe occupational classification systems. *Journal of Vocational Behavior, 5,* 177–196.

Meyers, D. (Host). (1996, January 18). *Equal time.* Fort Lee, NJ: CNBC.

Michener, J. (1992). *The world is my home: A memoir.* New York: Random House.

Milani, M., & Smith, B. R. (1985). *Rotational physics: The principles of energy.* Westmoreland, NH: Fanshaw Press.

Miller, D. C., & Form, W. H. (1951). *Industrial sociology.* New York: Harper & Row.

Miller-Tiedeman, A. (1980). Explorations of decision making in the expansion of adolescent personal development. In J. Whiteley & L. Erickson (Eds.), *Developmental counseling and teaching: The present and future of counseling psychology.* Monterey, CA: Brooks/Cole.

Miller-Tiedeman, A. (1982/1985/1992a). *Lifecareer®: How it can benefit you*. Vista. CA.: Lifecareer Foundation.

Miller-Tiedeman, A. (1987/1989). *How to not make it ... and succeed: The truth about your lifecareer®*. Vista, CA: Lifecareer Foundation.

Miller-Tiedeman, A. (1988). *Lifecareer®: The quantum leap into a process theory of career*. Vista, CA: Lifecareer Foundation.

Miller-Tiedeman, A. (1992b). *Life direction: The teeter totter of life*. Vista, CA: Lifecareer Foundation.

Miller-Tiedeman, A. (1996). Surfing the quantum: Notes of a Lifecareer® developing. In R. Feller & G. R. Walz (Eds.), *Career development in turbulent times: Exploring work, learning and careers* (pp. 105–113). Greensboro, NC: ERIC/CASS.

Miller-Tiedeman, A. & Tiedeman, D. V. (1983). Career: Simply life's gift. In C. Lynch, A. Miller-Tiedeman, & D. V. Tiedeman (Eds.), *Proceedings, Assembly to Advance Career* (pp. 27–42). Los Angeles: University of Southern California.

Mitchell, L. K., & Krumboltz, J. D. (1990). Social learning approach to career decision making: Krumboltz's theory. In D. Brown, L. Brooks, & Associates (Eds.), *Career choice and development* (2nd ed., pp. 145–196). San Francisco: Jossey-Bass.

Montgomery, B. (1990, July 2). Ill and broke, but not forgotten, ex-congressman Carl Elliott is honored as a profile in courage. *People Weekly, 33*, 99–100.

Morrissey, M. (1996, January). The transition from counseling student to counseling professional. *Counseling Today, 38*, 1, 10, & 14.

Murray, H. (1962, May 11). Prospect for psychology. *Science*, 438–488.

Myerson, B. (1997). Safeguards can't stem historic 554-point fall. *North County Times*, p. 1.

National Board for Certified Counselors. (1996). *Directions for Maintaining the NBCC Continuing Education File*. Greensboro, NC: Author.

NOVA. (1985, January 25). *Conquest of the parasites*. Boston: WGBH Transcripts.

Odajnyk, V. W. (1993). *Gathering the light: A psychology of meditation*. Boston: Shambhala.

O'Hara, T. (1996, April 22). Del Mar artist captures west on film. *North County Times*.

Oliver, G. (1975). *The pythagorean triangle*. Minneapolis, MN: Wizards Bookshelf.

Ornish, D. (1990). *Program for reversing heart disease*. New York: Random House.

Osipow. S. (1973). *Theories of career development*. Englewood Cliffs, NJ: Prentice-Hall.

Parsons, F. (1909). *Choosing a vocation*. Boston: Houghton Mifflin.

Persig, R. M. (1974). *Zen and the art of motorcycle maintenance*. New York: William Morrow.

Peterson, G. W., Sampson, J. P., Jr., Reardon, R. C., & Lenz, J. G. (1996). A cognitive information processing approach to career problem solving and decision making. In D. Brown, L. Brooks, & Associates (Eds.), *Career choice and development* (3rd ed., pp. 423–476). San Francisco: Jossey-Bass.

Petroski, H. (1989, Fall). H. D. Thoreau, engineer. *American Heritage of Invention and Technology, 5*(2), 8–16.

Pilzer, P. Z. (1995). *Economic paradigms* (audio cassette). Carlsbad, CA: Network Twenty-One.

Plummer, W. (June 1980). Interview with Ray Bradbury: The biggest influence on my life in that magical year was Mr. Electrico. *Quest*.

Popcorn, F. (1991). *The Popcorn report*. New York: Doubleday.

Prigogine, I. (1980). *From being to becoming: Time and complexity in the physical sciences*. San Francisco: W.H. Freeman.

Prigogine, I. (1983, May). Interview. *Omni, 5*(8), 85–121.

Prigogine, I., & Stengers, I. (1984). *Order out of chaos: Man's new dialogue with nature*. New York: Bantam Books.

Quinn, J. B. (1991). *Making the most of your money*. New York: Simon & Schuster.

Ramstad, E. (1996, January 3). AT&T calls it quits for 40,000 workers. *The North County Times*, p. A-7.

Reason, P., & J. Rowan (Eds.). (1981). *Human inquiry: A sourcebook of new paradigm research*. New York: John Wiley & Sons.

Redekopp, D., & Day, G. (1994). *Understanding work alternatives*. Edmonton, Alberta: Centre for Career Development Innovation.

Redekopp, D. E., Day, B., Magnusson, K., & Durnford, C. (1993). *Creating self-portraits*. Edmonton, Alberta: Centre for Career Development Innovation.

Redekopp, D. E., Fiske, L., Lemon, F., & Garber-Conrad, B. (1994). *Everyday career development: Concepts and practices—a guidebook for secondary school educators*. Edmonton, Alberta: Alberta Education, Learning Resources Distribution Centre.

Reynolds, D. K. (1984). *Playing ball on running water*. New York: Quill.

Rifkin, J. (1995). *The end of work: The decline of the global labor force and the dawn of the post-market era*. New York: Tarcher/Putnam.

Roe, A. (1956). *The psychology of occupations*. New York: John Wiley & Sons.

Roe, A., & Lunneborg, P. W. (1990). Personality development and career choice. In D. Brown, L. Brooks, & Associates (Eds.), *Career choice & development* (2nd ed., pp. 68–101). San Francisco: Jossey-Bass.

Rogers, C. R. (1942). *Counseling and psychotherapy*. Boston: Houghton Mifflin.

Rogers, C. R. (1951). *Client-centered therapy*. Boston: Houghton Mifflin.

Rogers, C. R. (1961). *On becoming a person*. Boston: Houghton Mifflin.

Rulon, P. J., Tiedeman, D. V., Tatsuoka, M. M., & Langmuir, C. R. (1967). *Multivariate statistics for personnel classification*. New York: John Wiley & Sons.

Salk, J. (1973). *The survival of the wisest*. New York: Harper & Row.

Sapolsky, R. (1994). *Why zebras don't get ulcers: A guide to stress, stress-related diseases, and coping*. New York: W.H. Freeman.

Sarche, J. (1996, April 12). Young pilot dies in stormy crash. *North County Times*.

Savant, M. V. (1997). Column: Ask Marilyn. *Parade Magazine*, p. 7.

Savickas, M. L. (1993). Career counseling in the postmodern era. *Journal of Cognitive Psychotherapy, 7*, 205–215.

Schein, E. H. (1993). *Career anchors: Discovering your real values*. San Diego, CA: Pfeiffer & Company.

Schimmel, A. M. (1993). *The mystery of numbers*. New York: Oxford University Press.

Schuré, E. (1961). *The great initiates*. West Nyack, NY: St. George Books.

Shah, I. (1972). *The elephant in the dark*. New York: E.P. Dutton.

Sharf, R. S. (1992). *Applying career development theory to counseling*. Pacific Grove, CA: Brooks/Cole.

Shilts, R. (1987). *And the band played on*. New York: St. Martin's Press.

Simonton, C., & Simonton, S. M. (1982). *Getting well again*. New York: Bantam Books.

Skutch, R. (1984). *Journey without distance*. Berkeley, CA: Celestial Arts.

Soelle, D., & Cloyes, S. A. (1984). *To work and to love*. Philadelphia: Fortress Press.

Spence, G. (Speaker). (1985). Santa Barbara Writer's Conference, Santa Barbara, CA.

Spiegel, D., Bloom, J. R., Kraemer, H., & Gottheil, E. (1989). Psychological support for cancer patients. *Lancet, 2*, 1447.

Stillman, H. (1996, August 31). Killing not same as murder. [Letter to the editor], *Los Angeles Times*, p. A-6.

Stockdale, J. B. (1978, April). The world of Epictetus: Reflections on survival and leadership. *Atlantic Monthly, 241*(4), 98–106.

Super, D. E. (1942). *The dynamics of vocational adjustment*. New York: Harper & Row.

Super, D. E. (1953). A theory of vocational development. *American Psychologist, 8*, 185–190.

Super, D. E. (1957). *The psychology of careers: An introduction to vocational development*. New York: Harper & Brothers.

Super, D., Savickas, M. L., & Super, C. M. (1996). The life-span, life-space approach to careers. In D. Brown, L. Brooks, & Associates (Eds.), *Career choice and development* (3rd ed., pp. 121–178) San Francisco: Jossey-Bass.

Swimme, B. (1989, April 28). *Workshop*. San Diego, CA.

Swimme, B. (1984). *The universe is a green dragon*. Santa Fe, NM: Bear & Company.

Teleshare 900. (1994). *Maverick Marketing Business Techniques*. Orem, UT: Author.

Thomas, L. (1980). The uncertainty of science. *The phi beta kappa: Key reporter 46*, 1–4.

Thurstone, L. L. (1947). *Multiple factor analysis*. Chicago: University of Chicago Press.

Tiedeman, D. V. (1968). *Information system for vocational decisions*. Cambridge, MA: Harvard University.

Tiedeman, D. V. (1996). The quantum career floats through the air. In R. Feller & G. R. Walz (Eds.), *Career development in turbulent times: Exploring work, learning and careers* (pp. 115–122). Greensboro, NC: ERIC/CASS.

Tiedeman, D. V., & Field, F. L. (1965). Guidance: The science of purposeful action applied through education. In R. L. Mosher, R. F. Carle, & C. D. Kehas (Eds.), *Guidance: An examination*. New York: Harcourt Brace Jovanovich.

Tiedeman, D. V., & Miller-Tiedeman, A. (1979). Choice and decision processes and career revisited. In A. M. Mitchell, G. B. Jones, & J. D. Krumboltz (Eds.), *Social learning and career decision making*. Cranston, RI: Carroll Press.

Tiedeman, D. V., & O'Hara, R. P. (1963). *Career development: Choice and adjustment*. New York: College Entrance Examination Board.

Tightwads ride recession. (1992, June). *Home Office Computing, 36*, 54.

Tillich, P., & Rogers, C. (1966, January). *A dialogue*. San Diego, CA: San Diego State University.

Toffler, A. (1970). *Future shock*. New York: Bantam Books.

Toffier, A. (1980). *The third wave*. New York: Bantam Books.

Van Buren, A. (1995, January 14). Pregnant girlfriend ruins college plans. *North County Times*, p. B-7.

Wagschal, P. H., & Kahn, R. D. (Eds.). (1979). *Fuller on education*. Amherst, MA: University of Massachusetts Press.

Waller, R. J. (1992). *Bridges of Madison county*. New York: Warner Books.

Waller, R. J. (1994). *Old songs in a new cafe*. New York: Warner Books,

Walls, R. T., Fullmer, S. L., & Dowler, D. L. (1996). Functional cognition: Dimensions of real-world accuracy. *Career Development Quarterly, 44*.

Weinrach, S. G., & Srebalus, D. J. (1990). Holland's theory of careers. In D. Brown, L. Brooks, & Associates (Eds.), Career choice and development (2nd ed., pp. 37–67). San Francisco: Jossey-Bass.

Weise, E. (1994, February 23). Crowd pelts protesters at funeral for gay journalist. *North County Times*, p. A-4.

Wilber, K. (Ed.). (1982). *Holographic paradigm and other paradoxes*. Boulder, CO: Shambhala.

Williamson, E. G. (1939). *How to counsel students*. New York: McGraw-Hill.

Williamson, E. G., & Hahn, M. E. (1940). *Introduction to high school counseling*. New York: McGraw-Hill.

Windle, J. W. (1993). *True women*. New York: Ballentine Books.

Wolf, F. A. (1981). *Taking the quantum leap: The new physics for non-scientists*. New York: Random House.

Yerzyk, T. (1996, September 7). Dittoheads prove writer right [Letter to the editor]. *Los Angeles Times*, p. A-6.

Young, R. A., Ladislav, V., & Collin, A. A. (1996). Contextual explanation of career. In D. Brown, L. Brooks, & Associates (Eds.), *Career choice and development* (3rd ed., pp. 477–512). San Francisco: Jossey-Bass.

Yunus, M. (1997, Spring). Soul from the ground up. *IONS: Noetic Sciences Review, 41,* 18–23.

Zambucka, K. (1978). *Ano ano the seed.* Honolulu, HI: Mana Publishing Company.

Zohar, D. (1990). *The quantum self: Human nature and consciousness defined by the new physics.* New York: Quill/William Morrow.

Zukav, G. (1979). *The dancing wu li masters: An overview of the new physics.* New York: William Morrow.

ABOUT THE ASSOCIATES

David V. Tiedeman, a former professor of education, Harvard Graduate School of Education, presently serves as vice president of The Lifecareer Group, and as a faculty mentor in education, Walden University. He formerly served as president of the National Institute for the Advancement of Career Education headquartered at the University of Southern California, where he retired as professor (emeritus) of higher and postsecondary education, continually seeking pioneering pathways into mind and matter in the human career. To the surprise of his old quantitative self, he's now gradually accommodating the understanding that matter over mind is not enough to life-as-career; matter over mind matters as well.

Tiedeman has authored numerous books and articles in the areas of measurement, statistics, and career development. He presently looks back on his half century in career development, asking himself many questions and looking into dreams for a better understanding of the play of consciousness in human career activity. That's where Tiedeman will be working as he watches Earth spin around through enough rotations to put the Gregorian calendar into the twenty-first century.

Lee Richmond is a professor of education and coordinator of the school counseling program at Loyola College in Baltimore, Maryland, where for the past ten years she also taught career development for Loyola's pastoral counseling program. Past president of both the National Career Development Association and the American Counseling Association, she has recently co-edited, with Deborah Bloch, a book entitled *Connections Between Spirit and Work in Career Development*, and co-authored, also with Deborah Bloch, a book entitled *Soulwork*. Lee is both a career counselor and a psychologist.

David Redekopp, Principle Partner of the Life-Role Development Group, has devoted over a decade to the promotion of career development and the better career development concepts and practices. He manages the Group's research and product-development initiatives, and trains hundreds of career development practitioners annually. Redekopp also serves as Director of Program Development with Concordia University College of Alberta's Career Development Department, and as Governor of the Canadian Career Development Foundation. He holds a Doctor of Philosophy in Educational Psychology from the University of Alberta, Masters of Educational Psychology (Counseling), University of Alberta, and Bachelor of Education, University of Winnipeg, and A Bachelor of Arts (Honors), University of Winnipeg.

Barrie Day, Principal Partner of the Life-Role Development Group, has a long history of career development work. He has been a public school teacher, assistant superintendent of a school board, Executive Director of Training Services within Alberta Career Development and Employment, and Executive Director of the Centre for Career Development Innovation. In the last few years, Day has engaged in group career counseling with hundreds of clients across Canada, written numerous career development guides and manuals, developed innovative intervention strategies and consulted with numerous organization on the integration of career development within organizational operations.

Jim Puplava, Certified Financial Planner, is President of Puplava Securities, Inc. He holds a Bachelor of Science degree in History and Economics and a Masters in Finance and Accounting. He was recognized with the Chairman's Award by Linsco/ Private Ledger Financial Service, Inc., Outstanding Client Service Award, and Outstanding Broker of the Year by *Registered Representative Magazine*. He hosts a daily Financial Sense show.

Laurie McMenamin, a Certified Hellerwork Practitioner, has participated in Advanced Hellerwork training. She is also experienced in Body Centered Therapy/ Breathwork, Expressive Movement, and Hypnotherapy. She has taught at the Academy of Health Professionals in San Diego, California, and works with women's healing groups and community health education programs. She has been licensed as a Holistic Health Practitioner since 1988. She presently practices in San Diego County and Portland, Oregon.

Calvin Rich has taught in the United States, Germany and China. His syndicated radio program, About Learning, and his TV spots, The Education Report, have been broadcast in the Northeast. He is currently working on his Ph.D., which includes research on the Jewish mystical path of Kabbalah. He presently studies with Chochmat HaLev in Berkeley, California.

Hal A. Lingerman received his M.A. from Harvard University and his M.Div. from Union Theological Seminary. He presently works with the North County Interfaith Council in Escondido, California, an organization dedicated to helping the homeless toward self-sufficiency. Lingerman is an ordained minister, speaker, counselor, university teacher, and workshop leader. His publications include *The Healing Energies of Music; Lifestreams: Journeys into Meditation and Music; Living Your Destiny; The Book of Numerology: Taking a Count of Your Life;* and *In the Presence of the Living Christ.*

INDEX

Miller–Tiedeman, A., 2, 13–14, 15,
    23–24, 35–36, 43, 50, 52, 54–
    56, 60, 76, 90, 98–99, 101, 112,
    122, 132, 143, 148, 152–153,
    159–160, 163–167, 169, 173–
    175, 179, 183, 193, 201–202,
    209, 225–231, 241, 271, 278,
    281, 289–293, 295–297, 300,
    314
Milne, A. A., 160
Miner, J. B., 27
Minnesota Employment Stabilization
    Research Institute, 28
Minnesota Jobs, 198
Mirror technique, 201–202
Mistakes, 12, 69–72, 151
Mitchell, L. K., 7, 34
Money management, 209–210, 214,
    221–238
    classroom/group exercises, 237
    college costs, 234–235
    development and paradigms, 223–231
    discussion questions, 236–237
    homework/test assignments, 237–238
    retirement, 234–235
    safety net, 231–232
    values, 233–234
Montgomery, B., 96
Moore, B. V., 27
Moore, C. W., 123
Morrissette, A., 146–147
Morrissey, M., 6
Morrow, T. J., 191–192
Mosaic, 194
Moses, 299
Mother of All Employment and Jobs, 194,
    197–198
Mother Theresa, 301
Motorola Corp., 309
Mozart, W. A., 91
Mr. Electrico, 82–83
Mueller, 114–115
Multicultural issues, 123, 203–204
Multi-sourcing income, 210–211
Murphy, M., 206
Murray, H., 77
My Turn (Reagan), 103
Myers, I. B., 275
Myers–Briggs Type Indicator, 275
Myerson, B., 66
Mythology, 73–75

N

National Board for Certified Counselors,
    13, 104
National Hockey League, 274
National Institute for the Advancement
    of Career Education, 165
National Institutes of Health, 106
National Institutes of Mental Health, 32
National Vocational Guidance Associa-
    tion, 26
New Careering, 2, 3, 48–95
    and personal development, 91–93
    and work, 84–88
    checklist, 219–220
    classroom/group exercises, 218
    classroom/group exercises, 95
    connections to past, 76–79
    developers, 50–51, 109, 134, 136,
        152, 188–189, 203–216
    differences, 15
    discussion questions, 217–218
    discussion questions, 94
    ethics, 59–60
    global economy, 18–190
    homework assignments, 95
    homework/test assignments, 219
    in action, 62
    in story, 81–83
    individual career theories, 185
    influence, 88–91
    job clients, 190–199
    Life–Is–Career, 200–202
    literature, 56
    practice, 183–220
    principles, 61–76
    professionals, 203–216
    reasons why, 13–15
    scientific assumptions, 57–59
New National Company, 25
New paradigm, 10–13
New Physics, 163, 172
New possibilities group, 206
Newton, Sir I., 4–7, 10, 27, 128–129,
    145, 161–162
Newtonian worldview, 4–7, 7–8, 11,
    30, 54–55, 71, 85, 114, 122,
    128–129, 143–145, 147–149,
    152, 154, 158–161, 163–164,
    166, 168, 171, 174, 225, 271,
    308
    career development, 5–7